MW01196987

SPATIAL REVOLUTION

SPATIAL REVOLUTION

ARCHITECTURE AND PLANNING IN THE EARLY SOVIET UNION

Christina E. Crawford

Cornell University Press
Ithaca and London

This book is freely available in an open access edition thanks
to TOME (Toward an Open Monograph Ecosystem)—a
collaboration of the Association of American Universities,
the Association of University Presses, and the Association
of Research Libraries—and the generous support of Emory
University. Learn more at the TOME website, available at:
openmonographs.org.

Publication of this book has also been aided by a grant from the
Millard Meiss Publication Fund of CAA.

First published 2022 by Cornell University Press

Printed in the United States of America

Library of Congress Cataloging-in-Publication Data

Names: Crawford, Christina E., author.
Title: Spatial revolution : architecture and planning in the early
　Soviet Union / Christina E. Crawford.
Description: Ithaca [New York] : Cornell University Press, 2022. |
　Includes bibliographical references and index.
Identifiers: LCCN 2020052687 (print) | LCCN 2020052688
　(ebook) | ISBN 9781501759192 (hardcover) |
　ISBN 9781501759208 (ebook) | ISBN 9781501759215 (pdf)
Subjects: LCSH: Architecture—Soviet Union—History. |
　Communism and architecture—Soviet Union. | Space
　(Architecture)—Soviet Union. | Spatial behavior—Soviet
　Union.
Classification: LCC NA1188 .C73 2022 (print) | LCC NA1188
　(ebook) | DDC 720.947084—dc23
LC record available at https://lccn.loc.gov/2020052687
LC ebook record available at https://lccn.loc.gov/2020052688

FOR DUKE, ISAIAH, AND OSKAR

CONTENTS

Color plates follow page 188

ACKNOWLEDGMENTS

I COMPLETED FINAL REVISIONS FOR THIS BOOK DURING THE GLOBAL COVID-19 pandemic, which gave me a renewed appreciation for the spatial debates discussed in these pages. Living under lockdown with a spouse and two children brought into stark relief the basic human need for restorative private space at one end of the spectrum (be that a living cell or home office), and communal public space on the other. The protagonists in these pages insisted that intelligently designed spaces could generate healthy social lives. As a trained architect and planner, I, too, believe that built environments can impact individual and collective well-being, and that certain spatial constructs span geography, politics, and time.

This project really began when I was welcomed into the Chernyi family as an AFS exchange student in Krasnodar, Russia in 1990–91, the final year of the USSR. It is thanks to their care and patience that I am able to speak and read Russian, have returned so many times, and remain deeply invested in Soviet culture and history. I have accrued more recent intellectual debts over the past decade working on this book. I am grateful to Eve Blau for the gift of Baku and for her assurance that with careful research and patience the stories would emerge (she was right). Thank you to Jean-Louis Cohen for his early advice to "follow the money," which led me to the three sites explored in these pages, and for modeling scholarly generosity. Thanks also to Maria Gough for accurately predicting that deep description would generate new knowledge about early Soviet design. In Baku, I am grateful to Amad Mammadov at the State Committee on Urban Planning and Architecture, Galina Mel'nikova at the State Archives, and Chingiz; and from stateside, advice from Sara Brinegar, Heather DeHaan, and Bruce Grant helped me to navigate the Azerbaijani capital. In Magnitogorsk, I offer thanks to the helpful staff at the Magnitogorskii kraevedcheskii muzei and Magnitogorskii Gipromez, and to Stephen Kotkin who sent me their way. Over the past year I have benefitted from the friendship of Evgeniia Konysheva, whose work on Magnitogorsk I have long admired. My interest in the surprising linear city of New Kharkiv is thanks to Jenia Gubkina. In Kyiv, Gena Donets and Alena Mokrousova each helped in myriad ways. Moscow was made so much more enjoyable thanks to the hospitality and intellectual stimulation provided by Nadya Nilina and Kolya Malinin. At Harvard, I am grateful to my GSD cohort, especially Peter Sealy, who has proven a friend for the long haul; to members of the Davis Center's writing and book proposal groups; and to my fellow Graduate Student Associates at the Weatherhead Institute for International Affairs for helping me capitalize on the interdisciplinarity of this work. A shout out goes to Daria Bocharnikova and Steven Harris for pulling together a community of congenial scholars under the umbrella of Second World Urbanity, including Richard Anderson, Diana Kurkovsky, Michal Murawski, Lukasz Stanek, Kimberly Zarecor, and Katherine Zubovich, with whom I look forward to continued collaboration. At Emory University, I thank my supportive colleagues in the Art History Department, particularly fellow architectural historians Sarah McPhee and Bonna Wescoat, and the Modern/Contemporary cohort of Lisa Lee, Susan Gagliardi, and Todd Cronan. My colleagues in Emory's Russian, East European, and Eurasian Studies Program, especially Juliette Stapanian-Apkarian and Matthew Payne, welcomed me graciously. This book has also benefitted from the Emory students in my graduate seminars—*Soviet Cities* and *Spatial Revolution!*—who proved to be astute manuscript readers and interlocutors.

Feedback on this final version of the book—when I could not see the forest for the trees—was particularly welcome. I am indebted to Johanna Conterio and Claire Zimmerman who gave the text a full read through and provided invaluable comments, and to Steven Harris for helping me to fine-tune the introduction. Thank you to staff and board readers at Cornell University Press, and the two anonymous reviewers whose recommendations made this book so much better in the revision. Thanks to acquisitions editor Roger Haydon, who partnered with me to secure funding and who demystified the publishing process for this first-time author with calm and humor; to Bethany Wasik and Karen Laun, who picked up where Roger left off; and to copy editor Irina Burns. If any inaccuracies remain, despite their efforts, the responsibility is mine alone.

Many research and publication grants funded this project. A Fulbright fellowship to Ukraine back in 2002, when I was in architecture school, started the wheels turning. Particularly impactful was a two-day trip to Kharkiv that opened my eyes to the city's remarkable Constructivist legacy. Critical archival forays to Azerbaijan, Russia, and Ukraine during my doctoral studies were funded by Priscilla McMillan and Maurice Lazarus research travel grants from the Davis Center for Russian and Eurasian Studies, a Peter and Mary Novak Ukrainian Fellowship from the Harvard Ukrainian Research Institute, a Jens Aubrey Westengard Scholarship from the Harvard Graduate School of Arts and Sciences, and a John Coolidge Research Fellowship from the New England Chapter of the Society of Architectural Historians. The Harvard Graduate

School of Design and the Canadian Centre for Architecture cosponsored the TD Bank Group-CCA Collection Research Grant for a fruitful summer of research in Montréal. A Merit/Term Time Fellowship from the Harvard Graduate School of Arts and Sciences and the Sidney R. Knafel Dissertation Completion Fellowship from the Weatherhead Center for International Affairs helped me to push through the first version of this project. A generous grant from Emory University's TOME/Digital Publishing in the Humanities program, led by Sarah McKee, made the open access version of this book possible, and a Millard Meiss Publication Fund grant from the College Art Association helped support the high-quality image reproduction.

My deep gratitude goes to the directors and staff at the archives and libraries who came through with permissions documentation during the pandemic. These include the Azerbaijan State Film and Photo Documents Archive (ARDKFSA); the Bentley Historical Library, University of Michigan; the Canadian Centre for Architecture (CCA); the Central State Archives of Supreme Bodies of Power and Government of Ukraine (TsDAVO); the Central State Cine-Photo-Phono Archives of Ukraine, named after G.S. Pshenychnyi (TsDKFFA); the Magnitogorsk Local History Museum; the Russian State Archive of Literature and Art (RGALI); the Russian State Archive of Documentary Films and Photographs (RGAKFD); the State Archive of the Azerbaijan Republic (ARDA); and the State Museum of Architecture, named after A.V. Shchusev (MUAR). I extend special thanks to the archivists at the Central State Archives and Museum of Literature and Art of Ukraine (TsDAMLM) who managed, during this difficult time, to track down specific citation information for many of the illustrations I used from their collection. I do not know how they did it with the archive officially closed—I am truly grateful. This book would not be as rich as it is in primary published sources without the help of Harvard and Emory University Libraries, and the Interlibrary Loan staff in particular, who managed to track down the most obscure rare books and pamphlets from 1920s USSR and convince other institutions to lend them. Thank you to Sage Publishing for permission to use previously published portions of chapters 7 and 8: Christina E. Crawford, "From Tractors to Territory: Socialist Urbanization through Standardization." in *Journal of Urban History* 44, no. 1 (January 2018): 54–77.

This book is, finally, the result of a family effort. Huge thanks to my dad, Lee, who served without complaint as a third parent to my boys over the past decade, and to my mom, Linda, who pitched in countless frequent flier miles and who came through at the eleventh hour to keep the boys busy during the pandemic. My sons, Isaiah and Oskar, have provided much-needed distraction and joy, and have given me innumerable reasons to make writing a book and teaching a Monday to Friday, 9 to 5 proposition. Most of all I am thankful to my husband, Duke, who loves this period and culture as much as I do, and who unquestioningly supported my leaving a stable professional career to follow an academic dream. This is for you.

GLOSSARY

Terms, Soviet Departments, and Institutions

Azneft: Azerbaijan state oil company

Baksovet: The Baku Soviet, the municipal Communist Party decision-making body

byt: everyday life, domestic habits

    meshchanskii byt: petty bourgeois way of life

    novyi byt: the new socialist way of life

control figures (*kontrol'nye tsifry*): predicted annual revenues for each branch of industry, which set hard limits on annual expenditures

disurbanism (*dezurbanizm*): extremely dispersed settlement—term used in the socialist settlement debate to refer to the theories Mikhail Okhitovich

dom-kommuna: communal house, usually with small sleeping quarters and common dining, recreating, laundry, and childcare facilities

genetic planning: conservative planning predicated on a balanced budget, such that capital expenditures on urban development are set by, and do not exceed, expected fiscal limits

Giprogor: State Institute for City Planning in the Russian Republic

Giprograd: State Institute for City Planning in the Ukrainian Republic

Gipromez: State Institute for the Design of Metallurgical Factories

GOELRO: State Commission for Electrification of Russia

Gosplan: State Planning Committee

gradostroitel'stvo/gradostroitel': city-planning / city-planner

icheri sheher: medieval Islamic city core of Baku

KhTZ: Kharkiv Tractor Factory

komandirovka: business trip

kommunalka: communal apartment

kommunal'naia khoziastva: communal or municipal economy

Kommunkhoz: Department of Communal Services

kvartal: residential superblock consisting of housing and common services, a term used from the early 1930s on

magistral': main arterial road, or highway

Magnitostroi: Magnitogorsk Design and Construction Trust; also, the common name for the entire Magnitogorsk construction project

MAO: Moscow Architectural Society

mikroraion: microdistrict, a large planned residential area with integral social services, but no production sector (post-WWII term)

NEP: New Economic Policy (1921–28)

New Kharkiv: *sotsgorod* designed and built for the Kharkiv Tractor Factory

NKVD: People's Commissariat for Internal Affairs

opytnyi proekt: experimental project

OSA: Society of Contemporary Architects, primary purveyors of architectural Constructivism

planirovanie/planovik: economic planning / economic planner

proektirovanie/planirovshchik: spatial planning / spatial planner

priviazka: practice of adjusting a standardized architectural type to conform to a specific site, and also the result of that practice (can be used as a verb and a noun)

rasselenie: settlement (really, re-settlement)

SA (*Sovremennaia arkhitektura*): Constructivist architectural journal published from 1926–1930—mouthpiece for OSA

sotsgorod (sotsialisticheskii gorod): socialist city that serves a population of +/-50,000 and includes all programs and services needed at the municipal level including residential, leisure, commercial, and governmental spheres, plus the infrastructural systems to knit these together and link them to the productive sphere (the factory), on which the *sotsgorod*'s existence is predicated

Sovnarkom: Council of People's Commissars

STO: Council of Labor and Defense

Stroikom RSFSR: Building Committee of the Russian Republic

teleological planning: aspirational planning concerned foremost with the *telos*, or goal, that the economic plan wishes to achieve

Traktorstroi: state entity set up to direct and oversee the delivery of the Kharkiv Tractor Factory (such an entity was also established for Stalingrad and Cheliabinsk)

TsK KPSS: Central Committee of the Communist Party of the Soviet Union

Tsekombank: Central Bank of Communal Services and Housing

urbanism (*urbanizm*): population-limited settlements accommodating all three spheres of everyday life (production, residential, socio-cultural)—term used in the socialist settlement debate to refer to the theories of Leonid Sabsovich

UkrGirpomez: State Institute for Metallurgical Factory Design in the Ukrainian Republic

Vesenkha/VSNKh: Supreme Council of the National Economy

zhilkombinat: housing combine—a planned, standardized residential block that includes housing, educational institutions, social and commercial services, and local commercial programming for a population of 2,000–3,000, the building block of the *sotsgorod*

Abbreviations for Archives

ARDA: Azərbaycan Respublikası Dövlət Arxivi (State Archive of the Azerbaijan Republic)

ARDKFSA: Azərbaycan Respublikası Dövlət Kino-Foto Sənədləri Arxivi (Azerbaijan State Film and Photo Documents Archive)

CCA: Canadian Centre for Architecture

DAKhO: Derzhavnyi arkhiv Kharkivs'koi oblasti (State Archive of the Kharkiv Oblast)

GARF: Gosudarstvennyi arkhiv Rossiskoi federatsii (State Archive of the Russian Federation)

MUAR: Gosudarstvennyi muzei arkhitektury im. A.V. Shchuseva (State Museum of Architecture, named after A.V. Shchusev)

RGAKFD: Rossiiskii gosudarstvennyi arkhiv kinofotodokumentov (Russian State Archive of Documentary Films and Photographs)

RGALI: Rossiiskii gosudarstvennyi arkhiv literatury i iskusstva (Russian State Archive of Literature and Art)

RGB/KGR: Rossiiskaia gosudarstvennaia biblioteka, Otdel kartograficheskikh izdanii (Russian State Library, Division of Cartographical Publications)

TsDAMLM: Tsentral'nyi derzhavnyi arkhiv-muzei literatury i mystetsva Ukrainy (Central State Archives and Museum of Literature and Art of Ukraine)

TsDAVO: Tsentral'nyi derzhavnyi arkhiv vyshchykh organiv vlady ta upravlinnia Ukrainy (Central State Archives of Supreme Bodies of Power and Government of Ukraine)

TsDKFFA: Tsentral'nyi derzhavnyi kinofotofonoarkhiv Ukrainy im. G.S. Pshenych-nogo (Central State Cine-Photo-Phono Archives of Ukraine, named after G.S. Pshenychnyi)

NOTE ON TRANSLITERATION AND TRANSLATION

ALL TRANSLATIONS IN THIS BOOK ARE MY OWN UNLESS OTHERWISE INDICATED. Working between four languages in the archives has made me particularly grateful for the clarity of the Library of Congress system, which I have used for transliteration, note, and bibliographic standards from Azerbaijani, Russian, and Ukrainian into English. I have favored Ukrainian over Russian spellings for locations that sit in contemporary Ukraine (Kyiv and Kharkiv, for instance, rather than Kiev and Khar′kov/Kharkov), but retained original spellings in quoted excerpts. I have also used commonly accepted Western spellings of certain proper names, such as Maxim Gorky rather than Maksim Gorkii, and Trotsky, not Trotskii.

SPATIAL REVOLUTION

INTRODUCTION

THE *DETROIT NEWS* REPORTER PHILIP ADLER TRAVELED THROUGH THE "SOVIET hinterlands" in the summer of 1929 to assess progress on the first Five-Year Plan (1928–32), Joseph Stalin's hyper-industrialization drive. He gave his Depression-stricken US readers a glimpse of the plan's material effects through the train window:

> The country's landscape is changing. Traveling in Russia by train or boat you see yellow smoke stacks of new factories rising among the golden cupolas of churches in every town and belching clouds of black smoke against the blue sky. You see everywhere new three-four-and-five-story apartment houses, workmen's dwellings—not blocks, but complete city sections—rising among the dilapidated ramshackles of yore. In the midst of thick forests, or on river banks you run into completely new cities of 5,000, 10,000, 20,000 inhabitants, with some new factory as a nucleus.[1]

Adler's reportage captured the Soviet Union amid a seismic shift from a rural landscape of thick forests and quiet riverbanks to a man-made industrial territory. Constructing these cities during the early years of the Soviet period was hard work that required a massive mobilization of materials and labor. Soviet administrators frantic to meet the plan's goals also had to contend with a rapidly evolving conceptual framework for socialist space-making. If capitalist cities are dense, hierarchical, and exploitative, Soviet economic and spatial planners asked at the time, how might socialist space be differently organized to maximize not only productivity but also equality and collectivity? These theoretical discussions were important—the future of a new kind of urban form rested on the correct formulations—but the plan's timeline was set. As the spatial debates raged on, concrete foundations were being poured. It was simultaneously a time of possibility and crisis.

The first Soviet industrialization drive in the late 1920s to the mid-1930s was one of unprecedented speed and unfathomable scale.[2] The first two Five-Year Plans for economic development projected the construction of thousands of new industrial enterprises in remote and sparsely populated locations like the Urals, Siberia, and the Soviet Far East. Eighty-seven new towns were to be built to accommodate a population of 4.5–5 million, and hundreds of additional workers' settlements were planned near existing urban centers. Over ten years, 6–7 million people were to be put to work and housed, all by the Soviet state.[3] These were official capital construction targets. To get at what was built and how, this book focuses on the evolution of the socialist spatial project in geographically peripheral but economically central locations where capital expenditure was greatest and design experimentation most intense. Three sites—Baku, Magnitogorsk, and Kharkiv—were selected by the Soviet government for rapid development in exceedingly difficult economic circumstances because each played an important role in early Soviet industrial growth. Baku, Azerbaijan was the Soviet oil bank; Magnitogorsk, Russia the model Soviet steel town; Kharkiv, Ukraine the source of a preexisting skilled workforce able to staff a Soviet machine-building industry. Each was a site where spatial planning arose early (between 1924 and 1932), where targeted capital improvements bolstered economic development, and where the precepts of socialist urbanism were tested on specific projects. These sites materialized despite conditions of economic austerity and technological inadequacy, and often due to harrowing human cost.

Architecture and planning activities in the early Soviet period were kinetic and negotiated. Up until the late 1930s, socialist spatial practices and forms emerged not by ideological edict from above but through on-the-ground experimentation by practitioners in collaboration with local administrators—via praxis, by doing. Questions about the proper distribution of people and industry under socialism were posed and refined through the construction of brick and mortar, steel and concrete projects. Complications produced by imperfect sites, impossible deadlines, and inchoate theories of socialist space-making forced practitioners to innovate. Ingenuity employed on one site was then harnessed by the burgeoning centralized planning apparatus to facilitate improvements on the next. The US journalist Anna Louise Strong noted this trend after touring a series of Soviet factory construction sites in the early 1930s. "Those who point to improvements made under capitalism through competition," Strong wrote, "overlook the improvements made in the USSR by passing on experience from one plant to another."[4] Each building project was an opportunity to fine-tune standardized architectural and urban models for installation elsewhere in the seemingly boundless Soviet territories. Successful urban units that bundled workplace and housing, evenly distributed social services, and robust municipal transportation were then planted on far-flung sites in other socialist states—and were tried in capitalist welfare states as well—for decades to follow.

This book contributes to and expands on early twentieth-century architecture and planning scholarship in three specific ways. First, it brings needed attention to constructed works of the early Soviet period, most instructive for their very materiality. Second, it is a history of the built environment that foregrounds specific economic conditions, linking the economy and space to bring the "spatial turn" to Soviet economic history. And third, it provides a wide geographical scope that zooms in and out to ally and compare specific industrial nodes where trans-Union and transnational exchanges of design expertise occurred.

Early Soviet architecture and urban planning projects have largely been framed as theoretical works, which is to say diagrammatic.[5] But what diagrams! Visionary urban schemes like those that emerged from the socialist settlement debate in 1929–30 retain currency in design schools today as exemplars of spatial and social innovation.[6] Insistence on celebrating seductive yet unbuilt paper projects has, however, pushed a pervasive narrative of disappointment and failure for early Soviet architectural output that simply does not jibe with lived experience.[7] Stories of design and construction projects in Baku, Magnitogorsk, and Kharkiv reveal how hands-on building experiments pushed Soviet architectural development and evolution. Investigation of building activities in Baku specifically also shifts the "start date" for Soviet architecture back before 1925, the commonly accepted year of initiation set by scholarship of the avant-garde.[8] Consideration of a wider variety of early Soviet design work—from paper to concrete—better situates avant-garde visionaries as well. Constructivist theoreticians and practitioners like Moisei Ginzburg, the Vesnin brothers, and Ivan Leonidov were active participants in the nitty-gritty tasks of building the Soviet environment.

In its first fifteen years, the Soviet Union passed through three economic periods: War Communism, the New Economic Policy, and the first Five-Year Plan. Economic planning and spatial planning were distinct fields of action in the early Soviet period. Economic, not spatial, planners determined the percentage of the state budget allocated to capital construction. Understanding the economic limits of change to the built environment provides a crucial corrective to architectural histories that hold the work of Soviet architects and spatial planners captive to expectations of what they might have accomplished in a friction-free context.[9] Creativity and innovation emerged on these sites in the face of fiscal and technological limits and design strategies like architectural standardization that were developed out of necessity impacted later developments.

The specific method deployed here, nodal history, engages in oscillation between multiple scales of inquiry, moving between single sites and the larger territories in which those sites are allied and materially connected. It is indebted to the concept of "circulatory localities" coined by Yves Cohen in his work to expose the prevalence of Stalinist borrowing in the 1930s and to actor-network theory, insofar as it is relational.[10] Nodal history pays most attention, however, to the impact of circulating ideas and people on the design of physical sites—the nodes themselves. This is the first comparative parallel study of Soviet architecture and planning to create a narrative arc across a vast geography, and is thus distinguished from recent publications that examine a single city over an extended timeframe, using that city as a lens through which to extrapolate broader economic, political, or societal themes. Sole-city monographs like Stephen Kotkin's *Magnetic Mountain*, on Magnitogorsk, and Heather DeHaan's *Stalinist City Planning*, on the Soviet transformation of Nizhnii Novgorod—which shares with this work a common protagonist, Aleksandr Ivanitskii—provided critical grounding for the episodes covered here. Nevertheless, the work of juggling multiple sites and pulling back to see the big picture has been undertaken without a paradigmatic roadmap.

An accurate mapping of this narrative quickly transgresses the political borders of the Soviet Union with pins dotting English garden cities, housing settlements in Weimar Germany, and oil extraction sites in the United States, among other locations. Sites like Baku, Magnitogorsk, and Kharkiv were nodes in a global network developed at the beginning of the twentieth century that freely shared experts, technologies, and materials. Ideas, both spatial and social, circulated even more readily, definitively upsetting Cold War assumptions about Soviet isolationism. Who is responsible for providing housing and social services to the working class? What are the constituent elements of the "good city"? What is the role of standardization and mass production in architectural design? How should the modern housing unit be spatially configured? All of these questions were posed in an international context, and the development of Soviet sites contributed heavily to the evolution of these debates. Conceptually, nodal history welcomes collaboration. It proposes that there is just one densely populated map, drawn without political borders, on which scholars collate corresponding research. The economic and spatial relations between researched nodes render political borders subservient to connectivities.

Praxis and Anti-Utopianism

The activity of praxis, critical to the projects built in the early Soviet period, is operative in both architecture and Marxism. In architectural discourse, praxis entails iterative movement between theory and practice.[11] Amanda Reeser and Ashley Shafer propose that praxis in architecture is marked by "uncertainty, improvisation, tactics, flexibility, and even chance."[12] Establishing a feedback loop between ideation and materialization allows architects to move through challenges that arise in design projects, and even to reframe roadblocks as opportunities. Architectural praxis is a nonlinear, trial and error process that is ultimately developmental. Good designers work this way intuitively.

The Marxist definition of praxis turns on Marx's XI Thesis on Feuerbach, which states that "philosophers have only interpreted the world, in various ways; the point is to change it."[13] For Marx, the "revolutionary," "practical-critical activity" of praxis was the means to enact change and the logical foil to utopian dreaming.[14] In the *Communist Manifesto*, Marx and Engels drew a stark line between their brand of scientific socialism and the "Utopian" socialists who came before them. Among their criticisms of utopia was one that Roger Paden calls the Metaethical Critique: if we agree that human nature is not fixed but negotiable, we must also agree that the form of utopia—or whatever you call the space of the future—cannot be definitively articulated.[15] The dynamic processes of history and social progress refute utopian projection, thus drawing up detailed blueprints of the future condition is a waste of time and effort. Picking up the anti-utopian thread, Vladimir Lenin wrote, "in Marx you will find no trace of Utopianism in the sense of inventing the 'new' society and constructing it out of fantasies."[16] Yet herein lies the fundamental conflict. Without a vision, no matter how cursory, it is impossible to embark on immediate construction.

In his critique of the Marxist-Leninist anti-utopian stance, philosopher Martin Buber stressed the proactive role of utopia. "What, at first sight, seems common to the Utopias that have passed into the spiritual history of mankind is the fact that they are pictures, and pictures moreover of something not actually present but only represented," Buber explained. "This 'fantasy' does not float vaguely in the air, it is not driven hither and thither by the wind of caprice, it centers with architectonic firmness on something primary and original which it is its destiny to build; and this primary thing is a wish. The utopian picture is a picture of what 'should be,' and the visionary is the one who wishes it to be."[17] In Buber's description, utopia is a concrete wish that drives the visionary to enact change. In the Buberian line of reasoning, the utopian plan can act as a kind of shovel-ready project, one that needs some refinement to address the particularities of the site, but one that nonetheless establishes the framework from which a new society is constructed.

The Marxist interdiction against utopia is one key reason for the precipitous ascendance of intense on-the-ground design activity during the first Five-Year Plan. When the dust cleared after the Russian Revolution and Civil War, the absence of a blueprint for the postrevolutionary condition left Soviet administrators struggling to define the shape of their new society. Here is where architectural praxis reenters the story. In the design and construction projects undertaken during the first decades of Soviet rule, spatial problems and their solutions revealed themselves through an intense engagement with context. Living blueprints developed in the making, an approach that Heather DeHaan calls "pragmatic planning," a combination of "science, pragmatism, and ideological correctness" rooted in site-specificity.[18] This type of planning practice was the only option available to the early Soviet state. Without preordained plans, construction had to proceed through experimentation, an activity that was congenial to Lenin's definition of praxis.

"At one time we needed [declarations, statements, manifestoes and decrees] to show the people how and what we wanted to build, what new and hitherto unseen things we were striving for. But can we go on showing the people what we want to build? No," Lenin asserted. "Even an ordinary laborer will begin to sneer at us and say: 'What use is it to keep on showing us what you want to build? Show us that you can build. If you can't build, we're not with you, and you can go to hell!'"[19] Although the "building" Lenin referred to here was analogical (he was addressing political education specifically), he was arguing that hands-on work was the only means to build the Soviet state. It was no longer the time for theories, manifestoes, or pictures of the communist future. It was time to build. Soviet architects and spatial planners had a mandate—and a lot of work to do.

Defining Soviet Spatial Planning

When the Bolsheviks issued the Land Decree on October 26, 1917, they assumed responsibility for all future development in the territories under their control.[20] Over the next fifteen years the Bolshevik, then Soviet, government operated under three distinct economic regimes, each of which engaged differently with capital construction. War Communism (1917–21) was a fully socialized, militarily focused command economy. The intertwined crises of civil war and economic collapse manifested in material destruction and abandonment of now-Soviet cities; proactive urban development was nonexistent. The New Economic Policy (*Novaia ekonomicheskaia politika*, NEP; 1921–28) was a so-called state capitalist economy in which limited private commerce coexisted with nationalized industry. In strategic cities like Baku, targeted development in transportation and housing infrastructure was critical to economic recovery. But for the USSR as a whole during NEP, urban development was sparse and of limited scope. The first Five-Year Plan (1928–32) marked a sea change in the Soviet state's attitude to capital construction. The plan's projective map was dotted nationwide with massive industrial complexes to be designed, constructed, and made operational within half a decade. The race to "overtake and outstrip" (*dognat' i peregnat'*) capitalist industry was on.[21]

The shift from limited development during NEP to hyper-development in the first Five-Year Plan is linked to a fundamental change in how the Soviet national budget was conceptualized. During NEP, a genetic (*geneticheskoe*) planning philosophy held sway. Soviet economic planners set annual "control figures"— projected revenues and expenditures—by considering historical tendencies both within and outside national boundaries and making educated guesses about the economy's future trajectory. Genetic planning was predicated on the notion of a balanced budget, and capital expenditures on urban development were set by, and did not exceed, expected fiscal limits. A teleological (*teleologicheskoe*) planning philosophy took over at the onset of the first Five-Year Plan. Teleological planning was concerned foremost with the goals that the plan wished to achieve. The control figure became, in the words of Leon Trotsky, "not merely a photograph but a command," which is to say that revenues and expenditures became aspirational, based on the telos that the state wished to reach rather than historical precedent.[22] What did this mean for the transformation of the Soviet built environment? Urban development under the plan was no longer curtailed by economic conservatism: space could finally enter the picture. With territories and resources that spanned continents, theorists could now consider how a socialist organization of space might differ demonstrably from capitalist modes.

In a command economy like the Soviet Union's, planning was understood first as an activity of state-controlled fiscal projection and oversight, and only second as an activity of physical projection and oversight.[23] These two interdependent yet distinct planning disciplines have specific names in Russian: *planirovanie* (state economic planning) and *proektirovanie* (spatial planning).[24] Both planning disciplines operated under the auspices of the State Planning Commission (Gosudarstvennyi komitet po planirovaniiu or Gosplan, established in 1921), although it was not until the first Five-Year Plan that spatial planners were given much of a role to play. During NEP, Gosplan economic planners were tasked to stabilize an economy wrecked by overly rapid nationalization, and because so much effort was put toward balancing the budget, little spatial planning occurred. Lenin's pet project to electrify the whole Soviet landmass—the GOELRO (Gosudarstvennaia komissiia po elektrifikatsii rossii or State Commission for Electrification of Russia) Plan from 1920—engaged both economic and spatial planning, and a limited number of critical sites, like Baku, did undergo spatial planning efforts during NEP. Nevertheless, Gosplan's monthly journal, *Planovoe khoziaistvo*, was devoid of articles related to capital construction through the 1920s, signaling that *proektirovanie* would have to wait until *planirovanie* figured out how to fund it.

Proektirovanie was a little-used term in the 1920s, which underscores the scarcity of spatial planning efforts. The discipline now well established as urban planning was a nascent field in all geographical contexts at the start of the twentieth century—in the Soviet Union, its arrival just happened to coincide with the shift in economic and political regime. Since both the state and the discipline were emergent, the precepts of socialist spatial organization were formulated in a rich field of interaction that included architects, engineers, economists, political theorists, state, regional and municipal administrators, and common citizens. According to one 1929 source, "in the entire USSR" there were only fifty spatial planning specialists, a small number attributable to the field's novelty, the inconsequential amount of work, and state neglect of educational programs to train future experts.[25] However, a small cadre of experts thought about and, in limited ways, modified the built environment. "City-building" (*gradostroitel'stvo*), a direct Russian translation of the German *städtebau*, was the term utilized by Aleksandr Ivanitskii, the author of Baku's first general plan, to describe this type of work.[26] Ivanitskii and his colleagues were not only the first generation of Soviet city-builders; they were also the last generation of Russian imperialist city-builders. To define socialist space, these experts bridged the gap between old and new, and researched and experimented with planning practices and architectural types from nonsocialist contexts they had studied and visited before the Russian Revolution. Ebenezer Howard's garden city was frequently cited as an apt model to house the proletariat. Ivanitskii gathered planning materials from the United States and France, among other countries, to find transferable policies for Soviet cities. Eclectic borrowing and intermingling led, finally, to new spatial configurations specific to state socialism.[27]

Socialist Space

What is socialist space? For Leonid Sabsovich, an economist at the Supreme Council of the National Economy, this was the burning question of the Soviet first Five-Year Plan. "In considering the problem of the city, our ideas are extremely constrained, and we are prone to use stencils, fed to us by our past and the present experience of contemporary capitalist countries, to design the modern concepts of our future," Sabsovich lamented. "Such an approach to this problem is totally incorrect. It does not account for the magnificent and unimaginable economic, social, and cultural shifts in our near future."[28] Although he was not a designer, Sabsovich attempted to provide the seeds of a spatial solution:

> The condition that will assist us in realizing [our socialist] objectives is above all the *"victory over the distance"* (*pobeda nad rasstoianiem*). By increasing industrial production several dozen times over, and enormously increasing and improving the means of transportation and communication, we will build new factories and plants not densely, but scattered over a wide area . . . *In our victory over distance, we will destroy the economic advantages of large cities as industrial and commercial centers . . . we will see enormous cultural growth of the entire population that will deprive the city of its current monopoly over culture.*[29]

As Sabsovich suggested, the practice of working on the existing city came under fire during the socialist urbanism debate in 1929–30, kicked off by these writings.[30] Sabsovich's "urbanist" solution was the *sotsgorod* (socialist city), a new hyper-communalized urban unit that bundled production, housing, social institutions, and recreation. The "disurbanist" camp in the debate, contra Sabsovich, deemed density of any sort inappropriate in the socialist context. In his provocative essay, "Not a city, but a new type of settlement" from 1930, disurbanist Mikhail Okhitovich argued that the city was an outmoded concept under socialism: "Instead of destroying the conflict between village and city (K. Marx), others suggest that we replace it with a *city* of industry and a *city* of agriculture; in place of a *new settlement* that would destroy village life and urban congestion (Lenin) they insert an *old city-like settlement*."[31] Okhitovich insisted on a new linguistic and spatial vocabulary to jettison the city once and for all in favor of decentralized settlement (more accurate, resettlement [*rasselenie*]).

Rasselenie conjures images of pioneering Soviet citizens turning away from the dense capitalist city to face the immeasurable depth and breadth of the Soviet landscape, moving through space, dispersing, searching for sites worthy of occupation. Maximum dispersion of the population away from prerevolutionary settings would, Okhitovich believed, make installation of a new socialist way of life (*novyi byt*) an easier task. Detachment from existing conditions would permit the light and air needed for the first green shoots of communal conduct to grow. This spatial condition of temporary detachment is consistent with Italian Communist Antonio Gramsci's "war of position," a strategy that promotes the construction of counter-hegemonic sites that model change for a gradual, nonviolent cultural transition from one state (here dense, hierarchical prerevolutionary urbanism) to another (diffuse, nonhierarchical socialist urbanism).[32] As further articulated by Frederic Jameson, socialist settlements adhere to the "enclave theory of social transition, according to which the emergent future, the new and still nascent social relations that announce a mode of production that will ultimately displace and subsume the as yet still dominant one."[33] The enclave must act as a demonstration project of a better way, visible but removed from the prevailing culture so that its clear superiority is legible.

The industrial-socialist nodes in Baku, Magnitogorsk, and Kharkiv were experimental enclaves. According to the People's Commissariat for Internal Affairs (NKVD) in 1929, "socialist cities are complete organisms, conceived and calculated from the beginning to the end . . . Governmental, and not private, design and construction of our living complexes is also a guarantee that the entire planning composition will be considered. Finally, the socialist city is constructed to provide maximal, equal comfort to the population, thereby eliminating the contrast between luxury and poverty."[34] In an environment designed for socialist clients, the socioeconomic inequalities endemic to the capitalist city would be tamped out altogether. One Soviet site's architectural and planning experiments to determine the shape of socialist space imparted lessons learned to subsequent test cases.

Diffuse, nonhierarchical, detached—these are all rather abstract characteristics to define socialist space. The French Marxist scholar Henri Lefebvre, frustrated by what he found to be insufficient spatial difference, claimed that under state socialism "no architectural innovation occurred," and further that socialism produced no "space of its own." The sites investigated in these pages refute Lefebvre's wholesale dismissal.[35] Under capitalism, architects typically concern themselves with the design of singular buildings that are isolated conceptually from their surrounding contexts due to property regimes that insist on the legal and spatial limits of private parcels. Shared property ownership under socialism, on the other hand, permits architects to consider social and spatial forms as codependent in what later Soviet architectural theorists referred to as "unified space."[36] As installed in the Soviet Union, socialist or unified spaces are notable for their massive scale, linear infrastructural systems needed to traverse that vast territory, and interdependent architectural elements.[37] The elements, expanding in scale, are the minimized domestic unit, institutions of social infrastructure (workers' clubs, schools, common laundries, etc.), and the self-sustaining superblock on which the first two elements sit, linked either to adjacent industry (early Soviet period) or state-run transportation infrastructure (later Soviet period).[38] Here architecture and planning are construed as bundles of relational networks in which no one program or spatial form stands alone, leading to inextricable community.

Socialist space also emerges from novel clients and architectural programs. As the architect El Lissitzky explained to a German audience in 1930, in the Soviet Union "the individual, private client has now been replaced by the so-called 'social commission,'" a group composed of the socialist state and the proletariat. This new collective client had three main concerns: industrial efficiency, reproduction of the workforce, and social equality—for the state, more or less in that order—and while only the last of these was distinctly socialist, the alchemical combination of production, residential, and sociocultural spheres yielded a list of interdependent architectural programs that sparked new spatial types. Soviet architecture's task, as Lissitzky put it, was "to comprehend the new conditions of life, so that by the creation of responsive building design it can actively participate in the full realization of the new world."[39] The programs of housing, health and hygiene, food and laundry provisioning, childcare, education at all levels, and edifying recreation were combined by Soviet spatial practitioners in numerous novel configurations, and worked and reworked to achieve the greatest collective efficacy. Once a tried and tested design was deemed successful by socialist designers and their state clients, intensive standardization ensued. A purported one-sixth of the world was diffusely colonized with standardized components at every scale from concrete panels to entire urban units.[40] Because the socialist state was client, landowner, and developer, Soviet architects and planners could envision and install spaces that exceeded physical and conceptual boundaries in ways heretofore unseen.

Ethics of Comprehensive Planning

The ambitious industrial goals set for the first Five-Year Plan were met, according to Soviet authorities, in four years. Policy analysts from capitalist countries that were suffering the effects of the Great Depression watched attentively as the plan unfolded, and many came to view the Soviet planned economy as a viable future alternative. Stuart Chase, the US economist who coined the term "New Deal," predicted in 1932 that the United States was in for structural changes, including "more collectivism, more social control of economic activity, more government 'interference,' less freedom for private business," in other words, the Soviet model.[41] However, geographical distance and tight control of foreign visitors to the USSR obscured the severe negative consequences of the plan, which the Soviets were at pains to conceal.

Philip Adler, one of those visitors whose itinerary was closely monitored, felt the effects of the means-ends logic of hyper-industrialization. "There is another side to the 'Pyatiletka' [the Five-Year Plan]," he intuited, "and it is this side that is responsible for much of the unrest that now exists in Russia. According to the semi-official *Izvestia*, some 3,000 peasant uprisings have broken out in the Soviet Union during the last nine months. Some reports even speak of a 'Civil War' that is now raging there." Adler noted that he did not see any violence with his own eyes, but that "there was a general feeling of discontent in the atmosphere, especially in the agricultural districts."[42] Grain grown in the countryside was earmarked as the primary Soviet export to fund capital projects like the Magnitogorsk Iron and Steel Works and the Kharkiv Tractor Factory, but the peasants, most of whom ran small-scale or subsistence farms, resisted. Because of unforeseen grain retention, export projections built into the economic model for the industrialization drive were rendered untenable. As Moshe Lewin put it, the great risk to the Soviet state was that "the countryside, if not properly controlled and mastered, could wreck the whole effort."[43]

Just a few months after Adler's visit, in November 1929, Stalin called for the rapid and total collectivization of Soviet agriculture, which initiated even more political unrest and violence in the countryside. Mobilized crews of activists streamed into peasant villages and conducted mass searches for hidden grain and livestock. Lev Kopelev, later a dissident author, recalled his participation in forcible grain requisitioning near Kharkiv when he was a young and fervent ideologue. "With the rest of my generation I firmly believed that the ends justified the means. Our great goal was the universal triumph of Communism, and for the sake of that goal everything was permissible—to lie, to steal, to destroy hundreds of thousands and even millions of people, all those who were hindering our work or could hinder it, everyone who stood in the way . . . Any single-minded attempt to realize these ideals exacts its toll of human sacrifice."[44]

To enact such sweeping changes to the Soviet built environment so swiftly during the first Five-Year Plan required conjectural choices by politicians that impacted real people and places and exacted tolls of complicity and human sacrifice. The archives attest to a Soviet obsession with numbers—tables, charts, and graphs crowd the yellowed pages of first Five-Year Plan projections and achievements. "Every day the papers printed the totals of tractors, automobiles and threshers produced," Kopelev remembered. "The dispassionate magnitudes of statistics, the figures for plans, returns, sums obtained held for us some spell-binding, cabalistic

Pythagorean power . . . Statistics, tables, totals were also posted on the struggle for grain."[45] These numerical lists and graphics gesture to the abstract compromises made during the plan. The Soviet government projected employing and housing 6–7 million people during the first two Five-Year Plans. We now know that in Ukraine alone, population losses from the Holodomor (death by hunger in Ukrainian, also known as the Terror-Famine) in 1932–34 are estimated at 4.5 million, with 3.9 million excess deaths and 0.6 million lost births.[46] In the technocratic language of quantification, the archival charts and graphs expose trade-offs of tractors for lives, an ethically reprehensible balance sheet if ever there was one.

On-the-ground engaged problem solving in each planning project detailed in this book stands in stark relief against the metaphysical political backdrop. The material spaces left by Aleksandr Ivanitskii in Baku, Ernst May in Magnitogorsk, and Pavel Aleshin in Kharkiv affirm that despite frustrations of schedule, funding, construction quality, and labor conditions, planning practitioners in the early Soviet Union held fiercely to a tangible goal of improving lives. Their work demonstrates that there are ways of planning and building that respond to the needs of the whole and that unfold under conditions of scarcity if necessary, through acts of determination and will.

Mining the Archives

Although they are named for convenience by geographical node, each section of this book focuses on a singular planning event or incident.[47] In Baku's case, it is the Baku General Plan, devised by Ivanitskii and his Baku client team between 1924 and 1927. The precepts that drove Union-wide planning after 1930—like state control of housing, equality in the distribution of items of collective consumption, and extensive green space—were tested and codified in Baku. In Magnitogorsk, the main event is the All-Union Open Design Competition for a new socialist city held in 1929 that communicated the potentials and limits of the socialist spatial revolution. The German architect Ernst May, who designed Frankfurt's successful worker housing program, enters and exits the picture after the competition, frustrated by the steel factory complex's insatiable appetite for labor and funding. For Kharkiv, the focus is the design and construction of the Kharkiv Tractor Factory and the New Kharkiv *sotsgorod* to house its workers built outside of the first capital of the Ukrainian Soviet Socialist Republic between 1930 and 1932. The near-impossible schedule of the first Five-Year Plan limited the options the Kharkiv designers could pursue, which made easily replicable architectural types and models particularly attractive. Once tested on an experimental site like Kharkiv, a type deemed successful joined the ranks of those ready for slight adjustment—a process known as *priviazka* in Soviet architectural discourse—and export to far-flung sites in the Soviet sphere.

Evidence on these events was gathered in Azerbaijani, Canadian, Russian, Ukrainian, and US state, local, and private archives and libraries. Gaining access to planning materials in post-Soviet states is challenging. An initial archival foray at the start of research naively targeted visual materials: maps, plans, drawings, and photographs. With hindsight, it is clear why such visual materials, maps especially, were difficult to access. Cartography was a practice linked to state security in the Russian imperial era, and the Soviets assumed similar policies. During the 1920s, a debate roiled about the "right of vision" and the degree of secrecy that should be maintained for civil maps; any map more detailed than 1:100,000 was classified. In 1935, after a period of relative openness, all maps and cartographic functions were placed under control of the NKVD (precursor institution to the KGB), and map sharing became a criminal offense. When the German army attacked the Soviet Union in 1941, all maps were taken out of public circulation and even removed from libraries. Pervasive secrecy surrounds the sharing of cartographic and planning materials even today. Employees of Giprogor, the Russian State Institute for City Planning, are banned from traveling abroad for a period deemed appropriate to their level of security clearance.[48]

Even when there is no purposeful archival stonewalling, early Soviet architecture and planning materials tend to be diffusely dispersed. Like the practice of planning itself, which drew in experts and funding from many different organizations and geographies, documentation on planning projects is spread throughout the archival landscape. Every branch of state power seemed to have its fingers in spatial planning projects; yet no one institution's material holdings provide a full picture. State Archives of the Economy, of the "Highest Organs of Power" (the Communist Party), of Literature and Arts, of Photographic, Cinematic, and Technical Documentation all hold materials that have proven useful in piecing together the stories of each event investigated here.

A last note on archival serendipity. The ghost of Pavel Aleshin, the Ukrainian architect and planner who authored the New Kharkiv *sotsgorod*, twice gifted historical materials of such depth and interest that he, among all the protagonists, came back to life through this research. Aleshin's archive resides at the Ukrainian State Archive of Literature and Arts in Kyiv. He was, judging by his papers, an unrepentant packrat. Aleshin's inability to discard proved useful not only for constructing the story of the Kharkiv Tractor Factory but also for Magnitogorsk. A thick envelope filled with photographs of competition design submissions accompanies his original copy of the Magnitogorsk All-Union Open Design Competition brief (a competition he did not enter). Some of these entries have not been previously published; they are the primary evidence that drives the analysis of the competition in these pages. Aleshin returned to assist the project again in Montréal, at the library of the Canadian Centre for Architecture. After inquiring of the librarian why Aleshin's name might be written on the flyleaf of a slim Soviet planning pamphlet, a cart piled with the forty-seven books from his professional library was wheeled out. With his emphatic underlines as evidence, it was possible to trace how Aleshin became acquainted with the theories and forms of the linear city model he utilized in Kharkiv.

If we take Aleshin as representative of the architects and planners active in the first decades of the Soviet project, our knowledge of their design practice also expands. Aleshin trained as an engineer, worked as an architect, and traveled extensively internationally before the Russian Revolution.[49] He was a renowned bibliophile, who began collecting art, architecture, and planning books in 1912, and who continued to amass such a valuable collection (over 6,000 volumes) that he was granted—and had to pay for—extra rooms in his Kyiv apartment to house the library after the transition to socialism.[50] On establishment of Soviet power, Aleshin became involved with large socialist construction projects and had to become knowledgeable about current debates. His library holds various types of architectural and planning texts published within the Soviet Union and outside its borders; he collected technical manuals, pamphlets, books on the theory, forms, and role of worker housing and the socialist city.[51] In short, his library demonstrates that technical and ideological training was necessary even for seasoned practitioners. Under the pressure of time, Aleshin utilized his research immediately on the design for the New Kharkiv socialist city. Read, design, read, adjust. Repeat.[52] Aleshin confirms that socialist space was established through praxis.

PART I

OIL CITY

Baku, 1920–1927

1

SOCIALISM MEANS HOUSING

The results of [our] examination revealed a seriously distressing picture. It turned out that despite the effort put in on the housing-construction front, a catastrophe was looming in terms of apartment stock. It became clear that the poor resolution to the housing question reflected very unfavorably on the oil industry.

—Azneft (1925)

OVER 2,000 KILOMETERS TO THE SOUTHEAST OF MOSCOW, THE STEEP STREETS OF Baku, Azerbaijan rise from the crescent-shaped southern shoreline of the Apsheron Peninsula. In 1920, a newly installed Soviet administrator standing atop the city's highest point would have gazed over a colonial urban grid, a medieval Islamic core, busy working piers, and finally out across the Caspian Sea in the direction of neighboring Iran (figure 1.1). Baku, the administrative and cultural center of the oil-rich peninsula, was a prized acquisition for the Soviets as it had been for the occupying Russians, English, and Turks before them. Unfortunately for this new overseer of the territory, fifteen years of strikes, wars, and revolutions in succession had wreaked havoc on the Apsheron oilfields and their infrastructure by the time the Soviets acquired control. With the Russian Civil War ongoing in regions north, east, and west of Baku, immediate recommencement of oil extraction was critical. The Bolshevik cause required fuel, and Baku would be the primary source.

Upon its appropriation into Soviet territory, Baku presented all of the standard characteristics and attendant challenges of a late nineteenth-century capitalist boomtown. It had a dense prerevolutionary urban core, poor worker housing stock, underdeveloped internal transportation, and industry within the city limits adjacent to residential areas. But to suggest that Baku was an average urban center would be

Figure 1.1. A view of Baku, looking from the Nagornoe Plateau toward the medieval Islamic city core (*icheri sheher*) to the working piers on the Caspian Sea, early twentieth century. Marianne Stigzelius Donation Archive at the Centre for Business History, Stockholm, www.naringslivshistoria.se.

to grossly understate the complex local relationship between oil and urbanism and the strategic centrality of the Apsheron Peninsula within the new Soviet economy.[1] Baku was one of the first Soviet cities to face head-on the transformation from capitalist to socialist city, and one of the first to undergo a formal general planning process, in large part because of oil. It is here that distinctly socialist urban practices emerge. First, through an attack on the housing problem and second, through holistic city planning with proletarian needs at the fore.

The shift to a socialist economy in Baku manifested first in the state takeover of the oil-bearing property. The Soviet government gathered land that ranged from large oil baron compounds to locally controlled plots to create a massive, lucrative territory. This territory was singly owned—by the Soviet state—but it was not singly administered. The urban center of Baku was overseen by the local municipal administration, the Baku Party Committee (Bakinskii sovet or the Baksovet). Azneft (a combination of Azerbaijan and *neft'*, or oil), the state oil company, controlled property affiliated with the oil industry and was the wealthier and more powerful of the two administrations. Azneft's first director, Aleksandr Serebrovskii, was instrumental in modernizing and socializing Baku's oil industry. He recognized that the success of these intertwined processes relied on an accessible and committed workforce, which required housing and transportation.

Baku became ground zero for experimentation with the socialist built environment, particularly in the first decade of Soviet control, from 1920 to 1930, and the narrative unfolds during the period of the New Economic Policy (NEP). NEP was a hybrid economic system, so-called state capitalism promulgated under the leadership of Lenin, who was pragmatic about the need to jumpstart the Soviet economy after the material destruction of the Revolution and the Russian Civil War, and the financial collapse brought about by full economic socialization, or War Communism. Under NEP, private trade was legalized, foreign concessions sought and granted, and small-scale manufacturing denationalized. Baku thrived during NEP, as Azneft sought out foreign precedents and expertise to modernize the Apsheron oilfields. It was common practice in the industry to test various drilling, extracting, and refining technologies. A propensity to experiment trickled down to other spheres of activity in Baku, like urban development.

What the Soviets inherited in Baku was much more than oil-rich territory; they also assumed a complex urban fabric and volatile political climate that together increased the gap between worker housing need and provision during the first years of socialist rule. Azneft learned that worker housing was "one of the most critical economic issues to confront the Baku oil industry," and that only when the housing problem was properly solved would Soviet oil production reach its full potential.[2] Under Azneft's leadership, Baku's urban planning and intractable housing shortages were addressed with the same open-ended approach applied to solving technological problems. After many false starts and a meandering search for solutions, the new Soviet leadership in Baku established the first templates for housing the working class.

Planning Prerevolutionary Baku

Prerevolutionary Baku was a city with copious plans, if not proper planning. The first prospective city drawing, a "plan of the city of Baku designated for the redesign of its defensive arsenals," was formulated in 1796. At least ten official city plans were drafted after this attempt and before the Soviets took power.[3] Baku came under Russian imperial rule in 1806, and the small fortress town was drawn and redrawn by Russian military planners as a seaport, trading center and, most important, a bulwark against neighboring Iran. Russian engineers placed a 350-meter glacis around the fortress and opened a new residential neighborhood to its north. The rectangular grid of the so-called *forshtadt* (from the German *vorstadt*, or suburb) established a rationale for future city growth, but individual structures often overstepped the neat block boundaries inscribed on the map. In short, Baku retained a frontier quality. Its density largely was confined to the area within the walls of the medieval Islamic city core (*icheri sheher*), an organic warren of small alleyways and courtyards, and the *forshtadt*. The city became a provincial capital only in 1859 when an earthquake destroyed the previous capital city of Shemakha.

Two factors conspired to draw a rush of outsiders to Baku and to instigate a late nineteenth-century building boom. In 1871, a local entrepreneur drilled the first successful modern oil well, industrializing the peninsula's extraction technology. Then, in 1872, Russian overseers of Baku elected to privatize land previously owned solely by the tsarist government. New landowners and long-term leaseholders could drill, extract, and sell whatever oil they could capture on their properties.[4] Land in Baku was bought up by foreign investors, the Nobel and Rothschild families among them, and the former regional capital was suddenly plotted on the map of international energy networks. The rush was on.

The effect of the oil boom on the physical shape of Baku was immediate. The population of the city grew over 700 percent between the 1870s and 1897, from 14,500 to 112,000.[5] Newly arrived workers lived on the city fringes and in villages adjacent to the oilfields that grew into informal worker settlements. Local Azeri and Armenian oil barons built their residences and institutions close to the natural center of Baku, along the old fortress wall and in the gridded Russian colonial city (figure 1.2). As Baku grew eastward along the Caspian shoreline, citizens complained to the local municipality of the uncomfortable proximity of oil concerns to residential quarters. In 1876, the municipality acted, forcing 147 factories to be dismantled, and their operations moved a minimum of two kilometers from the then-current edge of residential activity. Local industrialists slotted their relocated factories into preplanned gridded blocks to the east along the Caspian shore. This area, named the Black Town (*chernyi gorod*), was the first instance of a dedicated industrial zone in Russian planning practice.[6] The Nobel Brothers favored freedom from the grid and built their sprawling compound further to the east, in the so-called White Town (*belyi gorod*).

The former industrial zone between the old city center and the Black Town became a two-kilometer-wide swath strewn with the remnants of old factories. The engineers who drafted the Baku Plan of 1878 demurred from laying out a plan for this interstitial region, citing the lack of a proper land survey. The environmentally degraded properties stood to gain in value, nonetheless, with a scheduled completion of the Transcaucasus Railway just to the north of the region in 1883, a line that linked Baku to Tbilisi across the Caucuses Mountains. In the absence of active municipal planning, land-grabbers (*zakhvatschikov*) simply began building structures with occupation, not municipal connectivity, in mind. Haphazard buildings blocked east-west roads needed to link the old center and the Black Town. The head of the city government finally appealed to Baku's Russian governor in May 1882 for help to stave the fast, furious, and illegal occupation of the region: "We ourselves cannot address the new construction . . . simple homes are built incorrectly as mixed-up piles, resembling village outhouses (*saklis*). Similar structures rise day and night with the help of an entire crowd of workers."[7] In response to this plea, the governor charged municipal police to remove enough obstructing buildings to clear east-west passage.

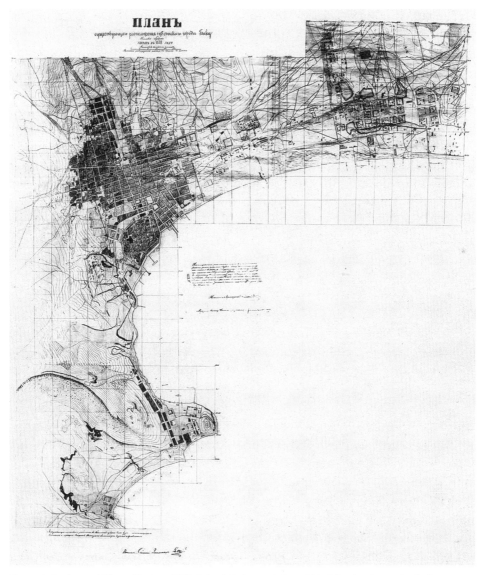

Figure 1.2. General Plan of Baku, 1878. *Icheri sheher* and the gridded *forshtadt* are the dark areas to the west. The sparsely developed sector just to their east is the area in which 147 factories were removed in 1876 in the interest of public health and safety. The relocated factories were slotted into preplanned gridded blocks two kilometers further up the Caspian shore. This area, filling in to the far east, was named the Black Town and was the first instance of a dedicated industrial zone in Russian planning practice. RGALI, f.2991, o.1, d.17, l.20.

When the Soviets took control of Baku, they inherited the 1898 plan of the city completed by the German engineer Nikolaus von der Nonne (plate 1). The colorful and seemingly rationally gridded plan was printed and sold as the official map of the city until 1918. Von der Nonne knew Baku well. He had served as Baku's city planning director from 1883 to 1895, after which he ran a private architectural firm in the city. In 1897, the City Duma (parliament) hired von der Nonne to undertake a comprehensive expansion plan for Baku, which he completed in sixteen months.

Von der Nonne laid a grid over the city in an attempt to bring unruly development under control and to guide rational future growth. The plan key holds four categories that make up the majority of the plan. Pink indicates constructed plots, most of which surround *icheri sheher* or sit against the Caspian seafront. Orange shows partially constructed plots that make up a large percentage of the plan and stretch to the north, west, and east of the constructed city. Light green designates existing and planned gardens and boulevards, which grow larger and more regular as they move away from the city center. Finally, and most tellingly, brown denotes parts of existing structures that conflict with newly regularized streets and seafront zone. Brown, therefore, is the color of friction. It can be seen veining through the medieval Islamic core and the tightly packed traditional neighborhoods to the north and northwest of the *forshtadt*. Although there likely was more conflict between existing and proposed conditions than the map discloses, the existence of this category nonetheless reveals a degree of planning realism. Topographic lines are also faintly drawn in the background of the plan, even if the grid largely ignores the hilly terrain.

Despite its temporal persistence, the von der Nonne plan was realized in ink alone. Private landowners consistently flouted regulating aspects of the plan, and successful commercial enterprises disregarded large-scale civic recommendations with tacit approval of the city government.[8] Von der Nonne had envisioned an ample public boulevard along the Caspian seafront, for instance, but the amenity was omitted in his final plan because the industrial piers were deemed too valuable by their owner, the Caucuses and Mercury Company, and by the city government.[9] Nonetheless, the last prerevolutionary plan for Baku made three specific proposals that the first Soviet general plan in 1927 would elaborate: implantation of green space at multiple scales, limited demolition to make way for better connectivity, and establishment of a model urban worker neighborhood at the city's northern border.

Proto-proletarianism in the Oilfields of Baku

In 1897, the City Duma voted to set aside land two to three kilometers to the north of the center for a so-called charity village (*blagotvoritel'nyi poselok*) to accommodate the poorest strata of Baku's population. This area became the site for the early Soviet-era Armenikend neighborhood. Assignation of a dedicated neighborhood for lowest class Bakuvians did little to improve living conditions for that sector of the urban population. The area set aside for the charity village filled in quickly with small-scale residential buildings, but suitable roads, water supply, and public institutions remained absent in the northern part of the city due to lackluster municipal follow-through. The numerous ad hoc worker settlements perched close to sites of oil extraction were even more remote and disconnected from municipal services.

Violence was common in Baku in the late nineteenth and early twentieth centuries, arising from both class and ethnoreligious conflicts.[10] Systemic abdication of responsibility for worker welfare by the prerevolutionary city administration and the owners and operators of oil extraction and refining facilities produced a growing set of grievances among the oilfield workers of Baku, who were among the Russian imperial subjects engaged in massive strikes that began in 1902. Like elsewhere in the empire's territories, a groundswell of discontent over poor wages, working conditions, and discriminatory ethnic policies in Baku led to a common push first for economic, and in some limited cases political and social, reform.

The oilfields were prime sites of economic and social inequality, as well as interethnic strife, that became retaliatory targets in the 1905 Revolution, the failed precursor to 1917. The dense industrial urbanity of Baku's oilfields fueled material destruction as fire moved quickly among the tightly packed wooden derricks and oil fed the conflagrations. Images in the international press showed plumes of smoke engulfing the formerly productive fields. US newspapers spun war reportage as a positive economic story: Baku's misfortune was a boon to the US oil industry. "The cloud that hangs over the burning oilfields of Baku, Russia [sic], has a silver lining from the point of view of American oil producers. These Trans-Caucasian fields, whose continuous yield of oil seems only to disclose new and inexhaustible supplies, have been the greatest oil competitors of America," the *New York Times* reported in September 1905.[11] The economic losses in Baku were devastating. Between 1904 and 1905, crude oil production on the Apsheron Peninsula dropped by 24 million barrels, or 32 percent.[12]

The condition of unrest was ripe for political agitation, and a young Joseph Stalin was among those socialist revolutionaries slipping into and out of Baku, stirring conflict and laying plans from 1907 to 1910. Stalin overlapped and collaborated during that time with fellow Bolsheviks Grigol Ordzhonikidze and Stepan Shaumian—both of whom would play important roles in Baku in the Soviet period—to take over oilfield district committees in the regions of Bibi-Eibat, the Black and White Towns, and Balakhany.[13] Because of debilitating strikes throughout the empire, the Russian railroad network was virtually at a standstill. Revolutionaries capitalized on the dysfunctional chaos and utilized oil transportation infrastructure to move people and supplies across the Caucasus Mountains. "In the tempest of the deepest conflicts between workers and the oil . . . I first discovered what it meant to lead large masses of workers," Stalin wrote in 1926. "There, in Baku, I received, thus, my second baptism in revolutionary combat. There I became a journeyman for the revolution."[14] Although Stalin's effectiveness as a political agitator was curtailed by repeated prison terms in Baku, the interrelationship of oil and political power was duly impressed on the future general secretary, and the city's importance to the socialist cause was ensured.

Economically neutral concessions by oil industrialists, such as guaranteed freedom of speech and assembly as well as the right to unionize and strike, appeased Baku's oilfield workers until 1913. The period from 1908 to 1913 also coincided with a decline in Baku's oil output and depressed prices for the oil that was extracted. In 1913, with "oil hunger" in Russia, and oil prices back up, as many as 40,000 oil workers took part in a general strike to protest a real wage decline of 10 percent and insufficient days of rest; in 1914, 30,000 workers took part. While the impetus for the strikes in 1913 and 1914 was economic (primarily a demand for higher wages), workers took the opportunity to make political demands as well. Strikers requested libraries and education in their native languages, schools with free books and breakfast for their children, and free days on Muslim holidays. Oilfield owners' concessions, when they came, addressed the workers' economic concerns and ignored political claims.[15]

When the Bolshevik government overthrew the monarchy and assumed titular power of all imperial territories in 1917, Transcaucasia (Armenia, Azerbaijan, and Georgia) refused to recognize it. For the following three years, Baku was seized and controlled by a series of short-lived governing bodies. A unified Transcaucasian Federation lasted for four weeks in 1918. From April through July 1918, the city was ruled by a dictatorship of the proletariat: the Baku Commune. The commune's executive body, the Baku Council of People's Commissars (Sovet narodnykh kommissarov or Sovnarkom), was chaired by the Armenian Bolshevik Stepan Shaumian. Under Shaumian's leadership, the Sovnarkom quickly enacted reforms that included expropriation of the oil and fishing industries, as well as banks and shipping companies.[16] These measures initiated regular oil shipments to Lenin's Bolshevik forces to the north, deliveries that had stalled during power shuffles over the previous months.[17] Upon increasing military pressure from British-led forces that surrounded the city, the Baku Sovnarkom resigned in July 1918 and was replaced by the British controlled government called the Central Caspian Dictatorship.[18] The British left Baku in August 1919, after which a precarious Azerbaijan Democratic Republic (ADR) held power through mid-1920.[19]

On April 28, 1920, the 11th Division of the Red Army definitively took Baku. The ADR was overthrown, and Azerbaijan was subsumed under Soviet rule. In the immediate aftermath of Baku's seizure by Soviet troops, Lenin made clear that the future success of the industrialized proletarian state hinged on the Apsheron Peninsula's petroleum products: "We all know that our industries stood idle because of the lack of fuel. However, today, the proletariat of Baku has toppled the Azerbaijani government and is in charge. This means that now we own a basic economy that is capable of supporting our industries."[20] Owning the Baku oilfields was not enough to ensure productivity on those fields. Over a decade of unrest and three years of mercurial governance had left Baku's oil industry in dire need of organization and renovation.

Azneft and the Rise of a Technical Leadership

Starting with the purposeful destruction of oilfields in the 1905 worker strikes, through the upheaval of the Russian Revolution and Civil War, Baku's oil industry had virtually collapsed. According to one diagram made for the 1927 city plan, Baku's oil extraction hit a prerevolutionary high of 677.4 million poods in 1901, a year during which it supplied approximately half of the world's crude oil (a pood is prerevolutionary unit of mass equal to 16.4 kg.) (figure 3.6).[21] Oil extraction dipped during the 1905 Revolution, rebounded slightly between the wars, but by the time the Soviets controlled the fields in 1921 volume had plummeted again to just 157.1 million poods, a staggering 77 percent decrease in production from its 1901 apex. Immediate reestablishment of industrial and urban order in the region was paramount. Upon gaining control of Azerbaijan, the Bolsheviks merged 272 private oil companies in Baku to create a single state-controlled company, Azneftkom, later shortened to Azneft.[22]

Technically savvy Soviet leadership was critical to ensure a swift return to productivity in Baku, and the men tapped to fill both the top economic and political positions were carefully selected (figure 1.3). Days before the official capture of Baku, at a meeting of the Main Oil Committee of the Supreme Soviet of the National Economy, the chairmanship of the Baku Oil Committee was granted to Aleksandr Serebrovskii, who had joined the Bolshevik cause in 1903.[23] Serebrovskii's revolutionary credentials were vast, but his technical know-how and experience with organizational logistics were most important to the role he played in the revival of Baku's oil industry. His technical expertise was earned on both sides of the machine, as it were. Starting in 1904, at the age of twenty, Serebrovskii labored as a fitter at the famed Putilov machine-building plant in St. Petersburg, and after the 1905 revolution he worked as a fitter in the Balakhany oilfields of Baku. At both sites, he doubled as a labor organizer under assumed names. After further arrests and close scrapes, Serebrovskii escaped Russia and landed in Brussels, where he learned German and French and earned a mechanical engineering degree. He returned to Russia on Lenin's command in 1913 and steadily ascended in the Bolshevik power structure. After the Russian Revolution, Serebrovskii served as deputy chairman of a commission to supply the Red Army, a post that was followed by a deputy chairmanship of the Commissariat of Transportation.[24]

Lenin sent Serebrovskii as an emissary to Baku to organize the Azerbaijani oil industry for imminent transfer to Soviet hands days before the Red Army marched upon and captured the city. Lenin equipped Serebrovskii with extraordinary

Figure 1.3. Aleksandr Serebrovskii, first director of Azneft (center left), and Sergei Kirov, first secretary of the Communist Party of Azerbaijan (center right). Azneft, *Obzor Azerbaidzhanskoi neftianoi promyshlennosti za dva goda nationalizatsii: 1920–1922* (Baku: Azneft, 1922).

power—later referred to as "Ilyich's Mandate"—to undertake three tasks as head of Azneft. Serebrovskii was to 1) organize and make productive Baku's oil industry; 2) guide smooth transport of oil where directed; and 3) use military force as needed to ensure the success of the first two tasks.[25] In addition to his post as the first director of Azneft, Serebrovskii also served as chairman of the Board of the All-Russia Oil Syndicate and as deputy chair of the Supreme Council of the National Economy (Vysshiy sovet narodnogo khoziaistva, VSNKh or Vesenkha), which oversaw the management of the entire Soviet economy, and most important, heavy industry. Although Azneft had a geographically circumscribed industrial footprint, Serebrovskii's Union-scaled positions helped to keep the technical and labor crises in the Baku oilfields on the national agenda.

Soviet Azerbaijan's head political position was filled in the summer of 1921, when the Central Committee in Moscow appointed former Bolshevik revolutionary, Sergei Kirov, as the first secretary of the Communist Party of Azerbaijan.[26] Kirov was an apt political choice to oversee a republic mired in industrial production issues, as he was one of the only members of the Central Committee with technical schooling.[27] Kirov's technical competence, paired with his mythic people skills—he was known to visit production sites to speak with workers directly—communicated seriousness of purpose by the central leadership in Moscow to boost morale and bolster extraction, refinement, and export of Baku's petroleum products.[28]

NEP in Baku: Technical Innovation, Capital Improvement

To address the broad economic distress brought on by War Communism and to draw much-needed foreign investment to support their modernization project, the new socialist state enacted a strategical retreat.[29] At the Tenth Party Congress in March 1921, Lenin convinced his colleagues in Moscow to pass NEP, a step back from full nationalization. The state would control all large enterprises (e.g., factories, mines, railways) as well as enterprises of medium size, but small private enterprises employing fewer than twenty people were allowed.[30] Under NEP foreign concessions were sought, and international companies lured to the USSR to capitalize on industrialization projects that the Soviets were unable to fund themselves.

This shift in economic policy had enormously positive implications in Baku, as Azneft was sanctioned to reengage with international fuel networks. Azneft hired foreign technical specialists to consult on modernization projects, and the Soviet Naphtha (Oil) Syndicate began export negotiations with foreign companies and states such as Standard and Vacuum Oil in the United States, and the French and Italian ministries of the Navy.[31] Under Serebrovskii's leadership, Azneft sought out highly qualified specialists to oversee oilfield production, drilling, and affiliated services; attracted foreign consultants; and imported new equipment from abroad.[32] For Serebrovskii, modernization of the oil industry was tied to Western technological advances, specifically US drilling and pumping techniques. In a 1922 *Pravda* article, he announced a partnership with the US firm International Barnsdall Corporation that would "provide the equipment, start drilling in the oilfields, and organize the technical production of oil with deep pumps."[33] The oilfields were swiftly modernized. Electrical rotary drillers replaced ancient percussive models, new oilfields were opened, and the volume of extraction significantly increased.[34] In addition, Azneft built two new pipelines and three refinery complexes. Long-term technical innovation occurred in the sea. In 1922–23, the Bibi-Eibat Peninsula south of urban Baku was enlarged with fill and steel pilings to take advantage of the oil known to reside underwater, and in 1925 the first offshore well was tapped from a steel and wood ramp. Finally, sophisticated electrical prospecting began in 1928, which allowed for more accurate geological surveying and mapping of rock formations and sediments.[35] The modernization project resulted in a surge in production and export: Baku's oil exports in 1926–27 doubled those of 1913.[36]

The temporary import of foreign technicians to consult on Baku's modernization did not constitute a unidirectional transfer of expertise from the West to Soviet engineers, as Yves Cohen has stressed in his writing on early Soviet technology. Instead, these meetings initiated a circulatory process of knowledge sharing that allowed Baku to become an important node in the international network of oil technology exchange.[37] R. C. Beckstrom, dean of the college of petroleum engineering at the University of Tulsa, returned from his short consultancy to the Soviet government in Baku in 1929, praising Soviet ingenuity through stories of rapid electrification of fields and anecdotal tales of the positive impact of the four-day work-week.[38] Technical expertise was absorbed, processed, transformed, and improved on in Baku for the wider Eurasian context, such that the city became known as the "Oil Academy" of the Soviet Union.[39] The institutes and training facilities for oil industry technicians established in the early Soviet period sustained the city's stature within the industry long after other extraction sites in the Urals and Soviet Central Asia had leapfrogged Baku in total volume.

The Housing Question

Living conditions for Baku's oil workers were notoriously appalling. Prerevolutionary photographs show warrens of ramshackle low-rise residential buildings with forests of derricks in the distance (figure 1.4). Oilfield strikes from 1903 through the establishment of Soviet power in Azerbaijan were primarily economically motivated, with higher wages and paid days off dominating worker demands.[40] The first mention of housing in strike literature occurs in 1908, when union representatives met with oil industrialists to discuss the construction of worker settlements away from the fields, but no material improvement resulted from the talks.[41] Not until 1913 did complaints of substandard housing join the strikers' more standard economic requests. A leaflet published by the strike committee demanded that residences be removed from oilfields and factory precincts and located instead in dedicated worker settlements. They argued further that oversight of improved housing should be run by sanitation committees staffed by the workers. Oil industrialists not only refused these demands, they forcibly removed striking workers from company-owned, substandard rental housing.[42]

Socialism and housing are inextricable. The provision of suitable, affordable housing for workers was a primary concern in two treatises written by Friedrich Engels: *The Condition of the Working Class in England* (1845) and *The Housing Question* (1872). Engels proposed in the latter that social inequalities could not be solved through housing reform alone. Once social equity was achieved with the overthrow of capitalism, resolution to the housing problem would necessarily follow. Though Engels detailed myriad causes of the working-class housing crisis under capitalism, he did not provide an actionable template for housing provision in a postcapitalist society. The newly installed administrators of socialist Baku had to enact this transformation through experimentation.

The Chief Oil Committee of the Russian Federation (Glavneftkom) raised the subject of worker settlements (*rabochie poselki*) in Baku the week before the Red Army took the city, in the same document that named Serebrovskii director of Azneft. Glavneftkom petitioned Vesenkha for the right to oversee worker settlement construction in Baku, and not, per protocol, to cede control to Committee

Деревня Балаханы

Figure 1.4. Prerevolutionary worker housing in the oilfields of Baku, the village of Balakhany. Azneft, *Obzor Azerbaidzhanskoi neftianoi promyshlennosti za dva goda nationalizatsii: 1920–1922* (Baku: Azneft, 1922), 15.

for State Construction (Komitet gosudarstvennykh sooruzhenii or Komgosor). The document described how the organization should be run: "Under the Baku Oil Committee [Azneft], a temporary construction management group will be formed for settlement construction and will be charged to work on existing settlement projects and to develop estimates."[43] In this structure, Azneft would coordinate with Komgosor and other state agencies as needed but would retain control over the process of rehousing the oilfield workers. What this meant in practice was that planning decisions would issue from and address local interests.

Azneft's early attempts to address the so-called housing question (*zhilishchnyi vopros*) were piecemeal and limited in scope. This was not for lack of aspiration, but for paucity of timely data. In the fall of 1920, the Minor Commission on the Construction of Garden-Cities in the Baku Region, composed of representatives from the Building Department of Azneft, Komgosor, the Baku Department of Communal Services (Bakommunkhoz), and the unions began to meet. The group's first order of business was to gather detailed demographic and geographic material for the territories to be planned, a task that proved difficult. For demographic numbers, the commission was forced to rely on 1913 census data that they ran through a complex mathematical formula to arrive at projective settlement populations. Existing maps and plans of the Apsheron Peninsula were scattered among various intractable departments such as the Geological Committee in Petrograd. After unsuccessful attempts to gain access to cartographic data, the committee took surveying matters into their own hands. They commissioned a topographical map for the whole peninsula, with special care to be paid to the location of industrial complexes.[44] At the end of 1920, the group also commissioned exploratory plans for worker settlements near the oil-field villages of Binagady, Bibi-Eibat, Sabunchi, and the White Town.[45]

The spatial relationship between drilling sites and worker housing was of particular economic concern to Azneft. The sole map in Azneft's *Overview of the Baku Oil Industry during Two Years of Nationalization, 1920–22* indicates the entire Apsheron Peninsula veined with solid and dashed red lines (plate 2). The key reveals that these lines trace known and proposed anticline axes, geological folds along which oil and gas drilling is most productive. A solid red line circumscribes urban Baku and runs directly through the industrial drilling sites of Binagady, Balakhany, Sabunchi, Romany, and Surakhany to the north and northeast of the city center. Dark clusters indicate villages at these sites, which are the residential quarters of oil workers that sit directly on the cherished fault line (plate 3). The campaign to move workers into more suitable settlements must then be considered doubly motivated. Azneft publicly justified settlement construction as a socialist right for the proletarian workers in Baku's nationalized fields. Behind closed doors, Azneft representatives stressed the importance of clearing the sprawling residential quarters from potential drill sites as soon as possible for solely economic reasons.[46]

The ideal location for an oil worker settlement had to satisfy two contradictory requirements. First, new settlements needed to be clear of all current and future extraction sites, which meant moving existing housing off the anticline axis and building new housing significantly away from the fields. Azneft screened itself by speaking to this economic motivation through the concerns of prerevolutionary oil barons. "Serious housing space shortages in the industrial and factory regions, and the unsanitary conditions of the majority of existing housing, long ago forced employers to begin building residential houses for their workers and laborers [in Baku]," Azneft noted in its 1922 *Overview*. "Employers, however, acted with great reluctance because the houses took up land that could be drilled for oil."[47] Like the barons, the socialist overseers of the lucrative peninsula wished to reserve all possible oil-bearing land for future exploitation.

In direct conflict with the first precondition to remove housing from sites of extraction was the need for residential areas to be located as close as possible to industrial sites so that commuting workers would be less dependent on Baku's poor transportation infrastructure. Serebrovskii had been deputy chairman of the Commissariat of Transportation for a brief period in 1919 and was particularly attuned to the importance of reliable connectivity. He repeatedly stressed in his communications back to Moscow that subpar transportation hindered productivity in the Baku fields by as much as 50–60 percent.[48] Settlement sites had to be found in the close middle ground: far enough away from the anticline axis to preserve future drilling rights, but close enough to the axis to ensure ease of labor conveyance. The locations had to be precise; all the more reason to insist on accurate surveys of the peninsula.

The housing question was shelved for much of 1921, when even more pressing shortages wracked Baku. Azneft coffers were effectively empty by February of that year. Azneft's bankruptcy was due to decreasing volume of oil and insufficient compensation for its export. Because of oilfield destruction through the wars, outdated drilling methods, lack of qualified workers, and insufficient transportation to the fields, oil extraction numbers in the first two years of Azneft's tenure were shockingly poor. From the previously noted 1901 high of approximately 540 million poods, the annual volume of extraction in 1921 dropped to just 62 million poods.[49] The majority of oil exported from Baku was thus drawn from pre-Soviet stores. Upon nationalization of the industry, this waning supply was shipped throughout Soviet territories without Azneft receiving currency, bartered goods, or services in return.[50] Azneft had no income. The company was unable to pay its workers in a timely fashion or offer them the most basic provisions. In March 1921, grain rations were reduced for workers in the industry, who were forced to forage for sustenance. In April, the oil workers who had not already abandoned their posts went on strike.

A Plenipotentiary Committee from the Council of Labor and Defense (Sovet truda i oborony or STO) arrived in Baku in August to address the collapse of the city's oil industry. The committee voted to institute the following measures immediately: "1) provide the oil workers with a living wage, as well as food, clothing and shoes; 2) provide the oil industry with technical materials and transportation resources; 3) establish single control of the industry [Azneft]."[51] With financial support from Moscow, Azneft was able to procure food and clothing, and to ensure payment to its workers. These local measures, supplemented by foreign technical assistance to modernize the industry, gradually increased oil outputs on the Apsheron Peninsula.

Plans for worker settlements were submitted to the Garden City Commission in the midst of the funding emergency. The cost for their realization: 42 million rubles gold. Not included in the estimate were the tramlines, water system and supply, and road networks necessary to connect tabula rasa settlements with industry and the city proper. In 1921, Azneft had neither the funding—nor the prospects for funding—to undertake such an ambitious project. Logistics support from Moscow for construction materials acquisition and transportation was not forthcoming, and the proposed four-year project schedule was also untenable.[52] Given strained labor conditions, Azneft opted to institute immediate, if less radical, housing solutions. Work toward a partial resolution to Baku's housing crisis ensued at a unit-by-unit scale.

Housing without Planning (or Socialism at the Scale of the Unit)

Azneft described a two-stage process of housing construction in their 1925 *Overview*. According to the company, 1920 to 1923 constituted a first phase of stopgap renovation work. The restoration of the oil industry hinged on provision of housing near the fields, but there were only enough suitable apartments to accommodate 50 percent of their workers, and certain key industrial sites like Zabrat had no housing at all.

The Building Department of Azneft examined the housing stock in Balakhany-Sabunchi and decided as a first step to renovate fifteen existing residential buildings for a total of 236 improved family apartments. Project managers economized on building materials by using reserve stores from Azneft's own warehouses and transporting them to the sites by animal cart. Further savings were obtained through a competitive bid process. Three of the lowest bidding contractors were granted a single building to renovate; this quickened construction and provided Azneft the opportunity to assess each team qualitatively. The whole first phase cost Azneft 172,000 rubles, a far cry from the 42 million required for a more systemic settlement solution to the housing question.[53]

In the two years that followed, Azneft threw labor and money "at the expense of the main oil industry" into addressing the housing question. The bootstrap efforts are described well in the company's five-year overview. "Dilapidated housing was brought to order, and abandoned boiler rooms, barns, workshops, and other premises, which the majority of the time consisted of nothing more than bare walls, were rebuilt and equipped as living quarters. Because of construction materials shortages, it was often necessary to create from two dilapidated structures one building that was more or less sufficient for housing."[54] By the end of 1923, Azneft had rehabilitated some 8,000 worker apartments throughout the Apsheron Peninsula. These units were considered "temporary residential stock" by the company, expediently located near the fields so that extraction could continue unabated.[55]

Azneft chose to supplement housing in the fields with existing apartments in urban areas of Baku. Inner-city housing was a mixture of largely self-built one- and two-story houses and some taller residential buildings in the gridded *forshtadt* (figure 1.5). In January 1922, Azneft rented from the Baku Executive Committee (Bakispolkom) forty-three residential buildings in the city and factory regions, a solution that provided nothing but grief for the company. "This [renting] effort offered absolutely no helpful results," the author of the *Overview* lamented, "since all of the houses turned out to be inhabited by people unauthorized by Azneft. It was impossible to evict them because there was no free residential space in the city in which to put them. Besides this, all of the rented houses needed expensive capital repairs and Azneft did not have the money for this. For this reason, renting became an unhelpful burden."[56] Azneft's own account reveals that no serious reconnaissance of the rented buildings was undertaken before the rental agreement with the city was signed. Not only were the buildings already inhabited by nonevictable, non-Azneft employees, but they also needed serious maintenance. Azneft pulled out of the agreement just three months into the lease and returned the majority of the units to the city administration. The abject failure of this episode reveals just how inexperienced the Azneft Building Committee was on questions of real estate development and management. The buildings they rented, sight unseen, tallied nicely against their deficit of worker units. But the problematic materiality of the buildings and their residents were issues that Azneft staff members were not even aware to consider in advance.

Official documentation offers little evidence of how workers responded to the first round of accommodations provided by Azneft—we hear workers' voices only through the mouthpiece of the union. The First All-Russian Conference of Oil Workers passed a resolution at the end of 1921 to initiate the rational, detailed, and implementable planning of dedicated workers villages in the Transcaucasus, which included the oil-bearing Baku, Grozny, and Embe regions.[57] But it was not until mid-1923 that the Presidium of the Azerbaijani Council of Trade Unions adopted a concrete proposal for the construction of worker villages in Baku.[58] Workers and their families to be housed can be glimpsed, fleetingly, in Azneft's *Overview* of the first two years of oilfield nationalization. The majority of illustrations celebrate the inanimate industrial infrastructure of oil, from derricks to reservoirs and pipelines. Workers appear periodically, engaged in the dirty, difficult manual labor of drilling. Although few illustrations show Azneft-sponsored social infrastructure, one rare photograph features a children's house of rest in the White Town (plate 4). Closely

Figure 1.5. Replanning the City of Baku photo series. Typical self-built one- and two-story housing in the urban center of Baku, 1928. Photo: L. Bregadze. RGALI, f. 2991, o. 1, d. 17, l. 17.

shorn oil workers' children stare at the camera, posed in front of a building most likely seized from the Nobels during nationalization, and commandeered for the purpose. There are no images of worker housing.

Azneft's first-phase housing program suffered from myopia, brought on by an absence of reliable data. The number of workers and families to be housed was unknown as was the number of salvageable units. The cost of undertaking new construction was no more than a rough estimate. Without information to plan forward, Azneft housing administrators were reduced to solving the problems immediately in front of them, which meant renovating existing stock, unit by unit. The magnitude of the housing crisis became clear only in 1923, when Azneft stepped back to assess the work done to date. Regardless of the amount of money, materials, and effort expended to house workers during the previous three years, the first "more or less full examination of the housing question" exposed a grim state of affairs:

> With about 45,000 people working for Azneft—120,000 including families— Azneft could provide only around 20,000 apartments, of which only about 50 percent were of sufficient quality to meet sanitary, hygienic, or technical norms. The crush in these apartments was extreme . . . In many barracks, beds occupied every corner, and workers would use them in succession, depending on when they were on duty or on watch. More than 7,000 industrial or factory workers lived in Baku and every day they wasted much strength and time getting from the city to the workplace.
>
> The conditions of some of this housing was so poor that residents were constantly fearful of collapse. This picture powerfully advanced the issue of building new apartments, and in 1923, Azneft began to construct new houses of the settlement type in areas specially designated for development.[59]

Azneft administrators were shocked by the data this report revealed. Despite the money spent to date, they had provided enough housing for only half of their workers, and half again of those units failed to meet the most basic hygienic standards. All told, suitable housing was available for just 25 percent of Azneft workers. The stark picture painted by raw numbers prompted reconnaissance of qualitative data as well. Although the text does not provide details of failed sanitary, hygienic, or technical standards, the mental image of shift after shift of oil workers cycling through a single barrack bed is enough to envision lives conducted under conditions of extreme domestic scarcity.[60]

The drive to begin new housing construction picked up speed and momentum once the director of Azneft became involved. Beginning in mid-1923, Serebrovskii was present at, and chaired, many of the housing-related meetings. He served as chair of the Committee on the Construction of Workers' Houses, a group composed of his own technical staff, union leaders, and representatives from the impacted industrial regions. Serebrovskii opened one October meeting not with an exploratory or descriptive report—as was customary for such working groups—but with pronouncements. All new worker houses would have concrete foundations. Only one-story houses would be built in the settlements to economize on construction costs. All work would be completed by January 1, 1924. Serebrovskii's assertive commands ensured that housing units came on line swiftly, but subsequent meeting minutes suggest that the aesthetic result was less than satisfactory. In the midst of the construction process, the committee requested that the Azneft Technical Bureau reconsider the typical window installation. To improve the look of the residential buildings, sashes were added to windows already installed, and standard window dimensions were enlarged.[61]

Hundreds of new houses were being built throughout Baku and the adjacent oilfields without anticipatory planning. Azneft was capable of providing materials and local logistics to amass a portfolio of housing units, but they did not have the expertise to consider the housing program holistically. Documentation of their early housing initiatives reveals that the sequence of construction decisions was often inverted. Small-scale material decisions were taken before large-scale infrastructural systems were considered. Take as an illustrative example the order of topics covered in one meeting of the Committee on the Construction of Workers' Houses. The group began by agreeing to prescribe a cement additive to the standard plaster mix so that interior walls would dry faster. This topic was followed by an accounting of the number of eight- and ten-length wooden boards needed for construction in each region. Only after these and other matters of fine unit-scale detail were discussed did the committee turn to those issues that a trained planner would have broached months before building materials arrived on site: open space design and the sewage system.

It may have been the interagency nature of these large-scale tasks that caused planning delay. Questions about the proposed sewage system had to be discussed by regional representatives who in turn were tasked to establish a special commission composed of engineers, architects, representatives of the technical inspectorate and Labor Ministry (Narkomtrud), and a sanitary doctor.[62] To construct a municipal system like a sewer, then, a deliberate administrative process was required. Conversely, individual buildings paid for and owned by Azneft solely could be constructed immediately without bureaucratic friction or municipal oversight. The fact remains, however, that through 1923 Azneft housing was renovated, rented, and built in a planning vacuum.

NEP: Local Plans under Centralized Planning

The main economic planning body for the new Soviet state was the State General Planning Commission (Gosudarstvennyi komitet po planirovaniiu or Gosplan), established in February 1921.[63] Unlike other significant governmental departments, Gosplan did not control any particular sector of the economy but rather served as planning adviser for both the long- and short-term economy of the Soviet Union as a whole, and its economists answered directly to the Politburo.[64]

Despite the planning commission's outsized brief, Gosplan had limited impact on Soviet economic policy in its first four years of existence (1921–25), a period Davies and Khlevnyuk deemed "the dictatorship of finance."[65] After War Communism failed to establish a firm foundation for the economy, Soviet authorities used the first years of the NEP to stabilize the budget and currency, seeking to achieve equilibrium in the economy between supply and demand. Such relative conservatism did not lend itself to big plans, and indeed, there was little aspirational physical planning undertaken at Gosplan during NEP.

Furthermore, centralized planning was not felt outside of Moscow in the early and mid-1920s. Baku, a city whose petroleum products were at the very center of the Soviet economy, was hardly a provincial town. But as the investigation into its NEP-era planning activity demonstrates, work on the city largely was financed by local oil and overseen by local administrators. Gosplan is not referred to in Baku planning documentation until 1924, when its planners in Moscow refused an official request from Azneft for land on which to build an oil worker settlement.[66] After this brief engagement, Gosplan again receded from view in the story of Baku's general plan, replaced by specialists deeply invested in the particulars of a site whose complexity could only be understood from the ground.

In 1923, the year Azneft began to construct ground-up housing, 550 new apartments in one- and two-story residential buildings were completed, at a cost of approximately 5,500 rubles per unit. In 1924, 750 apartments were added. The prevailing unit types were one- and two-room apartments with kitchen and veranda. Four schools, accommodating 2,000 students, were also built adjacent to the new housing.[67] According to Azneft, the construction work progressed smoothly. Local stone, lime, and sand were brought to the worksites on Azneft's own narrow-gauge rail line and by auto-transport. Delayed delivery of non-local building materials—alabaster, iron, gas piping, glass—often stopped work, however. Building materials factories located throughout Soviet territories were still under construction, so Azneft had to fight with projects in other corners of the USSR for access to the last surviving prerevolutionary stocks.[68] Without the support of Moscow, how was the construction financed? For the most part, Azneft paid for the work and materials out of its own coffers. In 1923 and 1924 combined, Azneft spent 1.9 million rubles of its money toward worker settlements and over 2.3 million rubles toward building materials. The Baksovet pitched in to provide some free transport, stones, and other building materials.[69]

For the first four years of its operation, Azneft relied on local technical staff to deal with the problem of worker housing. The ad hoc answers to Azneft's housing question are attributable to insufficient information: poor accounting of the people, housing units, materials, and territories under their purview. Without numbers to assess the shape and magnitude of the problem, an appropriately long-term answer was unreachable. Insufficient information in the realm of technical expertise also plagued the Azneft housing program. The state oil company needed to obtain outside knowledge on the settlement issue, and it did so through two imports: a national expert and US technical literature, machines, and houses.

Importing Expertise 1: The Well-Traveled, Well-Spoken Planner

The Azneft Building Committee resolved that it was high time to invite a housing expert to Baku. On October 29, 1924, Professor Aleksandr Ivanitskii arrived from Moscow to present a report on settlement construction at a joint meeting of the Azerbaijani Division of the All-Russian Union of Miners and representatives from various local organizations including Azneft, the Baku Department of Communal Services, the local Commissariat of Labor, and the City Health Commission. Ivanitskii was an engineer by training who was heavily involved in the Moscow Architectural Society as a section head, competition jury member, and lecturer on the issues of city planning. Like others of the first generation of Soviet planners, Ivanitskii was a specialist skilled in prerevolutionary tactics, well traveled and versed in European urban models, but eager to establish modes of practice appropriate to the new social and economic conditions.[70]

In a prepared talk, Ivanitskii shared his knowledge of small-scale residential construction in England. He illustrated his presentation with colored lantern slides of drawings and photographs of the projects he described in his report, many obtained during a research trip he took to England in late 1923 to early 1924. The housing situation in England, as Ivanitskii painted it, was remarkably similar to Baku's. Not only had World War I caused great destruction of existing housing stock, but it was also a period during which no new housing was constructed. By 1918, English municipal governments acknowledged that they would need assistance from the state to embark on a coordinated national housing campaign. The approved plan promised construction of one million new cottage-style apartments by the end of 1922. Ivanitskii noted that given the scope of the task and limited funding, architects exercised extreme design discipline. "[The English] sought to establish interior spatial standards devoid of extraneous decoration," he explained. "The plans of the apartments were developed purely from the point of view of economics, comfort, and hygiene."[71] To meet but not exceed these three criteria of economics, comfort, and hygiene must be the goal of all new housing in Baku going forward, stated Ivanitskii. He went on to share dimensional data for each domestic room type, followed by pricing data. He stressed in closing that the English postwar housing construction campaign answered so many important questions about small-scale residential construction, and generated such high-level scientific research, that its results needed to be utilized by the Soviet technical community, especially regarding the economization and standardization of housing types and household equipment.

At the conclusion of his formal report, Ivanitskii narrated a color slideshow that featured pre- and postwar worker settlements in England, France, and Wales.[72] Among his examples was Bournville, the model worker village founded by the Cadbury Company in 1893, and Port Sunlight, another model worker village built adjacent to the Lever Brothers' soap-making factory in Merseyside, northwest England, between 1899 and 1914 (figure 1.6). Each of these company towns provided social infrastructure including schools, a hospital, sports fields, and arts facilities in addition to housing. Ivanitskii ended his slideshow with images of regional plans on which worker settlements were shown in relation, and linked by road and rail, to sites of industry.

The chair of the assembled group proposed to extend the meeting to allow Professor Ivanitskii to share his opinions of the planned extensions of Azneft's worker settlements. Ivanitskii's incisive assessment of Baku's conditions revealed that he had done his research. He articulated two opposing points of view regarding the optimal location of worker settlements near Baku. The first option proposed that new worker settlements be placed in a ring close to the existing city and away from oil-bearing lands. The long-term benefit of such a scheme was that settlements in this middle territory would be subsumed naturally into the urban fabric as central Baku expanded. In addition, urban infrastructure such as roads, tramlines, electricity, water, and sewer systems would be more easily and rationally extended to these new areas. Ivanitskii characterized this as the "centralization" option, which made sense for the city administration, but which posed two dangers for Azneft. "First— there is the issue of transportation and private funding to transport the workers to industrial sites and back. Second—there are practical urban issues to deal with, including a large population, existing settlements that need to be transformed, renovation of structures, and difficult hygienic conditions. To solve these issues is very important not only from a humanitarian standpoint, but also from a cleanliness and production standpoint, as they are connected with the task to increase the quality and production of labor."[73]

A second "decentralized" option synthesized Azneft's position. In accordance with new housing already completed, the oil company advocated for worker settlements to be placed in closer proximity to the oilfields, tethered to sites of extraction. The degree of proximity was of primary concern to Azneft from the time of its consolidation. As Ivanitskii noted, the ideal settlement location was far enough away from the anticline axis to allow for further oil extraction in the future, but close enough to ensure easy transport of workers to the fields. This scheme had significant pitfalls for Azneft. Primary among them was the daunting and expensive task of creating an entire technical and social infrastructure separate from the municipality.

Although he provided an acute assessment of Baku's situation, Ivanitskii refused to provide a solution to the future settlement location problem or even to weigh

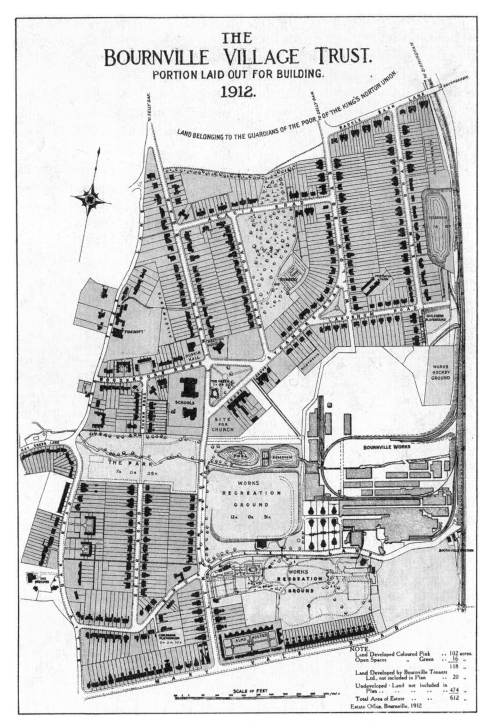

Figure 1.6. Bournville Works and Village, Bournville, England. Cocoa and Chocolate Works of Cadbury Bros., Ltd. Aleksandr Ivanitskii highlighted for his future clients in Baku the company's social infrastructure including schools, a hospital, sports fields, and arts facilities in addition to worker housing. Harvard Art Museums/Fogg Museum, Transfer from the Carpenter Center for the Visual Arts, Social Museum Collection. Photo: ©President and Fellows of Harvard College.

in on the housing construction underway. Instead, he was "more interested in the absence of a general plan than the plan of any individual settlement."[74] Consider for a moment the impact of this comment. In making it, the planner from Moscow ran the risk of irreparably alienating his hosts, most notably Azneft. Significant numbers of new worker housing units were already built and occupied by October 1924. That they were constructed without a general plan should be evident from the preceding history. But prior to Ivanitskii, no one had stressed the seriousness of this oversight.

The administrations of Azneft and the Baksovet had to be educated on the critical financial repercussions of building without planning. Ivanitskii warned the assembled that there was great risk of wasting money on costly engineering preparations for territories poorly suited to settlement construction. Before selecting a site, it was important to determine a rational road system congenial to Baku's difficult topography and to assess the proximity of existing transportation lines. To quantify the risk, Ivanitskii provided the group with startling numbers: "Construction without drafting a rational general plan threatens to increase all estimates—for the construction of roads, paving, planting, water piping, sewage—from 50–60 percent."[75] If Azneft captured these savings, Ivanitskii claimed, tens of millions of rubles could more aptly be allocated to increased housing capacity.

Additional economization was possible through intelligent planning of the typical worker housing units. Ivanitskii noted that his overall impression of completed Azneft housing was positive. The construction quality was solid, the units were spacious and light-filled, and they were, for the most part, comfortable and hygienic. Ivanitskii's criticism centered on the "luxuriousness" of the typical unit, which he considered excessive in area, volume, and ornamentation. "It is unpleasant to see acts of superfluous decoration that are unnecessary from an architectural standpoint and expensive," he stated. "All of these should be discarded, and residential architectural decision-making should turn to a more severe form, based on mass and space. The best decoration for the house is cleanliness and green all around. In order to move toward economic construction, it is necessary to reconsider all the needs imposed and understand the social implications, such that every hundred rubles spent on unnecessary decoration—which is, anyway, of a philistine character—is a subtraction from the beneficial spatial capacity of constructed living space."[76]

While his critique of Azneft's new worker housing began with a personal expression of distaste for decorative elements applied to the building exteriors, Ivanitskii took care to frame the problem of architectural style in terms of hygiene and economics. Simple, standardized units enhanced only by cleanliness and greenery were the least expensive to build. Ivanitskii suggested that once pilasters, moldings, and double-leaved doors were removed from typical unit designs, the Azneft Building Committee would find itself flush with unexpected extra funds with which to construct additional units. What was most important about Azneft's new worker units was that they had "nothing in common with the prerevolutionary type of housing," and they marked the beginning of a large-scale and ongoing effort to solve the housing question. "All of these flaws are easy to fix," Ivanitskii noted in closing.

Engineer / City-Builder / Planner

Aleksandr Ivanitskii made an immediate and deep impression on those members of the Baksovet Building Committee who attended his October presentation. The Moscow planner's critical remarks after his prepared talk were directed at both Azneft and the Baksovet and centered on one problem for which both organizations were accountable: Baku had no plan. Azneft was to blame for a myopic unit-by-unit construction campaign that left worker housing unconnected to regional transportation networks. The Baksovet was accountable for permitting Azneft to get so far without requiring systematic planning to benefit the urban region as a whole. If together Azneft and the Baksovet conceived of the housing crisis as more than a question of square footage and expanded their thinking to the scale of the region, more economical answers could emerge, the planner argued.

In the late fall of 1924, soon after his presentation for the institutions and organizations invested in solving Baku's housing problem, Professor Ivanitskii was hired for two separate though interrelated planning jobs. Azneft commissioned him to develop a comprehensive plan for Azneft worker settlements and detailed plans for four: Belgorod, Binagady, Montina, and Stepan Razin.[77] The timeline for this effort was extremely short since construction had already begun in some of these sites. Concurrently, the Baksovet engaged Ivanitskii to prepare a general plan for the entire city of Baku.

Who was this expert Azneft and the Baksovet entrusted with their territories? Aleksandr Ivanitskii was educated as a civil engineer, not as an architect, a fact that may explain his propensity to address function before composition.[78] He attended technical school in Kharkiv before receiving his ultimate degree in 1904, with honors, from the Institute for Civil Engineering in St. Petersburg. Upon graduation, Ivanitskii was retained to teach at the institute, and he also worked professionally on a wide range of projects. One of those projects was the reconstruction of the Marinskii Palace, for which Ivanitskii worked under the direction of preservationist and champion of classical revivalist practice, Leontii Benois.[79] In 1913, Ivanitskii moved to Moscow and started his own practice.

Ivanitskii was well traveled by the time he arrived in Baku, and he brought his experiences abroad to bear on his professional work. He was also well read and an exhaustive gatherer of urban precedents. Ivanitskii's writings are laced with concrete examples and quantitative data from planning work in Europe and the United States, and he regularly translated foreign planning tracts into Russian.[80] In one article in *Construction Industry* (*Stroitel'naia promyshlennost'*) he analyzed notable international planning and public building legislation to goad Soviet policy-makers into instituting similar measures. England, France, and Germany provided examples that a Russian public would expect. But by the end of a single long para-graph, Ivanitskii had also detailed laws in Sweden, Norway, Denmark, Belgium, Austria, and the United States. Ivanitskii noted that by 1923, all US cities with populations over 100,000 had instituted zoning plans, and large public and private funds had been expended on the efforts (St. Louis to the tune of $87 million, and Philadelphia: $70 million).[81] It would be impossible to apply capitalist examples to the socialist condition without some adjustment, Ivanitskii conceded. Nonetheless, proper coordination of industry, commerce, and public amenities would lead to municipal health, no matter the prevailing economic system.

Ivanitskii argued time and again that planning requires expansive conceptions of both space and time. The city, for Ivanitskii, was a complex organism that encom-passed more than the urban fabric within existing city limits. To understand how a city functions, the planner has to study the broader region. "Regional zoning is of major economic and social importance," he wrote. "Proper distribution of special purpose areas (central-administrative, commercial, residential, industrial, factory) provides the necessary framework not only for building a network of main streets, paths and all local transportation . . . but also for the development of social life, production, and trade. The social life of the city requires selection, proper distri-bution, and correct communication of its centers."[82] In Baku, this meant that the planner's scale of intervention was the Apsheron Peninsula. Likewise, the timescale of planning work had to extend beyond the present. Ivanitskii advocated for expan-sion plans that anticipated growth up to twenty-five to thirty years into the future. This period was selected because it corresponded to the amortization period for large infrastructural projects like tramways, water and sewer systems, and recon-struction of main railway junctions or ports.

Most important, planning requires site-specificity. Intense research and abun-dant data are necessary to determine the appropriate planning approach for a city. For Ivanitskii, data was king: demographic data, economic data, and especially data on existing physical conditions, for *without accurate preliminary surveys, serious planning work is impossible.*"[83] As it turned out the Baksovet, Ivanitskii's client for the city plan, was useless where data provision was concerned. Ivanitskii's tolerance for work without proper information, and his ability to invent work-around plan-ning tools, would be tested in Baku.

Importing Expertise 2: Americanization

Azneft director Serebrovskii traveled to the United States for several months at the end of 1924 as representative of the Presidium of the Vesenkha, which explains his absence from Ivanitskii's initial presentation in Baku. In his 1925 book, *The Oil* and Gas Industry in America (*Neftianaia i gazovaia promyshlennost' v amerike*), Serebrovksii explained that the goal of his trip was "to explore the conditions of the oil business in the United States, and to borrow from the Americans that which might be helpful for the Soviet oil industry."[84] He wished to see the US oil industry for himself and to garner US assistance to modernize the Baku fields. US press referred to Serebrovskii as the Soviet Rockefeller, a nickname that stuck throughout his 1924 and 1927 visits to the United States.[85]

Serebrovskii's visit was one of the first organized by Amtorg, the Soviet-American trade organization based in New York. On July 30, 1924, the day after his arrival in the United States, Serebrovskii visited the Manhattan offices of Standard Oil. Executive director Walter Teague entertained his Soviet counterpart and began talks that would lead to Serebrovskii being granted unrestricted visits to Standard's oilfields and logistical assistance to purchase US equipment. The sticking point in the initial talks between Teague and Serebrovskii was money. Azneft did not have sufficient cash reserves to purchase machinery outright; credit from US banks was impossible, owing to the lack of official Soviet-US diplomatic ties; and only Standard's senior partner, John D. Rockefeller, could authorize monetary assistance to Azneft.

Serebrovskii wrote to the elder Rockefeller to request a face-to-face meeting. Surprisingly, Rockefeller agreed. Serebrovskii recounted his visit with the US oil baron:

> [Rockefeller] was very well informed about things in Baku . . . and about our resources. He emphasized several times that they were willing to support Soviet industry on the condition that we be his allies . . .
>
> I proposed two arrangements. First, he would give a letter of guarantee to his bank to pay our supplier invoices from future earnings on petroleum products . . . Rockefeller thought for a long time, and then looked at me attentively and unexpectedly agreed. Second, he would give a letter to suppliers in which he would recommend us as buyers well known to him and recommend that we be given the same discount on invoices as Standard Oil. Rockefeller accepted this much more readily.
>
> It was around five in the afternoon, and tea was served. The old man poured tea for me, offered me cookies with jam, and then invited me to take a stroll. He walked quickly and for a long time, half an hour, and we went around the entire forest park. I was hardly able to keep up with him, and my leg ached. The two of us dined . . . In the morning I was awakened before dawn. The old man was going on a stroll before breakfast and wanted to talk along the way . . . After breakfast I bid him farewell and left.[86]

Two crucial agreements that would transform the Soviet oil industry were forged at the initial meeting over tea and cookies. First, Standard Oil would act as Azneft's sole creditor in the United States. US suppliers would bill Standard Oil directly for Azneft's machinery purchases, and Standard's bank would keep track of the debt to be paid from Baku's oil futures. Second, based on Rockefeller's personal request, Azneft would receive the same industry discount offered to Standard on all machinery purchased. With one meeting, Serebrovskii secured the most modern equipment for the Baku fields at a discount. Serebrovskii later learned what had caused Rockefeller to trust him so quickly: the patch on the bottom of his shoe. Rockefeller reportedly told his financial director, "This man can be trusted in debt. He is not a spendthrift, does not drink wine, does not smoke, and I like him."[87] By the time he left the United States, Serebrovskii had purchased more than $8 million worth of US machinery on behalf of Azneft—with Rockefeller's money.[88]

On his visits to oilfields in Pennsylvania, Texas, Oklahoma, and California, Serebrovskii also toured oil workers' residential quarters. In his 1925 book, published in London on the return trip, Serebrovskii included an image of the oilfields in Long Beach, California, a Standard Oil site that demonstrated one possible relationship between oil derricks and worker housing (figure 1.7). In the book, written primarily for his colleagues at Vesenkha, who were likely unaware of the full degree of the complications he was dealing with in Baku, Serebrovskii took the opportunity to stress the importance of worker housing provision again. "The workers and laborers of Azneft need housing. Historically this was not provided to them, and even now it is insufficient. It has been necessary to develop an extensive construction program that is even now incomplete; it was necessary to organize a number of construction offices for settlement construction. Finally, we have just organized an entire Construction Committee."[89]

Фиг. 106. Расположение вышек на промыслах в Лонг Биче, Калифорния. Вдали виден знаменитый Signal Hill, давший самые богатые скважины в Калифорнии.

Figure 1.7. Worker housing among oil derricks, Long Beach, California. Illustration from Serebrovskii's 1925 book on his travels to explore the US oil industry. A. P. Serebrovskii, *Neftianaia i gazovaia promyshlennost' v Amerike* (Moscow: Tsentral'noe upravlenie pechati VSNKh, 1925).

According to one account, he ordered a whole small town of worker cottages from American manufacturers to be shipped back to Baku.[90] Although this story is difficult to corroborate, Serebrovskii's trip to the United States did come less than a decade after leading US industrial corporations constructed entire company towns utilizing prefabricated housing types. In 1916, the Austin Motor Company shipped two hundred houses from the Alladin Company in Bay City, Michigan to Birmingham, England to accommodate their auto workers, and in 1918, Standard Oil made a record-breaking $1 million order with the Sears Roebuck & Company for 192 Honor-Bilt worker houses installed near coal fields in southwestern Illinois.[91] In both of these cases, the prefabricated houses were exclusively single-family types. A simple model from the first decades of the twentieth century, like the Sears, Roebuck and Co. Wabash Honor-Bilt Home from 1913, does exhibit certain architectural similarities with the Azneft "American" housing and with later worker housing designs for Stepan Razin. Shared details include single-story living arrangements, extended entry porches, shallow-hipped roof lines, and even, in some cases, double-columned porch supports (figure 1.8).

Thanks to Azneft's own reports, it is clear that Serebrovskii returned from his trip abroad laden with specialty literature and technical manuals on settlement planning. The US materials were handed over to Azneft's engineers to meticulously review, ingest, and process for the Baku context. Whether they were built from in-house designs or shipped from the United States, 110 "experimental American apartment types" (*opytnykh kvartir amerikanizirovannogo tipa*) were built in Baku's worker settlements in 1925. The express goal of this experiment was "to test the applicability of these types for all new Azneft housing and to explore new production organization and construction methods."[92]

A so-called American house is featured in Azneft's 1925 *Overview*, this one built in Shubany, a village in the hills west of Baku proper. The choice of location is unexplained, but it is not one of the new settlements designed by Ivanitskii. The photograph shows a three-quarter elevation of a single-story house (figure 1.9). The left edge of the photo clips the facade, making the building's full-length unknown. There is, however, a thick pilaster and chimney that appear to mark the centerline of the building, suggesting that this a so-called paired house, with mirrored units on either side of the center pilaster. The house is striking for its solidity, the generosity of its window openings, and its decorative excesses. The photograph highlights one unit's pedimented entry portico held up by four slender columns. An intricately profiled finial rises from the pediment. The covered entry porch is approximately four feet proud of the main body of the building, deep enough for two scale figures—one leaning on the balustrade, one standing at the back wall—to be cast in shadow. An off-center door sits behind the standing figure, and the remainder of the porch wall is taken up by tall double-leaved windows set off by contrasting surrounds. Compared to the stark settlement houses at Binagady, shown from afar in a photograph below it, the American house is the very exemplar of philistine taste that Ivanitskii condemned in his remarks months before.

Figure 1.8. The Wabash Honor-Bilt Home, Sears, Roebuck and Co., c. 1913. Extended entry porch and paired column supports are similar to the "American" houses built in the Soviet oilfields of Baku. Sears Holdings Collection.

Вверху: американский дом в Шубанах.
Внизу: общий вид поселка в Бинагадах.

Figure 1.9. "American" house in Shubany (top) and general view of the Bingady settlement (bottom), Baku, Azerbaijan, 1925. Azneft, *Obzor Azerbaidzhanskoi neftianoi promyshlennosti za piat' let nationalizatsii: 1920–1925* (Baku: Azneft, 1925), 70–71.

In addition to technical literature, Serebrovskii returned to Baku with new construction machinery. The machines that saved the most time and effort, according to Azneft, were those that extracted local stone for building blocks and dug pits for the sand used in mortar and concrete aggregate.[93] Serebrovskii also brought back examples of the latest American domestic appliances, such as gas stovetops, washing machines, and vacuum cleaners, in addition to packages of sanitary paper drinking cups for the Azneft headquarters in Baku.[94]

By Azneft's account, the US experiment was a success. The standard construction schedule was accelerated by 50–70 percent, and costs were reduced by 50 percent. The pilot project's positive outcome was due to three newly acquired resources: a complete set of technical-planning materials, modern construction machines, and the experimental construction itself. Together the brains, the brawn, and the built work provided Azneft with a model for a rationalized design and construction process. "In short," the company claimed at the end of 1925, "construction has developed an apparatus (*stroitel'stvo razvernulos' v apparat*), which begins to work broadly on Azneft settlement construction. In the near future, we will need to build up to 24,000 new settlement apartments that correspond to all of the requirements of our new cultural life."[95] In the coming year, Azneft's confidence in the apparatus would grow with the assistance of rationalized planning and implementation of new standardized housing types built proximate to the fields in the Stepan Razin settlement.

Azneft leadership was a perfect client group for the first comprehensive Soviet planning effort. The industrial project, they came to understand, began at the scale of the worker's unit, expanded to the scale of the settlement, and encompassed, finally, the whole oil-producing city-region. Azneft director Aleksandr Serebrovskii, in particular, a trained engineer and a seasoned logistician, understood that industries—from oil extraction to housing construction—reward technical innovation. He and his Soviet colleagues in Baku were of a mindset to accept external assistance, whether in the form of US drilling equipment or models for worker housing.[96] The latter import, a vetted worker housing model, demonstrated the benefits of developing a catalog of standardized residential types that Azneft could deploy with speed and confidence to address immediate housing needs in locations that supported the oil industry. The first housing models were architecturally derivative, but their rapid installation permitted construction to commence while new, indigenous Soviet housing types could be devised for installation at the edge of the oilfields and in the city of Baku.

2

FROM GARDEN CITIES TO URBAN SUPERBLOCKS

Of all the experiments in worker housing construction in the Soviet Union, it seems to me the most successful is the Azneft experiment. The Baku worker settlements are beautifully built . . . "These small towns are built by smart people," is what you think about them.

—Maxim Gorky (1928)

After four years of Soviet control in Baku, the city's socialist administrators were painfully aware that the provision of workforce housing was more than an ideological imperative. Housing was required to meet industrial production targets. The Moscow planner Aleksandr Ivanitskii, brought on to oversee the Baku planning effort, offered two logical options for the siting of dedicated worker settlements. A decentralized option would place settlements directly adjacent to oil extraction sites to limit the workers' commute but would also require significant capital outlay to build all housing, services, and utilities from scratch. A centralized option would locate settlements at the edge of the existing city to take advantage of proximity to municipal infrastructure but would necessitate significant transportation upgrades to convey workers from their residential quarters to the oilfields north of the city.

Ivanitskii declined to choose an alternative for Baku, but his incisive synthesis of the issues won him two clients—Azneft and the Baksovet—each of whom favored a different option. Azneft, the Azerbaijan state oil company, hired Ivanitskii to design four decentralized worker settlements in the territory between the city

and the anticline axis, along which drilling is most lucrative. At Stepan Razin, the
first constructed settlement closest to the oilfields, Ivanitskii and his team designed
everything from the settlement plan down to standardized housing types. By contrast, the Baksovet, the municipal Communist Party decision-making body, wished
to pursue the centralized settlement option at the city's northern edge. In the Armenikend neighborhood of Baku, Ivanitskii and team devised a standardized urban
block that could be replicated throughout the city grid.

The Baku settlement projects Stepan Razin and Armenikend yielded two planning paradigms of marked influence in the subsequent phases of the Soviet experiment: the garden-settlement, a modified and socialized version of the English
Garden City, and the urban superblock, a holistic residential quarter stocked with
communal green spaces and services.

Garden City to Garden-Settlement

Ivanitskii referred to the future Azneft residential areas that he was tasked to design
as "garden-settlements" (poselki-sady).[1] The term is a curious conflation of two
distinct planning paradigms: the garden city and the socialist worker settlement.
With "garden," Ivanitskii summoned Ebenezer Howard's To-Morrow: A Peaceful
Path to Real Reform from 1898, the book that established the garden city as an
antidote to England's heavily industrialized urban centers. Howard's garden city
is a population-limited model community (maximum 32,000 residents) placed at a
remove from large urban centers to permit political and economic autonomy and to
benefit from healthy, natural surrounds. To create a garden city, Howard explained,
6,000 acres worth of land is purchased by socially minded investors at depressed
agricultural land values and held in trust by them. As the city develops and draws
its own light industry, agriculture, and institutions, rents naturally rise. The trust-
ees' mortgage is then paid off, after which any excess municipal capital is plowed
back into a social fund to support local welfare.[2] Although Howard's model is well
known through its illustrative concentric diagrams, its author was less concerned
with the garden city's form than its function as an economically self-sufficient middle ground with the assets of both town and country.

Russians interested in city planning reform read about Howard's model as early
as 1904, but it was seven years before Howard's book was translated into Russian as Goroda budushchego (The City of Tomorrow, 1911), and another year
before the garden city received a proper exegesis in Russian.[3] In City Improvement
(Blagoustroistva gorodov, 1912), the architect Vladimir Semenov described and
parsed the formal and financial structure of the garden city, provided images of
Letchworth, the first constructed example outside of London, and translated Howard's original diagrams into Russian (figure 2.1). A Russian branch of the International Garden City Society was founded in St. Petersburg in 1913.[4]

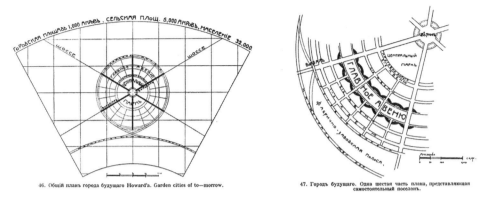

46. Общій планъ города будущаго Howard'а. Garden cities of to—morrow.

47. Городъ будущаго. Одна шестая часть плана, представляющая самостоятельный поселонъ.

Figure 2.1. Russian-language reproductions of Ebenezer Howard's diagrams from *Garden Cities of To-morrow*. V. Semenov, *Blagoustroistvo gorodov* (Moscow: Tipografiia P.P. Riabushinskogo, 1912).

Worker Housing and Everyday Life (*Rabochee zhilishche i byt*, 1924), by P. Kozhanyi, proves that the revolution did not quell Russian interest in Howard's settlement form.[5] The book's sole solution to the "housing catastrophe" in Soviet cities is the proletarian garden city (*proletarskii gorod-sad*).[6] Kozhanyi argued that because land holds no fiscal value in socialism, there was no economic pressure to build tall. Furthermore, the underdeveloped Soviet construction industry was best equipped to build low-rise cottage-style housing on the garden city model. How was the proletarian garden city sited, and what did it look like? Kozhanyi provided the following guidance: "Before constructing the garden-city, it is necessary to select a high, healthy, wooded area with access to running water . . . the whole city should be girded with wide agricultural bands and planted with agricultural products. Here, we realize the union of town and country (*smychka goroda s derevnei*)."[7] The proletarian garden city described by Kozhanyi is concentric just like Howard's diagram, with industry in a slim zone between the residential core and the exterior ring of agriculture. According to Kozhanyi, the garden city was a suitably Marxist spatial proposition because it would dissolve the urban/rural divide.

Baku's planner, Ivanitskii, had experienced firsthand the original garden city, Letchworth.[8] He understood his precedents, and he knew full well that the Azneft worker settlements could not be defined as garden cities. They were not fully economically or socially independent from the traditional city center of Baku, on whose services they would continue to rely. Ivanitskii instead cited worker settlements (*rabochie poselki*) just outside of the industrial cities of Birmingham, Bristol, Cardiff, Leeds, Liverpool, and Manchester as precedents, arguing that these were more comparable to the Baku case.[9] Garden-settlement, Ivanitskii's preferred term, does accurately describe the peri-urban Azneft worker regions he designed. They were settlements, which is to say agglomerations of worker housing proximate to industry but still closely tied to Baku. And, they were as garden-like as possible, under the hot, dry, salty environmental circumstances.

Azneft Garden-Settlements

Ivanitskii and his collaborators designed four oil worker garden-settlements for Azneft in 1925. Soon after his return from the United States in March of that year, Azneft director Serebrovskii presented to the Baku Executive Committee a potential site near the Stepan Razin ridge on the west side of Bulbul Lake for the Azneft settlement that would be the largest and most remote from the city center. The site was nearly equidistant from the historic oilfields at Balakhany, Sabunchi, and Surakhany, yet also comfortably removed from the anticline axis. Serebrovskii revealed that Azneft had already begun removing all residential structures in the village of Surakhany that sat on oil-bearing land to make way for more derricks. Ownership of housing units, whether urban or small-scale stand-alone structures like those on Baku's periphery, was not unusual in the postrevolutionary years because the locals had never been serfs. As Mark B. Smith notes, up to half of the urban housing stock in the USSR—like the structures in Surakhany—was still owned as "personal property" (*lichnaia sobstvennost'*) in the 1920s.[10] The displaced peasants would soon be homeless unless Azneft promptly decided where to build new housing for them.[11]

The Baku Executive Committee (Bakispolkom) approved the general settlement location for Stepan Razin but assigned Serebrovskii follow-up tasks to be completed before Azneft could proceed with construction. The Azneft and Baksovet Building Committees had to prepare together a report on worker settlement construction throughout Baku. In collaboration with colleagues from the Land Committee and the Department of Communal Services, Azneft had to work out a compensation plan for peasants whose arable land would be taken for the settlement. Finally, Azneft had to spearhead a special commission to define the most economical type of worker housing.[12] Designs for standardized worker housing types and the entire settlement plan for Stepan Razin were, in fact, already well underway when the committee made its request. Azneft had provided Ivanitskii and his team with sufficient survey data to allow them to move quickly, and their task was simplified because the settlement site was effectively a tabula rasa, since all existing peasant residents were being evicted per Azneft's plan. Ivanitskii had begun research and sketch designs for the Azneft settlements at the end of 1924, months before Serebrovskii asked official permission from the Baku Executive Committee.

Based on the drawings that remain, Ivanitskii's self-crafted assignment was to locate the settlements definitively within the Apsheron Peninsula to skirt the anticline axis; design a skeletal general plan for each settlement down to the street pattern and resulting blocks; and locate sites for transportation, civic, and recreational infrastructure. The earliest extant sketch from the effort is a diagram of the Apsheron Peninsula in which the areas of proposed settlements are shaded in pencil (figure 2.2). This diagram clarifies that the boundaries of each settlement were set by existing conditions that included rail lines, lake edges, and topographical anomalies. Binagady and Montina (1, 2), closest to Baku's urban fabric, are distinct and separate settlements in this first iteration, as is Belogorod (3). Stepan Razin was initially split into two sections (4, 5). The final peninsula-scaled plan indicates significant modifications to the conceptual framing of these settlements (figure 2.3). Binagady and Montina merge into a single urban entity that grows naturally from the northeast corner of Baku, allowing them to stand in for Ivanitskii's centralized settlement planning option. Belogorod is a middle ground option attached to the main rail line that connects Baku's central station to the oilfields, and it lies just northeast of the industrial district of the Black Town and preexisting communities on the Caspian shoreline.[13] Stepan Razin plays a decentralized role among the settlements. It sits as close as possible to the anticline axis without hampering future drilling potential and offers a short commute for the worker residents to the oilfields. Because Stepan Razin is so distant from Baku, it is largely self-sufficient, which makes it the settlement closest in spirit and design to Howard's garden city.

The individual settlement plans, delivered to Azneft at the end of 1925, share common scale, planning sensibilities, and constituent elements. Transportation connectivity is the primary concern of these designs. The detailed plan of the northernmost settlement, Binagady, shows the area bounded almost entirely by two rail lines that meet at the top (figure 2.4). The line that wraps the eastern edge connects Baku to the Russian city of Rostov, and the line along the western edge links the settlement to the oilfields and back to Baku. In this and each Azneft settlement plan, Ivanitskii's team carefully sited multiple passenger rail stations, indicated as long dark rectangles that sit adjacent to existing rail lines. These stations ensnare the settlements in the regional infrastructural network and serve as entry points in.

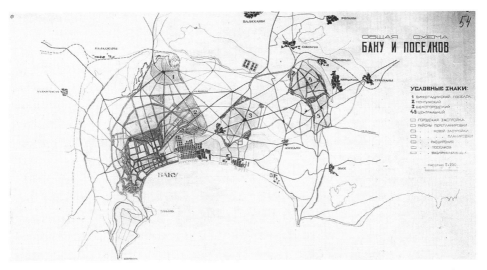

Figure 2.2. A draft plan of Baku, with proposed Azneft settlements shaded, 1924–25. 1. Binagady settlement, 2. Montina settlement, 3. Belogorod settlement, 4–5. Stepan Razin settlement. Boundaries of each settlement are set by existing conditions that include rail lines, lake edges, and topographical anomalies. Planners: Aleksandr Ivanitskii, Viktor Vesnin, Leonid Vesnin, et al. RGALI, f. 2991, o. 1, d. 17, l.54.

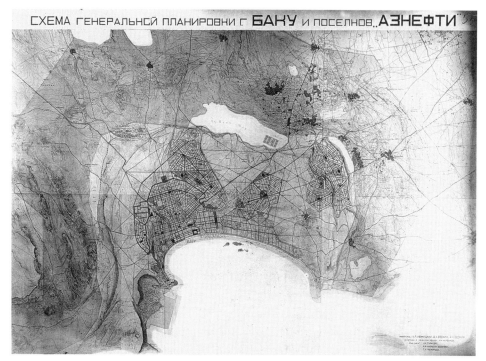

СХЕМА ГЕНЕРАЛЬНОЙ ПЛАНИРОВКИ г БАКУ и поселнов „АЗНЕФТИ"

Figure 2.3. A final plan of Baku and Azneft settlements, 1925. Binagady and Montina are a single urban entity, Belogorod lies just northeast of the industrial district of the Black Town, and Stepan Razin sits close to the anticline axis. Planners: Aleksandr Ivanitskii, Viktor Vesnin, Leonid Vesnin, et al. RGALI, f.2 991, o. 1, d. 17, l.55.

The two southernmost stations in Binagady are also the two northmost stations in Montina; these settlements adjoin along an east-west green spine (figure 2.5). The rail stations launch the geometrical logic of the site plans, as the Belogorod site plan demonstrates (figure 2.6). At Belogorod, a rail passenger who exits either of the two stations along the settlement's northern edge steps on to a plaza embedded in a green strip that buffers residential blocks to the south from train noise and smoke. At the south end of the plaza, the passenger is offered the option to walk down any number of wide streets that splay out and connect to multiple commercial and civic hubs, the centers of collective life.

Shared green space is second only to transportation connectivity in the designers' preoccupations for these site plans. All of the settlements are structured by a network of planted boulevards—long dark strips on the plans—that connect rail stations, parks, and commercial/civic hubs and that divide the settlements into smaller neighborhoods. Taking Binagady as the representative case, the Azneft garden-settlements are equipped with at least one sizable park that boasts a running track (the white lozenge-shaped space set in the shaded park area at the bottom of the plan), playing fields, and other recreational amenities. Small parks are sprinkled throughout each settlement, sometimes to serve as forecourts to civic buildings, but

Figure 2.4. A draft plan for the Binagady Azneft worker settlement, Baku, Azerbaijan, 1925. Planners: Aleksandr Ivanitskii, Viktor Vesnin, Leonid Vesnin, et al. RGALI, f. 2991, o. 1, d. 17, l. 58.

more often simply to provide gathering spaces among the residential blocks. Unlike in English examples, however, where "green" is simply achieved by allowing space to remain unbuilt, the planted lushness promised by shaded areas on the Azneft settlement plans would require infrastructural gymnastics to overcome the naturally desert-like climate and salty soil of the Apsheron Peninsula.

It is the small green spaces on the Azneft settlement plans that indicate allegiance to the work of Letchworth Garden City's architect-planner, Raymond Unwin. Ivanitskii was an avid follower of Unwin, and purportedly shook hands with the English architect at an international conference in London in 1924.[14] Unwin proved

Figure 2.5. A draft plan for the Montina Azneft worker settlement, Baku, Azerbaijan, 1925. Planners: Aleksandr Ivanitskii, Viktor Vesnin, Leonid Vesnin, et al. RGALI, f. 2991, o. 1, d. 17, l. 59.

a willing interlocutor and guide to the English planning and housing scene to Soviet architects and planners in the 1920s, including a high-ranking housing official who visited him in the UK to consult on one-room housing precedents for Soviet steel city, Magnitogorsk.[15] Unwin was a committed socialist from the time of his first job as an engineering draftsman in Manchester in 1885, and his subsequent writing and planning projects push spatial forms to generate a strong sense of community.[16] In his 1909 book *Town Planning in Practice*, Unwin argued that "the features which we deplore in the present condition of our residential areas have been largely due to the excessively individualistic character of their development." Under a private land

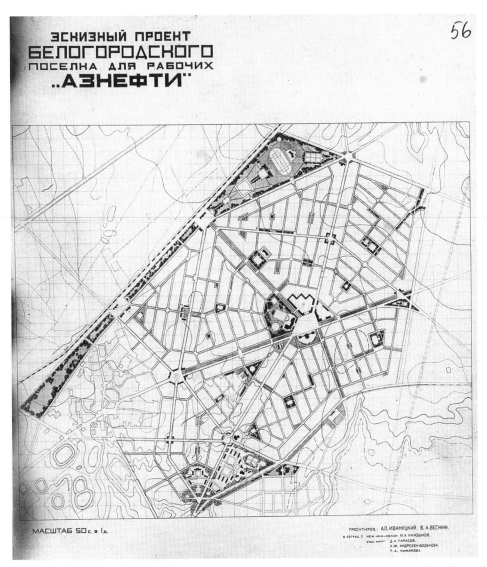

ЭСКИЗНЫЙ ПРОЕКТ
БЕЛОГОРОДСКОГО
ПОСЕЛКА ДЛЯ РАБОЧИХ
„АЗНЕФТИ"

56

МАСШТАБ 50с. в 1д.

ПРОЕКТИРОВ.: А.П. ИВАНИЦКИЙ. В. А.ВЕСНИН.
в сотрид. с мем. инж.-мелор. М.А. КНЯЗЫКОВ.
отд. инж.: Д.А. ТАРАСОВ.
А. Ф. АНДРЕЕВА-БОДУНОВА.
Т. А. ЧИЖИКОВА.

Figure 2.6. A draft plan for the Belogorod Azneft worker settlement, Baku, Azerbaijan, 1925. Planners: Aleksandr Ivanitskii, Viktor Vesnin, Leonid Vesnin, et al. RGALI, f. 2991, o. 1, d. 17, l. 56.

ownership regime, he noted, each site is developed as an isolated instance so that the benefits gained from pooling space and resources are irrevocably lost. Unwin foresaw a planning future in which there would be "opportunity for the common life and welfare to be considered first," and where it would be possible "to group the houses around greens, to provide playgrounds for the children, bowling greens, croquet or tennis lawns or ornamental gardens for the elders, or allotment gardens for those who wish for more ground than the individual plot affords."[17] Although the publication of *Town Planning in Practice* predated the Russian Revolution, the drawings that Unwin proffered for these common greens find their analogs in the modestly sized shared open spaces spread throughout the residential blocks of the Azneft garden-settlements.[18]

The land allotted for Stepan Razin straddles a rocky ridge and so offered limited layout options. The ratified plan divides the settlement into three sub-neighborhoods—two to the east, between the lake and the ridge, and one to the west of the ridge—each with its own civic/commercial plaza that radiates streets into the lobes of each section (figure 2.7). The hub and spoke development pattern in evidence at Stepan Razin, especially in the northmost lobe, bears a remarkable similarity to the western portion of Unwin's plan for Letchworth Garden City (figure 2.8). In *Town Planning in Practice*, Unwin repeatedly stressed the importance of providing an enclosed urban center—he called this a *place*, always in italics—that artfully orchestrates pedestrian and vehicular movement and encourages people to congregate. Most often the rail station and its plaza serve this purpose as entry to the town, but additional subcenters are also critical, as they serve as places "where the minor public buildings of the district may be grouped and where a definite central effect on a minor scale may be produced."[19] Unwin gave credit for this idea to the nineteenth-century Viennese architect Camillo Sitte, who advocated enclosed urban spaces as one means to combat the homogeneity of the urban expansion grid, exemplified in Baku by von der Nonne's 1898 plan.[20] In both Letchworth and Stepan Razin the entry point is the rail station; at Stepan Razin, the sole rail connection occurs at the northernmost tip of the settlement where the existing line dips toward Bulbul Lake. The semicircular rail station plaza empties into a trident of streets, the middle of which becomes the settlement's main north-south boulevard that leads, in turn, to its subcenters. As in all of the Azneft settlement plans, Stepan Razin is further divided by wide green boulevards, parks of various scales, and additional plantings that fill areas too steep to support construction.

After the general settlement plan for Stepan Razin was resolved, Ivanitskii and his planning team homed in on the area just south of the rail station to design the first phase of construction (figure 2.9). The rail plaza at the northwest corner of the drawing links to the southern subcenter along an urban spine, a double-wide planted boulevard lined with long, thin, multistory buildings. Flanking the spine, and surrounding the center and parks, are the small-scale residential buildings that compose the majority of the built fabric.

Stepan Razin's Standardized Housing Experiment

At the same time that the site plans for the Azneft garden-settlements were being resolved, a multidisciplinary team of specialists commenced design on a limited number of standardized worker housing types. For this task, Ivanitskii invited brothers Leonid and Viktor Vesnin to be his architectural collaborators. Ivanitskii

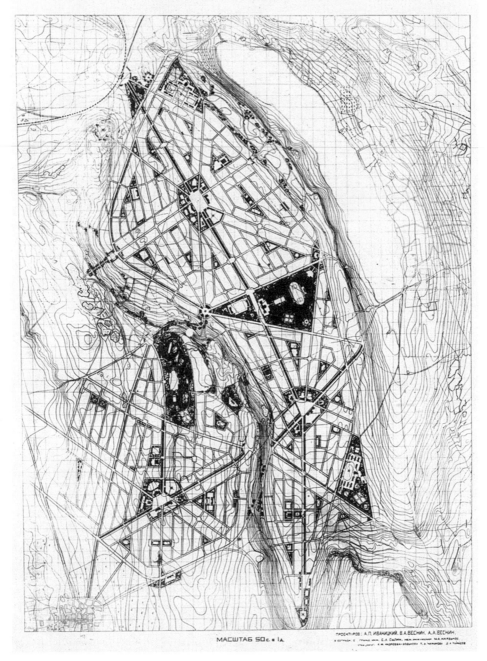

Figure 2.7. A draft plan for the Azneft Stepan Razin worker settlement, Baku, Azerbaijan, 1925. Planners: Aleksandr Ivanitskii, Viktor Vesnin, Leonid Vesnin, et al. RGALI, f. 2991, o. 1, d. 17, l. 57.

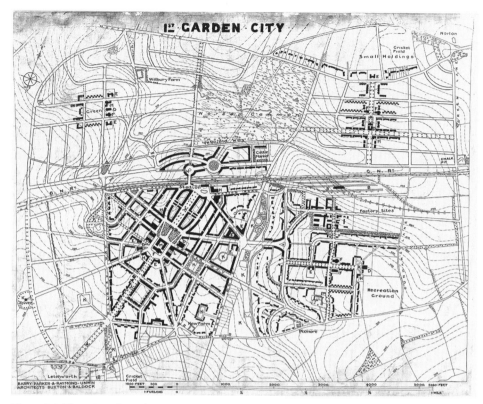

Figure 2.8. The original Garden City Masterplan, Letchworth, England, 1903. The town's civic hub and entry portal is the rail station, at the northern edge, from which spokes of planted boulevards emanate. Architects: Barry Parker and Raymond Unwin. © Garden City Collection (Letchworth Garden City Heritage Foundation).

and all three Vesnin brothers—Aleksandr, Leonid, and Viktor—knew one another through the Moscow Architectural Society, a prerevolutionary institution that took up the mantle of socialist concerns after the establishment of Soviet power. The society retained a conservative reputation, while also drawing members from among Moscow's architectural avant-garde including the Vesnins, leading Constructivist architects.[21]

Architectural Constructivism, a prevailing Soviet practice from the early 1920s through the mid-1930s, was functionally and socially motivated as well as aesthetically ascetic.[22] In his de facto manifesto for Constructivism, *Style and Epoch* (*Stil' i epokha*, 1924), the architect and theoretician Moisei Ginzburg argued that a new architectural style appropriate to the Soviet age must be motivated by practical, not visual, concerns. He explained that "the formation of a new way of life for modern man will provide a starting place for these quests [for a new style], which will model themselves on industrial and engineering structures." In the new Constructivist design process, "the goal that [the architect] will set himself will be not the unchecked fantasy of a detached idea, but the precise tackling of a task which

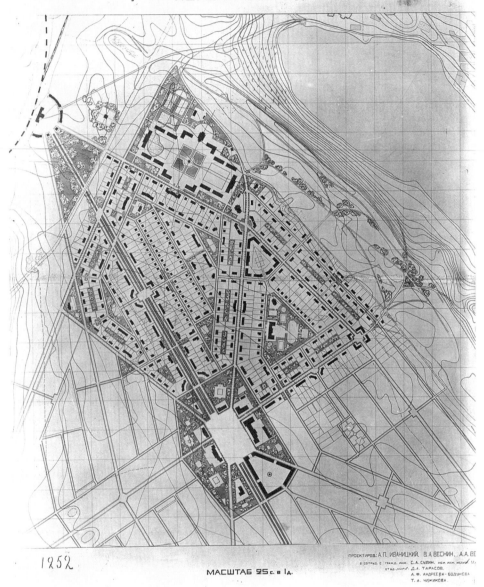

ЭСКИЗНЫЙ ПРОЕКТ ЗАСТРОЙКИ
ПОСЕЛКА „АЗНЕФТИ" ИМЕНИ С.Т.РАЗИНА
ПЕРВАЯ ОЧЕРЕДЬ

1252

МАСШТАБ 25с. в 1д.

ПРОЕКТИРОВ: А.П. ИВАНИЦКИЙ. В.А.ВЕСНИН. А.А.ВЕ
В СОТРУД. С ГРАЖД. ИНЖ. С.А. СУЛИН. ИНЖ. ИНЖ. МЕДИК М.
ОТВ. ИНЖ. Д.А. ТАРАСОВ.
А.Ф. АНДРЕЕВА-БОДУНОВА
Т.А. ЧИЖИКОВА.

Figure 2.9. A draft project for the construction of the Azneft Stepan Razin settlement, Phase 1, Baku, Azerbaijan, 1925. The rail station at the plan's northwestern edge serves as an entry point, and planted boulevards and shared parks stitch the settlement together. Dark dots and dashes indicate various worker housing types, from single- to multistory buildings, while larger social institutions sit in planted precincts. Planners: Aleksandr Ivanitskii, Viktor Vesnin, Leonid Vesnin, et al. RGALI, f. 2991, o. 1, d. 17, l. 9.

includes determinate data and determinate unknowns. The architect will then feel that he is not a decorator of life, but its organizer."[23]

Ginzburg conceded that it was difficult "to speak of a formal language" of architecture emergent from such a method. In other words: it was not clear what Constructivist architecture would look like. Ginzburg proposed two steps to crystallize a functional and formal language for Constructivism. First, the Constructivist architect must discard "all those various capitals, columns, consoles and brackets . . . the entire treasure-house of decorative elements." The visual result from stripping away non-essential ornamentation would be an architecture of "simple and clear expression." Like his modernist architectural colleagues Walter Gropius and Le Corbusier, Ginzburg supported his textual argument in *Style and Epoch* with images of grain elevators in Buffalo, New York, that exemplified unadorned volumes produced by a functional design process. Second, the architect must embrace "standardization of the building process, [and] mass production of individual and constituent parts of architecture using the machine method." Mass-produced architectural elements—from structural concrete blocks to steel frame windows—might limit the architect's aesthetic choices, but because standardization permits efficiency, the Constructivist architect is freed up to practice on "an amazingly grand scale—the scale of enormous ensembles, entire urban complexes."[24] Aleksandr Vesnin echoed Ginzburg's formulation of Constructivism, writing that "this primacy of function over decorative academicism has always existed, but today its base is considerably larger and more complicated— that of modern man, citizen of a socialist country."[25] The Vesnins had already proven this method and suggested certain aesthetic tendencies in their All-Union architectural competition successes. The most notable was their third place Palace of Labor entry from 1923, a design that, according to El Lissitzky, set the social, spatial, and formal tasks of Constructivist architecture.[26]

The research and utility-driven rationality of the Constructivist method was congenial to Ivanitskii's planning outlook. In 1919, he teamed up with Viktor and Leonid Vesnin on a competition entry design for an autoworkers' village in the town of Fili, which marked the beginning of the fruitful professional collaboration.[27] The Vesnins were also aware of the issues particular to sites of oil extraction. In 1922, the brothers took first prize in a competition to design three oil workers' villages in Grozny for Grozneft, the state-controlled company that was the Russian site's equivalent of Azneft. Ivanitskii brought them on to the Baku planning project in early 1925. Although the Vesnins' time working on Baku was limited—they were pulled away in late 1925 to oversee design for the Dnipro Hydroelectric Station in Ukraine—the standardized housing types they developed established an architectural language for Stepan Razin's worker settlements and socialist institutions.

Viktor Vesnin articulated three housing-related issues that the design team sought to address in Baku. First, they wished to ensure that worker housing was separated from industrial sites in dedicated settlements. Second, they looked to connect

housing and production through intelligent transportation planning. Last,—and
here is where architecture emerges—they hoped to "create a link between contemporary housing and the strong tradition and lifestyle of the local population," meaning that their designs for replicable worker housing in Baku sought to meld the best
attributes of modernity and tradition.[28] The housing for Stepan Razin was designed
during an ongoing sociopolitical debate about the *novyi byt,* or new socialist way
of life that architecture sought to inculcate.[29] Viktor Vesnin's comment suggests
that the design team was concerned that Bakuvians would find drastic changes to
the domestic environment alienating. Taking a softer line than he had previously,
Ginzburg explained in his book on socialist housing that Constructivist architects
"found it to be absolutely essential to create a number of ways to *stimulate* a transition to a higher form of everyday life, *without decreeing this transition.*"[30] Stepan
Razin was a design experiment to establish worker housing types able to bridge that
gap between a local past and a common socialist future.

Architectural tradition, in the case of Baku, was not easy to define. According to
Audrey Alstadt-Mirhadi, census data indicate that Baku housing types were varied
and often differed along ethnoreligious lines. Houses in the Muslim quarter tended
to open onto inner courtyards, while those in the Russian and Armenian quarters
opened on to the street.[31] These inner-city housing types and those in the oilfields
shared three architectural qualities: most were flat roofed, constructed of locally
quarried buff colored limestone, and incorporated architectural devices like balconies and verandas to provide much-needed natural shading and ventilation.[32]

By mid-1925, the Vesnin-led architectural team had developed for Stepan
Razin thirty-six house variants of one-, two-, and three-story houses.[33] A detailed
blueprint from late in that year shows the footprint of each house constructed
during Phase I development at Stepan Razin (plate 5). A small table in the drawing's upper right-hand corner indicates that just four house types were used to
create this 142-house section, making Stepan Razin a masterclass in architectural
standardization (plate 6).

Like Azneft's American houses, the Vesnin designs typically hold two mirrored
units per building, making them "paired" types. A combination of photographs,
drawings, and plans provides a partial catalog of these designs. Type I, seen in a
site photograph from November 1925, is a simple one-story paired house. A shared
dormer in the shallow-hipped roof marks the implied line of symmetry down the
middle of the broad facade (figure 2.10). The body of the house is constructed of
the traditional local stone—large blocks nestle against the completed building in
the photograph—but the stone is parged with cement and whitewashed, giving it a
smooth, modernist finish.

Common scale and architectural detailing among Stepan Razin housing type
variants suggest that the architects worked within a tight set of design parameters
to minimize cost difference between them. The houses share shallow-hipped roofs,
large front windows to illuminate living spaces, and entry porches created by open

Figure 2.10. Type I houses under construction, Azneft Stepan Razin settlement, Baku, Azerbaijan, November 22, 1925. Architects: Aleksandr Ivanitskii, Viktor Vesnin, Leonid Vesnin, et al. Canadian Centre for Architecture, PH1998:0011:014. Gift of Howard Schickler and David Lafaille.

exterior corners. A rectangular column marks the outside extent of each porch, and a knee wall or railing provides a measure of exterior privacy to the residents.

To manufacture visual interest at the ground level among the limited number of standardized housing types the architects used clever massing, color and finish variation, and unit orientation. In Stepan Razin housing Type XI, the most volumetrically sophisticated house design featured in a perspective drawing, the front windows push out to become bays, an inset window turns the corner from facade to porch, and the porch column sits back to allow the thin roof edge to cantilever over the body of the house (figure 2.11). At least three paint colors amplify changes of spatial depth: bays and columns are white, the main body of the house is gray, and the beams are black.

In one of the most common types constructed in the first phase, Type II, the symmetrical, paired units expand in width as they move from front to back, a massing strategy that offers the viewer perspectival heterogeneity from the street (figure 2.12). A deep open-air veranda at the front of the house composes zone one; the middle zone holds the shared living/sleeping space; the widest service zone sits at the back of the house, with a kitchen/dining area, separate shower and toilet stalls, and a door that leads directly outside from the kitchen. Running water, sewer, and central heating are all indicated. To further combat perceptual monotony, the

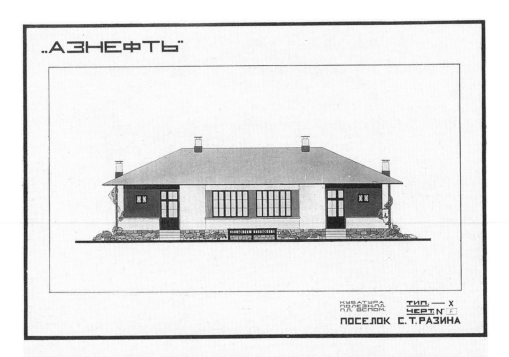

Figure 2.11. Type X (top) and Type XI (bottom) houses, Azneft Stepan Razin settlement, Baku, Azerbaijan, 1925. Architects: Aleksandr Ivanitskii, Viktor Vesnin, Leonid Vesnin, et al. RGALI, f. 2991, o. 1, d. 17, ll. 144–45.

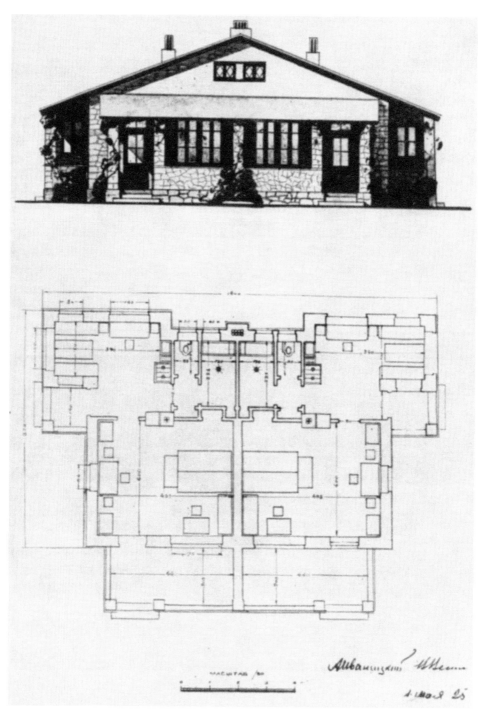

Figure 2.12. Type II house, elevation and plan, Azneft Stepan Razin settlement, Baku, Azerbaijan, May 1, 1925. The symmetrically paired units consist of three zones: deep open-air veranda at the front; shared living/sleeping space; service zone at the back, with a kitchen/dining area, shower and toilet, and a side door to the exterior. Architects: Aleksandr Ivanitskii, Viktor Vesnin, Leonid Vesnin, et al. V. G. Davidovich, and T. A. Chizhikova, *Aleksandr Ivanitskii* (Moscow: Stroiizdat, 1973), 52.

designers alternated the ridgelines of the houses in relation to the road, and in some cases local stone was left bare for textural variety (figure 2.13). In a hilltop panorama taken near completion of Phase I the whole collection of small-scale Stepan Razin housing types is arrayed in the foreground and middle distance as crowded oil derricks jockey for space on the horizon (figure 2.14).[34]

Figure 2.13. Type II (background) and Type III (foreground) houses, Azneft Stepan Razin settlement, Baku, Azerbaijan, November 22, 1925. Architects: Aleksandr Ivanitskii, Viktor Vesnin, Leonid Vesnin, et al. Canadian Centre for Architecture, PH1998:0011:015. Gift of Howard Schickler and David Lafaille.

Figure 2.14. A general view of the Azneft Stepan Razin settlement, Baku, Azerbaijan, November 8, 1925. RGALI, f. 2991, o. 1, d. 17, ll. 11–12.

Although the majority of Phase I houses constructed were one-room paired types like the examples described above, the architects also designed multiroom, multiunit, and multistory housing typologies for Stepan Razin (figure 2.15). Type V, built in limited numbers, has a footprint length nearly double that of the paired types and was likely intended for larger families.[35] Type VII stretches even further to accommodate four units in a long, low-slung body, the scale of which is broken down on the facade by an alternating light-dark paint scheme. Another four-unit type, Type XXIII, shown on the bottom of the drawing, is similarly long and low, but here the architects did not attempt to obscure the extreme linearity and repetition of the house. The syncopated rhythm of horizontal window strips and vertical doorways—capped at each end by a perpendicular side porch—accepts the additive aesthetics of multiunit housing in a manner that gestures at mass production, although these houses were built traditionally from masonry blocks.

Azneft began Phase II at Stepan Razin in 1926 to construct dense multistory buildings. The main spine of the settlement that ran from the rail station to central square was built up over the following two years with two- and three-story apartment buildings that riffed on the architectural language established by the small-scale units (figure 2.16). As in the paired houses, a two-story apartment type design is topped by a shallow-hipped roof and the building's volume is broken down through variation in color, depth, and limited ornamentation (figure 2.17). The constructed two- and three-story apartment houses at Stepan Razin were much more austere than the drafted design (figure 2.18). The entryways read as gaps sliced into the planar facade, and any semblance of neoclassical ornamentation was stripped away.

All of these housing types viewed together exhibit massing variety and material diversity to create a hybrid local-modern architectural language, as Viktor Vesnin proposed. The spectrum of exterior finishes as built ranged from local stone left bare, to walls parged and painted in an assortment of colors. Verandas, bays, and deep eaves were justified for their shading capacities, but they also contributed to volumetric complexity at the building, and perhaps more important, at the settlement scale.

The writer Maxim Gorky visited Baku in 1928, at the end of the second phase of construction at Stepan Razin. He noted, in particular, the pleasing heterogeneity of the settlement: "From a distance the settlement of Razin looks like a military camp: one-story gray houses, exactly like the tents of soldiers. But when I visited the settlement, I saw that each house was 'nicely done for its type' (*molodets na svoi obrazets*), and that together they make the beginning of an original and beautiful town. Almost every house has its own architectural physiognomy, and this makes the variety of types of settlements amazingly vibrant."[36]

Gorky highlighted the perceptive difference in the settlement's appearance depending on the length of view. Period photographs support his observation that the distant view was, indeed, camp-like. In aerial and long-range photos taken near

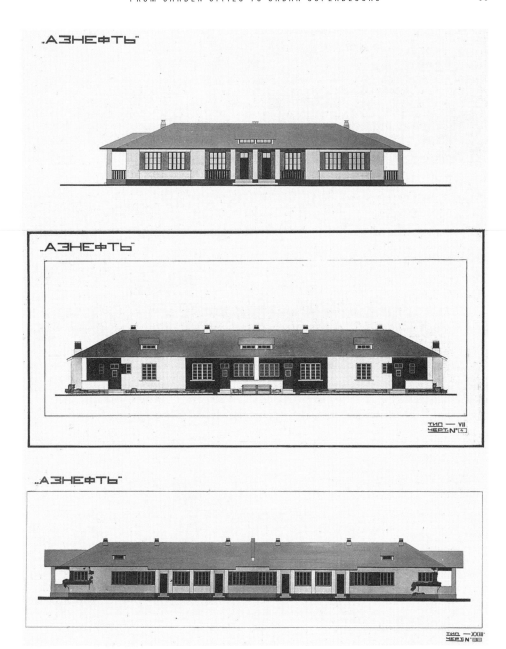

Figure 2.15. Type V (top), Type VII (middle), and Type XXIII (bottom) houses, all multiunit buildings, Azneft Stepan Razin settlement, Baku, Azerbaijan, 1925. Architects: Aleksandr Ivanitskii, Viktor Vesnin, Leonid Vesnin, et al. RGALI, f. 2991, o. 1, d. 17, ll. 141–42, 146.

the end of Phase I construction, Stepan Razin looked like a settlement built from a limited set of model houses in a short period—as it was. The types initially deployed were largely one-story, two- to four-unit houses set a similar distance apart that appeared more or less identical from afar. The starkness of the view was also not

Figure 2.16. "Construction from 1926–1928 before landscaping," Azneft Stepan Razin settlement, Baku, Azerbaijan, c. 1928. The boulevard leading from the rail station—the spine running through the middle ground of the photograph—is now lined with three-story apartment buildings. Single-story house types hold the foreground and background. RGALI, f. 2991, o. 1, d. 17, ll. 165–69.

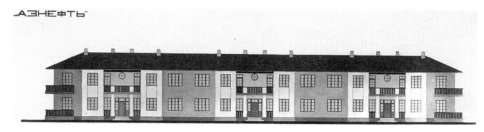

Figure 2.17. Two-story house type, Azneft Stepan Razin settlement, Baku, Azerbaijan, 1925. Architects: Aleksandr Ivanitskii, Viktor Vesnin, Leonid Vesnin, et al. RGALI, f.2991, o.1, d.17, l.140.

Figure 2.18. Two- and three-story house types, Azneft Stepan Razin settlement, Baku, Azerbaijan, 1926–28. Architects: Aleksandr Ivanitskii, Viktor Vesnin, Leonid Vesnin, et al. RGALI, f.2991, o.1, d.17, ll.162–63.

helped by the fact that the "garden" component of the so-called garden-settlement was not yet installed to soften the blank and dusty site. Once a viewer, like Gorky, was on the ground among the houses, however, the varied "architectural physiognomy" eclipsed the perception of sameness. Close range photographs show that Vesnin-designed types were artfully mixed, and that variegated topography of the site caused site-based construction adjustments from one house to the next. The number of steps to reach the veranda, the height of the foundation, etc., changed from house to house. For Gorky, the lasting impression of Stepan Razin was of its vibrancy, due in large part to the skilled deployment of slightly varied housing types.

The benefit of standardized housing design was by now clear to Azneft. In 1925 alone, the oil company completed hundreds of units in Phase I at Stepan Razin; they built 110 additional houses on other sites and planned to construct 1,000 more.[37] The economics of garden-settlement planning proved troublesome, however. Stand-alone two-family housing types, like the majority built in Stepan Razin's first phase, were costly to build and the density was too low to accommodate the volume of oil worker families in need of housing. Constructivist architect V. Kuz'min argued that the "house-cottage" at Stepan Razin was a prime example of a nonsocialist housing type, because while "we built a huge number of houses, [we] increased the cost of construction and wasted the workers' funds by not taking into account the difficulty of repairing and maintaining these houses."[38] Azneft's decision to move from individual cottage-style houses to denser multiunit buildings in subsequent construction phases was, according to Kuz'min, indicative of a maturation of the socialist approach to housing.

Armenikend: Workers' Settlement in the City

The Baksovet, Ivanitskii's municipal client, favored the centralized approach to settlement location and sought higher-density housing types from the start.[39] They selected the Armenikend neighborhood for an urban workers' settlement, a site at the northeast edge of the city in the area reserved by the Baku City Duma in 1897 as a charity village (figure 2.19). Armenikend was gridded and given numerical plot assignations by the von der Nonne plan in 1898, but it remained poorly connected to city services and was sparsely developed. Ivanitskii noted that by the 1920s, not more than 89 hectares worth of plots in Armenikend were built on (out of a possible 590), and the existing built fabric consisted of dilapidated one-story structures. Because of its relatively flat topography, Ivanitskii and his planning team considered Armenikend to be Baku's "most capacious and valuable land bank."[40]

The Baksovet had slated Armenikend for redevelopment before Ivanitskii began his work in Baku, but they halted the effort at the end of 1924 in deference to the general planning effort. By early 1926, Ivanitskii and his team, in collaboration with the Moscow architect Anatolii Samoilov, commenced design on a single urban block (*kvartal*) in Armenikend on which to experiment. Block no. 171—the Armenikend test block—would consist of "typical residential houses [that incorporate] more modern methods of development suited to local conditions."[41] These multiunit housing types would address new modes of socialist organization within the preexisting urban structure.

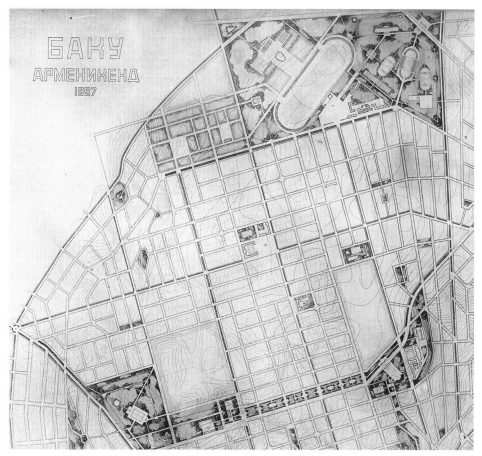

Figure 2.19. A detailed plan of the Armenikend region, Baku, Azerbaijan, 1927. Planners: Aleksandr Ivanitskii, et al. RGALI, f. 2991, o. 1, d. 17, l. 83.

From this point forward the block, not the living unit, became Baku's housing module. In the first round of site planning diagrams for the Armenikend test block, capitalist real estate logic held sway, as evidenced by the inclusion of lightly inked individual building plot lines (figure 2.20). In these diagrams, the planning team worked through twelve block variations that combined multiunit apartment buildings and open space. The first four "unacceptable" options, on the left-hand side of the diagram, are built up to and along the block's centerline. These scenarios prohibit natural ventilation through the block and recall Berlin's infamously dense *mietskaserne*, or New York's equally problematic dumbbell tenements. The fifth unacceptable variation is less dense but retains the capitalist plot structure. In the remaining "acceptable" site planning options (numbers six through twelve), the underlying plot lines are merely an organizing grid that differs in each variation and offers a geometrical structure for each composition. The acceptable versions invert the traditional capitalist development logic that prioritizes buildings over open space. Each of these acceptable block types for Baku is porous, with regular

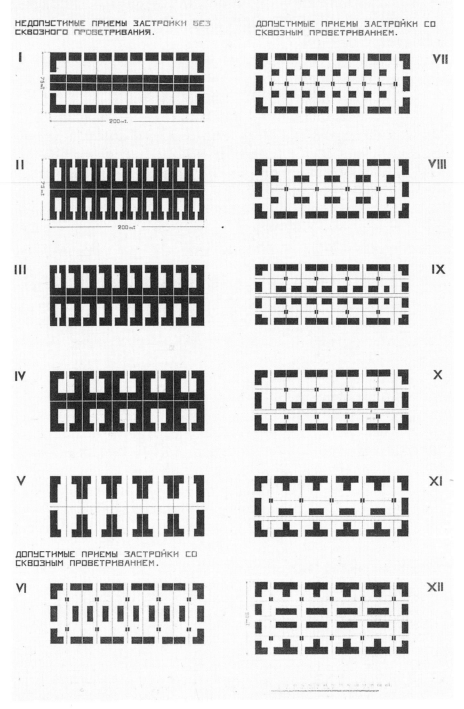

Figure 2.20. "Development schemes for blocks with individual plots (for small-scale construction)," Baku, Azerbaijan, 1926. I–V: unacceptable block development without through ventilation. VI–XII: acceptable block development with through ventilation. Architects: Aleksandr Ivanitskii, Anatolii Samoilov, et al. RGALI, f. 2991, o. 1, d. 17, l. 80.

openings from the street into a courtyard that hosts freestanding buildings. The shift in design scale from the plot to the block was not necessarily an ideological act by the socialist municipal client or the architects, but it was a spatial product of socialist land organization.

The following two sets of block variations dispense with plot lines altogether, rendering the block a conceptual whole (figure 2.21). At this point in the design process, a hard population density of 940 people per hectare was imposed, while site coverage (the percentage of the site occupied by buildings) remained the open variable. Early diagrams celebrate newfound design freedom by breaking the orthogonal grid. In the three variations on the upper left, housing units sit at forty-five-degree angles to the block edge, a compositional logic that is internal to the block rather than the street grid. These nonorthogonal plans yield low site coverage, at 24–30 percent, and require up to six-story buildings to maintain the proposed population. After brief experimentation, the designers homed in on orthogonal block schemes, seen on the right half of the diagram. These blocks hold low- to mid-rise apartment buildings that share landscapes and services. Site coverage in later iterations hovers between 30 percent and 40 percent, the height of the buildings is fixed at three stories, and the population becomes the block's variable (figure 2.22).

These planning diagrams provide an unprecedented glimpse into the design process for a first-generation Soviet urban block. First, the individual plot, the residue of capitalist land development, was inscribed by the designers then purposefully erased. Second, the designers imposed new limits—site coverage and population density on the block scale—to provide goals for the design and a measure of comparability among the iterations. Third, they altered the design limits to meet the economic and constructional reality of the context. In Baku at the end of the 1920s, buildings taller than three stories were anomalous because of limited access to modern building materials and a relatively unsophisticated residential construction workforce. The block diagram ultimately selected for design development (on the upper right) is not the densest in terms of population or site coverage, but it

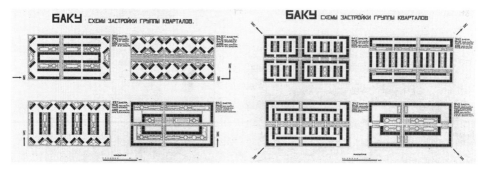

Figure 2.21. Block development schemes with 24 percent to 44 percent site coverage, Baku, Azerbaijan, 1926. Each of these schemes holds a hard population density of 940 people per hectare, while site coverage (the percentage of the site occupied by buildings) remains the open variable. Architects: Aleksandr Ivanitskii, Anatolii Samoilov, et al. RGALI, f. 2991, o. 1, d. 17, ll. 77–78.

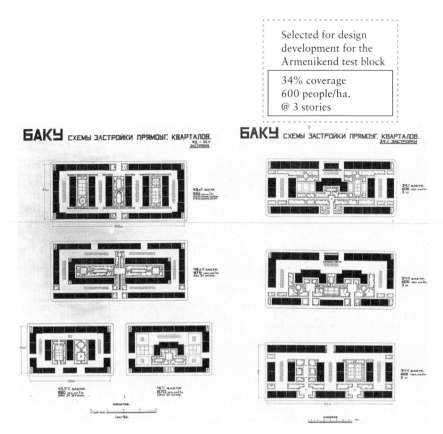

Selected for design
development for the
Armenikend test block

34% coverage
600 people/ha.
@ 3 stories

Figure 2.22. Development schemes for orthogonal blocks with 41–43.7 percent site coverage (left), and 34 percent site coverage (right), Baku, Azerbaijan, 1926. Site coverage hovers between 30 percent and 40 percent, the height of the buildings is fixed at three stories, and population is the block's variable. The scheme on the upper right-hand corner was ultimately selected for design development for the Armenikend test block, Block no. 171. Architects: Aleksandr Ivanitskii, Anatolii Samoilov, et al. RGALI, f.,2991, o. 1, d. 17, ll.,75–76.

maintains dedication to block scale design, porous site planning, generous internal common landscape, and three-story residential types.

The finalized plan for the Armenikend test block shows the design more or less as built (plate 7). The test block has 174 total units to serve 300 families (two- and three-room apartments were designed to hold two families each). Four apartment types, which range from one to three rooms, are distributed in three-story buildings that wrap the perimeter of the block and are separated periodically to allow passage from the sidewalk into the block interior.[42] With the exception of three small residential pavilions on the interior, the center of the communal block is left open for landscaped plazas at multiple levels and small garden plots. One service building at the center of the block's northern edge, divided into three sections, holds a laundry, kindergarten, and cooperative store.[43]

In June 1926, Ivanitskii and Samoilov presented their proposal for the Armenikend test block to the Baksovet Committee for Workers' Housing Construction. Ivanitskii provided the project overview and Samoilov walked the clients through the drawings. Though a subconsultant in Baku, Samoilov was at the heart of Soviet housing research in Moscow. From 1925 to 1932, a period that spans the Armenikend project, Samoilov worked at Gosplan SSSR, at the Building Commission of the Council of Labor and Defense, and at the Scientific-Research Institute for Norms and Standards.[44] He was engaged in the Union-wide effort toward architectural standardization, norm-setting, and rationalization of construction, and his professional rigor is evident in the Armenikend test block, which relies on typological design. Included in the team's initial report to the Baksovet are data about block density, open space ratios per resident, unit mix, price per unit and per family, and dimensional information for common programmatic elements like ceiling height, kitchen size, stair width, and overall area of each apartment type. When referring to unit mix and areas at Armenikend, the team utilized terminology and standards common to Soviet housing policy: a "room" is a bedroom or living room, and the sum of these areas provides a metric for living space (*zhilaia ploshchad'*). Nonliving space (*nezhilaia ploshchad'*) includes kitchen, entrance hall, bathrooms, corridors, pantries, and other service areas, even if those spaces are used for living purposes.[45] Tallied, living and nonliving areas quantify the total floor space (*obshchaia ploshchad'*) of a unit. This vocabulary persisted through the Soviet era.

Detailed plans and sections of the constructed Armenikend test block indicate that interior stairwells served two units per floor, six units per entryway; only units of the same type shared stairwells. All apartments were designed with double exposure (windows on two sides) to permit natural ventilation. Balconies, bay windows, and loggias provided ample natural light.[46] The living area of the Armenikend test block apartments averaged 7.6 square meters per person, which Ivanitskii favorably compared to European and US examples, calling the Baku units "generous."[47] Given that a 1926 Soviet housing census found that over half of Soviet families lived in a single room, and another tenth in just "part of a room (corner)," these units represented a marked improvement in spatial allocation.[48] A local comparison with the typical Stepan Razin unit also favors the Armenikend designs. Although the Stepan Razin Type II one-room unit boasted immediate access to the exterior and adjacent garden space, a single large room served the roles of foyer, living room, bedroom, and pass-through corridor to the kitchen in the back. The plan for Armenikend Type B unit, by contrast, shows a wide entry foyer that gives direct access to all rooms of the apartment (plate 8). Given that Type B was initially a communal apartment shared by two families, this foyer had two interrelated benefits: it obviated pass-through circulation and provided the unit's occupants immediate access to their family's private room and to the assortment of shared spaces within the apartment. A kitchen with pantry and a bath/shower alcove is on the immediate right upon entry to the apartment; the next door down the corridor leads to the water closet (toilet); and the door straight ahead leads to an extra communal space referred to as a dining room/

canteen (*stolovaia*). A wide balcony—this unit's direct opening to the exterior, effectively an additional room—is accessed from the two street-facing private rooms. Anticipating criticism of excess, Ivanitskii was quick to assure his clients that the Armenikend apartments were spatially and fiscally economical.[49] In their official resolution on the matter, the Baksovet agreed, noting that the units met hygienic requirements and the demands of domestic life.[50]

Not once, in the long meeting between the Moscow designers and their Baku clients, did the group discuss the Armenikend test block's proposed aesthetic character. The architectural language of the constructed neighborhood was decidedly Constructivist, as contemporary views attest (figure 2.23). The transformation from the so-called transitional, locally inflected architecture of Stepan Razin in 1925, to the spare, unabashedly modernist expression of Armenikend in 1926, had a couple of likely causes. While Armenikend was an extension of the city fabric, its relative fringe condition allowed for a greater degree of aesthetic experimentation than might have been possible either within Baku's historic center or at the first socialist settlement of Stepan Razin. The design of the Armenikend test block also coincided with a general strengthening of the Constructivist position within Soviet architectural discourse, especially for worker housing. In 1925, the same year that Armenikend was being designed, the Vesnins and Ginzburg founded the Association of Contemporary Architects (Ob″edinenie sovremennykh arkhitektorov, OSA) as a professional advocacy group for Constructivism. The OSA began publishing the journal *Contemporary Architecture* (*Sovremennaia arkhitektura*, SA) as the group's mouthpiece in 1926.[51] SA concerned itself with worker housing by sponsoring competitions, publishing designs, and sharing model examples from the USSR and Europe.[52] Through SA and European journals like *Das Neue Frankfurt*, also inaugurated in 1926 to follow the massive housing campaign in Frankfurt am Main, Germany under the direction of architect Ernst May, Soviet architects were aware that standardized flat-roofed multistory apartment buildings constructed of prefabricated parts were the ascendant norm.

In keeping with Constructivist rationality, the structures constructed on the Armenikend test block were flat roofed, planar, whitewashed residential buildings that enjoyed large windows and balconies. Volumetric dynamism—which the Armenikend test block had in spades—was the result of skillful placement of necessary architectural elements. There was no excess ornamentation. Although only four apartment types were utilized to create the block, it was a number nonetheless sufficient to generate variation at the building and block scale. The apartments had protruding entryways, long horizontal balconies, and vertical bays that moved forward and back against the "red line" of the sidewalk edge to create a spatially variegated experience for the passerby.[53] The block's facade alternated in light and shadow along the linear park to its south before the buildings turned the corner northward.[54]

Figure 2.23. "Workers' Town of Armenikend (Baku)." Photographers: T. Bunimovich, B. Kozaka, et al. *SSSR na stroike*, no. 1 (1930). N. A. Nekrasov Library, http://electro.nekrasovka.ru/books/ 3980/pages/12.

Birth of the Superblock

At the end of their June 1, 1926 meeting, the Baksovet Committee for Workers' Housing Construction sanctioned the Ivanitskii-Samoilov team to proceed with the detailed planning of the Armenikend test block. Provided all went well, slightly tweaked versions of the experimental case would be installed on Armenikend blocks nos. 172, 221, 222, 223, and 224 (figure 2.24). By November, however, a counterproposal for Armenikend was on the table, designed by a local technician (*tekhnik*) named Kniazev. The Baksovet Control-Audit Commission deemed Kniazev's design, tallying in at 91.16 rubles per square meter, more economical than the Ivanitskii-Samoilov design at 123.22 rubles per square meter. Ivanitskii complained in a letter to the new deputy director of the Baku Department of Communal Services that the exceedingly high estimates "drowned" the Armenikend test block design.[55] A group convened by the Baku Building Committee to investigate the matter discovered that their colleagues in Department of Communal Services had purposely overestimated construction costs for the Ivanitskii-Samoilov design so that in-house designs by their own staff would be built instead. Nevertheless, the five additional blocks earmarked originally as copies of Ivanitskii-Samoilov's Armenikend test block were built on the purportedly cheaper Kniazev design.[56] Kniazev's

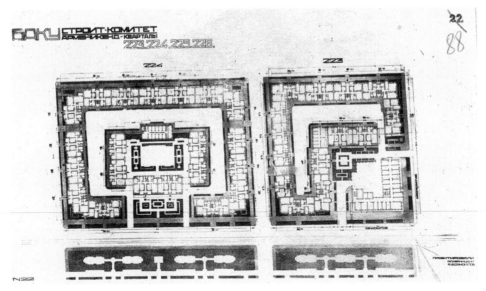

Figure 2.24. Designs for Armenikend blocks nos. 223, 224, 225, 226. Baku, Azerbaijan, 1926. These blocks were designed as variations of Armenikend test block no. 171, utilizing the same housing types. Local political jockeying caused this scheme to be scuttled in favor of a design by a Baku-based technician. Architects: Aleksandr Ivanitskii, Anatolii Samoilov, et al. RGALI, f. 2991, o. 1, d. 17, l. 88.

residential blocks, a dormitory featured in many images of the neighborhood, and other structures built in Armenikend took their architectural cues from the Ivanitskii-Samoilov Armenikend test block. The spare, white, multistory buildings that ran east-west along the linear park of Armenikend Boulevard visually marked the threshold into a new, socialized Baku.

Despite the fact that the Armenikend test block turned out to be a one-off installation for the Moscow team in Baku, Ivanitskii regarded the repeatable urban block, well designed and serviced as the key to socialized planning:

> What was created by our revolutionary overturn must . . . manifest as the decision to build whole blocks, precisely as is being done in Armenikend. When resolving the matter of the block, group of blocks, or even an entire neighborhood of the city, dwellings, laundries, kindergartens, etc. can be rationally distributed. But if you must resolve the issue separately per lot— nothing good will come of that, of course.
>
> Before everything else, I recommend the construction of blocks or groups of blocks as fully serviced complexes. Further, I recommend designating space within the boundaries of this block for household garden plots—that will still exist even with a fully socialized economy—clean inner-block courtyards, gardens and children's playgrounds.[57]

The urban block, as described by Ivanitskii, is socialist on two accounts. First, planning entire blocks for an entire urban region is possible only by virtue of land socialization. Under a socialized land regime, planners and municipalities have the luxury to disregard the fine grain of individual plots and instead focus on larger, more comprehensive solutions. Second, each of these carefully designed blocks incorporates essential supplementary social programs such as laundries, kindergartens, allotment gardens, and common-use green spaces. Other neighborhood-scale programs like upper schools and markets are allocated by larger catchment areas. For a practitioner like Ivanitskii, who lauded rationality, the benefits of repetitive block planning were immense. State-sanctioned block types could easily be deployed, and their use saved time, money, and effort in both the planning and construction phases of socialist city development.

If the urban block's inherently socialized nature was not reason enough for local administrators to support its use, Ivanitskii supplied them with economic justifications. In a typical prerevolutionary neighborhood of Baku, he argued, the typical block is extremely small. Small blocks require many streets, and in a modern city, streets are paved and have sidewalks and streetlights, infrastructure that is paid for and maintained by the local municipality. A large block—say a twenty-hectare block—"from the point of view of city improvements and planning, takes up four blocks in the old system, but eliminates four unnecessary streets. This means that the city economizes on the length of piping, paving, interior sidewalks, street lighting, etc. An extremely interesting prospect opens up if we go toward this type," Ivanitskii argued.[58]

The interesting prospect to which Ivanitskii referred was the superblock. The large residential block supplied with dedicated sociocultural and educational institutions, sports facilities, a central park, and service centers became a standard urban unit implanted throughout Soviet territories from the late 1920s on. In 1929, "urbanist" theorists like Leonid Sabsovich advocated the installation of housing combines (*zhilkombinaty*), fixed-population superblocks affiliated with sites of industrial production. The sole illustrative example of the *zhilkombinat* in Sabsovich's 1930 book *Socialist Cities* (*Sotsialisticheskie goroda*) is the Vesnin brothers' competition entry for the socialist settlement at the Stalingrad Tractor Factory (Stalingradstroi) (figure 2.25). These exact plans and axonometric diagrams also sit in Ivanitskii's archive alongside the diagrams he and his team produced for the Armenikend test block. For Stalingrad, the Vesnins worked through block-based plan options, calculated the population for each, then repeated the typical block to arrive at a target demographic. The Baku superblock predated the Vesnin superblock by three years. The fact that Armenikend and Stalingrad materials are mixed together in Ivanitskii's papers suggests that either Ivanitskii, the Vesnins, or both, acknowledged the debt of praxis at Baku.

The superblock proved a persistent planning paradigm throughout the Soviet era because it took advantage of socialist land ownership structure and was agnostic

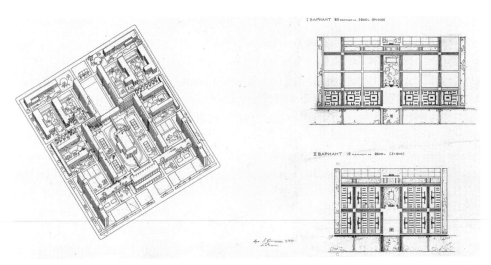

Figure 2.25. Competition design for a *zhilkombinat* for a *sotsgorod* at Stalingradstroi, Russia, 1929. Variant I: 20 combines @ 3,200 residents = 64,000 population. Variant II: 12 combines @ 2,600 residents = 31,200 population. Architects: Aleksandr Vesnin and Leonid Vesnin. RGALI, f. 2991, o. 1, d. 17, ll. 138–39.

about architectural language. In *Moscow under Reconstruction* (*Moskva rekon-struiruetsia*), a book that described and celebrated Moscow's 1935 General Plan, the chapter titled "Planning Residential Blocks" posited that notwithstanding a shift to architectural neo-classicism in the Soviet Union, housing and supplementary programs including landscape, schools, and cultural and commercial facilities would be designed symbiotically in Stalin's capital.[59] Later, during the Khrushchev era (1953–64), the Soviet housing crisis was addressed systematically with superblock microregions (*mikroraiony*) of prefabricated housing on Soviet city outskirts. The first *mikroraion* in Baku, designed in 1964, demonstrated conceptual fidelity to its predecessor, the Armenikend test block. Heavily trafficked streets surrounded the *mikroraion*, setting it off as a self-contained pedestrian precinct with all necessary amenities to serve the residential buildings that sat within it. Children walked to school without having to cross a street, and cultural and commercial facilities were all conveniently embedded within the block. Although the Armenikend test block was small compared to these later examples, it was nonetheless an exemplary test case for the workers' settlement in the city, demonstrating that the sociocultural and open space amenities enjoyed in garden-settlements like Stepan Razin were possible within a dense urban setting.

Socialist housing experimentation was particularly robust in Baku of the mid-1920s due to the importance of the site within the Soviet economy in combination with the city's physical and political dualities. Baku's two local magnetic poles for economic development—the oilfields and the city proper—were overseen by two political entities, Azneft and the Baksovet, sworn to cooperate, but each with

a vested interest in solving its own immediate housing problem in the territory
it controlled. Because Aleksandr Ivanitskii was in the employ of both, he and
his design team were able to experiment simultaneously on the two paradigmatic
conditions. For the first constructed decentralized settlement of Stepan Razin,
the planner leaned on his professional knowledge and firsthand experience of the
English garden city model, tweaked to meet the demands of a socialist context, an
abbreviated project schedule, limited material supply chain, and the Transcaucasian climate. For the Baksovet, Ivanitskii and his architectural collaborator Samoilov worked iteratively through block-based diagrams to arrive at a solution for the
centralized urban settlement of Armenikend. There, Ivanitskii and his team capitalized on another significant planning benefit of land socialization: the erasure
of private parcels to render holistic residential development possible. The Armenikend test block marked the invention of a new urban unit—the superblock—a section of the city grid on which residential units, shared open spaces, and additional
amenities such as laundries, childcare, and small shops sit in a pedestrian-friendly
precinct. The legitimacy of the superblock paradigm was immediately confirmed
by copycat blocks that filled out Armenikend in subsequent phases. Aerial photographs of the neighborhood taken in the early 1930s capture a vast grid of white,
flat-roofed, multistoried apartment blocks to convey, in one sweeping view, that
Baku's modernization campaign extended to worker housing as well as the oilfields. Could this modernization campaign extend to the whole of Baku's urban
fabric and even further into the Apsheron Peninsula? The Baksovet and Ivanitskii
sought to answer this question in the 1927 General Plan for Baku.

3

A PLAN FOR THE PROLETARIAT

I have stored the whole of Baku in me—in this way Baku is different . . .

I have had the opportunity to become acquainted with many cities in my work.
But this city, where construction is livelier than in other cities in our Union—it's
magic. Here, new plans are being realized.

—ALEKSANDR IVANITSKII (1930)

THE SOVIET PLANNER ALEKSANDR IVANITSKII WAS NOT PRONE TO POETICS. BUT FOR HIM,
Baku was nothing short of magical. The city held extraordinary status among others in the new Soviet Union, Ivanitskii stressed, because it was in Baku that socialist
construction was coming to fruition. Although the 1935 General Plan for Moscow has been cited as the working model for the Soviet city, Baku in the mid to late
1920s was its proving grounds.[1] In the geographically peripheral but economically
central city of Baku, concerns that drove most Union-wide spatial planning from
the first Five-Year Plan on were formulated and tested. These included state control
of housing, planned development of residential areas, limited journey to work, spatial equality in the distribution of items of collective consumption, stringent land-
use zoning, rationalized traffic flow, and extensive green space.[2] The first items on
this list—provision of housing, walkability, and collective services—were tested and
installed in Baku's experimental settlements of Stepan Razin and Armenikend. The
latter items—rationalized zoning, traffic, and green space networks—could only be
worked out at the city and regional scales, as they were in the first Soviet general
plan undertaken from 1924 to 1927 in Baku.

Hemmed in by oil extraction sites to the north, east, and west, and the Caspian
Sea to the south, Ivanitskii and his team had no choice but to grapple with the unruly
city of the present in the 1927 General Plan for Baku. Copious sketches, plans, and

photographs from Ivanitskii's archive make it possible to follow how the Baku planning process unfolded, and specifically how the planners worked creatively in the
absence of reliable data about existing conditions. The planning team developed a
diagrammatic language to distill information gathered from past cartographic work,
facts and figures from various branches of government, and firsthand observation.
Empirical data was critical to the plan's success, but a large degree of invention on
the planners' part was also required.

Ivanitskii's Azneft and Baksovet clients are actors in this story, acquisitive participants in the establishment of Baku's first socialist housing and general plan. They
were not universally enlightened; willful misunderstanding and obstructionism by
the Baksovet administrators and staff plagued Ivanitskii's five-year consultancy.
The big picture, however, is that the general planning effort in Baku built a cadre of
planning-savvy local administrators in addition to diagrams and projective maps.

The plan for Baku that emerged over the course of three years was a calibrated
mixture of capitalist and socialist urban models, and as such represents a transitional
response entirely appropriate to the time of its formulation, the NEP. Only by utilizing all planning tools available, regardless of derivation, could Ivanitskii bridge the
gap between the formerly capitalist petro-city and its socialist progeny.

Building Socialist Planning Clients during NEP

Baksovet, the client for the general plan, served under the Presidium of the Baku
Executive Committee (Bakispolkom), the city's highest governing body. For the plan,
the Baku Executive Committee was intermediary between the municipal government
and the state apparatus in Moscow, and most important, the overseer of the city's
budget. At their December 1924 meeting, the Baku Executive Committee allocated
1 million rubles for the 1925 building season, an amount that the Baksovet Building
Committee was not to exceed. Compared to the 4.2 million rubles that Azneft spent
on worker settlement housing over the 1923–24 building seasons, the Baksovet allocation is shockingly small. The problem for the Baksovet was fiscal sourcing. Unlike
Azneft, the municipality had no self-generated income.

V. S. Krylov, chair of the Baksovet Building Committee, proposed two funding
streams for the city's capital campaign. Long-term credit for construction would be
requested from "the center," i.e., Moscow, and the Building Committee would prepare
materials and propose terms to receive that credit from the Soviet capital. The more
lucrative, locally based fiscal source would come from the imposition of a 25 percent
industrial tax (*promnalog*), earmarked for residential construction.[3] The financial
and legal departments of the Baksovet were charged to research existing provisions
in the Russian Republic for the imposition of such a tax and to draw up an appropriate decree. The Baksovet protocol suggests that there was no codified system for
generating capital funding and that Soviet municipalities were left to guess how to
levy taxes, strong-arm constituents, and petition higher powers to finance a public

project and balance its own books. An early Soviet capital project had to "pay for itself," as a fictional NEP-era anecdote suggested.[4] Land allocation was one critical aspect of the project structure that the Baksovet did have under its immediate control. Despite the fact that the Baksovet and Azneft planning efforts overlapped, the oil company had to appeal to the city for permission to utilize nationalized land for their worker settlements. Having the same planner, Ivanitskii, at work on both plans simultaneously smoothed friction that the two projects naturally may have generated.

Both the Azneft and Baksovet client groups gained expertise through Ivanitskii, who brought knowledge about international planning practices to Baku. Like Azneft, the Baksovet Building Committee established a planning and construction library of Russian and foreign language books to bring their in-house engineers up to speed.[5] But high-ranking members of the Baksovet also wished to immerse themselves in firsthand precedent gathering. In February 1925, just months into Ivanitskii's consultancy, the Baksovet determined that a reconnaissance business trip (*komandirovka*) was in order. The Presidium of the Baksovet requested permission from the People's Commissariat of Foreign Affairs to send a commission to Europe. The purpose of the trip was to permit the three-person commission "to familiarize themselves with the achievements of Western European technology in the realm of worker housing and to learn about contemporary conditions of communal organizations and municipal improvements."[6] The travelers proposed to visit large urban centers in Germany, France, England, and Italy.

In their request, the Baksovet commission proffered two arguments in favor of the research trip. Commission members would gain firsthand knowledge of European precedents in civic improvement. The travelers would return eager to share best practices with colleagues in Baku, and they would be more able to engage intelligently with Ivanitskii and his planning staff on the forthcoming general plan project. Equally important, the commission members would enter into talks with foreign firms concerning orders for equipment "that cannot be produced in Russia." Parisian discussions would be with a firm specializing in garbage incineration systems.[7] In England, the trio would meet with the sewer equipment manufacturer, Adams. The Baksovet commission had already reached out to a number of Berlin-based infrastructural equipment firms with whom they would engage in face-to-face negotiation. Particular attention would be paid to Germany on the trip, given "the importance of social contacts, especially as they have the closest ties to us economically."[8]

The proposed European tour for the Baksovet commission had Ivanitskii's fingerprints all over it. He had extensive experience organizing research trips abroad. After graduating from the Institute of Civil Engineering in St. Petersburg in 1904, Ivanitskii traveled on several fact-finding trips through European cities. One itinerary, in 1910, covered Germany, Holland, Belgium, France, and Italy. Of that trip Ivanitskii later wrote that "the value of the research trip . . . was in learning the issues of overall improvement of residential areas. On the one hand, there were the urban design complexes of Paris, Berlin, Brussels, Antwerp, Amsterdam, Marseilles, Genoa,

Milan, Rome, and other cities. On the other hand, were issues of planning of smaller towns and sites of the 'garden city' type, and issues of constructing seaside resorts."[9]

When Ivanitskii was invited to speak about settlement planning in Baku, he did so on the heels of his latest trip abroad to participate in an international planning conference held in London.[10] All five English cities on the proposed Baksovet commission itinerary were the ones featured in his first presentation in Baku. For Ivanitskii, travel generated implementable ideas and effectively combated professional insularity. A grand tour of Europe, therefore, was the swiftest means to overcome provincialism in the Baksovet's administrative staff. Just as Azneft's director Aleksandr Serebrovskii returned to Baku from the United States with equipment, books, and washing machines, the Baksovet's commission returned with European models for worker housing and civic improvement.

Tracing and Mapping

Ivanitskii's planning team began their work on the Baku Plan in the late fall of 1924 but were immediately stymied by a paucity of contextual information about the city. Ivanitskii characterized the cartographic materials his team was given by the Baksovet as "incomplete and outdated," and the demographic data as "well below standard."[11] As the Azneft Building Committee had realized back in 1920, there were no accurate topographical and existing conditions plans of Baku. Unfortunately, the same situation held in 1924. In the absence of site-specific details, Ivanitskii gathered specialists from various disciplines—public health and municipal services specialists, economists, engineers—to frame broad planning objectives.[12]

When the planning team embarked on its work, the Baku municipal government began to capture and compile a detailed survey of the city, a task that stretched through 1925 and 1926.[13] Certain areas of the city were difficult to survey quickly and fell out of the planning scope of work. *Icheri sheher* was the first area eliminated from the general plan. Ivanitskii advocated for preservation of the historic Islamic quarter and argued that surveyors would be unable to accurately plot the irregular structures of the old town or assess archaeological findings while under the pressure of time. The Black and White Towns were also excluded from detailed planning once it became clear that Azneft would not readily open their industrial installations to municipal surveying crews.[14] While waiting for existing conditions surveys of the city proper the planning team, working largely from Moscow, collected all previous graphic representations of Baku that they could get their hands on, including maps from 1864, 1911, and 1913. They also began their own observational research and gathered social-scientific datasets to use as bases for their work.

Ivanitskii's Baku planning team adopted two exploratory drawing methods at the start of the process to build their knowledge of place and to pinpoint issues that the plan would later address. These methods align with James Corner's categories of tracing and mapping.[15] Tracing is defined as "equal to what is." In practice, a tracing can emerge from the planner placing a piece of translucent paper over an existing city plan and faithfully replicating the original. This is not a mindless task, however; through inscription, the tracer gains knowledge of the place being reproduced. Mapping, by contrast, is "equal to what is *and* to what is not yet." Mapping is a practice that requires invention. It may begin with a rough sketch of the existing condition, but it projects beyond it to elicit information not explicitly articulated before and to anticipate what lies ahead. For Corner, mapping is unquestionably superior as a creative method because, "unlike tracings, which propagate redundancies, mappings discover new worlds within the past and present ones; they inaugurate new grounds upon the hidden traces of a living context." Although maps that imagined a future Baku were the ultimate deliverables for the 1927 Plan, tracing was an inevitable and productive first step for cartographic engagement.

The earliest drawings by Ivanitskii's team are abstracted tracings of Baku's 1864 and 1913 plans. Labeling their 1864 tracing "a copy of a copy," the team drew the pre-oil boom urban fabric, carefully outlining the intricate block structure of *icheri sheher*, the rectangular grid of the colonial Russian *forshtadt*, the Russian and Muslim cemeteries, and the steep rocky ledge and quarry to the northwest of the built core (figure 3.1). This exercise would immediately heighten awareness of the historical and topographical materiality of Baku. The planning team's tracing of the 1913 plan—the von der Nonne plan of the city, printed as fact—reveals the earlier scheme's blatant disregard for the topographical complexity of the city and its blithe orthogonality (figure 3.2). Despite the 1913 map's questionable fidelity to existing

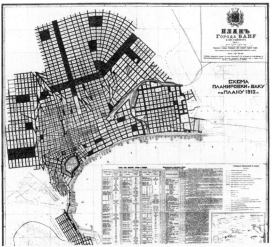

Figure 3.1. Plan of the Baku fortress and *forshtadt*, a "copy of a copy," based on the 1864 plan, drawn in 1924. Planners: Aleksandr Ivanitskii et al. RGALI, f. 2991, o. 1, d. 17, l. 19.

Figure 3.2. Scheme for the planning of Baku, based on the 1913 plan, drawn in 1924. Planners: Aleksandr Ivanitskii et al. RGALI, f. 2991, o. 1, d. 17, l. 23.

conditions, in tracing it Ivanitskii's team became acquainted with Baku's tendency to expand in a northeasterly direction. Redrawing von der Nonne's scheme also highlighted certain assets of the older plan, like the proposed open space network, rendered in a dark wash in their copy.

The team began mapping with a series of cartograms (*kartogrammy*) that they developed soon after completing the tracings.[16] A cartogram is a statistical map—a diagram that consciously retains a cartographic base while inserting quantitative data in a novel way.[17] Drawings categorized as cartograms might use color, shading, contour lines, hatches, dots, and small inset graphs or tables to "show geographically statistics of various kinds."[18] In producing such analytical illustrations for his initial work in Baku, Ivanitskii was tapping into practices long utilized by Russian social scientists.[19] Because of the advanced petro-technical apparatus in Baku, certain statistical data was available for use by the planning team, and its deployment on top of the outdated maps added a degree of contemporaneity. The combination of two forms of objective data—the survey-based map, no matter how outdated, and statistics—jibed with the assertion of planning as an analytical science more than an art, a claim that Ivanitskii was at pains to reiterate in many of his published texts. The resulting cartograms are fully engaged with both material and quantitative facts of Baku, and in crafting them, the planning team inventively layered varied types of information to perform interpretive acts on the city. Each cartogram makes an argument, for as Corner notes, "mapping is never neutral, [but] is perhaps the most formative and creative act of any design process, first disclosing and then staging the conditions for the emergence of new realities."[20] The cartograms, which are polemical drawings, reveal the planners' professional preoccupations and set the stage "for new eidetic and physical worlds to emerge."[21]

The 1913 Baku Plan was the planning team's base for all of the cartograms (figure 3.3). Ivanitskii's assistants reproduced it onto vellum sheets at a common scale. The final cartograms fall into two main categories. The first set is concerned with the infrastructural qualities of Baku and addresses questions of efficiency, organization, and modernization (figure 3.4). Topics in this group cover territorial growth from 1843, the paths of tramlines and electric cables, street paving materials, and property taxation. A second set centers on demographic issues including population density, "unhealthy" places in the city (dumps, swamps, etc.), and epidemic prevalence by region.

In highlighting water- and air-borne disease in the dense city neighborhoods as a primary planning concern, the Baku team was following a rationale set by European planners since at least the 1850s. Baron Georges-Eugène Haussmann's intensive modernization of Paris, undertaken after a series of cholera epidemics, was justified most convincingly as a public health intervention. In Germany, engineer Josef Stübben's influential book on urban planning *City-Building* (*Der Städtebau*, 1890), well-studied in Russia, didactically outlined the necessary provisions for

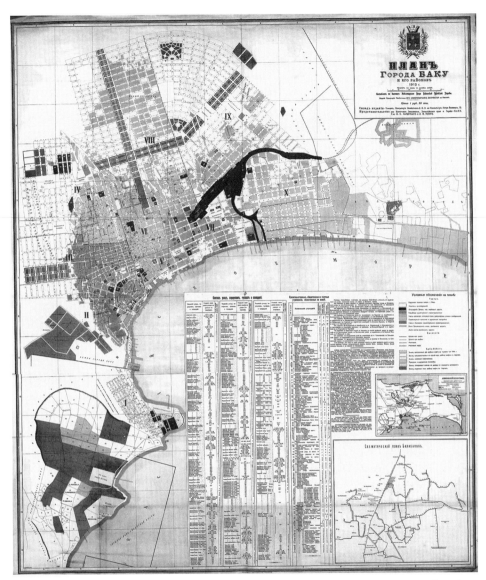

Figure 3.3. The 1913 Baku Plan. Inventarnoe biuro Bakinskoi gorodskoi upravy, *Plan goroda Baku* (Tiflis, 1913). Library of Congress, Geography and Map Division, G7144.B2 1913.I51.

urban health. Favorable soil, adequate sewage disposal, wholesome drinking water, fresh air, and greenery are all addressed in the first Soviet plan for Baku. Ivanitskii may have also gained knowledge of hygienic planning closer to home. In his work as a young planner for Leontii Benois in St. Petersburg, Ivanitskii likely came into contact with F. Enakiev, an engineer from the Ministry of Communications and the author of *Tasks for the Reform of St. Petersburg* (*Zadachi preobrazovaniia S.-Peterburga*, 1912), a book that proposed replanning the imperial capital according to hygiene and traffic movement.[22]

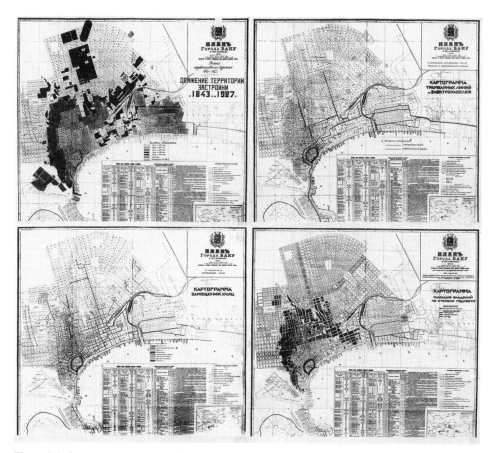

Figure 3.4. Cartograms, or statistical maps, that analyze the efficiency, organization, and modernization of the city of Baku, Azerbaijan, 1924. Read clockwise from upper left: Growth of territory by period, 1843–1927; Tramlines and electrocables; Taxes by quality of property; Paved streets. Planners: Aleksandr Ivanitskii et al. RGALI, f. 2991, o. 1, d. 17, ll. 32, 34, 43, 44.

The epidemiological cartogram for Baku places information about the occurrence of cholera, typhus, and dysentery in 1921 and 1923 in simple bar graphs over various regions of the city (figure 3.5). Cholera outbreaks in 1907, 1908, 1909, and 1910 were the result of the city's poor water and sewage systems, a problem addressed—but not entirely solved—by the Shollar Pipeline completed in 1917 that carried fresh water 170 kilometers from the Caucasus Mountains.[23] The epidemiological cartogram communicates the common threat of poor urban infrastructure and the unevenness of that threat across city neighborhoods. The one notable graphic aberration on the cartogram occurs in the industrial stronghold of the Black Town, the most easterly neighborhood of the city, which has spikes for typhus and dysentery that nearly match those for cholera. The civic danger of proximity between industry and residential life is encapsulated in the graphic cross-comparison of Baku's urban neighborhoods that the planners produced despite limited access to data.

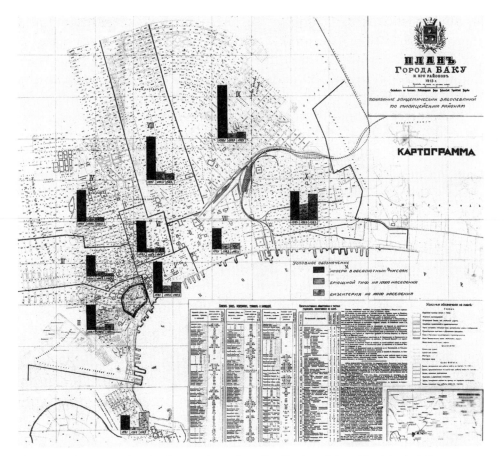

Figure 3.5. Cartogram charting the prevalence, by police district, of the epidemiological diseases cholera, typhus, and dysentery in 1921 and 1923. From a set of cartograms analyzing the population distribution, health, and well-being of the city of Baku, Azerbaijan, 1924. Planners: Aleksandr Ivanitskii et al. RGALI, f. 2991, o. 1, d. 17, l. 45.

Although each cartogram is a snapshot of a specific urban condition, the operative benefit of the effort arose in layering different types of data. Ivanitskii described the process of cartogrammatic discovery in a 1925 article on the Baku Plan:

By comparing these cartograms, which are exactly the same by scale and symbol, it is easy to orient one's self to those places that most need planning intervention, and the character of those interventions. It is easy to see that in parts of the plan surgery (*operativnoe meshatel'stvo*) is necessary, that is replanning. In those parts of the city the cartogram shows layered patches denoting places with primitive structures, swampy territories, places with unfavorable sanitary characteristics, and so on. In other situations, therapy or prophylactic planning (*terapiia ili profilaktika planirovki*) is needed, that is the regularization of the existing plan.[24]

Plotting the individual data sets on semitransparent sheets, and overlaying them on one another, allowed problem areas in the city to emerge. Certain regions, like the neighborhoods to the west of the old town that cling to the slopes of the Nagornoe Plateau are darkened in the cartograms by a density of problematic characteristics such as difficult topography, propensity for illness, and morbidity. This toxic combination, seen so clearly on the layered sheets, justified plan surgery—that is, total replanning. Prophylactic planning, on the other hand, was all that was needed in much of the rest of the city: minor street widening, grid correction, insertion of plantings, and public amenities. The team's mappings also included other types of diagrams that captured the path of the sun, thermal effects, and direction of the prevailing northern winds.

The interrelation of Baku's oil, demographics, capital construction, and territorial growth is the issue addressed in one remarkable diagram produced by the planning team (figure 3.6). On the x-axis of the graph runs a common chronology: from 1880—the beginning of the first oil boom—to 1930, five years into Baku's future.

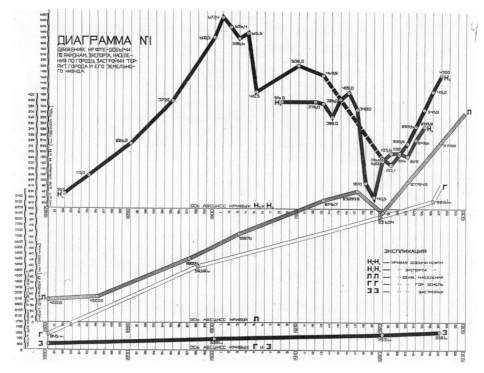

Figure 3.6. Diagram no. 1, Baku Plan, 1927. The interrelation of Baku's oil, demographics, capital construction, and territorial growth are shown in this diagram. On the x-axis of the graph runs a common chronology: from 1880—the beginning of the first oil boom—to 1930, five years into Baku's future. The graph charts five distinct data sets. First from the bottom runs a line that follows the fairly shallow rise of the number of structures built within the city (3); the second line charts the absolute urban area as the city limits expanded (Г); the third shows population growth (Л). Above a thin line of demarcation are the two prime generators of the city's growth: volume of oil extracted (Нд), and volume exported (Нэ). Planners: Aleksandr Ivanitskii et al. RGALI, f. 2991, o. 1, d. 17, l. 47.

The diagram charts five distinct data sets. First from the bottom runs a line that follows the fairly shallow rise of the number of structures built within the city (3); the second line charts the absolute urban area as the city limits expanded (Γ); the third shows population growth (Л). Above a thin line of demarcation are the two prime generators of the city's growth: volume of oil extracted (Нд), and volume exported (Нэ, exportation data, is plotted from 1908 on). These five indicators and their coordination illuminate the planners' desire to cross-reference the particular socioeconomic factors at play in Baku's urban growth.

Urban population control, a particular concern in Soviet planning from the 1930s on, is addressed in another diagram that plots two sets of data: the gross population of Baku beginning in 1859, at 135,000 residents, and the annual change in population growth (figure 3.7).[25] The planning team recommended that Baku's population growth taper from 7 percent annually to a steady 1.5 percent fifty years into the future. Interdisciplinary analyses such as this population projection drove

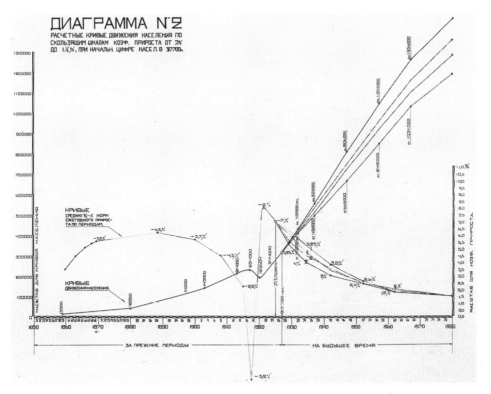

Figure 3.7. Diagram No. 2, Baku Plan, 1927. "Population curves on sliding scales from 7 percent to 1.5 percent, with an initial population of 317,700." The population lines (annual growth rate on the top and raw population on the bottom) cross at three anomalous moments. The first crossing indicates the drastic population decline during the Russian Civil War (1917). The second crossing marks a dramatic population increase in the first year of Bolshevik rule (1920). The last crossing, occurring in 1930, is projective. The actual population of Baku in 1970 was only 37,000 residents off from Ivanitskii's projection. Planners: Aleksandr Ivanitskii et al. RGALI, f. 2991, o. 1, d. 17, l. 48.

planning decisions like the expansion of municipal territory. The plan's prescience was proven in time. According to the 1970 Soviet census, the actual population of Baku was a mere 37,000 residents off from Ivanitksii's projection, and the city limit set by the 1927 plan was untouched in both the 1937 and 1954 general plan revisions. The Ivanitskii Plan accurately predicted the direction of growth and the territory required to accommodate it.

After the first round of drawing the team engaged in projective mapping, attacking problems identified by the cartograms and diagrams. The most detailed draft plan graphically inverts figure and ground to depict the volumetric conditions of Baku's urban fabric (figure 3.8). Here, and in all subsequent versions of the Baku

Figure 3.8. Draft of the Baku Plan, 1925. Planners: Aleksandr Ivanitskii et al. RGALI, f. 2991, o. 1, d. 17, l. 51.

Plan, built structures are rendered darkest, planted areas slightly lighter, and connective elements (streets, squares, and plazas) remain white. Although the graphic language accords with planning output produced concurrently in capitalist cities, the drawing also begins to suggest conceptual parity between material (black) and social (gray and white) infrastructure, a hallmark of socialist planning in subsequent decades.

Hammering Out the Tasks for Socialist Planning

Ivanitskii traveled to Baku at the end of May 1926 to update his clients on the plan's progress. Although the project was a year and a half in, Ivanitskii had little graphic material to show to the Baku Executive Committee and the Baksovet Planning Commission. He left the cartograms in Moscow because they were large, unwieldy, and would have been damaged in transit. Six of them, along with a draft version of the plan, had made their national debut at the first All-Union Sanitary Technical Conference in Kharkiv, in May 1925, and were not up to another long trip.[26] Ivanitskii did bring a handful of glass lantern slides, but the meeting was held early in the day and the room was too light for his audience to see them. He was forced to detail the team's preliminary research findings with little illustrative backup.

In his presentation to the Baku Executive Committee, Ivanitskii posed a singular question: how might disparate parts of Baku better connect? To answer it, he stressed that due to the territorial reach of the oil economy, the Baku Plan was not a city plan but a regional plan. He had already explained his reasoning for initiating the Baku Plan at the regional scale in a 1925 interview with the newspaper *Baku Worker* (*Bakinskii rabochii*):

> The project raises many issues regarding the growth and improvement over the next two to three decades of a rapidly expanding city like Baku. On one side are issues having to do with the growth of suburban industries and factory territories, rail lines and the port, and questions of integrating transport. On the other side are issues of sanitation and local education, construction of hospitals and schools, exercise and sports facilities. Large settlement construction developed by the exceptionally powerful economic organization, Azneft, in an area so close to the city of Baku, suggests that future expansion may simply merge the efforts. All of this leads us to consider not only the city but the whole region.[27]

Baku's expanding urban core would soon touch, and eventually subsume, Binagady and Montina, the Azneft settlements closest to the city center. Ivanitskii argued that it was simply impractical to plan discrete city sections without considering the implications of such expansion.

To determine the scope of planning work, Ivanitskii explained, the planner must understand that his target is "above all an expansion plan, a zoning plan, and a plan for communication between each of the regions as well as a plan of overall linkages within in the locality and beyond—with the province, the region and the entire country." He also made shrewd economic arguments for regional-scale planning, citing capitalist logic to do so. A city's productive capacity, he noted, relies on its ability to equally accommodate industry and commerce. Rational planning, per the US model, projects the territorial and infrastructural needs of industry so that economic growth is barrier free. But further, "a city plan that is technically well designed and economically feasible, and that considers the topography, soil properties, and technical requirements of different types of construction, *results in substantial savings in construction.*"[28] Planning is, in short, both a revenue-generating and cost-saving exercise.

Regional planning was of concern on the Apsheron Peninsula from the time of Baku's first oil boom in the 1870s. An detailed 1899 map of existing conditions plots the peninsula's undulating pockets of oil and privately owned oil-bearing parcels (plate 9). Baku is simply the most densely developed seaside area of a large mineral-rich territory subdivided by private interests. The map reveals that there was little infrastructure to link the peninsula as an interdependent whole, however. Individual industrialists like the Nobels built and maintained their own extraction sites, pipelines, refineries, and transportation. Under socialism, the peninsular region could planned holistically because land nationalization permitted thinking well beyond the private plot or even the municipality. The originating center of Ivanitskii's regional plan is *icheri sheher*, Baku's historic Islamic core (figure 3.9). Its dark urbanized center is surrounded by a ring of more diffuse settlement, which in turn gives way to a dark crescent of oil-bearing land in the middle of the peninsula. The city and oilfields are held in tension by a net of crisscrossing roads, trams, and rail lines. The Azneft worker settlements sit in the intermediate zone between them—the expansion zone—and benefit from the dense transportation network that connects the civil city and its industry. Beyond the oil lands, an amorphous gray zone reaches all the way up to the peninsula's north shore and fingers to the west, encompassing a number of dark patches planned as future urban subcenters. The entire peninsula is engaged and integrated.

Ivanitskii then addressed the spatial implications of demographic growth. The cartograms abstractly conveyed Baku's expansion since the oil boom in the 1870s, but two city scale drawings confirmed this fact territorially. The first shows the expansion of ratified municipal boundaries in 1877, 1898, and 1926, and proposes a new boundary for 1927 to increase the city's official footprint and incorporate the new Azneft settlements (figure 3.10). An accompanying drawing demonstrates that Baku, a consummate boomtown, grew in surges to create distinct morphological regions color coded and dated on the diagram (figure 3.11). The darker the swatch, the older the neighborhood. The diagrams capture Baku's tendency to expand in a

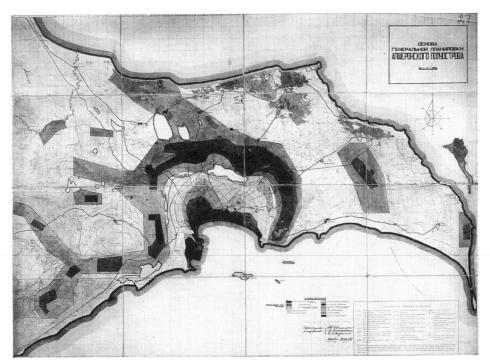

Figure 3.9. Apsheron Peninsula general plan (based on the 1899 Apsheron Plan), August 20, 1927. The dark urbanized center of Baku is surrounded by a light-colored ring of more diffuse settlement that gives way to a dark crescent of oil-bearing land. The city and oilfields are linked by transportation lines and the Azneft worker settlements sit in the intermediate zone between them. Future urban subcenters are indicated by gray zones throughout the peninsula. Planners: Aleksandr Ivanitskii et al. RGALI, f. 2991, o. 1, d. 17, l. 27.

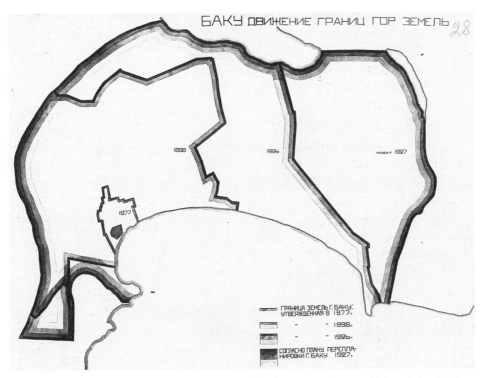

Figure 3.10. Expansion of city boundaries by year, Baku Plan, 1927. Planners: Aleksandr Ivanitskii et al. RGALI, f. 2991, o. 1, d. 17, l. 28.

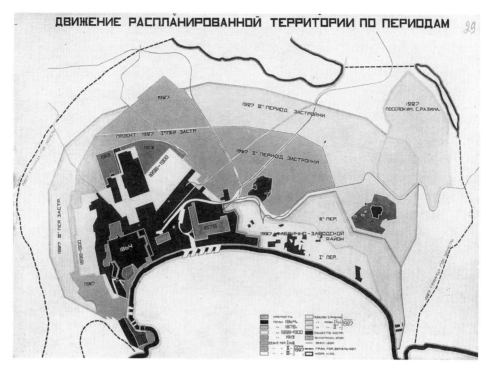

Figure 3.11. Territorial growth by period, Baku Plan, 1927. Planners: Aleksandr Ivanitskii et al. RGALI, f. 2991, o. 1, d. 17, l. 29.

northeasterly direction toward the oilfields, a direction that the 1927 plan would allow and yet also harness with a new city limit.

Ivanitskii explained to his clients that in German or US boomtowns growing at similarly steep rates as Baku, high density correlated with tall building. In Baku by contrast, high density correlated with "dwarf plots" (*karlikovie uchastki*), tiny parcels resulting from excessive subdivision. In the dwarf plot condition—which accounted for 40 percent of properties within the city limits—individual low-rise houses were constructed right up to the parcel line to maximize buildable area.[29] Small cobbled together structures sat cheek-by-jowl, which left insufficient open space and fresh air and prohibited the installation of municipal services such as running water or sewer. Disease spread quickly in these parts of the city. Beyond health concerns, the haphazard pattern of the dense built fabric impeded efficient passage through the city. The planning team's solution was to modify these dense neighborhoods carefully, taking "extreme care" to draw lines on the plan that would inconvenience the fewest possible residents. Ivanitskii referred to these sensitive interventions as "surgical measures" (*khirurgicheskie mery*).[30] Lastly, he recommended five regions of the city to receive detailed design attention. These included Bailov/Chemberekend, the Nagornoe Plateau/Region, Armenikend/Veer, Zavokzalnyi (rail station) Region, the Kirpich-Khana/Kani-tapa neighborhoods

Figure 3.12. Plan of the city divided by region, 1927. Key to regions that received detailed planning: 1. Bailov & Chemberekend Region; 2. Nagornoe Plateau & Nargornyi Region; 3. Armenikend & Veer Region; 4. Zavokzal'nyi Region; 5. Kirpich-Khana & Kani-Tapa Region. Planners: Aleksandr Ivanitskii et al. Diagram by the author based on RGALI, f. 2991, o. 1, d. 17, l. 30.

(figure 3.12). These five regions encompassed the entire northern and western territory of the city and required that the planners tackle the most challenging neighborhoods in terms of density and topography.

After Ivanitskii's presentations, the Baku Executive Committee and Baksovet Planning Committee passed identical resolutions that solidified six key tasks for the city's first socialist general plan:

a) The city territory must be zoned and distributed into industrial sites and sites for construction (city, semiurban, and settlement-suburban construction);

b) the city plan must be coherent and align technically with the proposed worker settlements;

c) the city plan must align with the railroad lines and the port;

d) a system of public squares and magistrals must be developed;

e) a system of green planting, playgrounds, and sports parks must be composed and grow gradually; and

f) unobstructed sewage and storm water systems must be installed.[31]

The administrators listened to Ivanitskii's proposals and then returned them as a formal mandate. At the regional scale, the city would be zoned into separate industrial and residential areas. The plan of the city would be cognizant of and work with worker settlements in the peri-urban regions and with rail and water transportation networks. The urban fabric would be knit together with boulevards, public squares, parks, and planting. Finally, municipal water and waste services would be provided to all neighborhoods. "Conclusive propositions" from the planning team were due no later than November 1926, five months from the date of the resolution.

The first socialist general plan for Baku is commonly known by two names: the 1927 Plan and the Ivanitskii Plan. As the temporal name indicates, the bulk of the plan was finished in mid-1927, not November 1926 as requested. In March 1927, Ivanitskii wrote to his clients to update them on planning progress and to send along a bundle of working drawings. His letter made clear that he felt extreme pressure to complete the work, and certainly wished to do so, but that there were many reasons for schedule setbacks. Ivanitskii received the long-awaited municipal survey only at the very end of 1926, and even after the long wait, it was imperfect. "A lot of time was wasted dealing with the numerous discrepancies and insufficiencies of the surveys," Ivanitskii complained. "In order to save money, the survey was not taken exactly along the regions to be planned. Further, old surveys were utilized for some sections that either were difficult or simply impossible to align with the new."[32] The planning team struggled to determine which aspects of the survey could be trusted. Given that roads were being punched through, houses demolished, and trees planted along their pencil lines, lack of confidence in the survey produced anxiety among the planning team.

A personal letter from Ivanitskii to his primary client, the deputy director of the Baku Department of Communal Services, revealed the two issues that caused the planner most emotional distress. The territory covered by the plan increased exponentially over the years, whereas funding had decreased. His fee for the detailed plan had recently been trimmed, and Ivanitskii was forced to accept it. "We are extremely exhausted by the lack of money for the project. I blame myself," he wrote of his capitulation, "but it doesn't help." Ivanitskii stressed that the plan needed to be completed professionally and responsibly, despite lack of funds. "I cannot crumple up the work or slapdash it, and I also cannot allow you to deploy the plan until all of the planning work is completed and applied to the overall master plan. I am doing everything I can to keep your work going: punching streets through, planning new neighborhoods, dividing the land into building plots, and so forth."[33] He promised to send neighborhood blueprints as they were completed, so that the city could begin construction in targeted areas without waiting for the comprehensive general plan. Ivanitskii requested that the client send him half of the amount that remained in the project budget to push the work through.

Ivanitskii was also concerned by the increasing "hostility, quibbles, stopped work, and curtailed job estimates" in his dealings with technical staff at the Baku Department of Communal Services, who appeared to be purposely torpedoing aspects of the plan.[34] Already, he had to stop faulty commencement of extensive tree planting in the city. The long east-west boulevard that Ivanitskii drew below the Armenikend district followed the line of the green cross in the von der Nonne plan and connected institutions and civic squares including the hospital, one of the city's main reservoirs, and the radio tower. Its location was carefully calibrated to waste the least amount of buildable land. "Now," Ivanitskii claimed, "the boulevard has been moved lower by someone, based on the alleged verbal agreement of M. A. Kniazkov, who energetically denies it. Dragged lower in the plan, the line of plantings takes up four free blocks below the reservoir, it falls on the sloping hillside, and denies Armenikend its correct shape."[35] The incorrectly located boulevard—already planted with trees—threatened to ruin the planned structure of the whole northern portion of the city. Ivanitskii enclosed a drawing that reiterated the proper location of the boulevard in protest and recommended "liquidation" of the erroneous plantings.[36]

The 1927 Baku Plan: Stitching the City

Ivanitskii and his planning team completed the final version of the Baku General Plan in August 1927. The client had narrowed the scope of the plan due to "budget economization" and simply to get the work in hand. The main deliverables were just six drawings: a comprehensive plan of the city within municipal boundaries and five detailed plans of the city's most troublesome regions. Ivanitskii made clear in his final report that budget limitations did not allow for detailed technical development of citywide standards such as the longitudinal and transversal street sections or the planting system, though he would provide diagrammatic recommendations.[37] Nonetheless, he felt confident that the structure of the plan, and the municipal boundaries set by it, would serve Baku through 1957, when the city's intense growth would taper.[38]

The general plan is a large pencil drawing thick with information, composed of four equal sheets assembled to make the whole (figure 3.13). The planners divided the city into five height and density zones. The darkest and densest areas correlate with *icheri sheher* and the *forshtadt*, followed by other built-up sections of the city closest to the Caspian shoreline. Areas to the north, west, and east become less dense and are thus are shaded in a gradient that lightens as it grows away from the center.

The shaded blocks are the body of the plan, whereas the streets and open spaces—the nervous system and organs—are rendered in stark white and black. The white

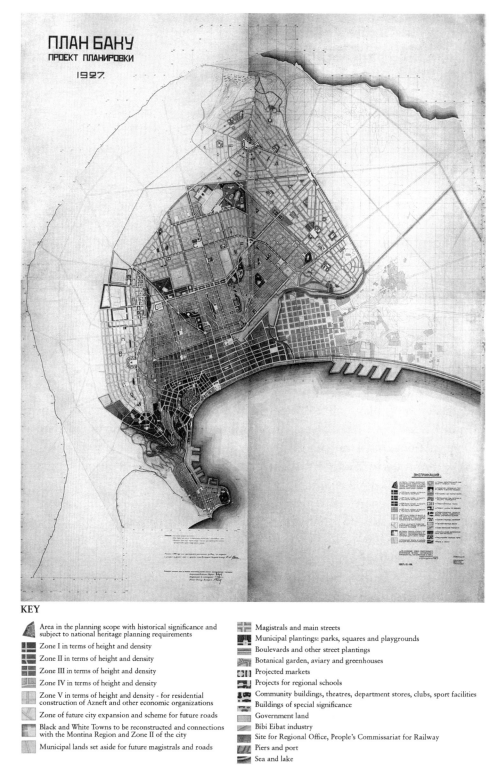

KEY

Area in the planning scope with historical significance and subject to national heritage planning requirements	Magistrals and main streets
Zone I in terms of height and density	Municipal plantings: parks, squares and playgrounds
Zone II in terms of height and density	Boulevards and other street plantings
Zone III in terms of height and density	Botanical garden, aviary and greenhouses
Zone IV in terms of height and density	Projected markets
Zone V in terms of height and density - for residential construction of Azneft and other economic organizations	Projects for regional schools
	Community buildings, theatres, department stores, clubs, sport facilities
Zone of future city expansion and scheme for future roads	Buildings of special significance
Black and White Towns to be reconstructed and connections with the Montina Region and Zone II of the city	Government land
	Bibi Eibat industry
Municipal lands set aside for future magistrals and roads	Site for Regional Office, People's Commissariat for Railway
	Piers and port
	Sea and lake

Figure 3.13. Baku Plan, 1927. Planners: Aleksandr Ivanitskii et al. RGALI, f.2 991, o. 1, d. 17, ll. 152, 153, 154, 155. Key diagram by the author.

strips and openings that run through the plan are the network of streets and squares that Ivanitskii referred to as the city's "nerves."[39] The longest and widest white strips are the magistrals (main thoroughfares) that connect disparate parts of the city. Baku's organs are the black patches on the plan that indicate parks, sports grounds, planted boulevards, and civic institutions. Ivanitskii explained the relationship between the systems:

> The magistral is one important aspect that creates social organization in the city plan. The additional parts are the squares and the locations set aside for public buildings. If we construct a massive system of magistrals and squares but indicate no proper locations for public buildings where they can command a certain radius, then the plan is not correctly socially organized. We consider by contrast European and American cities that are built by private-capitalist concerns, in which you don't see such organization in the plan. Indicated on our plan are also locations for a square and a public building in each city region. Each region will have its own central square (of cultural or adminis-trative function)—this creates organization in the plan.[40]

According to Ivanitskii's logic, the Baku Plan was socialist because the streets, squares, and public buildings worked together across the breadth of the city, and yet each neighborhood was also provided with its own center to ensure distributive equal-ity of civic institutions and places of leisure. The unjust hierarchies that Ivanitskii witnessed in capitalist cities were combated in the Baku Plan by spatial diffusion of important connective streets and public programs, especially green space. Both of these important aspects of the plan are covered in turn.

Connective Logics: Magistrals

The principal solution to Baku's connective problems, and the main organizational tool of the 1927 plan, was the magistral: a wide road, or boulevard. These arteries served to connect main spaces in the center efficiently with one another and with industrial enterprises outside the city. Surface transportation followed these lines, inscribing them on the collective consciousness.

When design for the Baku Plan began, the city's street network was a messy tan-gle, the result of the medieval Islamic core clashing with the middle-scale Russian colonial grid and the large-scale industrial grid. Ivanitskii determined that the city's dysfunctional street network was the core problem to be solved. "Baku, an indus-trial city with significant economic activity, needs a structure to its plan to maxi-mize linkages between outlying regions and industrial regions that lie to the north, east, and south of the city. Further, the crazy circulation (*beshenaia tsirculiatsiia*) in the city does not accommodate public masses, trucks, etc., that also require clear

magistrals. In the city these do not exist."[41] Here, Ivanitskii raised two separate
street-based issues: poor connectivity between the center and the outlying regions,
and traffic congestion in the center. To address the first, the planning team linked
the city, new worker settlements, and industrial sites with rail and roads. Careful
attention was paid at the regional scale to topography and existing rail and pipeline
networks to determine efficient trajectories. Urban congestion required a more inva-
sive solution since dense neighborhoods had to be cut through to remove blockages.
Before the plan was completed Torgovaia Street (now Nizami), that runs parallel
to the Caspian coast from the Black Town to *icheri sheher*, began in the east at 84
feet wide and progressively narrowed as it moved westward to 70 feet, 50 feet, 35
feet, and finally just 28 feet wide by the time it landed in the oldest part of the city
as Torgovaia Lane. The traffic jams that resulted from this one bottleneck, even in
1927, led to "catastrophic effects" on city movement.[42]

The planning team designed six magistrals in detail that included the seaside boulevard, the east-west link between the Nagornoe Plateau and the Black Town, and
the north-south road that connected the shore to the middle of the Apsheron Peninsula (figure 3.14).[43] In an accompanying construction phasing diagram, magistrals
are clearly legible as white lines that cut through existing fabric and link civic spaces
(figure 3.15). The first phase of development on this plan is darkest—generally, near

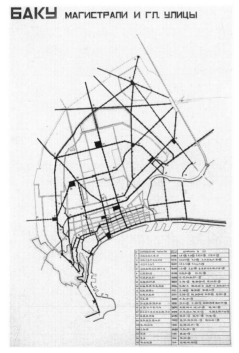

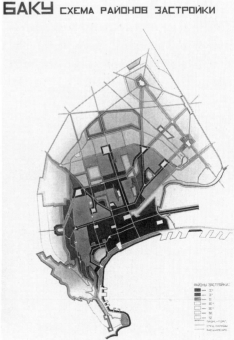

Figure 3.14. Magistrals and streets, Baku Plan,
1927. Planners: Aleksandr Ivanitskii et al.
RGALI, f. 2991, o. 1, d. 17, l. 60.

Figure 3.15. Construction phasing by region, Baku
Plan, 1927. Planners: Aleksandr Ivanitskii et al.
RGALI, f. 2991, o. 1, d. 17, l. 61.

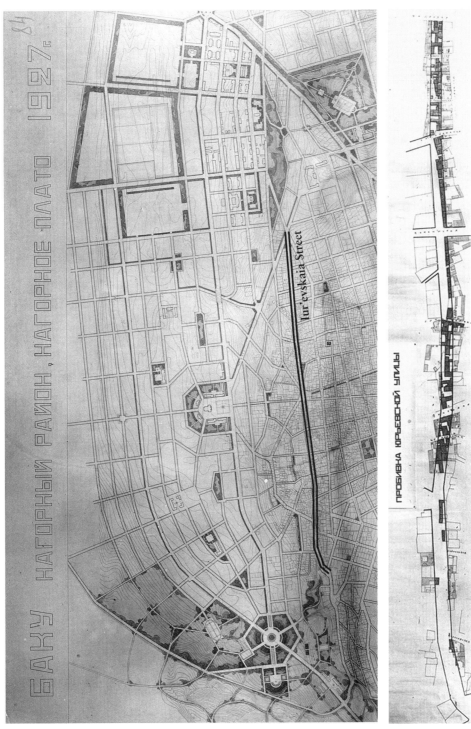

Figure 3.16. Iur'evskaia Street located on the detailed plan of the Nagornyi Region and Nagornoe Plateau, Baku Plan, 1927. Planners: Aleksandr Ivanitskii et al. Diagram by the author based on RGALI, f. 2991, o. 1, d. 17, l. 84.

Figure 3.17. Punching through Iur'evskaia Street. Planners: Aleksandr Ivanitskii et al. RGALI, f. 2991, o. 1, d. 17, l. 71.

the Caspian shoreline—but the magistrals are arms that reach into poorly developed areas to set the stage for future growth. Later Soviet general plans used Ivanitskii's 1927 magistral skeleton to situate strategic capital improvements.

The magistral that received the most design attention was Iur'evskaia Street (now Nariman Narimanov Avenue) that runs north-south along a steep slope from the Nagornoe Plateau down toward *icheri sheher* (figure 3.16).[44] Because of its difficult topography, the Nagornoe Plateau was one of the most poorly planned and constructed neighborhoods in Baku. It suffered from microparcelization (dwarf plots), and the majority of the tiny houses sat haphazardly in relation to one another and blocked routes of passage. Ivanitskii proposed planning surgery to "punch through" (*probivat'*) the neighborhood to create a magistral for tram and bus traffic. The ghostly footprints of each structure impacted by the proposed demolition show through the vellum sheets the planners laid over the survey (figure 3.17). Ivanitskii tallied that 496 structures would have to be removed to install a proper network of magistrals. An additional 214 structures would be demolished for construction of squares and open space. The team evaluated the age, height, character, and monetary value of the 710 affected structures and determined that 552 (77 percent) sat on dwarf plots of just 42–49 square feet. "This fits one room," Ivanitskii told his clients, "and in that room sometimes there is one apartment, sometimes a few. These are unbelievably (*neveroiatnye*) poor structures in terms of quality and sanitary conditions!"[45]

In the summer of 1928, local photographer Lavrentii Bregadze documented the neighborhood, the structures, and the Bakuvians affected by the magistral clearance project. These photographs follow the nineteenth-century practice of capturing the process of urban modernization midstream.[46] On July 5, 1928, Bregadze captured demolition and construction work at various points along the path of Iur'evskaia Street. The majority of the shots were taken from a slightly elevated vantage point and provide deep views of the ongoing urban transformation.

One photograph, likely taken from a rooftop, shows overlapping layers of single-story houses as they recede into the distance and climb the hill to the west (plate 10). Piles of dirt, stone, and wood sit on the edges of an emerging pathway through the dense quarter; women wrapped in black chadors stand out against the light-colored footpath. Bregadze often posed his human subjects to mark the scale of intervention. In one image, a multigenerational group stands in the middle of a cleared passage (plate 11). A line of children takes the front: a white-shirted child stands before a fully covered woman, two barefoot boys, and a naked toddler. In the background, clearing work proceeds. Pairs of men carry planks piled with rubble, and mules and carts stand ready to transport it away. Another photograph along the future magistral's path captures a scene in which clearing has concluded (figure 3.18). The generous width of the street is measured by more than a dozen figures who stand in a single line across the clearing and still do not reach the buildings on either side. Neatly orthogonal buildings line the cleared, modernized path of movement.

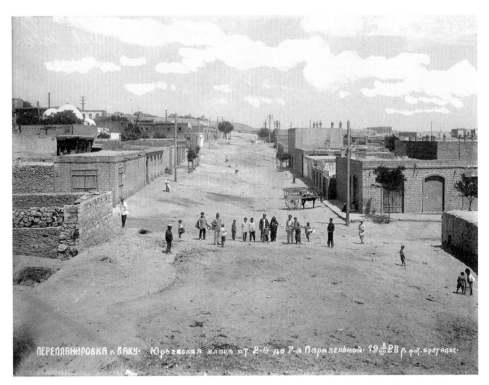

Figure 3.18. Replanning the City of Baku photo series, documenting the removal of houses along Iur'evskaia Street on July 5, 1928. The width of the street is measured by more than a dozen figures who stand in a single line across the clearing. Orthogonal buildings line the cleared path of movement through the Nargornyi Region. Photo: L. Bregadze. ARDKFSA, Inv. 5-378.

Ivanitskii attentively followed major demolition and construction work in Baku from his office in Moscow. On a copy of the plan drawing, he hand-notated the major infrastructural projects underway and referred to the Bregadze photographs that documented the planning interventions (plate 12). Ivanitskii was aware of and sensitive to the physical labor and massive displacement his plan required. He argued, however, that "the experience at Iur'evskaia proved that it was the right thing to do."[47] The magistral would be a lifeline for those citizens shown in the Bregadze photographs, providing modern transportation links, pedestrian infrastructure, greenery, and open passage for installation of electricity, water supply, and sanitation.

The planning team also devised a taxonomy of street sections for the Baksovet that covered eight widths and configurations (figure 3.19). All of the dimensions are given in feet, and indeed, the profiles were adapted from US data and precedents.[48] Type I, the widest typical profile, is a 154-foot-wide boulevard that accommodates four lanes of auto traffic, two tram lines, a generous tree-lined pedestrian walkway in the center and ample shaded sidewalks on either side. On the other end of the spectrum is the 56-foot-wide Type VI that holds just three auto lanes, one tree-lined sidewalk, and another narrow unshaded sidewalk (Iur'evskaia, for all of the trouble, came closest to the modest Type VI).[49] Iur'evskaia's reconstructed profile, roadbed,

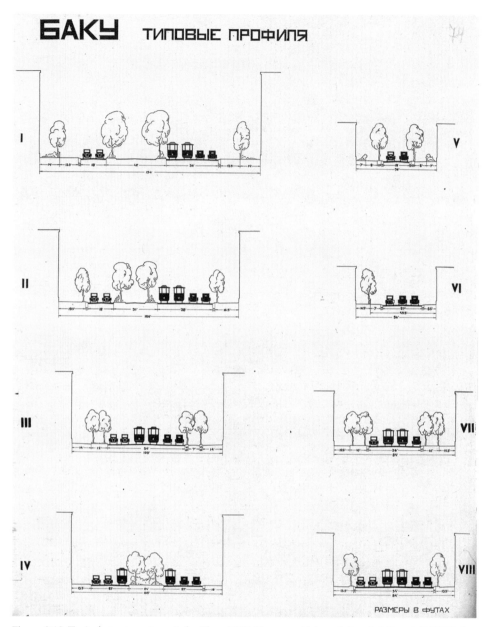

Figure 3.19. Typical street sections, Baku Plan, 1927. Planners: Aleksandr Ivanitskii et al. RGALI, f. 2991, o. 1, d. 17, l. 74.

and slope were designed to handle tram and bus traffic to bring the neighborhood, finally, into the citywide street network.

Magistrals and secondary streets were widened throughout the urban center of Baku in accordance with a new "red line"—the boundary between the public way

Figure 3.20. Karl Marx Street during reconstruction (left; February 20, 1933) and after reconstruction (right; May 15, 1933). Photos: L. Bregadze. ARDKFSA, Inv. 5-224, 5-223.

Figure 3.21. Gogol Street during reconstruction (left; February 20, 1933) and after reconstruction (right; May 15, 1933). Photos: L. Bregadze. ARDKFSA, Inv. 5-270, 5-349.

and the building plot—such that 1,200–1,300 properties would be "cut" over time.[50] Streets not dimensionally adjusted were nonetheless upgraded with asphalt paving, proper sidewalks, and street trees. Bregadze also captured the process of street modernization (figures 3.20–3.21). In his photos of Karl Marx and Gogol streets, "before" shots from February 1933 show muddy trenches ready for the installation of the concrete water and sewer pipes that lay to the side. On Gogol Street, mounds of discarded cobblestones sit on the obstructed sidewalks, a pile of primitive two-person moving pallets holds the right foreground, and a lonely donkey and cart stand in the middle of the trench. By May 1933, reconstruction was complete. The smooth asphalted surface of the street bed is separated from the asphalted sidewalk by a curb, and street trees and electrical poles sit safely in the pedestrian zone.

Greening the City

Given "the hot climate, the dry and dusty air, the incredible density of construction, and most of all rapid industrial growth . . . city greenery takes on a much greater degree of importance in Baku than in any other city of the USSR," Ivanitskii argued.[51] The Baku 1927 Plan's green spaces—rendered in black on the general plan—included planted boulevards, parks, squares, playgrounds, and sports fields that together served as the lungs of the city to filter particulates and create much-needed shade. Greenery, Ivanitskii stressed, "is important from the perspectives of social health, city improvement and to increase the cultural conditions of life (*kul'turnye usloviia zhizni*)."[52]

Ivanitskii gathered extensive transnational data on the benefit of plantings to urban residents and stressed that greening was an issue that transcended politics and economics. "Where working masses have a voice in the direction of municipal economics," he wrote, "they want more plantings closer to houses, to shade playgrounds, and within 500–600 meters from workplaces. Plantings are necessary for life—democratic and proletarian populations value them in the construction of the city."[53] In capitalist countries the land on which greenery sits has a monetary value that planners have to account for in the project budget, but socialist planners do not have to factor in land costs. They do have to convince the client to leave space free that could otherwise be built on. Ivanitskii argued that green space's value is qualitative: greenery increases the desirability of all programs that surround it, so in a socialist city plan, greenery must be equitably and regularly distributed. The system of plantings he and his team proposed created an extensive green network that infiltrated all regions of the city (figure 3.22).

In making his case for green Ivanitskii summoned data from European and US sources, most notably a 1923 report from the Pittsburgh Planning Commission. The Pittsburgh report compared open space ratios (green space per capita) for all significant US cities that ran from 5.92 square meters per person in New York City to 51.33 square meters for Washington, DC, with an overall North America average of 12.0 square meters (Baku's ratio was a paltry 1.8 square meters by comparison). To incite the competitive spirit of Soviet policymakers, Ivanitskii advocated a US-sized ratio of 12.0 square meters for Baku, although 4.2 square meters was the legislated norm in the Russian Republic.[54] The Baku Plan finally settled at a ratio of 6–7 square meters of green space per resident on the regional and the city scale.[55] Ivanitskii also cited the United States for its novel park classification system, which ranged in scale from large regional reserves to local playgrounds for small children.[56] "We have paused on this question—the question of classification of open spaces—because this is not at all the way we work in the USSR," Ivanitskii wrote in his final report. "But it is well known that such classification plays a great role in general planning and especially the planning of green spaces."[57] By utilizing standardized modules—street types, park types—the unknowns in a planning project can be limited, Ivanitskii argued. Planning is more rational with typological design, making it easier to calculate and price an equitable spread of green area across territory.

In his discussion of open space cost ramifications, Ivanitskii focused on three US parks for which he had obtained pricing data: Warinanco, Cedar Brook, and Echo Lake Parks. All three were located in greater Elizabeth, New Jersey, and were

БАКУ СИСТЕМА НАСАЖДЕНИЙ

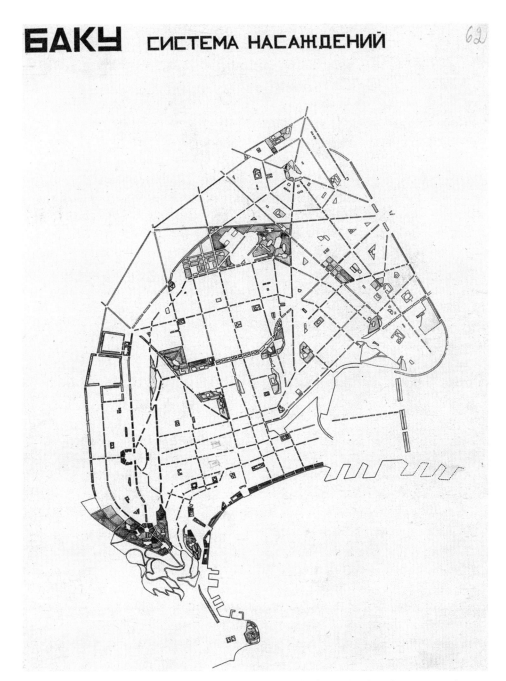

Figure 3.22. System of plantings. Baku Plan, 1927. A network of green boulevards connects Baku's park and open space systems. Planners: Aleksandr Ivanitskii et al. RGALI, f.2991, o.1, d.17, l. 62.

designed in 1923 by the Olmsted Brothers landscape architectural firm. Ivanitskii
noted that land cost doubled the overall cost in each case, such that the final price
tag for Warinanco Park, the largest of the three, was almost $700,000. Lest they be
warned off such expenditure, Ivanitskii employed a cunning capitalist argument for
his NEP-era clients. "The Americans," he wrote, "whose wealth of experience with
park issues we utilized here, have a saying: 'Parks pay the city back.' The Bakuvian
saying will be the same, such that in Baku, parks will 'pay.'"[58]

The 1927 Baku Plan provided exhaustive area calculations in page after page of
fold out spreadsheets so that the recommended capital improvements could be accurately priced. Ivanitskii and his team tallied the cost of greening and determined
that it was not going to be cheap. "In Baku, this [planting scheme] means a lot of
money," Ivanitskii admitted.[59] Installation of the planting plan would take twenty to
twenty-five years, and the Baksovet would expend 250,000–300,000 rubles to make
it happen. This was, however, just a small amount more than the city was spending
at the time for a noncoordinated collection of street trees and open spaces.

Ratifying the Plan

Once Ivanitskii's team completed the six critical drawings for the plan, they put their
pencils down. Much work remained, however, to describe what had been accomplished. Over the course of 1928, Ivanitskii compiled a massive four-volume report
on the project, which was a necessary requirement for the plan's official approval
process. In late 1928, the Baku clients engaged an expert panel of three eminent
planners to adjudicate the plan.[60] Professor G. D. Dubelir taught at the Institute of
Transportation in Leningrad and was the author of the influential manual *City Planning* (*Planirovka gorodov*, 1910) that first introduced Russian engineers to planning
trends in Western Europe and the United States. In the Soviet period, Dubelir specialized in the optimization of road networks in his position as director of the Leningrad and Moscow Highway Institutes. Professor Z. G. Frenkel' was the author of
The Fundamentals of General Urban Improvements (*Osnovy obshchego gorodskogo blagoustroistva*, 1926). Frenkel' knew Baku well; in his lectures and texts, he
cited it as the only city in the Soviet Union with a modern system of daily garbage
collection.[61] The third expert panel member, L. A. Il'in, was the chief architect of
the city of Leningrad at the time of the expert review, but his influence in Baku was
greatest over the long term. Il'in moved to Baku in 1929 shortly after participating
in the plan's adjudication, and over the next few years he adjusted the Ivanitskii plan
to meet the new demands of Moscow-influenced ensemble planning.[62]

The expert opinion submitted in January 1929 was brief and complimentary.
The panel found the project "reasonable and in good faith, in accordance with local
physical, geographic, economic, demographic, and social conditions, as well as with
the provisions of modern science and the art of urban planning."[63] In other words,

the Baku Plan managed to be both local and universal; it was tied to the particulars of its site and also in line with international planning standards. The experts ratified a distilled version of Ivanitskii's report and in so doing they articulated the tasks of Soviet planning. At the fore was the economy. The Baku Plan organized the entire Apsheron Peninsula to accommodate the oil industry, fruitful plots were left free for future exploitation, and proximate housing and services for the oil workers were provided. The plan was also responsive to the limits of the nascent socialist economy. By recommending dense construction and adjustment to the existing fabric instead of destruction, Ivanitskii's team made the most of restricted capital funding. Lastly, the plan sought to improve urban dwellers' quality of life through sensitive building orientation and increased greenery. The experts' final determination was that the plan "should be seen as a general project of redevelopment of the city . . . that can be taken as the basis for the development of working drawings necessary for implementation."[64]

In January 1930, an entire year after the expert opinion was submitted, and five years after planning work had begun, the Presidium of the Baku Executive District Committee summoned Ivanitskii to Baku to present the plan for official approval. Ivanitskii opened his remarks with gracious acknowledgment of the many collaborators who worked on the plan over the half decade. "This is not an individual work, but a seriously collective work," he stressed. "I am the one presenting this report formally, but I speak for the whole Baku Department of Communal Services. . . I feel myself to be one of their co-workers—if not forever, at least for the past five years, which is a long period of time. I have stored the whole of Baku in me—in this way Baku is different. I can only say that the interests of Baku have become very close to my heart."[65] Ivanitskii presented the plan's chronology and explained the causes of the protracted process. Despite the setbacks, the plan was a tenable long-term proposal for controlled urban growth, and this was the aspect of the project that the executive committee needed to consider and approve. "This is in no way a negative condition to find yourselves in," Ivanitskii assured his clients. "You should make your desires [for the future] known now, when there are a lot of ideas, a lot of options on the table, when you can be objective, while the project is just one of any number of variants. City planning, which comes to fruition over twenty to forty years, is not impacted by the fact that we are deciding on the plan so far in the future."[66] Most important, he stressed, the plan required quick ratification. Although Baku was one of the first cities in the Soviet Union to begin a general planning process, it now faced competition from other cities for limited state funding. "To accelerate the implementation of your plan it is necessary to deal with lending credit. I know Tsekombank (the Central Bank of Communal Services and Housing): they would rather give money when they know that the plan is well developed and that no other significant changes are coming."[67] The stage was set for the executive committee to give the 1927 Baku Plan its stamp of approval.

In the five years between Ivanitskii's first appearance in Baku and this final one, the balance of power had shifted. Newly acquired knowledge of and experience with the science of city planning empowered the members of the executive committee to interrogate the plan and its planner. The questions they posed ranged from the programmatic to the climatic to the operational. Was Ivanitskii convinced that the stadium was on the optimal site? Why was there no public beach included in the final scheme? On what basis were schools sited on the plan? Was the allocation of 7.5 square meters of green space per person sufficient for decent quality of life in the city? Was the plan in line with anti-aircraft defense measures, and were representatives from the military command consulted as experts? How were Baku's harsh northerly winds to be mitigated? What did the city need to do to ensure that the plan would be followed?[68] When the barrage of questions tapered, the floor was given back to Ivanitskii.

Speaking off script, the planner addressed the questions one by one with answers that exhibited his breadth of research and deep knowledge of the city. The client group had proven its capacity to absorb the complexity of the planning task, so Ivanitskii did not shy from technical details. He cited international norms from memory and provided statistics where needed. He spoke at length about the characteristics of each of the regions planned in detail and ranked their desirability to justify the phasing for municipal improvements. Ivanitskii also made clear that the plan was not complete. He urged his clients to understand the deliverables as portions of a larger regional plan, yet to be undertaken:

> All of Apsheron should be planned, the main highways need to be laid out, and the land must be zoned. We must determine which land will be for military purposes, which will become industrial land, which will be set aside for railways, the port, beaches. Finally, we need to determine where the population will settle, and plan these areas in more detail. This is a giant undertaking but you yourself understand what kind of results it will yield. While in other places planning generalities are sufficient, this little Apsheron Peninsula presents such a valuable territory [for our Union] that we must develop a thorough technical plan.[69]

Although Ivanitskii had insisted from 1925 that the Baku Plan needed to encompass the entire peninsula, the project's many scheduling and funding setbacks limited the plan's ultimate scope to the urban core. Professional ethics forbade him from presenting his work as more comprehensive than it was.

Ivanitskii's answers quelled the committee, whose chair, Frolov, opened the debate and moved to vote on the language of the final resolution. At 10 o'clock at night on January 11, 1930, the Presidium of the Baku Executive District Committee approved the 1927 Baku Plan with three addenda. First, Torgovaia Street would be extended to merge with Gubernskaia. Second, the planning committee was, in the future, to engage economic issues alongside physical planning issues. Lastly, the Presidium resolved that "the main task of the Planning Committee is to consider measures for the organization of socialist everyday life (*byt*)."[70] From then on, any adjustment to the space of the city would be judged against its ability to instill suitably socialist habits in Baku's citizens.

Socialist Urban Theory Arrives in Baku

In all of the archival documentation about housing and planning Baku, from 1920 to 1930, there is sparse mention of socialist ideology. The concerns of Azneft and the Baksovet were practical and immediate. Baku's growth was dependent on oil, and the city's importance to the Union fluctuated with its ability to extract this primary resource. Reliable labor was needed to get the oil industry back up and running, so Azneft and the Baksovet built housing, transportation, and limited social services to draw and retain a labor pool. When Ivanitskii arrived in Baku at the end of 1924, he introduced his clients to a more complex set of concerns. Most important, he taught them to conceive of planning as a tool to plot future expansion. Building a single house, or even a whole workers' settlement like Stepan Razin, was myopic, he stressed. Planning, on the other hand, optimized the overlapping systems of oil, transportation, sanitation, public services, housing, and greenery to make the most of capital expenditures.

Why then, after five years of planning, and at the end of a long ratification meeting, was the relationship of physical planning to socialist ideology suddenly of utmost concern to the Presidium of the Baku Executive District Committee? The final written question submitted to the planner provides context. Ivanitksii read the question aloud to the client group, then offered a curt answer:

Q: You are closely acquainted, no doubt, with the new questions of city building as published in *Economic Life* (*Ekonomicheskaia zhizn'*). Namely, shouldn't we avoid piling ourselves up large cities and instead build small towns for 10,000–15,000 people?

A: This is an issue that keeps coming up. Personally, I think that we are not "piling things up" in this plan but are instead creating a place that will be good for life. Many different organizational patterns are possible that still completely satisfy the demands of socialist *byt*. Let us end with this.[71]

Socialist city-building kept "coming up," as Ivanitskii put it, because all of a sudden it was a topic of intense debate in the national press. The questioner referred to *Ekonomicheskaia zhizn'* in particular, the daily newspaper published by the Council of Labor and Defense. Starting in December 1929, the newspaper kicked off a regular series titled "Toward a socialist *byt*" (*Navstrechu sotsialisticheskomu bytu*). In more than thirty articles published over the course of that month, economists, architects, and politicians weighed in on the construction of socialist cities that were rising chaotically and poorly planned during the fulfillment of the first Five-Year Plan. The socialist city debates were centered in Moscow. There is no evidence that Ivanitskii played an active role in these discussions, but as a Moscow-based planning practitioner and colleague of some of the most vocal participants, like the Vesnins, he was undoubtedly well versed in the main points of the debate. The Baku Executive District Committee's concern was that the project they were about to adjudicate might not align with emerging trends in socialist city planning.[72]

Before the vote on his plan, Ivanitskii requested the opportunity to offer a conclusion on the "ideological status of the socialist city." He opened with an exegesis of the Moscow debates. There were two prevailing concepts for the socialist city that were diametrically opposed to one another, he explained. One concept, the brainchild of the economist Leonid Sabsovich, proposed a city with socialist infrastructure and *byt* consisting of large residential buildings—house-communes (*doma-kommuny*)—with separate units for each of the 2,000–2,500 residents. The private rooms in the *doma-kommuny* were of minimal dimensions, to be used for rest, sleep, and intimate relations only. All other daily activities would take place in public institutions embedded in the building. The second socialist city concept, promoted by the sociologist Mikhail Okhitovich, proposed single-room, individual houses strung linearly through open territory. "If the other city [Sabsovich's] had an expression of vertical volume, this one [Okhitovich's] has a horizontal volume," Ivanitskii explained. They both derived from the same principle of the full socialization of *byt* and total socialist organization, but they arrived at different conclusions regarding the form of residential buildings, and following this, the project of the city plan.[73] In the official transcript for the meeting, the surnames of both socialist city protagonists are misspelled, as "Sapsovich" and "Akhotovich," and none of the signatories to the minutes caught the mistakes. Socialist city ideas may have circulated among the Baku administration, but the particulars were fuzzy at best.

Ivanitskii divided his analysis of these concepts into two categories: issues emerging from unresolved population caps and those having to do with block size. His population critique was aimed directly at Sabsovich, whose outside limit for a socialist city unit was set at 50,000 residents. Ivanitskii used the socialist city at Zaporizhzhia, near the massive Dnipro Hydroelectric Station, as an example of how difficult population caps would be to institute in practice. In Zaporizhzhia, planners designated an initial population for the city at 250,000–300,000 with predicted urban growth at 500,000–600,000 residents. "But if you stop at a city plan for 50,000 residents, then the work required to run a huge energy station is complicated by artificially fragmenting the population and forcing them into groups of small cities," Ivanitskii argued. "This may even be contrary to the necessities of a healthy economy."[74] By raising the specter of economy, Ivanitskii spoke directly to the concerns of the assembled.

If Baku's workforce was forcibly fragmented into population-capped housing combines, municipal transportation would need to expand yet again. In the Sabsovich scheme, the city would also be required to provide potentially redundant public services for each urban unit. Ivanitskii noted that he had discussed with Sabsovich personally these and other issues prompted by forced urban fragmentation, but that the economist could not answer the concerns satisfactorily. Okhitovich's theory, architecturalized into diffuse single-room pavilions set in the landscape by Moisei Ginzburg, "has had unfavorable results in terms of the sanitary-technical systems," Ivanitskii told the group, "because to install a sewer in a city which consists of individual rooms is a task that simply cannot be solved."[75]

In closing, Ivanitskii sympathized with the members of the committee before him who were tasked to choose a system for urban organization but who were faced with "undeveloped schemes on which the highest party and state echelons, specifically Gosplan, has not even yet made their own judgment."[76] Common frustration with the nebulous, evolving goals of Soviet city planning united the planner and his clients in their final meeting. It was a frustration echoed in all corners of the USSR during the 1929–30 building season. Theoretical ground continued to shift while construction targets for the first Five-Year Plan loomed.

The process by which Baku was planned is an example of design praxis *par excellence*. The planning team began with intense research on the city's morphology, economy, demography, and social and cultural practices. They then moved on to draft designs and final recommendations. Two years separated the completion of deliverables from the plan's final ratification, ample time for Ivanitskii to synthesize the effort's most important takeaways—to turn practice into theory. Spatial preoccupations and solutions that became hallmarks of socialist planning were brought to light and pushed forward in the Baku 1927 Plan. First, the plan advocated regionalism. Both planner and client recognized the entire Apsheron Peninsula as the proper scope of planning work for the city of Baku. Second, housing and industry were acknowledged as inextricable. Worker settlements, the first priority of the Baku Plan, were located proximate to, but not on top of, valuable oil-bearing lands. Hundreds of units of worker housing—though still not nearly enough—were designed and constructed with hygienic economy. Third, linkages across urban space and into the periphery were highlighted as crucial. Long clear lines of communication—magistrals—were inscribed on the city to connect neighborhoods previously divided by topography, density, and distance. Four, public institutions and services were evenly distributed throughout the plan and acted as local centers of gravity. Finally, a planting plan was instituted to bring quality of life to the dusty city and provide spaces for public leisure.

The story of the Baku Plan confounds one of the most stubborn assumptions about Soviet planning: that it was, from the start, administratively and geographically centralized. In its period of inception, from the mid-1920s to the early 1930s, Soviet planning benefitted from the absence of central direction, and from an open dialogue with a community of experts inside and outside of the Soviet Union, both distinctive features of NEP. The Baku planning effort was not driven by the demands of the state apparatus in Moscow, nor was it administered by a state entity in the Soviet capital. Planner Aleksandr Ivanitskii was a private practitioner hired by a local administration, and together client and contractor devised the planning tasks with little to no oversight from Gosplan, the state planning body. As such, the 1927 Baku Plan represents a period of revolutionary experimentation in Soviet spatial planning that, despite later centralization, left a significant legacy. This locally grounded effort produced a plan that stood the test of time and the vagaries of style. The 1927 Baku Plan effectively shaped the rational growth of the city in the decades to follow and provided a practical guide for socialist planning after the 1929–30 socialist urbanism debates had run their course.

PART II

STEEL CITY

Magnitogorsk, 1929–1932

CHAPTER 4

THE GREAT DEBATE

We are building our industry from the bottom.

We can construct everything in the light of the very latest word in technology. Our factories will, therefore, be equipped with the newest, the strongest, and the best machines.

We build on a vacant lot.

Well, what of it? There we can build according to a plan.

—M. ILIN (1931)

ALEKSANDR IVANITSKII WAS SUMMONED TO BAKU MORE THAN TWO YEARS AFTER completing the city's first general plan to assuage his clients' political panic. The Baku Plan was completed quietly in 1927, and it provided his client, the Baksovet, with more than a decade worth of implementable municipal improvement projects. The Baksovet's request to see Ivanitskii in January 1930 was prompted by the Union-wide debate on the proper organization of socialist industry and labor sparked at the onset of the first Five-Year Plan. Suddenly, socialist urban form was a topic of interest at the highest levels of Soviet power, and the Baksovet was in possession of a general plan that did not directly address concerns raised in the Moscow debates. Ivanitskii confronted his clients' anxiety with measured critique and dismissal of the most radical socialist city models in circulation. While his assurances persuaded Baku's Soviet leaders to ratify the city plan, the clients acknowledged the debate in their final vote, stipulating that going forward, "the main task of the Planning Committee is to consider the measures for the organization of socialist *byt* [everyday life]."[1]

The great socialist urbanism debate was, indeed, a new development that erupted at the end of 1929 in response to the first Five-Year Plan. In April 1929, the Council of People's Commissars of the USSR (Sovnarkom) ratified the plan, a full year and a half into its official term (the first Five-Year Plan was to have begun in 1928). The Supreme Council of the National Economy (Vesenkha) and the State Planning Committee (Gosplan) had to scramble to define a spatial planning platform for the new industrial sites already under construction and those slated to commence. The beginning of the socialist urbanism debate can be traced to when the Vesenkha economist Leonid Sabsovich began to lecture and write about the plan's possible sociospatial implications. Sabsovich, Gosplan chair Gleb Krzhizhanovskii, and other so-called nongradualists argued for extreme haste toward industrialization. The Soviet Union could catch up to and overcome capitalist countries in just ten to fifteen years if, and only if, the USSR mobilized a fully socialized labor force that would be created through the construction and inhabitation of carefully crafted physical environments designed to instill socialist practices.

Although he was not the first to connect space and political consciousness, Sabsovich renewed a call for radical reconfiguration of *byt* in the design of housing and social services. He argued that it behooved the Soviet state to utilize the massive sums spent on capital construction to shape social practices simultaneously. Sabsovich coined, among other terms, *sotsgorod* (socialist city) and *zhilkombinat* (housing combine) to name unprecedented spatial organizations he envisioned. His controversial proposals sparked the first intellectual discussion about why and how socialist spatial practices should differ from those inherited from capitalism.

The Magnitogorsk Iron and Steel Works was the preeminent first Five-Year Plan show project, touted by the Soviet publicity machine both inside of the USSR and internationally as the "enormous city of steel, the new Gary [Indiana], created by the dictatorship of the proletariat."[2] Propagandistic publicity about Magnitostroi—the commonly used name for the construction project—cut across media and ranged from children's books, to architectural journals, to documentary films. Carefully framed stories and images of the construction project aimed to elevate Magnitogorsk, and the Soviet state by extension, in the public imagination.[3] Inconvenient truths about Magnitostroi's problematic schedule, labor conditions, and housing provisions were generally cropped from view. In a special issue about the industrial giant, even *Krokodil*, the leading satirical magazine in the USSR, tempered its anecdotes and ditties with a laudatory opening paragraph: "In its scope, Magnitostroi exceeds all construction projects that rise through the will of the proletariat in the vast space of the Soviet Union."[4] Effusive affirmation of the project first, jokes second.

For the authors of the first Five-Year Plan and the discussants in the socialist urbanism debate, Magnitogorsk was foremost a concept rather than a physical place. Actual Magnitogorsk, located on the east side of the Ural Mountains at the edge of Asia, was incomprehensible to the urbane Muscovites plotting its development. Conceptual Magnitogorsk, by contrast, was a blank slate waiting to be populated with aspirational ideas. Held up as the prime site to test models of socialist space-making, conceptual Magnitogorsk played a critical role in the evolving settlement debates. While theorists battled over the proper location, density, and form of socialist settlement, conceptual Magnitogorsk floated above the fray as a site of possibility. The Union-wide design competition for the socialist city of Magnitogorsk—launched in December 1929 at the height of the debate—provided the chance for all sides to apply physical form to their ideas.

The economic and political conditions of the first Five-Year Plan made massive capital projects like Magnitostroi possible. If Baku can be characterized as a typical NEP-era planning effort, in which local leaders determined the scope of planning and the fiscal balance sheet was regularly examined to determine the feasibility of implementation, Magnitogorsk marks the ascendance of a radically different economic model. At the onset of the plan, the Soviet Union shifted to a full command economy, and market forces were disregarded in favor of rapid industrialization. Profit garnered from other sectors of the Soviet economy were pumped into high profile projects like Magnitogorsk. The abstract shift of numbers from one column—agriculture—to another—industry—on a spreadsheet in Moscow set into motion forced agricultural collectivization, manufactured famine, and massive migration from the countryside to construction sites such as Magnitostroi, hungry for labor.[5] In a single month, June 1931, the population of Magnitogorsk rose by 50,000; many of those new residents were deported *kulak* (landowning) peasants forcibly removed during collectivization and sent as penal labor to help construct the steel factory in the Urals.[6]

From Genetic to Teleological Planning

How was it possible for Union-wide capital construction to accelerate so precipitously at the start of the first Five-Year Plan? What fundamental change in the Soviet Union's economic outlook made extensive capital outlay possible when it had not been just months before? To engage in spatial planning and infrastructural improvement under NEP, Baku reminds us, state enterprises and municipal administrations had to secure either self-generated (Azneft) or local collective funding (the Baksovet). National and local budgets had to be balanced, and plans had to pay for themselves.

A skim through Gosplan's monthly journal, *Planned Economy* (*Planovoe khoziaistvo*), from the NEP years (1923–26) reveals that the planning committee gave little press to theoretical or practical questions of socialist capital construction. Over these three years, the sole author of articles on capital projects was L. N. Bernatskii, head of Gosplan's Building Section (*stroisektsion*), a department launched in March 1922.[7] Bernatskii struck a circumspect note in his inaugural article as head of the section, writing that "construction is not a self-sufficient sector of the economy, or an end in itself, but one that is performed only on the instructions of other sectors."[8] Over the course of his tenure as section head he changed his tune and shifted to advocating for construction projects as a means to jumpstart the Soviet economy. In 1924, in the midst of an attenuated financial crisis, Bernatskii stressed that the rise of Soviet socialism depended on investment in the built environment. "Construction is one of the primary factors in the economic and cultural development of the country; without the latter, construction cannot move forward, but the successful development of the country is also impossible without construction," he wrote. "The state is obliged to take this into account and mobilize all possible measures to assist with construction of all types."[9] If an economic downturn limited construction, Bernatskii continued, then it was important to prioritize building in the regions most likely to spur economic development, namely the Central-Industrial, Ural, and Caucasian oil-bearing regions. The majority of his colleagues at Gosplan, and the economists at the People's Commissariat of Finance (Narkomfin), disagreed, asserting that large-scale construction projects would occur when, and only when, the national budget stabilized.

Gosplan's primary task, as directed by the Politburo, was to achieve this stability in the Soviet economy by balancing supply and demand. A fiscally conservative approach known as genetic (*geneticheskoe*) planning prevailed for most of NEP. Genetic planners sought to achieve economic equilibrium by looking at past economic trends and monitoring current international market conditions to plan forward according to historical probabilities. The means to this end were "control figures" (*kontrol'nye tsifry*). Gosplan vice chairman Grigorii Grinko defined them for a US audience. "What are these control figures? Annually in advance they . . . fix the amounts of capital to be invested in industry, transportation, and agriculture, in housing and public construction. In a word, the control figures lay down a general economic plan for this huge country with a population of 150 million people for a year in advance."[10] Control figures predicted annual revenues for each branch of industry, which in turn set hard limits on that branch's expenditures for the year. Annual control figures played a critical role during NEP.

In 1925, three economic planning teams commenced work at Gosplan to draft plans for a different temporal scope. A general plan team considered ten- to fifteen-year prospects for the Soviet economy; a five-year or "perspective" plan team took on half a decade; and a control figures team dealt with annual budgetary concerns as they had since 1923. Because the general plan never got off the ground, and the first Five-Year Plan was not ratified until mid-1929, control figures effectively directed all Soviet economic policy for seven years.[11] An economy predicated on year-to-year planning is a shortsighted one. Under such a regime, Soviet administrators could address only the issues immediately before them, which rendered large-scale capital construction projects with multi-year completion schedules impossible to entertain. The stopgap manner in which Azneft handled housing shortages in early Soviet Baku befits this broader economic context.

Bernatskii recognized that housing was the construction type most suitable to tackle under the strict control figure system. The granular scale of housing could be addressed with targeted, small-scale offensives such as renovation of existing housing units, renovation of other building types into housing, and as a last resort, new construction. Bernatskii did broach the subject of architectural typification (*tipizatsiia*) as early as 1925, linking the domestic scale of housing to national scale planning via building standardization. "The question of the choice of types becomes a planning question, especially if one takes into consideration that the development of housing types allows for standardization that, with mass production, is one of the keys to affordable, quality construction," Bernatskii explained. "This is the healthy foundation on which a better plan for capital construction can be brought to life." In the meantime, Bernatskii proposed immediate construction of cheap one- to two-story wooden houses instead of costlier multistory brick or reinforced concrete structures. He acknowledged that such structures were "not altogether modern," but that a "truly economic form of capital construction—built not on capitalist, but socialist foundations—will take some time."[12]

By 1928, a small chorus of voices began to challenge the perspicacity of control figure planning for capital construction. In the previous five years *Planovoe khoziaistvo* published just twelve articles related to capital construction; in 1928 alone, there were fifteen. One particularly astute article by A. Gordon determined that control figure planning crippled capital construction projects in two interrelated ways. First, the state's fiscal planning timeline wreaked havoc on the seasonal construction industry. Before annual construction could begin, ideally in March, contracts had to be signed and building materials procured, but due to delays in plan ratification, building trusts were left guessing how much funding they would be allotted, which led to "an element of randomness" in how projects were estimated and run. Second, the conservative psychology of control figures tamped down aspirational projects. "Drafting a financial plan begins with the control figures, but [these numbers] are nothing but a claim to material and financial resources; a claim that is made with the assumption that it will be trimmed back. In this way the plan cannot escape the actual state of things (the status quo), because 'claims' are limited not only by the planning assumptions of the coming year, but by the estimates (supposedly the balance sheet) for the current year."[13] Simply put, even though the control figures were a sorely inaccurate prediction of fiscal activity, they were taken as a reflection of an inescapable economic reality. Those wishing to make budgetary claims for the coming year were forced to hew closely to the previous year's request. In order that their budgets did not decrease from one year to the next, local administrations might pad the claim with new, sacrificial line items, but radical expansion of revenues or expenditures was not expected.

This pointed critique of status quo control figure planning was representative of a philosophical shift occurring within Soviet leadership concerning the purpose of economic planning. Leading the charge, and methodological change in tenor, were two economists at the top of the Gosplan hierarchy: two-time director Krzhizhanovskii, and statistician and theorist Stanislav Strumilin, who worked together to draft the first Five-Year Plan. Both economists advocated the teleological (*teleo-logicheskoe*) method of planning, which was concerned with the *telos*, or endpoint of the planning effort. Vesenkha deputy chairman and Central Committee member, Yuri Piatkov, described the new projective planning attitude as follows: "We deliberately depict a model of industry to ourselves as we want it, so that it may be brought into existence. In other words, we set ourselves a definite purpose and a task dictated by our will (*volevaia zadacha*). We free ourselves from the clutches of what is given by history; we break the old bounds and gain considerably greater creative freedom."[14] Compared to genetic planners, who looked to the past to keep the economy in equilibrium, teleologists planned forward, striving toward unprecedented goals.

At the second Gosplan conference in March 1927, Strumilin explained that with the new teleological approach, the first Five-Year Plan would "*redistribute* the productive forces of society, including labor and the material resources of the country *at the most rapid possible tempo*, with the goal to *maximally* satisfy the current needs of the working masses and to *very quickly* bring about the full reconstruction of society according to the principles of socialism and communism."[15] Strumilin's redistribution proposition exploded the sector-based structure of control figure budgetary distribution to consider the Soviet economy holistically. The productive inputs of labor power and material resources would be shared between branches of the economy and could be shifted around as needed to support those sectors—mainly industrial sectors—tasked with the most ambitious goals. Teleologists like Strumilin viewed rapid industrialization as the most expedient means to achieve economic self-sufficiency, which would make reachable the ultimate *telos*: communism. Fuel and power, iron and steel, and the machine-building industries were given top priority in the first Five-Year Plan. Labor, expertise, capital, and material resources were mobilized and shifted to those engineering projects like the Magnitogorsk Iron and Steel Works deemed best able to move the Soviet Union toward autarkic, fully socialist status.[16]

In August 1929, Krzhizhanovskii wrote that "recently, our attitude toward planning the economy has changed—in its methodology and in the assessment of those materials that we choose to utilize . . . We no longer look with such credulity at the columns of control figures."[17] According to Grinko, control figures evolved "from a mere *estimate* of the general progress of the national economy during the coming year . . . into *the* annual *plan* for the development of the national economy."[18] Control figures transmogrified from statistical reflections of "the actual state of things" to prescriptive, aspirational targets. Grinko's control figures for the first Five-Year Plan show overall capital investment in the USSR for the 1928–33 period more than doubling the 1923–28 allocations, and investment in industry alone nearly quadrupling.[19] The years from 1929 to 1931, when budgetary caution was thrown to the wind, became known as the "period of exaggeration" (*period uvelicheniia*).[20] In that exaggerated space of budgetary difference were 12 billion rubles to spend on the construction of industrial facilities.[21] Funding to build housing and social services to serve workers at these sites was often bundled together with factory construction funding, although as Magnitostroi demonstrates, these support programs frequently fell victim to overspending on the industrial installations themselves.

Acknowledging the Problem of Socialist Space

Before 1929, Soviet city planning (*gradostroitel'stvo*) was largely an engineering enterprise. Practitioners like Ivanitskii, trained as civil engineers, summoned proletarian rights as was expedient to ensure that sanitation, connectivity, and other nuts-and-bolts municipal issues were addressed. The relationships between natural resources, heavy industry, housing, and social infrastructure in a socialist city were designed masterfully in Baku, but socialist spatial theory, as such, was absent.

Finally, in mid-1928, the economist S. A. Bessonov rang the alarm in his article, "The Problem of Space in the First Five-Year Plan." In his investigation of large-scale, cross-regional systems like rail under socialism, Bessonov became convinced that the poverty of Soviet spatial theory would lead to misappropriation of first Five-Year Plan funds. "We will invest about 20 billion rubles in the coming Five-Year Plan. It should be obvious that we need to determine the spatial characteristics of such a huge capital investment alongside quantitative and qualitative terms," he cautioned. "The masses do not live by industry, or by region. They live non-districted lives—they are spaceless, so to speak. Capital construction, as it is now considered, does not speak to the minds and hearts of the workers and peasants."[22] Rail, electricity, and people, Bessonov argued, are naturally fluid and territorially unhampered. If the drafters of the plan disregarded the massive spatial implications of their work, the opportunity to dissolve regionalism—to take advantage of the socialization of land ownership and the vast territorial expanse of Soviet space—would be lost.

Enter Leonid Moiseevich Sabsovich, the critical figure who would bridge the gap between economic and spatial planning during the first Five-Year Plan. From 1927 to 1930, Sabsovich, an economist in the planning department of Vesenkha, was one of the most prominent and articulate advocates for teleological planning and rapid industrial growth rates. Sabsovich stood out for his ability to use quantitative data to address social concerns and was the inventor of two key concepts: *sotsgorod* and socialization of everyday life (*obobshchestvlenie byta*).[23]

Sabsovich's first so-called hypothesis on the proper orientation for the Soviet economy, from August 1928, proposed that the USSR did not need decades to overtake advanced capitalist countries, destroy class structure, and build socialism—fifteen years would suffice.[24] Industrial self-sufficiency was not an end in itself, however. Construction of socialist culture also needed to advance apace. "In creating the general plan of development of our country, we must be planning the construction of socialism broadly," he wrote in the pamphlet *USSR in 15 Years* (*SSSR cherez 15 let*). "The working class has to understand that socialism is not some kind of ideal, far into the future, but is instead a practical goal that is feasible to reach in the next one-and-a-half decades."[25] If there was a proper sense of urgency to affect cultural change at the same rate as factories were rising, social and economic transformation would progress hand in hand. This message resonated with many party officials, who understood NEP as seven years marred by cultural compromise. No matter their potency, Sabsovich's ideas were disseminated only at the pleasure of officials at the top of the Communist Party hierarchy, and indeed, directly behind Sabsovich stood Valerian Kuibyshev, chairman of Vesenkha and one of Stalin's principal economic advisers. In a period characterized by paper shortages, *USSR in 15 Years* enjoyed three print runs in 1929, the last two at 13,000 and 30,000 copies, respectively.[26] The pamphlet and the ideas that it held were markedly influential in setting the accelerated pace of industrialization ratified in the final version of the first Five-Year Plan.

Sabsovich's message was optimistic and aspirational. To help his readers grasp the scope of his predictions, he quantified the results of steep and steady industrial growth using the Magnitogorsk Iron and Steel Works as his example of a "great work" (*velikaia rabota*). By fiscal year 1942–43, he explained, the budget for heavy industrial construction would be 33 times that undertaken in 1929. If the equivalent of 7.5 Magnitogorsk factories were built in 1927–28, approximately 240 such factories would be built per annum fifteen years hence.[27]

Sabsovich claimed a strong relationship between environmental and social transformation. He communicated his enthusiasm for the issues in play through frequent textual stresses:

> The new structure of life, even the construction of this new life, requires a new type of person. We need to remake man. Of course, this is a task of extraordinary difficulty. But it is being [*bytie*] that determines consciousness. *The notion that a person is inherently conservative and difficult to alter is patently false.* You could say that man is inert—and this is true, but not in the everyday sense of the word. In an environment of technical, economic, and social stagnation, a person acquires the inertia of stagnation and becomes a so-called conservative. *In an atmosphere of rapid technical, economic, and social transformation a person acquires forward momentum and undergoes rapid change and adaptation to meet the changing conditions of his existence.*[28]

Here, Sabsovich insisted that Soviet citizens living in "stagnant" physical circumstances—cities constructed under the capitalist system, communal apartments carved out of bourgeois residences—were destined to retain old modes of everyday life and interpersonal interaction. Conversely, radical alteration of the environment could induce new citizens into being.

This was not a new idea, but rather a restatement of the Marxist postulate that matter (specifically, "the mode of production of material life") determines consciousness.[29] Trotsky devoted an entire book to this issue in 1923. "On the question of everyday life [*byt*]," Trotsky wrote, "it is patently obvious that each individual is the product of his environment rather than his creator. The conditions and customs of everyday life, even more than economics, develop 'behind people's backs' as Marx says."[30] Logic follows that if space shapes behavior, everyday environments are key sites of political intervention. To ensure the ascendance of *novyi byt* (the new socialist way of life), traditional household relations and responsibilities would have to be completely reconceived, Trotsky argued. The two "intimately connected" processes that would pave the way to the new socialist interpersonal relations were a) increase in education and cultural levels of the working class, and b) state-organized improvement of their material conditions.[31] As Katerina Clark notes, Trotsky and other Marxist theorists believed that "through its *byt*, that is, thorough the ordinary and everyday, society would, paradoxically, attain the extraordinary."[32] Whether material betterment manifested as full-fledged house-communes or not, it was incumbent on the socialist state to relieve women of housekeeping and childcare duties at the very least, Trotsky concluded. Alexandra Kollontai, director of the Women's Department of the Communist Party (*zhenotdel*), went further to advocate the dissolution of the nuclear family altogether under socialism, a proposition that would require total reconfiguration of domestic spaces. "There is no escaping the fact: the old type of family has had its day," Kollontai wrote in 1920. "In place of the individual and egoistic family, a great universal family of workers will develop." Like the institution of the state under complete communism, the family would "wither away not because it is being forcibly destroyed by the state, but because the family ceases to be a necessity."[33] But the road to emancipation for Soviet women was destined to be a hard one until the state provided physical spaces to support new modes of living.

Although the attack on *byt* was framed primarily as a social issue before the first Five-Year Plan, it was ultimately economics that motivated *byt* transformation. Gender-balancing programs advocated by Trotsky and Kollontai such as canteens, laundries, and live-in and drop-off nurseries would permit Soviet women to practice domestic independence and, crucially, to enter the workforce. At the Fifteenth Congress of the Communist Party, held December 1927 in Moscow, architects were among those entreated to help construct the *novyi byt*. "In preparing a practical plan it is not sufficient to raise the question of cultural revolution for women workers in a general way," a female architect, Comrade Zaborskaia, argued. "A tremendous amount of work is needed here, and in working out the Five-Year Plan we must pay serious attention to the emancipation of women. We must strive to . . . avoid a situation in which industry is constructed along socialist lines while new apartments still have the same old kitchens, the same troughs, and the same washtubs. If the old prerevolutionary way of life is implanted in small living units or even in large apartment buildings, if old bourgeois rubbish is piled up in new apartments, who is going to speak for socialist construction?"[34] In Zaborskaia's opinion, a worker living in a poorly designed apartment surrounded by outmoded objects would perpetuate prerevolutionary modes of living. In one pamphlet released during the first Five-Year Plan, Zaborskaia's point was illustrated by a Soviet working woman tormented by freakishly large, threateningly sentient pots and pans, dishes, and silverware (figure 4.1).

Вот что может померещиться домаш-
ней хозяйке после целого дня работы.

Figure 4.1. "This is what the housewife imagines after a full day of work." M. Il'in, *Rasskaz o velikom plane*, 3rd ed. (Moscow: Ogiz—Molodaia Gvardiia, 1931), 193.

Domestic spatial conditions were grim during NEP, when workers and peasants flooded into cities ill-equipped to handle the population influx. Between 1926 and 1939, at least 23 million Soviet peasants traveled to urban centers to look for work and to escape starvation, a rate of rural-to-urban migration that David Hoffman claims is unprecedented in world history.[35] In Moscow during that same period, 4 million square meters of housing was added, but that was still less than 10 percent of domestic space actually needed; the housing bank was a stunning 46 million square meters short.[36] Stopgap housing solutions like the communal apartment (*kommunalka*) were put in place, a condition in which residents—sometimes extended families—were granted a single room within a subdivided prerevolutionary bourgeois or aristocratic residence. Common entry, corridor, kitchen, and bathroom facilities became battlefields for interpersonal conflict.[37] Newly arrived peasants who lived in such overcrowded housing contributed to a ruralization (*okrest'ianivanie*) of Soviet cities, and village moral codes became entrenched in urban contexts.[38] Overall, these were inauspicious conditions for crafting new Soviet citizens, as Sabsovich noted.

With the first Five-Year Plan superseding NEP, Sabsovich picked up where Trotsky and Kollontai left off, arguing for direct intervention into the proletarian material environment. It was precisely within the realm of socialist everyday life—from the domestic unit to the urban scale—that Sabsovich developed a body of theory that sparked the great socialist spatial debates of 1929–30.

Urbanism: The Problem of the City and Victory Over Distance

By mid-1929, the inaugural building season of the first Five-Year Plan was underway, and it was patently discouraging. The first year of the plan, when the relative growth of capital construction would be greatest, was destined to be the most difficult. But if the Soviet building industry was barely functional before the plan, now ambitious targets paired with cost-reduction mandates revealed gaping cracks in the project delivery system. Technical difficulties were made more intractable by the glaring absence of theory. As Catherine Cooke explains, "to people who needed to intellectually understand the place of their small actions within the total context of their social and political purposes, the lack of any Marxist-theoretical description of how the total environment-building process related to those larger purposes was more than unsatisfactory: it too had a crippling effect on their real activity."[39] The technical staff and workers laboring on poorly advancing construction sites had no vision to motivate their work. Without spatio-ideological directives from above, construction workers on the Donugl, Beketov, and Avtostroi sites took it upon themselves to organize "socialist settlement" working groups, to discuss the ways in which socialism might influence architecture, planning, and the building industry. "The abnormality of this situation is obvious," Sabsovich wrote of the theoretical vacuum in which these workers toiled. "It should be clear that we must devise ways to penetrate the consciousness of the increasing range of workers involved in the construction of new workers' settlements."[40] Large-scale, structural thinking about the territorial organization of industry and housing was critically needed.

The crisis of weak socialist spatial theorization came to a head in July 1929, when Sabsovich published "The Problem of the City" (Problema goroda) in *Planovoe khoziaistvo,* and presented the essay as a speech to the All-Union Association of Scientific and Technical Workers to Assist Socialist Construction in the USSR (VARNITSO). VARNITSO, in turn, republished the speech as the pamphlet *Cities of the Future and the Organization of a Socialist Way of Life* (*Goroda budushchego i organizatsiia sotsialisticheskogo byta*) because, in their assessment, the problem of the socialist city demanded the attention not only of the technical intelligentsia but of the general Soviet public.[41] Sabsovich made three main points. First, he asserted that economic, cultural, and urban arenas were interdependent, and that the problem of the socialist city deserved proper formulation. Second, he insisted on solely future orientation for all spatial interventions. Third, he argued for decentralization, a process made possible by modern technology.

"The problem of the city is one of the least developed problems of the future growth of our Union," Sabsovich began—a statement would have been difficult to refute at the end of 1929.[42] The first Five-Year Plan (ratified three months prior) should, he argued, have been a plan for economic development and for building socialism. Unless the national economy, socialist culture, and the city were considered together, none would succeed. Because culture and everyday life were only cursorily addressed in the plan, the question of how to organize humans and industry to inculcate socialism remained unformulated. There was a sense of urgency to address the issue, given the tempo of change, "*for if development of industry, agriculture, and transportation should create the material basis for the possibility of building socialism, the restructuring of our towns and villages should also create conditions for the direct implementation of the socialist way of life.*"[43] In Sabsovich's formulation the achievements of the general plan and the problem of socialist space were inexorably linked.

Sabsovich cautioned that the rapid tempo of socialization did not justify falling back on tested urban models, however. Historical precedent needed to be exorcized in any future urban intervention. "In considering [the problem of the city] our ideas are extremely constrained, and we are prone to design our future using stencils given to us by our past or contemporary capitalist countries. Such an approach to this problem is totally incorrect. It does not account for the magnificent and unimaginable economic, social, and cultural shifts in our near future. If we want the correct approach to the problem of the city, we must pay much more attention to our future than our past or present." Soviet cities were a lot like capitalist cities both because they originated as capitalist cities and because, in the absence of theory, Soviet designers continued to utilize nonsocialist urban precedents. Ivanitskii and other city-builders (*gradostroiteli*) trained before the Revolution had, until the late 1920s, tweaked capitalist organizational systems for use in socialist contexts without much concern for ideological taint. Sabsovich's design philosophy was fundamentally avant-garde; if planners put on blinders to the past, they could invent spatial forms as unprecedented as the advent of Soviet socialism. Existing cities and those being built on old models required immediate and "radical restructuring" at the very least, wrote Sabsovich. The dense and centralized modern city was the product of the capitalist epoch, the hub of industry, trade, transportation, economic power, and population concentration; the "control center" for administrative, spiritual, and cultural life. It was also the site of inequity and disease. To radically restructure the urban condition under socialism, "the first question that we must ask is whether the city will continue to play the same role in the country as it is currently playing."[44] What if instead of allowing economic development to cluster in cities, per the Weberian law of agglomeration, other concerns entered locational decision-making, like the well-being of the working class?[45] "Enormous overcrowding, living in stone cells cut off from nature—all of this ugliness associated with the capitalist system . . . are we forced to continue to build in this way?" Sabsovich asked. "This question can easily be answered in the negative: we should not and cannot do this!"[46]

Sabsovich's main spatial proposal was to "transform NEP Russia into socialist Russia" through decentralization, effectively instantiating Engels's and Lenin's prognosis of diffuse spatial organization under socialism.[47] In 1914, Lenin wrote that the socialization of labor would lead to "redistribution of the human population (thus putting an end both to rural backwardness, isolation and barbarism, and to the unnatural concentration of vast masses of people in big cities)."[48] In Sabsovich's plan, new socialist settlements (*poseleniia*) associated with industrial and agricultural complexes would take the place of existing cities and villages altogether. Technology was the key to enacting this decentralized spatial model:

> The condition that will assist us in realizing these objectives [to care for the life and health of the workers] is above all the *"victory over the distance"* (*pobeda nad rasstoianiem*) . . . [With] the vast number of large power plants and the possibility to transmit energy over long distances, we can to a large extent free ourselves from the attachment between industry and the fuel base and we will be able to distribute industrial enterprises with much greater territorial freedom in the interest of placing settlements in the most suitable location for the workers.
>
> By increasing industrial production several dozen times over, and enormously increasing and improving the means of transportation and communication, we will build new factories and plants not densely, but scattered over a wide area, closer to nature . . . *In our victory over distance, we will destroy the economic advantages of large cities as industrial and commercial*

centers . . . and the enormous cultural growth of the entire population *will deprive the city of its current monopoly over culture.*[49]

Finally, with the "victory over distance," an appropriately revolutionary slogan for socialist spatial practices was coined. What did it mean? As Sabsovich explained, the immense Soviet landmass would be conquered by the electric grid expanding ever eastward. In citing the emancipatory potential of electric power, Sabsovich tapped into enduring party enthusiasm for electrification that first emerged in the GOELRO (Gosudarstvennaia komissiia po elektrifikatsii rossii, or State Commission for the Electrification of Russia) Plan of 1920, Lenin's pet project to electrify the rural territories of the entire Soviet Union in ten years' time (plate 13).[50] The map for the GOELRO Plan shows blue dots for existing generation stations and red for proposed, each of which radiates a light pink circle to indicate the service area. The pink circles overlap and meld together to create contiguous—though still partial—electrified territories. The rails, roads, and telephone/telegraph wires that crisscrossed the geographical expanse of the Union would connect these far-flung nodes. Instead of being tethered to sites of fuel extraction or urban rail hubs, settlements could occur in remote corners of the country, utilizing the nascent Soviet science of logistics.

Cities of the Future and the Organization of a Socialist Way of Life forwarded no concrete urbanistic or architectonic proposals. This was because the problem of the socialist city, while undoubtedly "a problem not of tomorrow, but of today," still needed great development, according to Sabsovich. His choice to remain graphically mute was wise: without images to scrutinize, critics deferred assessment of the possible material effects of his propositions. Sabsovich did begin to make some of the programmatic recommendations that elicited harsh criticism in his later book, *Socialist Cities* (*Sotsialisticheskie goroda*, 1930), but all of these were restatements of ideas devised by Kollontai and other early Soviet social theorists. A section on child-rearing in *Socialist Cities*, for instance, proposed that children live independently from their parents in "Baby Homes" and "Children's Cities," which would be better equipped to raise the next generation in proper socialist fashion.[51] Sabsovich also recommended communal food preparation, dining, laundry, etc., to forward socialization of everyday life.

Large Five-Year Plan show projects like Magnitogorsk and the DniproHES hydroelectric station, sited by proximity to natural resources, did not have ready-made villages to accommodate factory workers. Instead, Sabsovich explained, socialist settlements large and comfortable enough to attract an outside cadre of workers had to be "erected completely from scratch on a practically empty site." A fully socialized city would lose a dependent and gain a worker when women's domestic and child-rearing responsibilities were lifted. Therefore, for each working couple willing to relocate to one of these remote, efficient factories, twice the typical housing allowance could be spent to construct the social and cultural amenities needed to enact a socialist *byt*.[52] With this optimistic economic logic, Sabsovich laid the groundwork for Magnitogorsk to become the site of a groundbreaking socialist city.

Disurbanism: Not a City but a New Type of Settlement

In the apocryphal tale, a young man entered the Typification Section of the Building Committee of the Russian Republic (Stroikom RSFSR) unannounced and asked to consult with the section chief Moisei Ginzburg. The stranger "drew attention to himself by his extraordinary appearance—he looked like some American Jules Verne-like character with the clothes he was wearing and the beard beneath his chin."[53] Mikhail Okhitovich, the stranger, was a sociologist at the Marx-Engels Institute who had decided to seek out architectural collaborators for his theory of socialist spatial organization. Okhitovich had discovered anew Engels's argument that cities inevitably would "wither" under socialism. According to architectural historian Selim Khan-Magomedov, Okhitovich was the first theoretician to follow Engels's argument to its logical conclusion: that socialism would result in a rejection of compact settlements altogether.[54] In making this logical leap, Okhitovich repudiated communality as the ultimate goal of socialism, and instead saw in socialist space the means to complete individual freedom. He named his concept "new resettlement" (*novoe rasselenie*), a term that became synonymous with the more descriptive label "disurbanism" (*dezurbanizm*).

Okhitovich's disurbanist theory was predicated on the assumption that socialist land nationalization would allow industrial installations to disperse as needed to reach raw materials and energy resources. The supporting electric grid would gradually cast a net over the entire territory, destroying once and for all the need for people and production to cluster in cities. Although they arrived at different morphological conclusions, Okhitovich and Sabsovich agreed that technology was the key to future settlement patterns. Disurbanism could be so radically diffuse because modern transportation, communications, and electrical systems were indifferent to spatial concentration. Before he entered into discussions with architects, Okhitovich imagined that disurbanist dwellings would be individual, single-story, light metal, moveable structures connected to national networks along a single road. The expensive centralized sanitary-technical services of the capitalist city would be replaced by small local biological cleaning plants connected to the little metal houses by short plastic piping. The theory of spatial dispersal was original and sound per Marxist ideology; the architectural resolution was naive. Hence Okhitovich's decision to seek out Ginzburg who was, as chapter 2 discussed, a theorist of socialist space in his own right.

The alliance that developed between Ginzburg and Okhitovich to define the proper organization of socialist space was certainly unlikely. Ginzburg was, at the time, leading the Soviet state's laboratory to design communal unit types while Okhitovich summarily dismissed the *dom-kommuna* (house-commune) as belonging to the "prison or workers' barrack" classification.[55] Although their ideas about form may have differed, Ginzburg and Okhitovich did share a belief in process as a way to reach form. For Ginzburg and OSA this was the so-called functional method, and for Okhitovich it was the process of disurbanization.[56] After a series of intense discussions, Ginzburg and the majority of OSA members (though not the Vesnin brothers) became staunch advocates of disurbanism. At Ginzburg's request, Okhitovich expounded his dispersal theory in "Toward the Problem of the City" (K probleme goroda), published in SA in mid-1929.[57] Okhitovich's own sketch diagrams illustrate this most thorough statement of disurbanist theory.

Okhitovich was a sociologist. He was interested in probing the social functions of city, housing, and settlement, and was keen to intervene in the discipline of architecture, so primed to effect societal change yet at such great risk of conservatism. His essay ranged widely, but it carried two main themes. First, Soviet architects needed to understand that the epochal shift to socialism required new methods of design, not just new programs. Second, the concentrated form of the capitalist city was outmoded and inappropriate to socialism. Okhitovich's ultimate proposal, laid out in the final paragraphs, was to enact total decentralization.

First: new epoch, new method. The architect has the potential to play a special role in the construction of socialism, Ohkitovich claimed, but only if he correctly formulates the task. From where does this proper outlook arise? From Marx, of course. "Karl Marx (we are talking about the scientific method of Marxism) is the only preparation needed at present for the architect who is interested in the proper formulation and possible resolution of the problems of today and tomorrow's architecture, because his 'client' is the common interest; his 'master' today is the proletariat, tomorrow: classless humanity," explained Okhitovich. "And so, while today it is impossible to build without capital (in small letters), in the future it will be impossible to build without *Capital*."[58] With this play on words (that works in both Russian and English), Okhitovich stressed the importance of reformulating the architect-client relationship to align with the new socialist mode of production. If the architect views humanity, writ large, as his client, he is more apt to consider the social rather than economic or technical impacts of his design decisions. As a concrete example, Okhitovich cited the contemporary trend in Soviet architecture for setting sanitary-technical norms to economize on worker housing, which he considered antihumanist and wrong-headed. "It appears that houses are built to meet public rather than physiological needs . . . Six square meters [per person] is the bare minimum. Ten is better. Twenty: wonderful, but ideal? What is ideal is to live in the fresh open air." The capitalist architect has no choice but to carry out orders for particular buildings, to repair, to replan existing cities. The task of socialist architects of the coming epoch, on the other hand, is "not to construct buildings, but to 'construct,' that is to devise the social relations of production." An enlightened architect who "constructs" considers how each structure is linked to the means of production and national systems because "the interior structure of the cabin as a whole will depend on which of these industries are outside of it."[59] The socialist architect's duties thus span from the intimate to the continental scale, which are inextricably connected.

The dense, centralized city was in Okhitovich's crosshairs. The first two hand-drawn illustrations in his essay indict the "historic concept of the contemporary city" and the "regional-concentrated contemporary capitalist city" (figure 4.2). The first is undoubtedly a diagram of Moscow, with its three concentric rings and a "feudal kremlin" at the center. The second diagram is a slight modification that includes subregions within the concentric structure. The wealthiest citizens live centrally near the seat of power and institutions, and the working class are relegated to the industrial suburbs. In subsequent "decentralization" diagrams, the center is evacuated, and its components—first institutions, then housing—are flung beyond the outer ring (figure 4.3). "We ask ourselves," he wrote, "where will we resettle these 'unloaded' people and businesses? Answer: not on the basis of clustering, but on the principle of maximum freedom, ease, and the speed of connections and communications."[60] In Okhitovich's vision, the city would empty, and its liberated population would move off into the landscape and attach loosely to far-flung industrial enterprises. Again, the key was to understand the whole of the Soviet Union as a productive machine. "The distributive planning of business enterprises must form the possibility to organize assembly line production on the scale of the entire national (then the world) economy," Okhitovich explained. "Cultural institutions will be planned and will specialize in relation to the 'interests' of the production plan. Service institutions are also included that may not be fixed to a particular place."[61] His description evokes an image of a massively expanded Fordist assembly

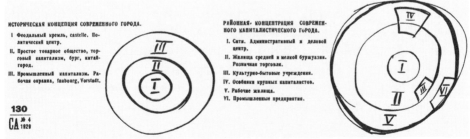

**HISTORIC CONCEPT OF
THE CONTEMPORARY CITY**

   I. Feudal kremlin. Political center.
  II. Simple trading community, commercial
     capitalism, burg, "kitai gorod" (the traditional
     commercial quarter of Moscow).
 III. Industrial capitalism. Worker outskirts,
     faubourg, vorstadt.

**REGIONAL-CONCENTRATED
CONTEMPORARY CAPITALIST CITY**

    I. "City". Administrative and business center.
   II. Residential quarter for the middle and
     bourgeois classes. Retail trade.
 III. Cultural-community institutions.
 IV. Mansions of the major capitalists.
  V. Worker housing.
 VI. Industrial enterprises.

Figure 4.2. Hand-drawn diagrams that analyze and dissect capitalist urban forms. M. Okhitovich, "K probleme goroda," *Sovremennaia arkhitektura*, no. 4 (1929): 130. Key diagram by the author.

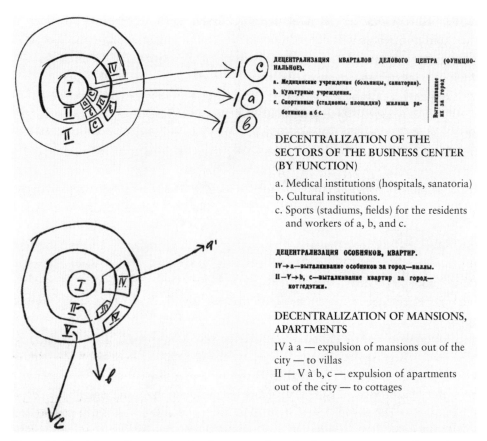

Figure 4.3. Hand-drawn diagrams showing the process of socialist disurbanization. M. Okhitovich, "K probleme goroda," *Sovremennaia arkhitektura*, no. 4 (1929): 132–33. Key diagram by the author.

line draped over the Eurasian continent in which the rail, roads, and electric lines of the USSR would shuttle increasingly complex assemblies to their final destinations. Okhitovich imagined cultural institutions also traveling along these lines to serve the dispersed population. He conceded that his proposal was composed of the same elements as a traditional city, albeit in radically dissipated form.

Okhitovich's proposal was not a formal solution. Instead, he identified a historical process that would enact continual shifts in spatial relationships:

If one talks about its essence, then this new complex will be called not a point, a place, or a city, *but a process, and this process will be called disurbanization.*

Urbanization is the phenomenon of universal gravitation to production centers, of production centers to each other, of trade centers to production centers, cultural centers to population centers, housing to production, commercial activity to places of work, etc. The farther from the center, the worse the housing conditions.

Disurbanization is the process of centrifugal force and repulsion. It is based on just such a centrifugal tendency in technology . . . [which] reverses all former assumptions. With disurbanization, proximity is a matter of distance and community is a matter of separation.[62]

In its obsession with process and transformation over time, disurbanism was the most Marxist of all spatial propositions. The arrows that point away from the urban ring in Okhitovich's diagrams of disurban processes are the centrifugal forces of technology poised to spin programs away from the center and each other. Okhitovich asserted that modern transportation and technology obviate the need for either physical proximity or community. A future socialist society would be territorially liberated.

Population dispersal schemes developed by Soviet spatial theorists in response to the first Five-Year Plan were part of an international movement in early twentieth century planning. At the same time that Ivanitskii was designing the regional expansion plan for Baku, and Okhitovich was envisioning disurbanization in the USSR, the Regional Planning Association of America (RPAA) emerged with similar preoccupations in the US context. Like some of his Soviet counterparts (most notably Okhitovich), RPAA theoretician Lewis Mumford believed that the new technologies of electricity, radio, telephone, and automobiles would be agents of territorial freedom. Modern systems would make population concentration unnecessary, so the new scale of planning intervention would be the region, or even the nation. Mumford wrote in 1925 that "regional planning . . . sees people, industry and the land as a single unit," a triad that was strikingly similar to Soviet theories of the time.[63] The RPAA member and economist Stuart Chase later admitted, "we were mildly socialist, though not at all communist; liberal but willing to abandon large areas of the free market in favor of a planned economy."[64] For Broadacre City, his decentralization proposal germinated in the 1920s that took the Jeffersonian grid as its organizational skeleton, Frank Lloyd Wright likewise pinpointed the motor car, electrical intercommunication, and standardized machine-shop production as inventions that would condition new dispersed settlement patterns. Wright wrote that "given the simple exercise of several inherently just rights of man, the freedom to decentralize, to redistribute and to correlate properties of the life of man on earth to his birthright—the ground itself—and Broadacre City becomes a reality."[65] Wright lamented in *Pravda* that the capitalistic US economic system "interferes with [correct town planning] and makes [it] impossible," and he made it clear that Broadacre would require full state control of property and utilities to institute land redistribution.[66] If Broadacre were implemented, the "ultra-capitalistic centers" would disappear over the course of three or four generations, Wright asserted.[67]

In the Soviet Union, the antagonistic relationship between urbanism (Sabsovich) and disurbanism (Okhitovich) hinged on the degree of dispersal. In Okhitovich's view, any system that clusters programs, tends toward a center, and fosters communality is simply replicating old forms of settlement. "The process to eliminate the contradiction between city and countryside is not the process of urbanizing the village, as some supporters of the socialist city believe, nor is it agrarization of the city . . . Neither horizontal (territorial), or vertical (airspace) crowding nor congestion is eternal. They arose out of the centripetal character of capitalism. The theory of socialist cities is a theory of the bourgeois form of socialism, and therefore it is utopian, reactionary."[68] Although he did not mention Sabsovich by name, this comment revealed Okhitovich's familiarity with Sabsovich's "socialist city" concept that was suddenly garnering so much press at the end of 1929. In allying Sabsovich's socialist city with Utopian (bourgeois) socialism, Okhitovich threw down the gauntlet. Though Sabsovich was also interested in destroying the capitalist city and in territorial dispersal, he envisioned Soviet territories sprinkled with deeply communal, population controlled, industrial-social nodes. Compared to Okhitovich's spatially liberated, granular, individualized vision, Sabsovich's proposal was downright urban.[69]

A heated debate between Sabsovich and Okhitovich continued in tit-for-tat essays and articles, but the two theorists were soon joined in their efforts to formulate a socialist urban platform by a host of experts who gathered under Gosplan's auspices at a watershed November conference.

Discussion at the Club for Planning Workers

At the beginning of November 1929, with reports streaming in about the poor results of the inaugural first Five-Year Plan building season, and the 1930 building season looming, a heightened sense of urgency developed within the party to rationalize planning and construction. On November 4, *Pravda* published "Lack of Planning and Anarchy in City Construction" (Besplanovost' i anarkhiia v stroitel'stve gorodov), an article accompanied by a cartoon. The text was an invective that chronicled myriad planning and construction snafus in cities throughout the Union. In Dzerzhinsk, a new workers' settlement built near a factory had to be demolished when it became clear that prevailing winds were blowing harmful chemicals directly into the residential quarter. Also in Dzerzhinsk, it was discovered that the town water supply was located immediately downriver from the factory's chemical outfall. In Novorossiisk, a new rail line cut the city center in half, such that the only way for citizens to travel between the two halves was by boat across the harbor. The list of absurd planning mishaps went on. The accompanying cartoon made light of the geographically dispersed examples by crowding them together in a single fictional space of disaster (figure 4.4). The actual situation was more tragic than comic, not only for the inhabitants of these and many other poorly planned sites but also for the state's fiscal officers. The article's author noted that "it is decidedly unhelpful to throw away tens of millions of rubles on schemes that worsen the conditions of the working class," a clear if mild statement of a systemic planning crisis.[70]

In light of the crisis, Gosplan convened a discussion on the problem of the socialist city at the Moscow Club for Planning Workers, held over two sessions at the end of November 1929. The stated purpose was to "gather together those active in the field, theorists, architects, pedagogues, doctors, political organizers, and

A workers' settlement in Dzerzhinsk had to be demolished because it was located downwind of airborne discharge from a chemical factory.

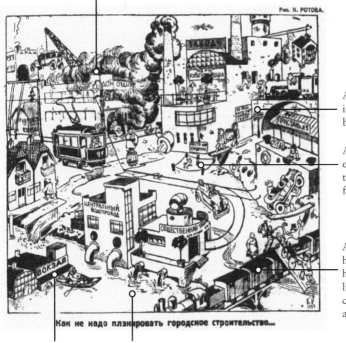

A wharf and a silicate plant in Dzerzhinsk are being built on the same small site.

At Briansk, a site 'big enough for a dog' in the town center was allocated for the new airport.

At Novorossiisk, 'the town has been cut into two halves by the new railway line, and they can only communicate by boat, across the harbor.'

Ivanovo-Vozhnetsk railway station has begun construction on land subject to flooding.

The intake of Dzerzhinsk town water supply is located immediately downriver of a chemical outfall.

Figure 4.4. "How not to plan city construction . . ." The cartoon makes light of the geographically dispersed examples of poor construction during the start of the first Five-Year Plan by crowding them together in a single fictional space of disaster. *Pravda*, November 4, 1929. Diagram by the author based on Catherine Ann Chichester Cooke, "The Town of Socialism" (PhD diss., University of Cambridge, 1974), 150.

participants from all institutions and organizations who, in some way or another, deal directly or indirectly with the question of city-building," and to elicit concepts, debate, and ultimately to hash out a general line for socialist spatial planning.[71] The list of conference speakers reveals heterogeneity of expertise. In addition Gosplan staff there were representatives from Vesenkha and the People's Commissariats for Trade, Health, Transportation, and Internal Affairs; architects and engineers; an electrical factory worker; and not least, Nadezhda Krupskaia—Lenin's widow—representing the People's Commissariat for Education.[72] Sabsovich represented Vesenkha, and he gave a speech on the first day that advocated for full and rapid socialization of life through entirely new types of settlements: socialist cities. Okhitovich did not participate. Despite the increasing amount of press each theorist was receiving at the time of the conference, the conflict between urbanism and disurbanism was little addressed during the proceedings.[73]

Twenty-one speakers held forth over two days, each addressing the planning crisis through the lens of a particular area of expertise such as health, transportation, and social reformation. The speeches were typically short and contained few new ideas, but the fact that all of these factors were discussed in a common forum was itself a step toward establishing a comprehensive Soviet spatial planning platform. In the weeks leading up to the conference *Pravda* published numerous articles on construction mismanagement occurring throughout the USSR. Lack of coordination between overlapping agencies and organizations was the source of many of these construction gaffes. Miscommunication plagued both the logistical and theoretical realms of socialist city-building. The Gosplan economist G. V. Puzis noted in his speech that by his "rough accounting there are 21–22 institutions working on the question of new city construction. I have recently had the opportunity to work with six of them. Discussions always begin: 'we build poorly, without planning, putting houses in the wrong places, incorrectly utilizing the territory, etc.' All conclude that it is necessary to build in some other way, to construct the socialist city according to a plan that all parties can agree upon."[74] But that elusive other way was always left unresolved, feeding more mishaps. At the end of the first day of the conference, Strumilin lamented that already a year into the first Five-Year Plan, "we are seriously late in posing these questions, Comrades."[75]

An architect for the People's Commissariat for Education, Aleksandr Zelenko, laid out a number of administrative proposals in the opening paper of the conference that subsequent speakers referred to and generally agreed with.[76] He stressed that the establishment of a consistent and intelligent city planning platform was key to the macroeconomic health of the USSR. Despite the fact that 1.35 million rubles were spent on residential construction in 1929, and 8 billion would be spent in the following four years, engineers and architects addressing socialist housing were working in a vacuum of "any kind of directive data—they are helpless."[77] They were helpless on two fronts: they had no guiding principles to drive their design work and no recourse to stop the chaotic and poor quality housing that was being built nonetheless. The first order of administrative business was to create Union-wide architectural and planning norms under the direction of Gosplan. Zelenko's proposed list of norms ranged in scale and included the design of industrial and agricultural city types; standard residential buildings for each of these city types; and temporary housing of a demountable character. In addition, he proposed that rules be established for the distribution of communal services and for the relationship between green space and built fabric.[78] The second order of business was to widely disseminate these norms as enforceable planning laws. Any project that deviated from the norms would be disallowed or subject to immediate work stoppage.

Zelenko's morphological proposal was a linear city strung along a transportation or communication line and organized according to the principles of industrial production. The residential quarter was composed of repetitive blocks designed to accommodate 2,000–3,000 residents each, and thus affirmed both the concentrated density and the terminology of Sabsovich's socialist city-building block, the *zhil-kombinat*, or housing combine. On other issues, particularly child-rearing, Zelenko flatly rejected Sabsovich's more radical *byt*-reforming proposals. He recommended a robust system of nurseries, kindergartens, and schools to support working mothers but made no recommendation to separate children's and parents' living quarters.

This restrained approach suited other conference participants like Krupskaia, who advocated transitional societal change instead of rapid cultural overturn, especially where the family was concerned. In her speech Krupskaia asked incredulously, "so we send the children away to special children's homes where they can pick flowers or work in workshops away from society? Neither the children nor the working mothers would agree to this. Children belong in the thick of life. It is important, therefore, that children be close."[79] Sabsovich rebutted this direct swipe in his speech that followed, noting that where the constitution of the socialist family was concerned, "Nadezhda Konstantinovna approaches the problem much too bashfully."[80] Although Sabsovich and Krupskaia represented positions on opposite ends of the child-rearing spectrum, varied opinions emerged at the conference regarding the proper physical and interpersonal relationship between socialist children and their birth parents. The question of socialist child-rearing remained unresolved at the end of the conference.

The main themes of the Gosplan conference aligned with those outlined in Zelenko's opening paper. Planning of the socialist city should be driven by industrial needs. Union-wide architecture and planning norms should be set, published, and policed. Standardized architectural types should guide all design decisions at all scales, in all contexts. Local density (block-based housing) should help to economize residential construction. New cities should provide communal services to support the socialization of life. These were not inherently spatial recommendations, but rather practical administrative steps, immediately implementable planning solutions that steered clear of global theory. Decentralization, dispersal, urbanization, and disurbanization—the concepts that threaded through the writings of Sabsovich and Okhitovich—were all active processes that implied spatial transformation, but they were also abstract and difficult to act on.

Although actionable spatial proposals were largely absent from the conference, the event as packaged for publication gained a distinct forward orientation. The conference proceedings were published within a couple of months by the Gosplan press under the title *K probleme stroitel'stva sotsialisticheskogo goroda* (Toward the problem of constructing the socialist city). "*K*" (toward) implies a bodily or intellectual orientation, a distinct prospective lean. It is also possible that the book's editors sought to suggest intellectual allegiance with another forward leaning text well known in Soviet architectural and planning circles at that time, Le Corbusier's *Vers Une Architecture* from 1923 (a title translated in Russian as *K arkhitekture*, or Toward an Architecture).[81] By the time the socialist settlement debate was in full swing the Paris-based architect had visited the Soviet capital, gained a notable commission in the Tsentrosoiuz building, and exerted even more pointed influence on Moscow's architectural scene through burgeoning friendships with Moisei Ginzburg and others. Le Corbusier's critical commentary on OSA's disurbanist schemes, and his own plan for Moscow, were a year into the future.[82] Regardless of its provenance, the intention of the conference publication title was clear: the experts on socialist city-building had convened, and together they turned to face the future.

The Debate Goes Public: A Journalistic Fever Pitch

The specialists gathered at the Gosplan conference voted to unleash a publicity juggernaut to stimulate a Union-wide discussion on socialist city-building. The response by the Soviet press was immediate. *Pravda* reported on the conference after each day of proceedings and began a regular "Socialist City" feature on the day after the conference closed. In December, major newspapers like *Pravda*, *Izvestiia*, *Komsomol'skaia pravda*, *Ekonomicheskaia zhizn'*, *Vechernaia Moskva*, and *Za industrializatsiiu* began carrying regular articles devoted to the topic of the socialist city. Architectural and cultural journals *Sovremennaia arkhitektura*, *Stroitel'stvo moskvy*, *Literatura i isskustvo*, and *Revoliutsiia i kul'tura* opened their 1930 publishing seasons with sections or entire issues on socialist city-building.[83]

Ekonomicheskaia zhizn' (Economic life), the Union-wide daily newspaper of the Council of Labor and Defense, published a review of the conference's first day of speeches, and thereafter commenced a regular series titled *Navstrechu sotsialisticheskomu bytu* (Toward a socialist *byt*). In December alone, there were five installments of the series, each with multiple articles that addressed many facets of the socialist urbanism debate. Unlike *Pravda*, which buried articles on the socialist city in its back pages, *Ekonomicheskaia zhizn'* placed the debate up front.[84]

What is remarkable about this regular series is the degree to which it left the question of socialist settlement open for debate.[85] The polemical positions on Soviet city-building arose not from the paper's editors directly but from the wide-ranging experts and nonexperts selected to weigh in on the topic. The paper reported that the People's Commissariat of the Workers' and Peasants' Inspectorate had established a special commission on the question of socialist *byt* consisting of nine subcommittees: cooperative services; residential construction; standardization; new business types; children's *byt*; recreation; professionalization; finance; and education.[86] An open call for ideas, communicated with enthusiasm in bold caps, was published the following day:

SHARE YOUR EXPERIENCE, YOUR PROJECTS, AND PROPOSALS ON ALL QUESTIONS RELATED TO THE ORGANIZATION OF SOCIALIST *BYT*. TELL US ABOUT ALL OF YOUR PRACTICAL ATTEMPTS AND ACHIEVEMENTS IN THIS REALM, DOWN TO EVERYDAY TRIFLES.

THE PAGES OF *EKONOMICHESKAIA ZHIZN'* WILL BE OPEN FOR
PERMANENT COVERAGE OF THESE QUESTIONS. WRITE TO *EKO-
NOMICHESKAIA ZHIZN'*, COMMUNICATE YOUR PROPOSALS AND
WISHES.[87]

The call ended with a promise that the commission on socialist *byt* would use the
submissions in its work to develop official recommendations.

In a December issue of *Ekonomicheskaia zhizn'*, theoretical-architectural alli-
ances finally crystalized in the public eye. The architects asked to participate in
the debate included Aleksandr Vesnin and Moisei Ginzburg who, despite coedi-
torship at SA, found themselves on opposing sides. Aleksandr and Viktor Vesnin's
article stressed the need "first to resolve the general questions of the organization
of *byt*—only then can we plan cities."[88] They were particularly concerned that
socialist familial structure was not resolved, which made housing typologies impossible to design. The Vesnin proposals hewed to Sabsovich's recommendations, which
by this time were well known to those following the socialist city debate. Sabsovich's only contribution to the *Ekonomicheskaia zhizn'* series was a scathing take-
down of Okhitovich. In his article "'Rabid petty bourgeois,' or the car salesman"
('Vzbesivshiisia melkii burzhua' ili kommivoiazher avtomobil'noi firmy), Sabsovich
attacked what he saw as the disurbanist's reliance on automotive transport and his
vision of solo living. "Okhitovich does not understand 'our conditions' that are to
be reconstructed along socialist lines. But he does know (and is this good?) trends
in urban development in capitalist countries, many of which he describes in his
reports, and from which he derives his 'decentralized' settlement and his 'automobile' socialism."[89] At the core of Sabsovich's urbanism was extreme communality,
and he just could not square individualism with socialism. The Vesnins called for
new population-limited settlements for 20,000–50,000 residents made up of house-
communes because "collectivization of *byt* is possible only when large numbers of
people live together and are able to create regular social connections." Though their
text in *Ekonomicheskaia zhizn'* was not illustrated, their *zhilkombinat* designs for
Stalingrad—also found in Ivanitskii's files—later served as illustrations for Sabsovich's *Socialist Cities*.

Ginzburg allied with Okhitovich. The *Ekonomicheskaia zhizn'* series gave Okhitovich his first opportunity to spread the disurbanist vision to a Union-wide audience. He took direct aim at Sabsovich:

The difficulty with the problems of settlement and housing in our time is the
result of a few people trying to resolve them in an overly simplistic manner.
Instead of destroying the contradiction between village and city (K. Marx),
they suggest that we place a *city* of industry and a *city* of agriculture; in place
of *new resettlement* to destroy village life and urban congestion (Lenin) insert
old settlement—of an urban type. The second part of the problem is just as
simplistically understood—the type of dwelling.

It is for some reason believed that under socialism the dwelling type must be the house-commune (*dom-kommuna*). Why?

The *dom-kommuna*—again, it is only a *new name* for an old thing . . .

Socialist resettlement, the only one possible, will put an end to the idiocy and barbarity of rural life. The means to make this happen is the automobile and not the "socialist" crush proposed by L. Sabsovich.[90]

Whereas in earlier texts Okhitovich was not concerned with "terminological quarrels," by the end of 1929, terminology had become a cudgel to use against Sabsovich. He claimed that the moniker *sotsgorod*, Sabsovich's invention, pointed right back to the same congested agglomeration that characterized capitalist cities. The dense house-commune, furthermore, was a housing form destined in its crush of residents to instill the same everyday habits that traditional crowded urban dwellings had done. What form of settlement and housing was most appropriate to socialism, then? "In place of urban congestion, urban clusters, urban concentration of people, buildings, we will have nonurban, *decentralized* resettlement," Okhitovich proposed. "In place of the forced proximity of people in an urban setting—the maximum distance of dwellings from each other should be based on auto transportation. In place of a separate room for each worker create *a separate structure*."[91] Okhitovich envisioned light single-person structures arranged along roads traversed by automobiles. Parroting Okhitovich's recommendations, Ginzburg advocated decentralized settlement composed of small, nonmonumental, portable structures strung along the lines of transportation.[92]

Magnitogorsk at the Center of the Debate

Magnitogorsk appeared in *Ekonomicheskaia zhizn'* mid-December. A full-page spread that focused on how to build new cities bundled articles on Stalingrad, where a Ford tractor factory was under construction, Magnitogorsk, and Nizhnii Novgorod, the future site of a Ford automobile factory. Magnitogorsk sat temporally and conceptually in the middle of this trio since Stalingrad was nearing completion, and Nizhnii Novgorod was months into the future.[93] Magnitogorsk, instead, floated in a paradoxical state of concrete uncertainty. The article claimed that Magnitogorsk would be composed of a variety of commune types in which each adult would be allocated seven to ten square meters of living space in a centrally heated building with modern water and sewer, a canteen, a workers' club, a library, and reading rooms. Although the schooling system was unresolved, a proposal to construct boarding schools was under consideration. Each house-commune would have a dedicated round-the-clock nursery, and services would be provided to relieve women from housework.[94] These specific details and their budgets indicated that the program for the workers' residential area was set, but the article abruptly concluded with no indication of a groundbreaking or completion date.

Magnitogorsk's specificity was the result of blowback from a failed schematic city plan designed in the fall of 1929 at Gosproekt under the leadership of architect Sergei Chernyshev.[95] Chernyshev's scheme for Magnitogorsk, presented to the Sovnarkom at the end of October, showed a two-phase plan made up of a temporary settlement and a permanent city that included the factory, factory administration, and worker housing. Housing came in two main variants: four-story buildings that lined streets and small cottages at the city's periphery—not dissimilar to Baku's Stepan Razin settlement. Wide boulevards connected the two city sections. Chernyshev complained in his accompanying report that the primary planning stumbling block was the constantly changing population target for Magnitogorsk: 20,000, then 50,000, 60,000, and finally 70,000 residents.[96]

Nikolai Miliutin, the former commissar of the People's Commissariat for Finance, immediately took umbrage with the schematic plan for Magnitogorsk, which he viewed as unforgivably traditional and petty bourgeois. Writing as chair of the State Commission on the Construction of Socialist Cities (*Pravitel'stvennoi kommissii po stroitel'stvu sotsgorosdov*), Miliutin wrote a withering critique in *Izvestiia* a few days after seeing Chernyshev's scheme.[97] The perceived offenses of the design are best conveyed in Miliutin's own words:

> We really have not fully posed the question about the social character of the construction of our cities, of Soviet urbanism. As a result, we are witnessing a phenomenon that should be inconceivable under the dictatorship of the proletariat: in our new construction we are following the worst traditions of the last century. *The construction of our cities (including new ones) is completely saturated with the spirit of the petty bourgeois and emerges from their vulgar byt.* There is not even a hint of a new social order . . . We can and we must sweep away and obliterate the concept of home ownership, we can and we must build on the basis of social order, we must demand from our housing and public works binding decisions on the tasks of organizing the new socialist way of life . . . *To the new generation we must provide new dwellings* . . .

> On October 23 the Sovnarkom of the Russian Republic listened to an informational report "On the progress of the construction of Magnitogorsk." *The authors correctly set the tasks of the plan but could not solve them.* Complete services were planned for the convenience of the new city's population, including nurseries, schools, hospital care, kindergartens, factory kitchens, etc. The social order was given. But how was it solved? Yes, the old way. The workers' village was made up of a group of houses and cottages with kitchenettes and small flats, half of which face north . . . The calculation of population was taken from typical capitalist relations . . . with "overhead"

consisting of the wife and children. In other words, one person engaged in productive labor shall feed three dependents, half of whom are able-bodied.

Where is the organization of a socialist way of life? Where is the hygienic location of dwellings? Where is the emancipation of women? Where is even a hint of the public education of children? In Magnitogorsk, the first purely Soviet city in the USSR, we are not bound by the past. We must demonstrate to the world the will of the proletariat to build a new collective life![98]

Miliutin made two critical points in his diatribe, starting with the assertion that demographic accounting is at the heart of urban design. As long as the population projections for Magnitogorsk were based on a traditional nuclear family unit, architectural solutions would tend toward larger unit types, whether communal servicing was provided or not. In addition, he noted that novel programming was not enough to overcome poverty of architectural imagination. Even when the planning team for Magnitogorsk was working with the correct programmatic building blocks—from communal nurseries to factory-kitchens—they fell back on traditional forms. As the client for the Narkomfin Building, Moscow's most celebrated Constructivist house-commune, Miliutin wrote with firsthand knowledge about the architectonic potential of a fully socialized *byt*. If Magnitogorsk was to be the project that exemplified a new world order, forward thinking and inventive architects (like the Milinis-Ginzburg team at Narkomfin) had to be running the show.

The October scuffle over the correct form and programs for the socialist settlement of Magnitogorsk may well have prompted Gosplan's November conference. It certainly alerted the Sovnarkom to the seriousness of the problem. Miliutin's critique had its desired effect, for two weeks later, on November 12, the Sovnarkom issued a corrective decree on the construction of Magnitogorsk. The decree stipulated that Magnitogorsk should be a "purely proletarian city, fully linked with the work of the Magnitogorsk plant . . . a significant experiment in constructing the new type of city, which will provide maximal socialization of *byt* to the degree possible during this transitional period."[99] It went on to prescribe the same programs reported in the *Ekonomicheskaia zhizn'* article a month later, with enough detail to provide direction to architects of the future city. The communal services and cultural programs would be placed in the center of the city with close ties to the residential buildings. Children of all ages would be accommodated in a special children's city (*spetsial'nyi detskii gorod*), made up of nurseries through boarding schools. Interiors would be designed to provide ample sunlight as well as sanitary technology. Finally, in designing the buildings, a full account was to be taken "to utilize all achievements of advanced modern architecture—in particular, the work of the Stroikom RSFSR."[100] Miliutin's direct influence on the language of this official pronouncement comes in this final stipulation. His friend, Ginzburg, was at the time the head of Stroikom RSFSR's special commission to create standardized residential unit types. The efficient, spare, modern architectural forms that the commission devised would be the building blocks for the most prominent new socialist city in the Union, Magnitogorsk.

The *Ekonomicheskaia zhizn'* articles devoted to the problem of socialist city-building in December 1929, the most intense month of discussion on the topic, laid out a range of possible programs and forms, but two common arguments emerged. First, all authors agreed that first Five-Year Plan construction projects had a dual role to reform social habits (install socialist *byt*) at the same time that they established the Soviet industrial complex. Second, the authors agreed that old style (prerevolutionary, petty bourgeois, Western) and uncoordinated city-building efforts stood in the way of realizing these necessary societal changes. There was no consensus on the urban or architectural form of this new socialist settlement.

It should not be surprising that a strict party line on the correct constitution of socialist space was unformed at the end of 1929: the topic was still in its infancy. Only in July of that year did Sabsovich grab the attention of the economic planning community with his essay "The Problem of the City" in *Planovoe khoziaistvo*. Still, months passed before socialist urbanism was deemed an issue worthy of widespread concern. The Gosplan conference, held at the end of November, was the first time that socialist settlement was put under the microscope.

The twelve-year delay in addressing the relationships between the socialist economy, ideology, and space can be chalked up to economics rather than ideology. The shift from fiscally conservative genetic planning to aspirational teleological planning at the start of the first Five-Year Plan made massive capital construction projects possible: 12 billion rubles were to be spent on building the Soviet industrial complex from 1928 to 1933. But what exactly was to be built with that money, what would those industrial and residential installations look like, and how would they cause people to act? The questions had not been posed because so little had been built since the revolution. There can be no doubt that the Union-wide discussion about the problem of socialist space that led up to the Magnitogorsk design competition was prompted by the abysmal reports coming back from construction sites around the USSR. The unfortunate city of Dzerzhinsk, subject of innumerable satirical cartoons that highlighted its planning snafus, became a cautionary tale. Unless socialist spatial precepts, forms, and laws were established immediately, the second building season of the first Five-Year Plan was destined to produce more Dzerzhinsks.

5

COMPETITION AND VISIONS

At a recent meeting on the construction of Magnitogorsk at the Building Committee of the Russian Republic, the workers of Magnitogorsk asked: was it possible to undertake experimental construction not at Magnitogorsk but at some other site? It turned out that arguments about the plan had completely stopped construction, there was nothing they could do about it, and come next year there simply would not be room enough for everyone. If you asked why this was happening you would receive the following answer: because each person carries into Magnitogorsk his own new project for the socialist city expecting the concretization of it at the current moment, and each chooses not to see that the resolution of that question is impossible.

—G. V. Puzis (1929)

The Gosplan economist G. V. Puzis was sent to Magnitogorsk in the second half of 1929 to revise the economic plan of the city. In his speech at Gosplan's November conference on socialist settlement, Puzis described to his colleagues the chaos and confusion he encountered on the Ural steppe. Magnitogorsk, he reflected, seemed weighed down with too many irreconcilable ambitions. Workers justifiably worried that disagreements about conceptual Magnitogorsk—the experimental socialist city being shaped through debate by theorists like Leonid Sabsovich and Mikhail Okhitovich—only served to attenuate provisionality in actual, material Magnitogorsk. While a collection of officials in Moscow drafted the brief for the most important design competition of the first Five-Year Plan for an end-of-1929 release, construction workers and their families were living on the site of the future steel city in dugouts, tents, yurts, and single-room barracks.

Magnitogorsk's origin story has been told myriad times and with great archival depth.[1] This particular narrative focuses on the conceptual version of Magnitogorsk that emerged in text and drawings in late 1929 and early 1930. It forges links between the socialist urbanism debates roiling in Moscow, the drafting of the Magnitogorsk design competition brief, and the competition entries submitted for the most prominent new socialist city in the Union. Although the natural outcropping of iron ore known as Magnetic Mountain, and the Iron and Steel Works, were the prime reasons for the site's development, they sit distantly in the background of this portion of the Magnitogorsk story, as they did for the designers drafting competition submissions in other Soviet cities distant from the Urals.[2]

The All-Union Open Design Competition for Magnitogorsk, announced at the end of December 1929, elicited proposals for the design and construction of a socialist city adjacent to the metallurgical plant in the Urals, and for typical residential communes. The brief was exhaustively detailed: the competition entries would test the possibilities of *byt* transformation in urban and architectonic form and would materialize the programs and relationships discussed in the socialist urbanism debate. To understand the role this competition brief played in the evolution of the socialist spatial project requires borrowing a concept—the instaurational text—from the urban historian Françoise Choay. Choay defines the instaurational text as a written framework for constructing new spaces; it is intellectual work that spawns physical worlds.[3] By following the conceptual apparatus of the competition brief, it was believed, Soviet designers would finally provide to the jury and public alike images of the new socialist world that could be examined, assessed, critiqued, and hopefully, embraced.

Arrival at the Mountain

Magnitogorsk was born in 1918. In April of that year Vesenkha announced a competition to design a metallurgic plant in the Urals modeled on the US Steel Plant in Gary, Indiana. This mythic plant would produce "all of the steel that Russia might need."[4] Although it is unclear whether the competition ever occurred—the Russian Civil War began and further information has been lost—the giant iron-ore mountain and the territory surrounding it became lodged in Soviet imaginations as critical to autarkic industrial goals. Work on the Magnitogorsk Iron and Steel Works restarted in 1926 with the establishment of the State Institute for the Design of Metallurgical Factories (Gipromez), but lack of internal technical expertise hamstrung the project from its inception.[5] In 1927, Vesenkha engaged the Chicago-based design-engineering firm Henry Freyn and Co., the company responsible for designing the Gary plant that Magnitogorsk strove to emulate, as technical consultants for the burgeoning Soviet metallurgical industry.[6] Design work on Magnitogorsk commenced in the Leningrad office of Gipromez with the assistance of Freyn engineers, while a parallel effort continued at the Urals branch of Gipromez, an office that would soon be renamed Magnitostroi.

The site for the future factory city was determined by a geological anomaly: a mountain made almost entirely of iron ore that sat alone in the middle of the steppe. As it developed, unplanned, the production zone for the Magnitogorsk Iron and Steel Works consisted of the mountain, a mine to its immediate north, the factory site to the west of the mine, a rail yard nestled between mine and factory, and an industrial lake along the whole western edge, created by damming the Ural River at the city's southern border (figure 5.1). Rail lines marked the city's northern edge, heading west to Ufa, east to Kartaly. In the absence of planning, workers' residential accommodations—such as they were—sprung up within the production zone, in a slice of land between the mine and factory territories.

In March 1929, the first twenty-five people arrived in Magnitogorsk. Through that year, the only construction activity at the site consisted of laying track to connect with the nearest rail station 145 kilometers away, building a small brick

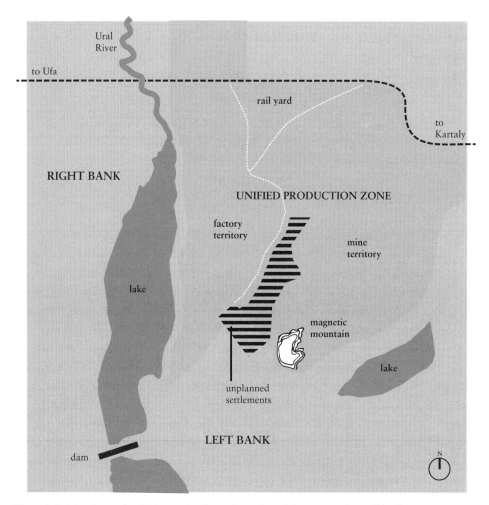

Figure 5.1. Magnitogorsk, 1930. Map by the author, adapted from *Sovetskaia arkhitektura*, no. 3 (1933): 29.

factory, and a few wooden barracks. By the end of 1929 there were purportedly already 6,763 workers on the factory site, a population number that did not account for their family members or people not working in construction.[7]

Magnitogorsk at the turn of the decade was a site of extremes, on which the openness of the windswept steppe contrasted unfavorably with crowded, poorly built living quarters. Workers and their families who were either enticed or forced to make the long trip to the construction site found no proper living quarters on arrival, a problem that intensified with the precipitously expanding population.[8] Photographs show the housing options that were made available to this population or that were built by the workers themselves. For families, the most private option was a stand-alone "dugout" house, constructed from turf harvested on the steppe (figure 5.2). For singles, the administration pitched a tent city and built wooden barracks, while some enterprising workers constructed their own yurts (figure 5.3). S. Gugel', director of Magnitostroi in the later 1930s, estimated that just forty-three proper residential buildings—wooden barracks—were built in the winter of 1929–30 to accommodate a population upward of 10,000 residents (figure 5.4). As it was, the open-plan barracks housed not just the sleeping quarters of workers and engineers but also socialist organizations, banks, the municipal

Первые жилища на Магнитке.

Figure 5.2. Family dugout, "first housing in Magnitka," Magnitogorsk, Russia, 1929. Magnitogorskii kraevedcheskii muzei.

Figure 5.3. Yurt housing, Magnitogorsk, Russia, 1929. Magnitogorskii kraevedcheskii muzei.

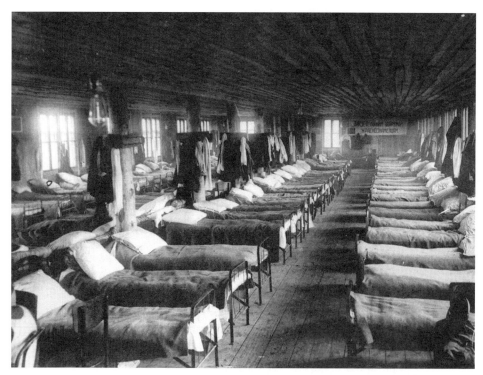

Figure 5.4. Open-plan wooden barrack housing, Magnitogorsk, Russia, 1929–30. Barracks held not only sleeping quarters but also socialist organizations, banks, the municipal government of Magnitogorsk and the Komsomol, stores, hospitals, schools, and worker clubs. Magnitogorskii kraevedcheskii muzei.

government of Magnitogorsk and the Komsomol (the Young Communist League), stores, hospitals, schools, and worker clubs.[9] So pervasive and despised was barrack life that Gugel' anticipated "there will be a city-wide celebration in Magnitogorsk on the day when the existence of a cultured city allows us to abandon these barracks. We'll burn them to the ground."[10]

The designers of the industrial side of the project, the Iron and Steel Works, encountered difficulties that prefigured those faced by the designers of the socialist settlement. Neither the Leningrad nor Ural offices of Gipromez could keep up with the shifting production goals that, with each revision, changed the scale of the plant they were tasked to design. In its first 1928 iteration, the future Magnitogorsk Works was projected to produce 656,000 tons of pig iron. Over the next year and a half, the target was raised from 1.1 million, to 1.6 million, and finally 2.5 million tons by the start of 1930, a number that amounted to a four-fold increase.[11] After two years in the Soviet Union, the Freyn engineers produced a 700-page report filled with charts and graphs that was intended as a roadmap for the project. Construction drawings for the plant were notably absent. In hopes of fast-tracking construction, the Soviet government reformulated its foreign assistance contract from consultancy to concession. The Cleveland engineering firm Arthur McKee and Co. won the bid to become became both designer and part owner of the Magnitogorsk Works in March 1930 and arrived on site in early summer. Responsibility for the design of the plant was handed off to the new US engineers. The design of the city was a far more ideologically freighted endeavor, and one that would take much longer to resolve.

Magnitogorsk Competition Brief as Instaurational Text

The official brief for the All-Union Open Design Competition for the Socialist City of Magnitogorsk was crafted in Moscow by a collection of officials in November and December 1929.[12] At a predraft meeting, attendees were reminded that much more than a factory was to be built out beyond the Urals—the project raised critical questions "about how to build socialist culture."[13] One thing was certain: disorderly conditions on the ground in Magnitogorsk had no bearing on the design competition brief. Instead, discussants, who included Leonid Sabsovich, Vesenkha representative and chief theorist of socialist urbanism, referred to Magnitogorsk as a bare site (*golyi uchastok*) on which a model socialist city could be built according to prevailing urban theory.[14] The text's drafters had clear direction from Sovnarkom's November 11 decree, which stated that Magnitogorsk was to be "purely proletarian" and a "significant experiment in constructing the new type of city."[15] After verbal scuffles over terminology (was it a "city" or "settlement"?), family structure (should socialist children live with their parents?), and housing typology (how tall should the buildings be?), the final version of the brief was released publicly at 10 am on December 22, 1929. Interested competitors had six weeks to formulate their design proposals.[16]

This brief is arguably the most important textual artifact from the 1929 socialist urbanism debate (figure 5.5). The stapled eight-page brochure—small enough to tuck into a book—presented the ground rules for an entirely unprecedented urban culture, one anchored by industry and predicated on new social relations. It represents a fleeting moment when visionary theorists and state officials (in some cases these were one and the same) agreed on how socialist space, and the people within it, should be organized to break all ties with capitalist models.

Françoise Choay's concept of the instaurational text helps to situate the Magnitogorsk competition brief in its time. Choay defines instaurational texts as "those writings which have the explicit aim of developing an autonomous conceptual apparatus in order to conceive and build new and unknown forms of space." Their goal, in other words, is "to provide a theoretical support and foundation for spaces, whether already built or projected."[17] Choay breaks these texts into three categories: architectural treatises, utopias, and writings on urbanism. The focus here is on the first two, the treatise and utopia, which are explicit "mechanisms for generating built space." Both treatises and utopias are projective; what separates them is the degree of autonomy allowed the designer. A treatise stipulates principles and makes rules—it provides the framework for future space but leaves room for interpretation. A utopia, by contrast, is a totalized imaginary—it sets both the shape of future space and the relationships between its parts. With a treatise there is loose structure but freedom for the designer, while with utopia there is clarity but constraint.

Utopia is a concept to be summoned with caution in the context of Soviet history since Marx and Engels explicitly rejected it. Utopian socialism, the flawed precursor to their Scientific socialism, pictures clearly what the ideal future society will look like. Scientific socialism instead submits that events in the present continually shape the future. History and social progress are dynamic—and human nature is likewise negotiable—so there can be no fixed spatial model of the future (read: utopia). "We cannot outline Socialism," Lenin announced in assent with this line of reasoning in 1918. "What Socialism will look like when it takes on its final forms we do not know and cannot say."[18] The philosopher Martin Buber later found fault with this line of reasoning in *Paths in Utopia*. How, Buber asked incredulously, is it possible to build socialism, or anything, without a vision in the mind's eye of what shape that future might take? In asking this question, Buber put his finger directly on the quandary that Soviet planners faced at the start of the first Five-Year Plan. The lack of a clearly articulated vision of Soviet space, or rules with which to create it, resulted most often in Dzerzhinsks: haphazard, chaotic construction projects that did not align with the ideological imperatives of the socialist state. A concrete vision—call it utopia or simply a replicable model— would have given Soviet planners "something primary and original which [was

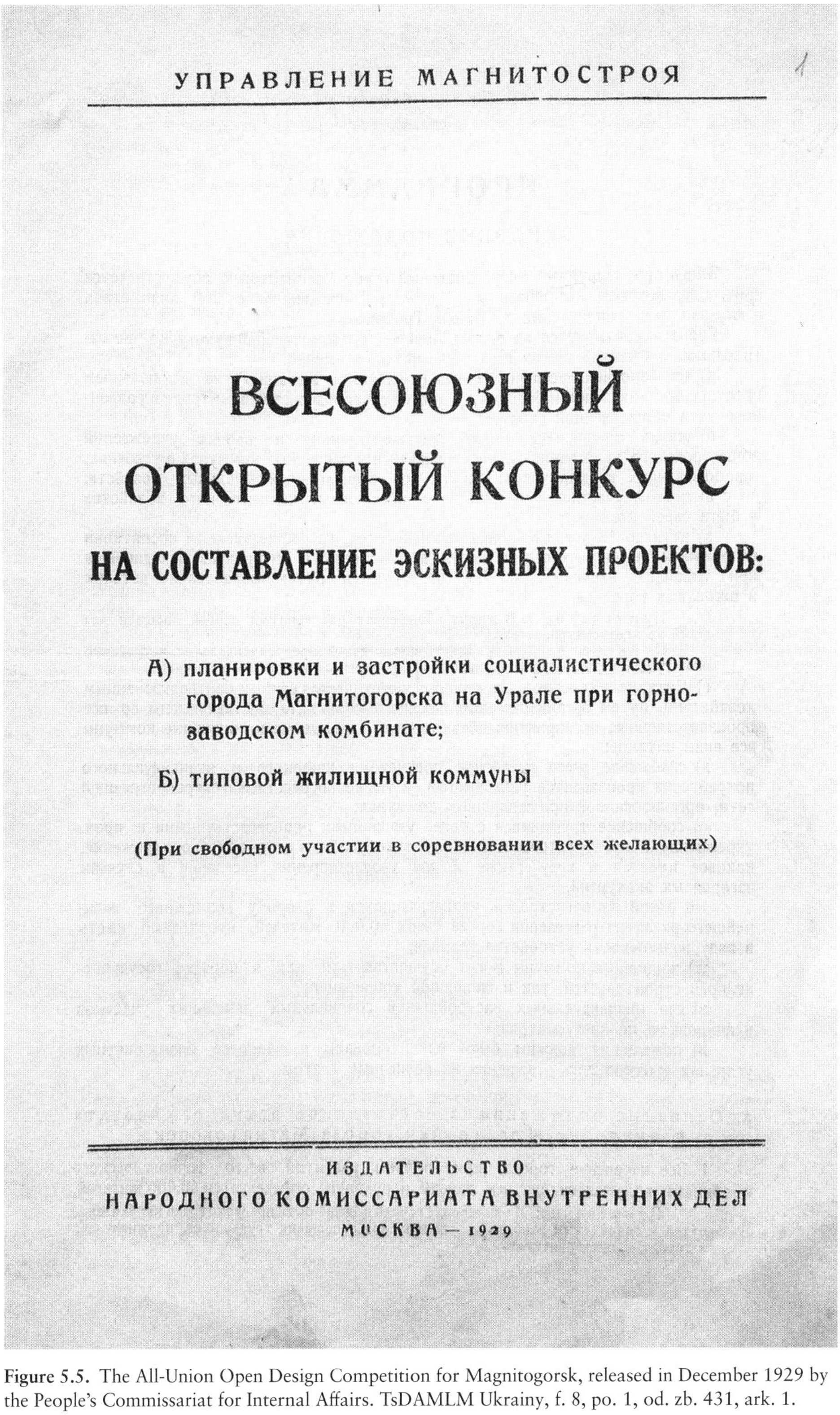

УПРАВЛЕНИЕ МАГНИТОСТРОЯ

ВСЕСОЮЗНЫЙ
ОТКРЫТЫЙ КОНКУРС
НА СОСТАВЛЕНИЕ ЭСКИЗНЫХ ПРОЕКТОВ:

А) планировки и застройки социалистического города Магнитогорска на Урале при горно-заводском комбинате;

Б) типовой жилищной коммуны

(При свободном участии в соревновании всех желающих)

ИЗДАТЕЛЬСТВО
НАРОДНОГО КОМИССАРИАТА ВНУТРЕННИХ ДЕЛ
МОСКВА — 1929

Figure 5.5. The All-Union Open Design Competition for Magnitogorsk, released in December 1929 by the People's Commissariat for Internal Affairs. TsDAMLM Ukrainy, f. 8, po. 1, od. zb. 431, ark. 1.

their] destiny to build," as Buber put it.[19] Defined as an instaurational text, the Magnitogorsk competition brief can be analyzed as the long-awaited concrete vision for generating Soviet built space.

The Magnitogorsk competition brief constitutes its own category of instaurational text that sits between Choay's treatise and utopia. The final approved brief is more than treatise but less than utopia; it is a suggestive but not wholly prescriptive text. Each of the published prize-winning entries shares certain characteristics like a commitment to minimal private living quarters, common public servicing, and state-run child-rearing. The competition brief defines these issues, treatise-like, as the axiomatic principles for the city's design. The remainder of the brief veers toward utopian projection, providing specific area, volume, and relational direction to the designers, from the scale of the living cell to the city. Design teams were given the liberty to invent architectural forms, but only to the extent that their solutions met the many programmatic and dimensional limits imposed by the brief. The brief that at first glance is no more than a technocratic bundle of lists yields a clear polemical program for the design of socialist settlements on close reading. An inchoate urban model is woven into the language of the competition brief, but the text remains shy of a priori form.

Axioms of Socialist Urbanism

The brief for the All-Union Open Design Competition for the Socialist City of Magnitogorsk requests designs for a newly planned industrial city on the east side of the Ural Mountains, 260 kilometers southwest of the village of Troitsk (see the appendix for the English translation of the brief). This new site, hundreds of kilometers from any significant cartographic locale, is to be planned "on the basis of a complete socialization of cultural, educational, and everyday life of all workers."[20]

Competitors are asked to design two projects: a socialist city (*sotsialisticheskii gorod*, or *sotsgorod*) and a typical residential commune (*tipovoi zhilishchnoi kommuny*, or *zhilkombinat*). Both of these terms—*sotsgorod* and *zhilkombinat*—emerged from the writings of Sabsovich between 1929 and 1930; it is worth clarifying the relationship between them before detailing how they were posed to the competition entrants.[21] Per Sabsovich's definition, a *sotsgorod* is a city with a population of 50,000–60,000 that includes all programs and services needed at the municipal level. These include residential, leisure, commercial, and governmental spheres, plus the infrastructural systems to knit these together and link them to the productive sphere (the factory), on which the *sotsgorod*'s existence is predicated. The *zhilkombinat* is the building block for the residential sphere only, a smaller urban unit with a population of 2,000–3,000 people. These standardized units that hold residential buildings, local schools, a workers' club, and other limited recreational facilities must be duplicated until the overall desired urban population of the entire city is reached. Twenty-five *zhilkombinaty* at 2,000 residents each is needed to reach a *sotsgorod* population of 50,000, for example.

The main regulations (*osnovie polozheniia*) for the planning and construction of the model socialist city, listed at the very front of the Magnitogorsk competition brief, can be organized into three axiomatic categories that structure the details to follow: socialist demographics, socialist *novyi byt*, and socialist construction. First, under the axiom of socialist demography, the brief stipulates that "all adult residents (men and women), except for the elderly, the disabled, and the sick, are involved in productive labor and of various kinds of social work." The new industrial city will be a productive city foremost, and women will be among the working population.

The next four points support the axiom of socialist *novyi byt* (the new everyday life). Covered by this axiom are directives related to housing type, child-rearing, meal preparation, and provisioning. Residential communes will be the only housing option provided, and complete socialization of life will rely on each worker identifying with and contributing to the communal unit to which they belong. "Aside from production work and visits to city institutions, the life of the workers is concentrated in the housing commune and its environment, liberating the working people from the worries of maintaining individual property, and permitting active participation of the working people in the collective economy and *byt* of their commune," the brief stipulates. With the full instantiation of the *novyi byt*, women are liberated from household tasks, most important childcare and cooking. In Magnitogorsk, children under sixteen years of age (the age of able-bodied productivity) will live "under socialized care and in closed nurseries, kindergartens, and boarding schools located near the adult dwellings, not isolated in children's and school campuses" (this last note may have been a minor concession to Nadezhda Krupskaia, Lenin's widow, who vigorously disapproved of separating children from their parents). The degree to which fully socialized parents will be involved in the lives of their offspring is ambiguous in the Magnitogorsk brief. Children will be physically proximate—in institutions located near adult living quarters—but space for children is not to be provided in the living quarters of married couples. Freedom from cooking is ensured by the fact that "meal preparation for the entire population of the city is carried out by a centralized food processing plants that deliver all types of food to each manufacturing facility, public agency, and residential commune." Cooking will occur in factory-kitchens and bakeries, and all meals will be consumed in canteens. Lastly under this axiom, "supplies for the entire population—items of general and individual consumption—will be handled by a department store and a commodity supply network organized by the residential communes."[22] Unlike during the NEP, when small businesses supplied consumer goods that the state was unable to provide, the new socialist city will be entirely free of private enterprise.

Finally, there is the axiom of socialist construction, which covers guidelines for conveyance, construction organization, land regime, and general building orientation. Busses and automobiles will provide transportation for workers to "more remote manufacturing locations and institutions" and on "countryside excursions." This provision implies that residential communes will be located close enough to the production zone that laborers can walk to work. The residential communes will be constructed by the state as housing cooperatives, and no land will be provided to individual builders. All premises will be "oriented with regard to the most favorable sunlight conditions." This rather specific environmental directive may have arisen from ongoing mass housing research and construction in Germany, undoubtedly known to the Magnitogorsk competition brief drafters. While no specific solar angle is prescribed in the Magnitogorsk brief, awareness of heliotropism is expected in submitted designs.

The regulations stipulated in these three axiomatic categories set the basic parameters for competition submissions. The following two sections of the brief provide detailed information for the separate (though interrelated) design projects required of competition entries: the socialist city and the typical residential commune. Both projects are described through program elements, dimensional attributes, and in certain cases relationships between building and site. These are the strict rules of operation that give urban and architectural shape to the general principles presented in the brief's opening paragraphs.

Socialist City of Magnitogorsk

The competition brief stipulates that the socialist city of Magnitogorsk will be built and sustained by proletarian labor. Details for designers begin, therefore, with specific demographic targets. The entire population of the socialist city at full development of the metallurgic plant, silicate factories, and mines will be 50,000 residents, a number to consist of 68 percent able-bodied adults, 24 percent children younger than sixteen, and 8 percent elderly and disabled. These residents will become socialist citizens through programmatic and spatial conditions designed to install the *novyi byt*. Workers will enjoy communal living and servicing; cultural, educational, and recreational opportunities; and state-provided health care. Cultural life will be centered on the Palace of Labor and Culture with its library reading room, meeting rooms for trade unions and health education, and separate theater and cinema buildings. The primary recreational site for the city will be the Park of Culture and Leisure with a stadium, playing fields, and sporting clubs. A network of public squares and boulevards will offer passive leisure, and municipal greenhouses will furnish the planted matter.

The residential educational institutions required in the brief cover three stages of young life. The youngest citizens, up to age eight, will be taken care of in kindergartens and specialized daycare facilities for disabled children. Students up to working age, from eight to sixteen, will be accommodated in large schools with a maximum population of 800. These schools will have grounds large enough for planting crops and raising animals as part of the standard curriculum. In *Socialist Cities*, his 1930 book, Sabsovich argued that there would be blanket cost reductions for agricultural food products "due to the fact that farms *can employ children as a necessary element of their upbringing and education*, as well as the elderly and the feeble, who are not useful in other productive labor."[23] Juvenile and elderly gardening and animal husbandry in service of communal food provision would wrest productivity out of the least able-bodied members of the population. For working age youth over the age of sixteen, the brief requires inclusion of a higher technical school (*vyshee tekhnicheskoe uchebnoe zavedenie* or VTUZ) with metallurgical, chemical, and mining departments, on a site near the factory grounds.

The communal services specified in the competition brief are broken down into food provision and sites of everyday civic life. The city of Magnitogorsk will be catered by a centralized food processing plant to prepare hot meals and baked goods. The plant, located next to a rail line, will have specialized sausage, cheese, confectionery, and beverage production facilities to feed 30,000 people in its first phase, with expansion possibilities for an additional 20,000 in the near future. Critical but ancillary food production programs include a slaughterhouse, industrial refrigerators and food warehouses, and a disposal plant. Sites of everyday civic life include venues for shopping (a department store); communications (mail, telegraph, telephone, and radio); laundry; bathing (bathhouse and pool); and a number of technical services like a garage, fire station, repair shops, an incineration plant, and crematorium. Finally, the health of city residents will be overseen in a 400-bed hospital and a central health clinic with two regional branches: one convenient to the industrial complex, the other to the residential area. The description of the wellness program in the competition brief is exhaustive. It details myriad hospital departments—from maternity to morgue—as well as separate isolation units, laboratories, birth homes, and other specialties.

The items that elucidate the particulars of socialist construction in Magnitogorsk give specific temporal, topographic, and relational direction to the competition entrants. Most important in the context of the first Five-Year Plan is the schedule. City construction is to be phased over the first two Five-Year Plans—30,000 residents will be accommodated by the end of the first, and the additional 20,000 by the end of the second. The demographic limit set on Magnitogorsk is not a hard one, however, for the brief stipulates that "the city should be planned to accommodate further expansion in future, after the first two five-year plans." The indication toward expansion—although buried among requirements and other data points—sets the competition brief in conflict with Sabsovich's texts. In *Socialist Cities*, Sabsovich unequivocally supported hard population caps for future urban centers. "We must consider that *in a socialist city, public life and the collective private life of the population will be developed on an immeasurably large scale, larger than the space available in our cities. Therefore, it is advised that the socialist city should be built to accommodate a population of no more than 50,000–60,000 people.*"[24] Sabsovich's argument in favor of fixed demographics hinged on the inextricable interdependencies of full socialization. Production, housing, education, and communal servicing are suspended together in a delicate web. Unexpected inputs or outputs from any of these constituent elements threaten to destroy the communal balance, so the population of a socialist city must be planned for, reached, and frozen. This was exactly the argument that Ivanitskii used against the fixed-population model in discussions with his Baku clients in January 1930 when he cited the industrial city of Zaporizhzhia as his example of why population caps do not work in practice. If the 300,000-person city were planned as a collection of so-called socialist cities, each with a maximum population of 50,000, urban territory and urban life would be artificially fragmented. Redundant roads, utilities, and institutions built for each of these urban units would place an undue fiscal and managerial burden on the greater municipal government.[25] The Magnitogorsk brief satisfies each position, albeit obliquely. The 50,000-person population target matches Sabsovich's model, but the door is left open for organic urban growth beyond that target, per Ivanitskii's suggestion.

Additional pragmatic planning details also fall under the axiom of socialist construction. Magnitogorsk will be serviced by the "most modern scientific municipal improvements including district heating, water supply, sewage, electrification, and gasification provided by the combined factory installations," the brief stipulates. Taking a lesson from the Dzerzhinsk fiasco, where the city was built downstream of industrial outflow, the Magnitogorsk brief states the precise source of the city's water supply—groundwater aquifers on the Ural floodplain—and the downriver location of sewerage outfall. The "open steppe nature of the city" requires softening, the brief notes in the conclusion of this section. Tree planting, especially in the zone between the factory and residential areas will be necessary. Lastly, the entrants are asked to pay particular attention to the topographic conditions of the site, the location of the production area (already under construction), and the existing rail lines when designing the street network. All of these items and their locations were included on a 1/5000 site plan attached to the brief that has since been lost.

Typical Residential Commune or *Zhilkombinat*

The competition brief next turns to instructions for the design of the typical residential commune, or *zhilkombinat*. Here, the socialist demographics of the communal sub-unit are further refined. Each residential commune, a complex of buildings, will be designed for a capacity of 1,500–3,000 people of all ages who will occupy their own respective sectors. Issues related to socialist construction principles are straightforward. Buildings within the residential commune are allowed to be no more than four stories.[26] The ceiling height of residential spaces will be 2.8 meters (just over 9 feet), and the common areas from 2.8 to 4 meters. The exception to this rule is a large theater space with a minimum 4-meter ceiling height. The limits placed on building and floor height, while seemingly benign, greatly impact the architectonic language of the entries. Not all design teams abided by this rule. The OSA team led by Ivan Leonidov, whose Magnitogorsk competition entry is best known in the West, baldly disregarded the height restriction with slim residential skyscrapers distributed in a diffuse checkerboard pattern.

The balance of the residential commune section of the brief provides details to ensure installation of the *novyi byt*. The axiomatic principles of the model socialist city, noted at the front of the brief, gesture toward social reconfiguration, but the radical and controversial aspects of the new socialist life become clear here. First and foremost, the nuclear family is entirely liquidated, a process envisioned by Soviet feminist Aleksandra Kollontai nearly a decade before. To enact this process, the population of every Magnitogorsk *zhilkombinat* is divided into four age groups—babies (0–4), kindergarteners (4–8), school-aged children (8–16), and adults (16+)—each of whom will live in a specially designed sector of the commune. The separation and atomization of each citizen will permit, perhaps paradoxically, a more robust collective sphere, or so argued Sabsovich:

> In the socialist city, houses should be constructed in such a way that they provide the greatest convenience for the worker's collective life, collective work, and collective recreation. They should also provide the most comfortable possible conditions for individual work and individual leisure. *These houses should not have separate apartments with kitchens, pantries, etc.* for individual domestic use since all of the worker's everyday needs will be completely socialized. In addition, *they should not include space for private family life, because the idea of family, as we now know it, will no longer exist.* In place of the closed, isolated family unit we will have the "collective family" of workers, in which isolation will have no place.[27]

In this prescription for socialist housing outlined in *Socialist Cities*, Sabsovich summarily eradicated the spaces in which the middle relational scale of the nuclear family might flourish, such as the kitchen table or sitting area within the apartment. All socializing and recreating would occur in "social condensing" spaces like canteens and worker clubs. Either the worker would engage in solo work and leisure in her single room, or she would immerse herself in the collective.

The Magnitogorsk brief assumes nearly all of Sabsovich's recommendations. Competition entrants are instructed that sleeping accommodation for adults can be designed for singles or for two to three people (the unit mix is unspecified). The sleeping rooms—for that is what these spaces are exclusively for—will be designed at 9 square meters per person for a single, 7.5 square meters per person for all other types. To make such tight quarters feasible, the brief specifies that all furniture within the sleeping quarters will be collapsible: folding beds, sofas, cupboards, and so on. The social condensing spaces, on the other hand, will be ample: 2–3 square meters per adult will be allocated to these programs located either in the residential buildings or in separate buildings connected by heated passageways.[28] Designers must provide space to accommodate two scales of communal interaction for the residents. At the local level, each group of sleeping rooms is to be provided a pantry with a gas stove for heating food, a social room for greeting guests, a bathroom, showers, a washroom, toilet, laundry basin, and a common balcony. At the commune level, residents will share dining, laundry, and club facilities; and a commercial area replete with a hair salon, a solarium, and sports playing fields. Limits to full communality are set by population volume: the dining room should hold at maximum 25 percent of the adult population of the *zhilkombinat*, and the club 20–30 percent. Nonetheless, just a quarter of the adult population eating in the canteen at the same time would tally 570 people, a large enough crowd to engender a sense of community.[29]

And where are the children—the future socialist individuals—in this new arrangement? Without exception, they live separately from the people who spawned them. "*The question of joint dwelling for children and their parents can only be answered in the negative*," stressed Sabsovich. "Infants are best located in special buildings where the mothers can visit for feeding . . . Preschool and school-age children should spend most of their time in spaces designed for their learning, productive work, and leisure. It is clearly pointless to provide space for them in the same dwelling as their parents, where they would return at night. Therefore, *house-communes should only be built for adults*."[30] In the Magnitogorsk competition brief, adults and children are duly separated. Children are allocated learning and living sectors by developmental stage and are to be accommodated in state-run dormitories: nurseries for children up to age four and kindergartens for four- to eight-year-olds. Competition entrants are asked to provide adjacent play yards for the children, and otherwise should refer to requirements set by the People's Commissariats of Health and Education for dimensional and relational criteria related to these programs. Older children will live in boarding schools (*internaty*), in which the structure of everyday life mimics that of the adult sector. The brief stipulates that each dormitory room will accommodate sleeping groups of up to ten children. As with the adults, social condensing spaces will be provided for the children at the local and community scale. Toilets, showers, a linen closet, and washing up sink are shared by sleeping group. Common areas for the whole school include a dining room to accommodate half of the children; classrooms; a library and reading room; a red corner; and a large room for entertainment and sport. The schools for all ages must be connected to the rest of the commune by heated passageways.

The residential commune as described in the Magnitogorsk competition brief was controversial in its time on relational and temporal terms. Controversy number one surrounded the proposition that familial relations be dissolved in toto. The residential commune was to be the solvent, breaking apart deep interpersonal relations between partners and between parents and children. Sabsovich conceded that "some of these rooms (or maybe all) must have a door or sliding partition to connect to adjoining rooms through interior circulation, if the husband and wife wish." Yet he stressed that "there should be no joint living space for husbands and wives."[31] The conjugal door might satisfy immediate sexual desires, but emotional attachment between spouses was a need left unaddressed. As for state-run child-rearing, Krupskaia was not the only Soviet thought leader to question the utility of breaking filial ties. Nikolai Miliutin proposed a more measured approach to socialist child-rearing in the transitional period in his book *Sotsgorod* (1930), suggesting that "in building special institutions for the life and education of children (closely connected with the adults' home) we are establishing only the necessary conditions so that parents, when they wish, may send their children to these institutions . . . This will not, however, mean compulsion."[32] Krupskaia, for her part, stressed that cross-generational interaction was of benefit to both children and adults, and not just in the transitional period. "When people talk about kids, they often seem to be thinking of them as disorganized, hooligan-like interferers," she wrote. "But the new socialist house should be organized so that kids can grow in it, develop, learn from adults how to organize themselves, without annoying or disturbing anyone. And, of course, when building, you cannot economize on every centimeter. *It is necessary to sew the housing clothes for [cultural] growth, anticipating the development of the inner life of the house, its social life.*"[33] Because she advocated for cultural growth, Krupskaia was lumped with the so-called gradualists, who understood the transition from old to new ways of living under socialism as a process that would likely take some time.

Another controversy had to do with tempo. In November 1929, the Gosplan Presidium member N. A. Paskutskii noted that "we are living in a transitional period," and he stressed that the rapid tempo of socialist construction would, in itself, bring about sharp changes in the lives of the working class and laboring peasants.[34] Intensifying this seismic cultural shift by forcing radical domestic changes too quickly was unwise, Paskutskii argued. The Magnitogorsk brief takes no such equivocal stance: the proposed residential commune was expected to immediately and totally instantiate the new way of life. According to antigradualist Sabsovich, that was its primary asset. To make his argument in favor of the residential commune, Sabsovich first denounced the retrograde Chernyshev version of the Magnitogorsk city plan:

The invention of any kind of "transitional forms" (*perekhodnye formy*) of dwelling is simply unjustifiable opportunism. The original plans of the new socialist city Magnitogorsk, for example, called for the design of dormitory style rooms for four people; it also called for family rooms for a husband, wife, and two children . . . The authors of these projects cite the backwardness of the workers, who apparently are unprepared for the abrupt transition to the *novyi byt*. These authors are advised first to get rid of their own backwardness and prejudices before they assign them to the workers.[35]

In Sabsovich's opinion, there was no benefit to proposing half solutions in deference to the transitional state. He hung his argument on the workers themselves, for whom he purported to speak. The workers were ready for radical change, he asserted—it was the socialist intelligentsia who could not imagine, and were discomfited by, the idea of full communalization. The first Five-Year Plan was the opportunity to overthrow the past and build the future in the here and now, claimed Sabsovich. The Magnitogorsk brief shares this prospective lean forward.

The remainder of the Magnitogorsk brief lays out the substantive submission requirements. The sheer volume of material expected of entrants communicates that this is much more than an "ideas" competition. Design teams are asked to provide a general plan of the city to indicate residential, public, and administrative structures; their parcels; various types of green spaces; and the schematic locations of water and sewer mains. Typical street cross sections are also required. Detailed drawings of the residential commune must include plans at various scales; sections with structural systems; elevations; and axonometric and perspective views. An explanatory text must provide basic information about the scheme and is to be accompanied by a detailed cost estimate (inclusive of the formulas used to generate the results). Additional tables must calculate the area and volume assigned to each program and the percentage of the residential commune allocated to each age group by area and volume. This is an enormous amount of information to generate in six weeks.

Visions of Concentrated Collectivism

The deadline for receipt of competition entries at Magnitostroi's Moscow office was February 2, 1930. Entries were to be submitted under a verbal or graphic slogan (*pod devizom*), to obscure authorship and ensure judging fairness. In addition to the seventeen open entries received, the competition organizers invited five well-known design teams to submit proposals: MAO, OSA, Kartoizdatel'stva NKVD (the cartographic office of the People's Commissariat for Internal Affairs), the Stroikom working group, and a team led by Sergei Chernyshev, the project's previous architect.[36] In total, the jury deliberated over twenty-two schemes for the socialist city of Magnitogorsk and residential commune to select four prizewinning designs that would, as a consequence of their success, become the property of Magnitostroi.

The jury was composed of a variety of experts in urban planning matters. Former Commissar for Education, Anatolii Lunacharskii, chaired the jury and was assisted by vice chair, Nikolai Miliutin. Among the specialists who adjudicated the competition were local administrators from Magnitostroi and the Ural regional government; representatives from the People's Commissariats for Internal Affairs, Education, and Health; the Construction Committee of the Russian Republic; the Women's Department of the Central Committee; the All-Union Central Soviet of Trade Unions; the Central Committee of the Young Communist League; and Moscow architects Viktor Vesnin, Ivan Mashkov, and Andrei Ivanov.[37]

In their detailed report, the jury divided entries into two categories: "concentrated city planning" (*kontsentrirovannaia planirovka goroda*) and "linear city planning" (*lineinaia planirovka goroda*). The formal divergences between the two submission types can be explained by the sociospatial theories that drove them. Entries from the concentrated group hewed to the urbanist writings of Sabsovich, while those from the linear group followed Okhitovich's disurbanist theories. Notable concentrated city entries came from MAO, Kartoizdatel'stva NKVD, and Chernyshev, as well as the prize-winning anonymous teams Black Square, Roman Numeral Five, Two Lines, and Three Lines. Because the competition brief requested a city plan stocked with dense 3,000-person residential communes on Sabsovich's insistence, the prevalence of concentrated city entries is not surprising. The disurbanist schemes submitted by OSA and Stroikom (a team also made up of OSA members) were the sole members of the "linear city" group whose designers disregarded the call for dense residential communes.[38]

As the jury's grouping implies, the concentrated planning schemes share significant formal and organizational characteristics, chief among them embrace of controlled density. On the whole, these entries are cognizant and respectful of the difficult existing conditions on the site. Each of the concentrated city submissions places the future city to the southeast of the intersection of factory, lake, and dam, and between Magnetic Mountain and another hill to the south (figure 5.6). Site planning geometries for the concentrated city designs are generated by connecting the factory gates with the open southeasterly swath of land, and all entries provide a green buffer between the factory and the residential sector of the city. In nearly every case, a single residential commune type is repeated in a regular grid pattern, with strips of green space acting as expansion joints between quadrants. Long midrise housing bars run north-south, almost to an entry. This orientation allows for optimal east-west insolation on the broad sides of the residential buildings.

The site plan of the co-second-place-winning Black Square team entry, a representative concentrated city example, indicates the factory and its snarl of rail lines lightly penciled in at the bottom (west) of the drawing (figure 5.7). The factory gates open onto a green buffer zone that offers access to an administrative center to the left and a cultural/recreational center to the right, while straight ahead stretches a three-kilometer axis lined with identical residential communes. An axonometric

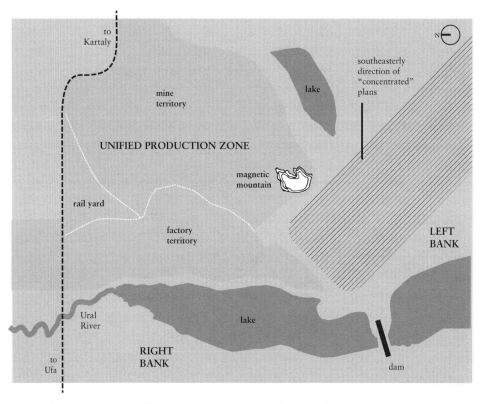

Figure 5.6. Siting key to the All-Union Open Design Competition for Magnitogorsk design entries, 1930. Map by the author, adapted from *Sovetskaia arkhitektura*, no. 3 (1933): 29.

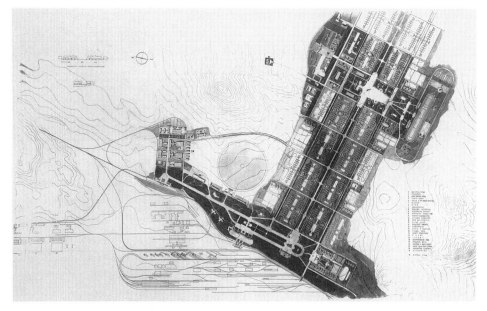

Figure 5.7. Black Square team *sotsgorod* plan, All-Union Open Design Competition for Magnitogorsk, 1930. 2nd prize (tie). Designers: F. B. Bialostotskaia, Z. Rozenfel′d, and B. Rozenfel′d. TsDAMLM Ukrainy, f. 8, po. 1, od. zb. 431, ark. 61.

drawing of the typical residential commune shows a bilaterally symmetrical design (figure 5.8). The long southeasterly park axis—one mirror line—runs through the middle of the scheme. Each of the two residential clusters stretched along the sides of the green spine is entered through a central communal building that marks the second mirroring axis. From the communal entry, residents move right or left through heated passageways to five five-story residential blocks oriented perpendicular to the communicating corridor. At the end of the sequence sits an educational building that once again faces the linear park. Detailed plans and sections explain the complex circulation of the typical residential building (figure 5.9). On the ground floor, a regular grid of slim columns holds most of the building off the ground to allow for open air passage beneath and between the residential bars. A large common stair in the main entryway brings residents up to a single-loaded corridor on the first residential floor. Pairs of shallow single-exposure sleeping cells at 8 and 9 square meters each—one room per worker, with a shared bathroom for

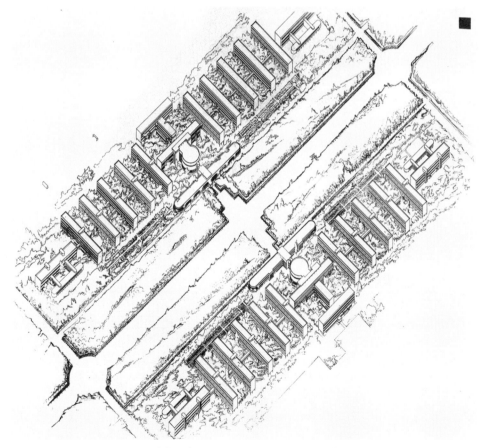

Figure 5.8. Black Square team *zhilkombinat* axonometric projection, All-Union Open Design Competition for Magnitogorsk, 1930. 2nd prize (tie). Designers: F. B. Bialostotskaia, Z. Rozenfel′d, and B. Rozenfel′d. TsDAMLM Ukrainy, f. 8, po. 1, od. zb. 431, ark. 68.

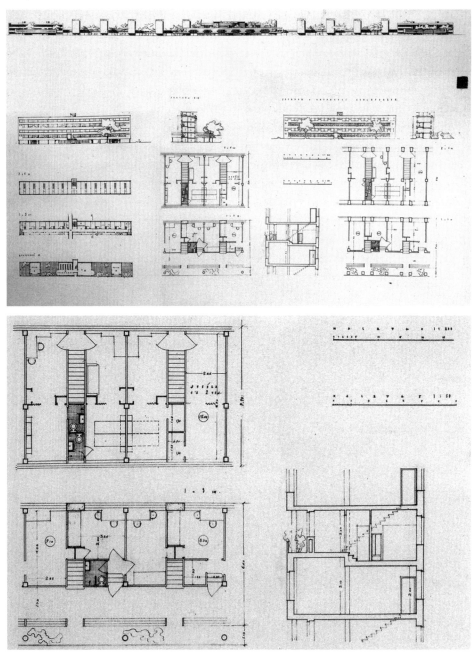

Figure 5.9. Black Square Team *zhilkombinat* elevation (top), residential building plans and sections (middle), and detail of paired skip-stop floors (bottom), All-Union Open Design Competition for Magnitogorsk, 1930. 2nd prize (tie). Designers: F. B. Bialostotskaia, Z. Rozenfel'd, and B. Rozenfel'd. TsDAMLM Ukrainy, f. 8, po. 1, od. zb. 431, ark. 52, 55.

the pair—are directly accessed from this second story hallway, as are narrow stairways that climb up to the second residential floor. Long double-exposure units on the second floor, each with its own toilet room, accommodate two people each in

15 square meters. There are no private kitchens in any of the units. The sequence repeats on the third and fourth residential floors. The clever circulation design, with a common corridor only every other floor, is a variation of the so-called skip-stop section that would have been well known to jury vice chair Miliutin who was by this time living in the penthouse of the skip-stop Narkomfin Building in Moscow, designed by his friend, Moisei Ginzburg.

The competition brief is richest in instruction for the residential commune, or *zhilkombinat*, and it is at this scale that the concentrated entries are most inventive. The axonometric drawing of the Three Lines team *zhilkombinat*, for instance, is detailed enough that it invites the viewer to inhabit the complex (figure 5.10). Residential, communal, and educational buildings, arranged in a dynamic zipper pattern, surround a park with a running track. Open spaces of various sizes, surfaces, and degrees of privacy nestle between the interlocked buildings. In the drawing, the edges of the complex bleed into planted open spaces on the east and west, while another identical residential commune sneaks into the frame at the southern edge to suggest a regular repeating pattern that is borne out on the large site plan (figure 5.11). Other site plans among this group, like that submitted by the Roman Numeral Five team, share similar organizational principles and aesthetics (figure 5.12). The Roman Numeral Five *zhilkombinat* is composed of thin,

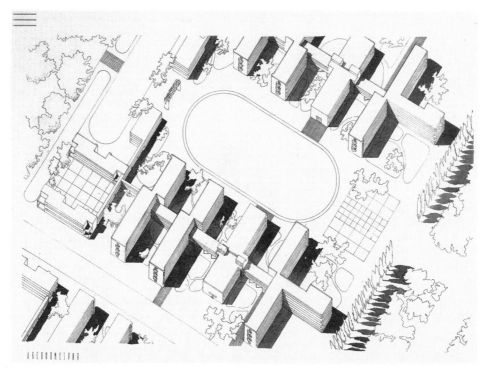

Figure 5.10. Three Lines Team *zhilkombinat* axonometric projection, All-Union Open Design Competition for Magnitogorsk, 1930. 3rd prize. Designers: R. Val'denberg, S. Leontovich, and D. Meerson. TsDAMLM Ukrainy, f. 8, po. 1, od. zb. 431, ark. 67.

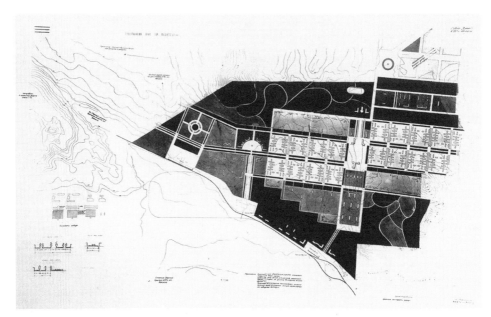

Figure 5.11. Three Lines Team *sotsgorod* plan, All-Union Open Design Competition for Magnitogorsk, 1930. 3rd prize. Designers: R. Val'denberg, S. Leontovich, and D. Meerson. TsDAMLM Ukrainy, f. 8, po. 1, od. zb. 431, ark. 63.

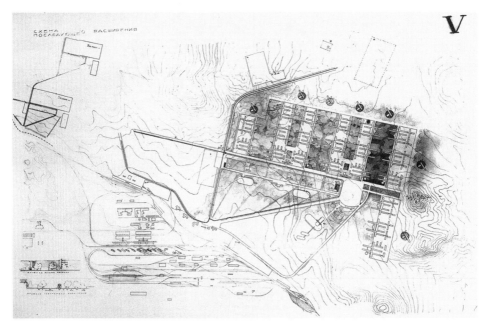

Figure 5.12. Roman Numeral Five Team *sotsgorod* plan, All-Union Open Design Competition for Magnitogorsk, 1930. 2nd prize (tie). Designers: R. Brilling with students of VKhTI: N. Gaicharov, M. Semenov, V. Armand, and V. Semenova. TsDAMLM Ukrainy, f. 8, po. 1, od. zb. 431, ark. 62.

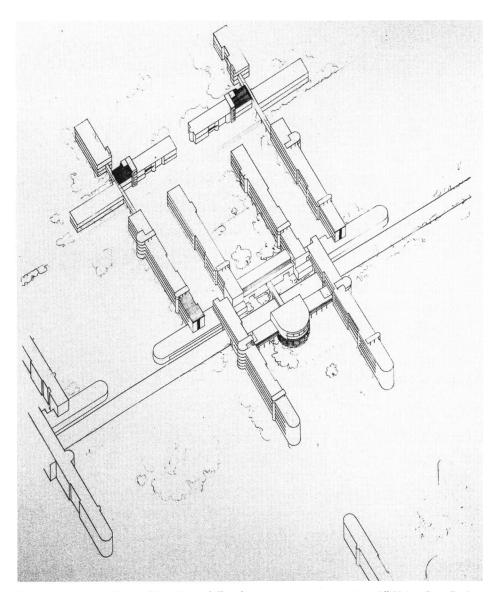

Figure 5.13. Roman Numeral Five Team *zhilkombinat* axonometric projection, All-Union Open Design Competition for Magnitogorsk, 1930. 2nd prize (tie). Designers: R. Brilling with students of VKhTI: N. Gaicharov, M. Semenov, V. Armand, and V. Semenova. TsDAMLM Ukrainy, f. 8, po. 1, od. zb. 431, ark. 69.

rectilinear housing bars with broad east-west faces that intersect—just barely—with perpendicular communal buildings (figure 5.13). A shared open space is captured between buildings connected by heated passageways. Dormitory schools for children of various ages fan out at the extremity of the composition and are surrounded by green space intended for gardening and animal husbandry.

The architectural and planning commonalities between these latter two submissions can be explained not only by their historical and professional context—the architectural language is redolent of Constructivism, ascendant in Moscow at the time—but equally by the brief itself. The programmatic requirements, population targets, four-story height cap, prerequisites of heated connections between all facilities, optimal east-west insolation, and small sleeping cells conspire to support programmatically articulated, insistently horizontal complexes of slim, linked buildings. The construction cost estimate required of each submission also forced designers to be cognizant of architectural economization. The buildings are rectilinear and aesthetically spare. The designers employed expressive rounded forms only where needed programmatically, for example in theater spaces. The brief proposed formal solutions through a combination of suggestion and requirement as similar competition entries confirm.

Although it was considered one of the most successful open entries, the jury found faults in the Black Square scheme that can be extrapolated to other concentrated city entries. At the urban scale, the jury resolved that the stretched (*rastianutaia*) planning of the socialist city created a "lengthy path between factory area and the institutions of public use, especially for the most distant residential communes on the opposite side of the city." The jury failed to note, or chose not to consider, that while a southeasterly-tending site plan at its most attenuated would preclude a walking commute for workers at the remote end (up to 4.7 kilometers away from the factory in the Black Square case), the fixed locations of Magnetic Mountain at the southern edge of the production zone, and the lake and river to the west, made more advantageous residential siting impossible. For the *zhilkombinat* design, the jury reprimanded the Black Square team for exceeding (by one floor) the four-floor height limit set by the brief. They speculated that the relatively open ground floor of the housing bars was inspired by Le Corbusier, whose technique to raise buildings on slim columns was "often used in recent competition work." The jury determined that there was little reason to utilize such a costly detail. Lastly, they expressed dislike of the "single residential commune type."[39] They were generally unsatisfied with the communes among the concentrated planning group because while they were "rational in terms of volume, they were extremely monotonous and did not address the question of insolation and the necessity for relief from such repetition."[40] The jury's censure against architectural monotony comes across as a particularly unjust critique when the submitted designs are checked against the competition brief. To design a plausible residential commune to accommodate many demographic categories and programs is a challenging task under the best of circumstances. With a six-week deadline and a city to plan besides, artful deployment of a single *zhilkombinat* design—as the competition brief requested—was all that could plausibly be expected from entrants. The jury's disappointment with the repetition of a single commune type reflects poorly on the competition instructions and timeline more than the results. But it also prompts an important urban design question that the Soviets would grapple with for the next sixty years, namely: what are the psychological limits of typological standardization? Baku's Armenikend test block of 1927 was deemed a successful exemplar for residential standardization, but that may have been because it was not, in fact, repeated. The Magnitogorsk competition designs, on the other hand, demonstrated in graphic form the potential aesthetic pitfalls of scaling up superblock standardization.

Visions of Dispersal and Freedom

The OSA and Stroikom design teams elected to abide neither by the suggestions nor the requirements of the competition brief. Instead, their linear planning proposals for Magnitogorsk follow disurbanist directives set out by Okhitovich, though OSA's proposal is closer to meeting the spirit of the residential commune requested in the brief than the Stroikom proposal.

The linear scheme proposed by the OSA Brigade originates at the production zone and stretches to the southeast like the concentrated schemes, but formal and conceptual similarities end there (figure 5.14). Whereas the concentrated entries accept the singular gravitation pull of the factory, the OSA design introduces a second pole of activity: a giant collective farm (*gigant-sovkhoz*) twenty-five kilometers to the southeast. The OSA design is an extraordinarily attenuated residential commune that links these industrial and agricultural production areas. A dramatic single-point aerial perspective illustrates the basic structure of the design (figure 5.15). The line of settlement is divided into three equal strips along its length; the width of these strips determines a regular cadence of lines scored in the perpendicular direction to create a perfectly square mega-grid, open and ready to accept a wide variety of programmatic and formal insertions. As Andrei Gozak notes, OSA's scheme is a "model of organization," an ideogram more than a resolved urban design proposal.[41] In the competition drawings and models, OSA's gridded blocks are filled with a mix of housing, cultural, and recreational facilities that include children's sectors, communications centers, and large-scale cultural and recreational facilities (figure 5.16). One repeated block holds low-rise residential buildings built of wood and glass arranged in a checkerboard pattern (*v shakhmatnom poriadke*) (figure 5.17). Both block and buildings imitate, at nesting scales, the grid of the site plan. Each typical checkerboard commune holds eight buildings with thirty-two residents each, for a total population of 256. Four-story square residential buildings hold stacked pairs of sleeping units in each corner and double-height shared spaces with common bath and shower facilities, an exercise room, and spaces for collective rest and cultural work. The height of these residential buildings, the size of the individual sleeping cells, the assortment of communal programs, and the relative density of the housing here are all in line with the requirements of the competition brief.

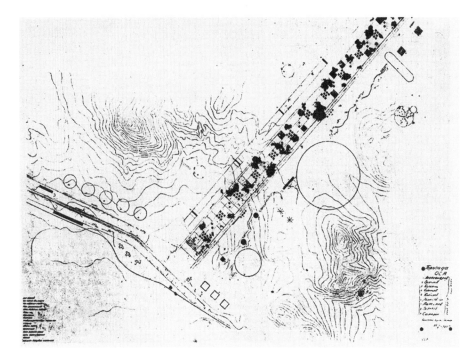

Figure 5.14. OSA Brigade *sotsgorod* plan, All-Union Open Design Competition for Magnitogorsk, 1930. Designers: I. Leonidov with P. Aleksandrov, A. Ermilov, S. Kibirev, G. P'iankov, S. Samarin, and Kuz'min, Kuznetsov, and Maksimov. *Sovremennaia arkhitektura*, no. 3 (1930), 1.

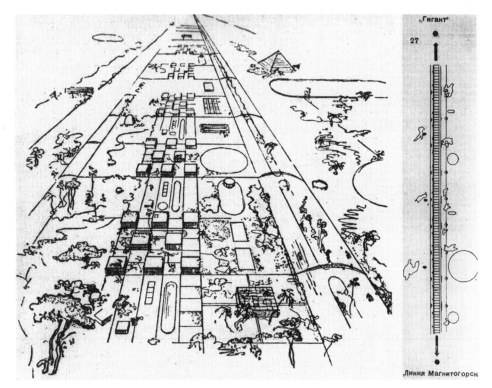

Figure 5.15. OSA Brigade perspective and diagram of the line of settlement, All-Union Open Design Competition for Magnitogorsk, 1930. Designers: I. Leonidov with P. Aleksandrov, A. Ermilov, S. Kibirev, G. P'iankov, S. Samarin, and Kuz'min, Kuznetsov, and Maksimov. *Sovremennaia arkhitektura*, no. 3 (1930), 3.

Figure 5.16. OSA Brigade model of the typical mega-grid block variations, All-Union Open Design Competition for Magnitogorsk, 1930. Designers: I. Leonidov with P. Aleksandrov, A. Ermilov, S. Kibirev, G. P'iankov, S. Samarin, and Kuz'min, Kuznetsov, and Maksimov. TsDAMLM Ukrainy, f. 8, po. 1, od. zb. 431, ark. 53.

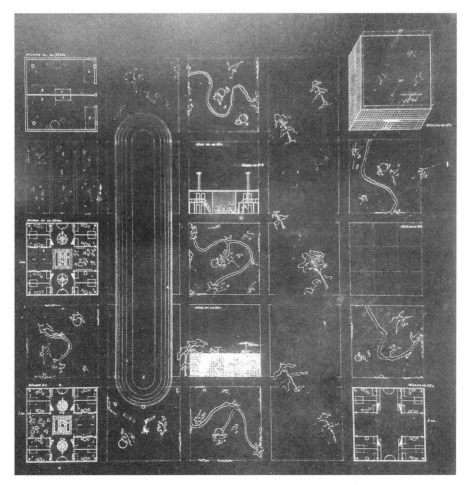

Figure 5.17. OSA Brigade model of the typical mega-grid block variations, All-Union Open Design Competition for Magnitogorsk, 1930. Designers: I. Leonidov with P. Aleksandrov, A. Ermilov, S. Kibirev, G. P'iankov, S. Samarin, and Kuz'min, Kuznetsov, and Maksimov. TsDAMLM Ukrainy, f. 8, po. 1, od. zb. 431, ark. 49.

The OSA submission exceeds the brief's four-story height limit many times over in a skyscraper (*neboskreb*) block that is most evident in perspective drawings of the project (figure 5.18). Using the same housing floor plan as the low-rise buildings, two twenty-eight-story residential towers meet the 256-person population target of the neighboring low-rise block while retaining more open space on the ground. This high-rise planning logic was well practiced by 1930. "Towers in the park" urban schemes like Le Corbusier's Ville Contemporaine (1922) and Plan Voisin (1925) were known to the Soviet architectural community in general, and members of OSA—Le Corbusier's primary interlocutors on his visits to Moscow—in particular. The planning merits of building tall were offset by Soviet technical and economic realities, however. Steel, the future fruit of the Magnitogorsk industrial complex, was a rare commodity in 1930, and one earmarked for industrial, not residential, construction.

While OSA's submission was original, spatially dynamic, and evocative, it was plagued by questions of feasibility. As the jury noted, municipal services, transportation, and communications would be difficult to supply in such an attenuated

61. ОБЩИЙ ВИД ПОСЕЛКА. НЕБОСКРЕБЫ.

OCA

Figure 5.18. OSA Brigade residential perspective, All-Union Open Design Competition for Magnitogorsk, 1930. Designers: I. Leonidov with P. Aleksandrov, A. Ermilov, S. Kibirev, G. P'iankov, S. Samarin and Kuz'min, Kuznetsov, and Maksimov. TsDAMLM Ukrainy, f. 8, po. 1, od. zb. 431, ark. 51.

development. In the journal *Stroitel'stvo Moskvy* (Moscow construction) the architect Nikolai Dokuchaev added a formal critique of the scheme when he asked, "how, in the random and chaotic distribution of the residential and communal buildings—which is interesting only as an image—are we supposed to see a novel solution to the socialist city, instead of just another village of some self-build dacha association?"[42] But it is precisely the open and readily transformable framework of the mega-grid that places this scheme in opposition to traditional fixed-goal general planning. The OSA scheme is a skeletal framework that allows for varied possibilities and transformation over time. It is, most important, an organizational infrastructure that welcomes the process of dispersal over large territories that Okhitovich called "disurbanization."

Okhitovich himself, joined by architects Mikhail Barshch, V. Vladimirov, and N. Sokolov, authored the linear Stroikom submission. Their general plan, titled "A New Resettlement of Mankind" (*novoe rasselenie chelovechestva*), is drawn at a scale much larger than the 1/5000 required by the competition brief because the scheme is premised on regional, not city, planning (figure 5.19).[43] The industrial production zone at the center is supported by multiple agricultural zones twenty-five kilometers or more remote from the factory complex. The roads to connect industry and agriculture are the lines along which diffuse settlement will develop. On the general plan and project diagrams, these eight settlement ribbons (*lenty*) register as dark lines that radiate from the southern shore of the industrial lake and the production zone. A long multi-sheet drawing describes the constituent elements of a typical ribbon (figure 5.20). An automotive road runs down the center of the sinuous line. A communal service building at each kilometer (the so-called kilometer station) holds a canteen, provisions store, library, barber/hair salon, garage, and two motorcycles for communal use. Nurseries, boarding schools, and public recreational facilities flank the station (figure 5.21).

Fine-grained organization in the Stroikom scheme is loose and driven by personal choice, in keeping with Okhitovich's philosophy that socialism leads to individual freedom. Each socialist citizen should have the right, explained the design team, "not only to impact the collective, but also to deepen work on himself. Not only to engage in public action, but also in concentrated thinking." The architectural vessel for introspective self-improvement is the stand-alone living cell (*zhilaia iacheika*), a single occupancy cube sitting on thin columns that looks out over the landscape (figure 5.22). Any citizen could build the simple and lightweight living cell using structural elements kept on hand at the kilometer station. Location, orientation, and proximity to other cells would be a matter of personal preference. As the diagrams and axonometric view reveal, the system does not preclude communal living. The cells can be constructed in clusters, rendering density and communality a choice in the Stroikom scheme. To underscore once and for all the conceptual distinction between urbanist proposals that force shared living in a single large structure and this disurbanist scheme of cellular units, the Stroikom team adopted the motto: "not a house-commune, but a commune of houses."[44]

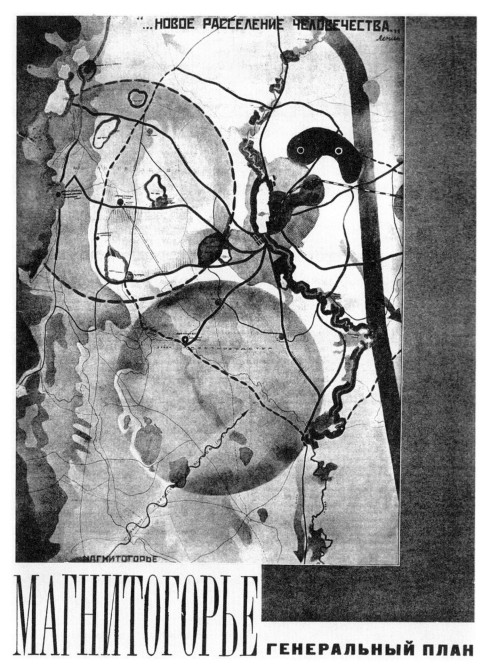

Figure 5.19. Stroikom RSFSR team general plan, All-Union Open Design Competition for Magnitogorsk, 1930. "New Resettlement of Mankind—Lenin." Designers: M. Barshch, V. Vladimirov, M. Okhitovich, and N. Sokolov. *Sovremennaia arkhitektura*, no. 1–2 (1930), 39.

Dokuchaev homed in on a common critique of the Stroikom scheme. "A little individual house [on stilts], with a personal auto beneath, is the authors' solution to the Leninist charge to create 'a new resettlement of mankind which destroys

Figure 5.20. Stroikom RSFSR team, typical resettlement ribbon plan, All-Union Open Design Competition for Magnitogorsk, 1930. Inscribed on the drawing are the maxims "End of the separation of city and countryside—Marx-Engels" and "End of the distinction between city and countryside—Marx-Engels." Designers: M. Barshch, V. Vladimirov, M. Okhitovich, and N. Sokolov. TsDAMLM Ukrainy, f. 8, po. 1, od. zb. 431, ark. 58.

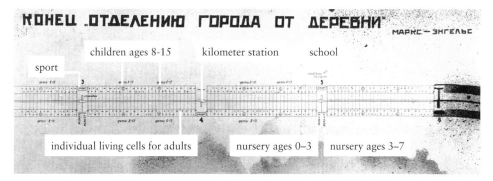

Figure 5.21. Stroikom RSFSR team, typical resettlement ribbon plan detail, All-Union Open Design Competition for Magnitogorsk, 1930. Designers: M. Barshch, V. Vladimirov, M. Okhitovich, and N. Sokolov. Diagram by the author based on TsDAMLM Ukrainy, f. 8, po. 1, od. zb. 431, ark. 57.

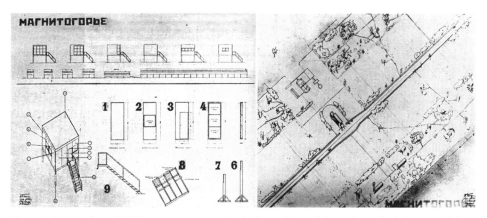

Figure 5.22. Stroikom RSFSR team, axonometric of urban scheme (left), and standard elements of the individual living cell (right), All-Union Open Design Competition for Magnitogorsk, 1930 Designers: M. Barshch, V. Vladimirov, M. Okhitovich, and N. Sokolov. *Sovremennaia arkhitektura*, no. 1–2 (1930), 44, 48.

rural backwardness and isolation, and the inhumane concentration of masses in the large cities.' Here, the little house is cut off from urban density, and the auto abolishes rural isolation. A truly 'genius' answer to the problem."[45] Dokuchaev's snide remarks aimed at Okhitovich's chief spatial principle of *"to every worker and laborer—his own space."*[46] In the socialist urbanism debates taking place

in Moscow at the end of 1929, there was a general consensus that collective living was the ultimate goal for Soviet society; only the timeline for and degree of
change was unresolved. The free-floating individual living cells designed by Stroikom for Magnitogorsk simply flew in the face of prevailing logic at the time. They
are not urban, dense, or collective. Further, the resonant image for the Stroikom
scheme—the stand-alone elevated box—looks and acts nothing like the residential commune requested in the competition brief or any of the other entries to
the competition. Sabsovich landed the most direct, if childish, hit against Stroikom's living cell by referring to it as an "izba on chicken legs" (izba na kur'ikh
nozhkakh).[47]

Surprisingly, the jury reacted more favorably to the rule-breaking submissions
than to those that met the brief's requirements. They declared that although linear
settlements were still untested in practice, the proposals' only significant defect
was their considerable length, for which "the issues of electrification, telephony,
and water supply would be difficult and expensive to resolve."[48] Linear settlement
systems and their housing types were, furthermore, "truly interesting and positive
ideas that fully answer Lenin's decree for the task of socialist settlement." And
although "not one made an entirely detailed design project for the city," the jury
nonetheless proposed that a small section of either the OSA or Stroikom design
be installed as an experiment in Magnitogorsk.[49] Both linear schemes do share a
common commitment to process over totalizing vision and to granular versus monumental construction. These characteristics made it possible for the jury to imagine
implanting one of the linear proposals as a seed project that could grow and be
tested with time.

What Now?

After all of the collaborative energy exerted by individuals and groups on both sides
of the Magnitogorsk competition—to craft the perfect brief, to design the model
settlement, to select the most promising vision for socialist urbanism—the results
were disappointingly inconclusive. The jury found that the submitted proposals
"did not fully satisfy the requirements of the competition brief, and further, that
among the total number of projects submitted, six did not satisfy the competition
requirements even on formal grounds." In addition, they determined that "all of the
projects proposed were unsatisfactory with regard to the socialization of everyday
services for the population." Based on this assessment, the jury opted not to award
a first-place prize. Two second-place awards were given, as well as a third- and two
fourth-place awards. In an apparent effort to temper their critique, the jury concluded that because Magnitogorsk was "the first experiment in constructing new
cities, the whole competition provided positive results which we will be able to use
in future studies."[50]

The jury's unenthusiastic response to the submissions meant that the competition was of no service to the residents of Magnitogorsk insofar as it yielded no officially endorsed project to construct. The Magnitostroi administration disregarded the jury's recommendation to implant a fragment of one of the linear schemes on site, and the concentrated city entries likewise remained on paper. Despite the competition organizers' and participating designers' best efforts, the socialist city of Magnitogorsk was no closer to being built in March 1930 than it had been in January.

The jury's prediction that the Magnitogorsk competition was a "first experiment" likely to prompt more theorizing, discussion, and (ultimately) construction was accurate, however. In his book *Sotsgorod*, published soon after the competition, vice chair of the jury, Nikolai Miliutin, rolled out his own urban model he called the Linear City.[51] He included in the book diagrams of the Black Square, OSA, and Stroikom schemes for the Magnitogorsk competition as close, but imperfect, predecessors to his model. His own proposal "for a plan according to the functional-assembly-line system" was a "correction" of the plans of OSA and Stroikom and was "devoid of their shortcomings" (figure 5.23).[52] Miliutin's version runs north-south along the left bank of the lake. The program is distributed in strict linear bands starting with the Ural River, followed by a park, a residential sector, a green buffer, and finally the industrial zone, which is bordered at the far eastern edge by a rail line. Members of the jury were strictly forbidden from participating

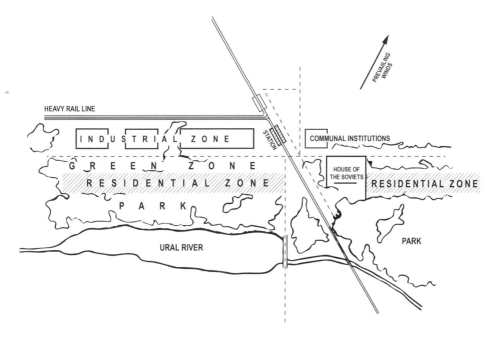

Figure 5.23. A site plan diagram for a linear city at Magnitogorsk, Nikolai Miliutin, 1930. Diagram by the author based on N. A. Miliutin, *Sotsgorod: Problema stroitel'stva sotsialisticheskikh gorodov* (Moscow: Gosudarstvennoe izdatel'stvo, 1930), 28.

in the competition even as consultants, so this scheme was purely speculative and designed after the fact.[53] Its purpose seems to have been to introduce readers to the idealized linear city model as tested on a well-known site recently covered in detail by the Soviet press.

In 1931, the German architect Ernst May, generally a proponent of linear planning, dismissed Miliutin's speculative proposal for Magnitogorsk. By then, May had learned for himself that topographical and industrial conditions on the site prohibited a clean linear solution like Miliutin's. May wrote that "quite obviously, the linear city is to a large extent influenced by local geographical conditions. For instance, Miliutin's proposal would not work for the city of Magnitogorsk, simply because the terrain there is restricted by the fourteen-kilometer-long dam on the one side and the iron-ore mountain on the other, thus precluding any kind of parallel development."[54] The competition entrants, and eventually May, came to understand that physical realities stood in the way of easy solutions. Magnitogorsk was not at all a tabula rasa site. Contextual conditions would drive the city's design.

Did the Magnitogorsk competition brief, the primary instaurational text of the first Five-Year Plan, act as a mechanism for generating built space? Yes, and no. Yes, because from its opening operational principles to its concluding salvo of detailed requirements, the brief sparked the pivotal creative task of the first Five-Year Plan, namely the formulation of a buildable, replicable model socialist urban form. It conjured an image of future socialist space in the mind's eye before pencil was put to paper through its treatise-like framework of ground rules and utopian-ready set of architectonic details. The competition designs that resulted from the brief, especially the concentrated city examples, share remarkable organizational and formal similarities because the text specifically directed the creative work. No, because despite the creative output that resulted from the text, the competition did not generate actual built space on the site for which it was written.

Unlike Baku, and Kharkiv to come, where on-the-ground research and construction led to real-time development of new design processes, urban relationships, and architectural forms, the socialist city competition for Magnitogorsk was largely an intellectual project. Magnitogorsk prompted more theoretical and less material activity than the other two sites for a number of reasons, but perhaps most saliently for the prosaic facts of geographical distance and intensity of the industrial construction project. Because it was so remote—over four days from Moscow by train—few of the officials or designers charged to plot its future set foot on the site. This distance permitted the material fact of the Magnitogorsk *sotsgorod* to be deferred in favor of its conceptual potential. In addition, the factory complex was perpetually siphoning funding, workers, and materials from the residential quarter.

Although the gap between intellectual work and actual construction was undoubtedly a tribulation for the workers living in substandard housing on the Ural steppe, it would be unjust to brand the theory generated in the name of Magnitogorsk a failure. If we choose to characterize the All-Union competition brief as an instaurational text—the purpose of which was to stimulate the development of model spatial solutions—it is possible to judge the competition positively, even though it produced no winning scheme. The text did drive the development of urban and architectural types by the next round of designers hired to solve the Magnitogorsk *sotsgorod*: the Soviet architect Sergei Chernyshev and the German architect Ernst May.

6

FRANKFURT ON THE STEPPE

Are you convinced then that Magnitogorsk is a city? A big city, even though
much of it is still in wooden barracks? And that to build this city alone was no
small problem? But—the city of Magnitogorsk is only incidental. It is, in essence,
still mainly a construction camp, whose purpose is to erect the Magnitogorsk
steel mill. This gives an idea of the magnitude of the steel mill that needs such a
city to build it.

—Anna Louise Strong (1931)

Through the winter of 1929, life for the growing population at
Magnitogorsk proceeded, albeit uncomfortably. Workers on site might have been
aware that the important All-Union Design Competition to design their future
quarters was taking place through reportage in the local newspaper *Magnitogorsk
Worker* (*Magnitogorskii rabochii*), which began publication on January 1, 1930.
They may also have guessed that the inconclusive results of the competition signaled an extension of makeshift housing conditions.[1] As the English-language
Moscow News reported almost two years later, the city was "in essence, still
mainly a construction camp."

Despite the absence of comprehensive planning, Magnitogorsk continued to
expand. The site held 40,000 people in September 1930. By December, the population stood at 60,000 residents, a number already well in excess of the competition
brief's long-term maximum population of 50,000. By mid-1932, one contemporary account estimated that there were 200,000 people living on site in temporary barracks and dugouts.[2] The designs submitted to the All-Union Open Design
Competition for Magnitogorsk had concerned the construction of a conceptual
apparatus for model socialist city-building. By any measure, Magnitogorsk met

the demographic threshold of "city" by mid-1930, though it remained far from a model socialist one.

The postcompetition months involved the efforts of two designers, Sergei Chernyshev and Ernst May. Chernyshev, the Moscow architect whose previous plan for the city was maligned by Miliutin in 1929, returned to design Magnitogorsk in September 1930. German architect May, the former director of the Municipal Planning Department in Frankfurt am Main who oversaw the design and construction of 15,000 new housing units in that city, began development of a general plan and housing for Magnitogorsk a month later. Each architect was hired by a different client, and their projects overlapped and conflicted. A second competition between these two architects forced both clients and designers to engage in late-breaking, on-the-ground praxis.

Foreign architects who worked for the Soviet government during the first Five-Year Plan, like May, faced unprecedented economic, technological, and theoretical conditions that precluded direct importation of architectural and planning models from the West. Over the period of their consultancy, from 1930 to 1933, the building typologies (and resolve) imported from Germany by May and his architectural brigade were bent to the particulars of Soviet conditions, as the narrative of their design work for the city of Magnitogorsk reveals. An experimental urban block known as the Kirov District remains in Magnitogorsk as material testament to that architectural exchange.

Shifting Priorities

A seismic shift in Soviet sociospatial theory was already underway in the months following the Magnitogorsk competition. Newspaper columns devoted to the socialist city debate had petered out by mid-1930, and on May 16, the Central Committee of the Communist Party (Vsesoiuznaia kommunisticheskaia partiia bol'shevikov or VKPb) issued a "Resolution on the work to restructure *byt*," that unequivocally communicated the Soviet leadership's position that the socialist urbanism debate was over. The resolution opened with critique, noting that "along with the growth of a movement toward a socialist *byt*, extremely unreasonable semi-fantastic schemes exist. It is therefore extremely harmful to individual comrades (Yu. Larin, Sabsovich, et al.) to attempt in 'one jump' to clear those obstacles to the socialist reconstruction of *byt* which are rooted . . . in the country's economic and cultural backwardness." Sabsovich was reproached by name—he was on the outs. His proposals for swift and total refashioning of daily life were suddenly deemed "semi-fantastic," and unsupportable by the USSR's most powerful political executives.

Economic realities explain the Central Committee's change of tune. As the price tag for heavy industry construction escalated, "soft" construction projects like housing, communal services, and cultural and recreational facilities slipped down the State's list of priorities, as the resolution made clear:

> We need to focus maximum resources on the rapid industrialization of the country at this moment, which creates real material preconditions for a radical remaking of *byt*. Projects to redevelop existing cities and construct new ones [that] have appeared recently in the press . . . are intended to be funded exclusively by the state, with immediate and complete socialization of all aspects of the working people's *byt*: food, housing, education of children with separation from their parents, elimination of domestic bonds between family members, an administrative ban on cooking, and so on. The implementation of these harmful, utopian undertakings, which do not consider the material resources of the country and the degree of preparedness of the population, would lead to an enormous waste of resources and a brutal discrediting of the idea of the socialist transformation of *byt* altogether.[3]

The Central Committee's resolution dispensed with vision, and instead stressed the paucity of state resources and the intractability of the populace. If the first Five-Year Plan was to meet its stated targets, state resources would be funneled to heavy industry, full stop. Complete socialization of *byt* was impossible—the economics did not work. Even more problematic than funding shortfall, the resolution claimed, was theoretical overextension. The "utopian" schemes of Sabsovich did not take into account the "preparedness of the population," which is another way of saying that these schemes ignored the transitional nature of Soviet society. Nadezhda Krupskaia, who had waged a similar critique in the previous months, was vindicated.

The remainder of the resolution was a list of action items that confirmed the closure of the debate. The Central Committee gave the Sovnarkom fifteen days to develop rules for the construction of workers' settlements and residential buildings in newly built and existing cities and towns. These guidelines, which echo design instructions in the Magnitogorsk competition brief in many ways, include accommodation for some communal services to support the transition to a socialist *byt*. The Central Committee stipulated that new workers' settlements at large enterprises (like Stalingradstroi, Dniprostroi, Magnitostroi, Cheliabstroi) would be separated from the industrial zone by a sufficiently wide green axis, and that roads, means of communication, and municipal infrastructure like water, electricity, canteens, clubs, schools, and medical care must be provided. Maximum hygiene and convenience would be ensured, and measures taken to reduce the price of construction. The resolution also sought to stave off administrative dysfunction. All party organizations were instructed to ensure "maximum resource mobilization" for

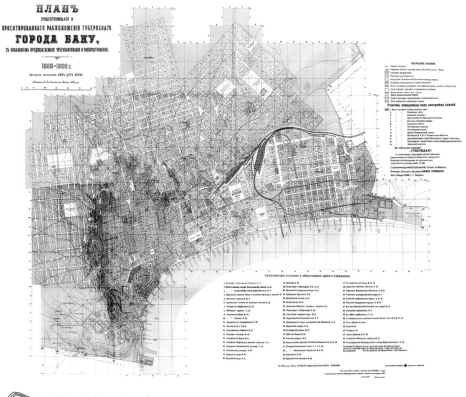

Mountainous terrain

Municipal boundary

Built-out plot

Empty plot

Transcaucasian State Railroad right of way

Cemeteries, existing and proposed

Portions of buildings that depart from street regulations

Existing piers and wooden structures

Transcaucasian State Railroad line

Horse-drawn tram line

Gardens and boulevards, existing and proposed

Portion of the city's profitable land

Plate 1. A plan for the City of Baku, Azerbaijan, 1898. Planner: Nikolaus von der Nonne. Library of Congress, Geography and Map Division, G7144.B2 1900. F6 1992 MLC. CC-PD-Mark. Key diagram by the author.

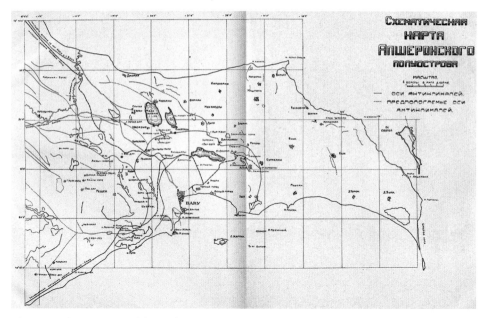

Plate 2. A schematic map of the Apsheron Peninsula. Red lines trace the anticline axes, geological folds along which oil and gas drilling is most productive. Azneft, *Obzor Azerbaidzhanskoi neftianoi promyshlennosti za dva goda nationalizatsii: 1920–1922* (Baku: Azneft, 1922).

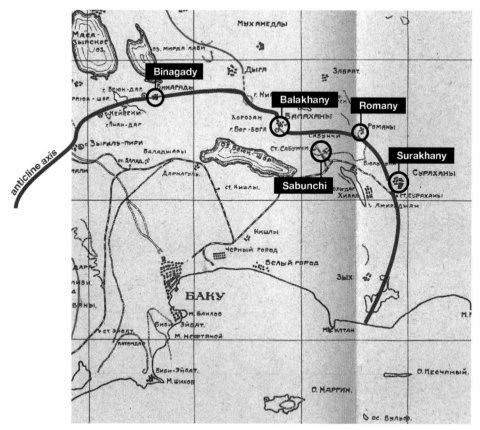

Plate 3. Map detail showing the location of pre-Soviet worker villages that sit directly on the cherished fault line. Diagram by the author based on the map in Azneft, *Obzor Azerbaidzhanskoi neftianoi promyshlennosti za dva goda nationalizatsii: 1920–1922* (Baku: Azneft, 1922).

Дом отдыха для детей нефтеработников в Белом городе

Plate 4. House of rest for the children of oil workers in the White Town, Baku. Azneft, *Obzor Azerbaidzhanskoi neftianoi promyshlennosti za dva goda nationalizatsii: 1920–1922* (Baku: Azneft, 1922), 265.

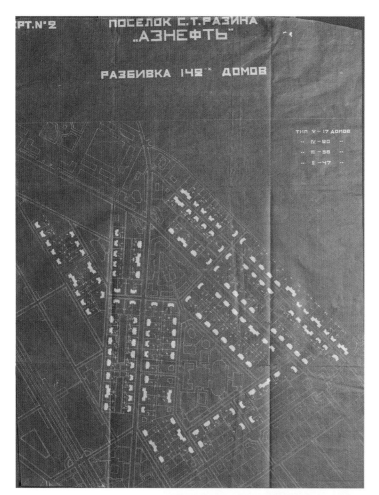

Плате 5. Site plan of the 142 houses planned for the first phase of construction in the Azneft Stepan Razin settlement, 1925. Planners: Aleksandr Ivanitskii, Viktor Vesnin, Leonid Vesnin, et al. RGALI, f. 2991, o. 1, d. 17, l. 10.

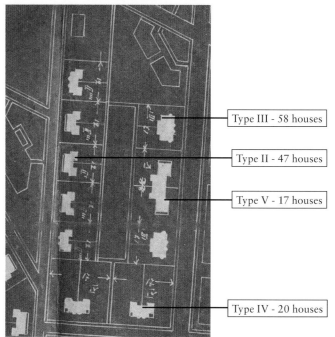

Type III - 58 houses

Type II - 47 houses

Type V - 17 houses

Type IV - 20 houses

Плате 6. A detailed plan of the four primary worker housing types and their quantities planned for the first phase of construction in Azneft's Stepan Razin settlement, 1925. Planners: Aleksandr Ivanitskii, Viktor Vesnin, Leonid Vesnin, et al. Diagram by the author based on RGALI, f. 2991, o. 1, d. 17, l. 10.

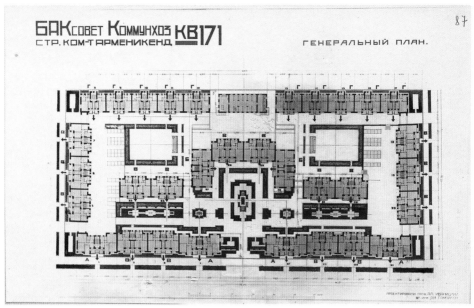

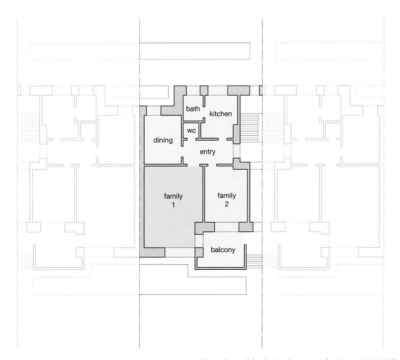

БАКсовет Коммунхоз KB171
СТР. КОМ-Т АРМЕНИКЕНД ■ 171   ГЕНЕРАЛЬНЫЙ ПЛАН.

Armenikend Test Block 171	Approved unit mix	Living norms + dimensions
3-story buildings	Type A (3-room/2-family, 27.5%): 48 units	240 s.m. average / unit
174 apartments	Types Б/В (2-room/2-family, 45%): 78 units	138 s.m. / family
300 families	Type Г (1-room/1-family, 27.5%): 48 units	7.6 s.m. / person
shared laundry building		22.8 cu.m. / person
playgrounds + garden plots		51 s.m. open space / person

Plate 7. Armenikend Test Block (Block 171), Baku, Azerbaijan, 1927. Architects: Aleksandr Ivanitskii, Anatolii Samoilov, et al. RGALI, f.2991, o.1, d.17, l.87. Detailed information about the block, unit numbers, and mix from ARDA, f. 1933, o. 1, d. 353, ll. 29–37.

Plate 8. Apartment Type B, a two-room unit, Armenikend test block, Baku, Azerbaijan, 1927. These units were shared by two families, each of whom were given a single private room. Gathering and utility spaces were communal (in blue). Identical Type B units are mirrored on both sides. Architects: Aleksandr Ivanitskii, Anatolii Samoilov, et al. Drawing by the author based on RGALI, f. 2991, o. 1, d. 17, l. 87.

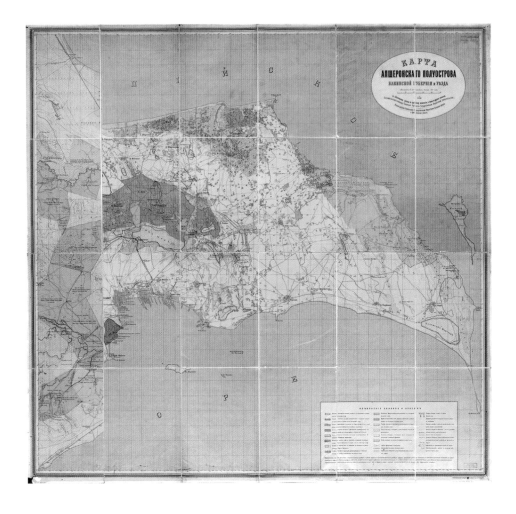

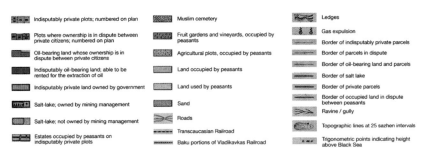

	Indisputably private plots; numbered on plan		Muslim cemetery	Ledges
	Plots where ownership is in dispute between private citizens; numbered on plan		Fruit gardens and vineyards, occupied by peasants	Gas expulsion
	Oil-bearing land whose ownership is in dispute between private citizens		Agricultural plots, occupied by peasants	Border of indisputably private parcels
	Indisputably oil-bearing land; able to be rented for the extraction of oil		Land occupied by peasants	Border of parcels in dispute
	Indisputably private land owned by government		Land used by peasants	Border of oil-bearing land and parcels
	Salt-lake; owned by mining management		Sand	Border of salt lake
	Salt-lake; not owned by mining management		Roads	Border of private parcels
	Estates occupied by peasants on indisputably private plots		Transcaucasian Railroad	Border of occupied land in dispute between peasants
			Baku portions of Vladikavkas Railroad	Ravine / gully
				Topographic lines at 25 sazhen intervals
				Trigonometric points indicating height above Black Sea

Plate 9. Map of the Apsheron Peninsula in the Baku Governate, 1899. Zemlemier Dmitriev and Kartograficheskoe Zavedenie A. Il'ina, *Karta Apsheronskago poluostrova Bakinskoi gubernii i uiezda: s oboznacheniem granits po sudebnomy mezhevaniiu, a takzhe i drugikh sviedienii* (Baku: Bakinskoe upravlenie gosudarstvennykh imushchestv, 1899). Library of Congress, Geography and Map Division, G7142.A6G46 1899. D5. Key diagram by the author.

Plate 10. Replanning the City of Baku photo series, documenting the removal of houses along Iur'evskaia Street on July 5, 1928. The elevated vantage point captures the Nagornoe Plateau's character before the street was "punched through." Photo: L. Bregadze. RGALI, f. 2991, o. 1, d. 17, l. 125.

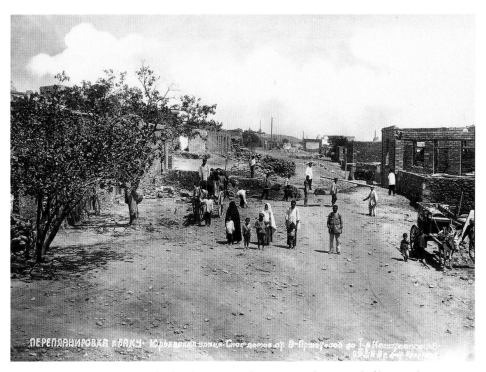

Plate 11. Replanning the City of Baku photo series, documenting the removal of houses along Iur'evskaia Street on July 5, 1928. The photographer often posed his human subjects to mark the scale of intervention. Photo: L. Bregadze. RGALI, f. 2991, o. 1, d. 17, l. 123.

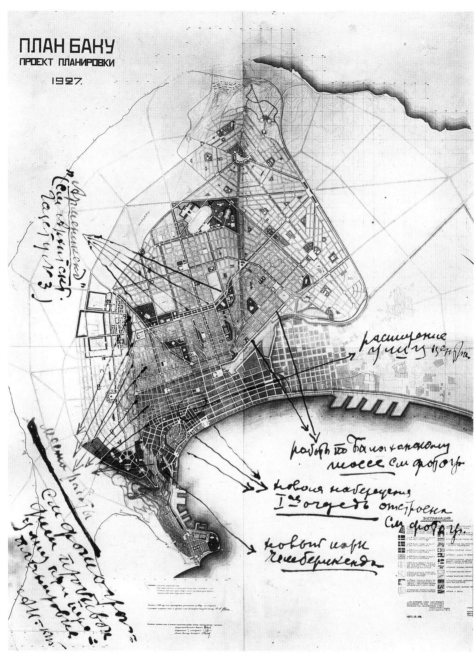

Plate 12. Baku Plan with Ivanitskii's hand notations, 1927. Read clockwise from the lower left-hand corner: *places of work [Iur'evskaia]—see photographs of the street punch-through from the replanning—A.I.-skii -; "Armenikend" see [unclear] Newspaper, no. 3; widening of the street in the center; work on Balakhanskoe shosse—see photo; work on the seafront boulevard, 1st phase completed—see photo; new park in Chemberekend.* Planners: Aleksandr Ivanitskii, et al. RGALI, f. 2991, o. 1, d. 17, l. 115.

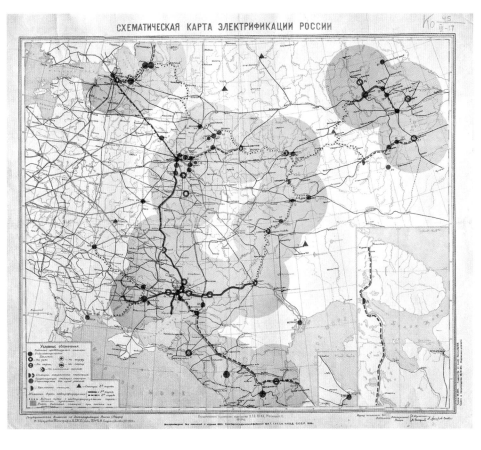

СХЕМАТИЧЕСКАЯ КАРТА ЭЛЕКТРИФИКАЦИИ РОССИИ

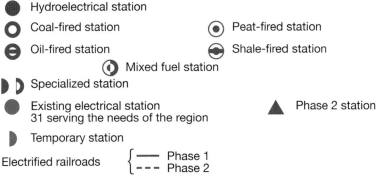

Hydroelectrical station

Coal-fired station

Peat-fired station

Oil-fired station

Shale-fired station

Mixed fuel station

Specialized station

Existing electrical station
31 serving the needs of the region

Phase 2 station

Temporary station

Electrified railroads { — Phase 1
--- Phase 2

•••• Waterways with electrified transshipment points

Area of electrical service when plan fully developed

Plate 13. GOELRO Plan for the Electrification of Russia, 1920. Planners: Gosplan USSR. RGB/KGR Ko 45/III-17. Key diagram by the author.

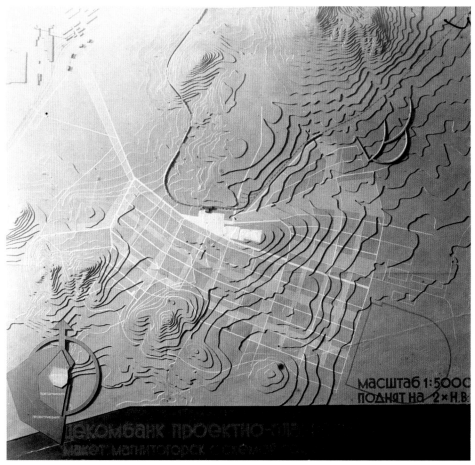

масштаб 1:5000
поднят на 2 × н.в.

декомбанк проектно-пла
макет: магнитогорск

Plate 14. A topographical model of the Left Bank socialist settlement scheme, Magnitogorsk, Russia, 1930. Architects: Tsekombank / Ernst May Brigade. The bowed shape of the housing area is explained by its location between the mine and industrial lake to the north and a row of hills to the south. MUAR, Negative VII-572.

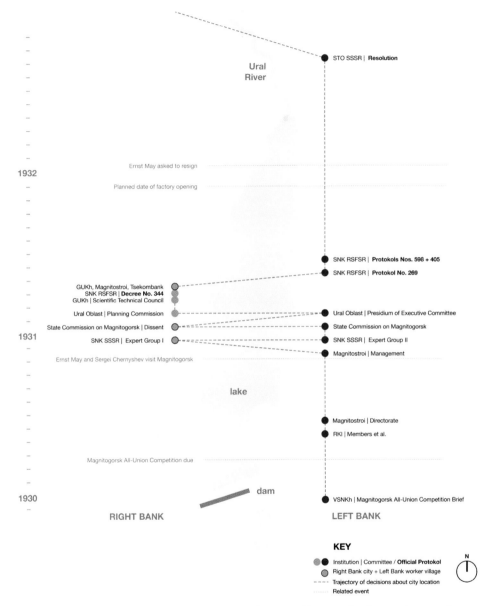

Plate 15. A spatio-temporal map of decisions about the optimal location for the socialist city of Magnitogorsk, 1930–33. From November 1930 to June 1931, the location of the city shifted between the left and right banks seven times. Graphic by the author based primarily on the Magnitogorsk timeline for 1929–1932 at GARF, f. A-314, o. 1, d. 7667, ll. 184–92.

Plate 16. Kirov District "sectional housing," Magnitogorsk, Russia, 1931–34. Architects: Standartgorproekt / Ernst May Brigade. Photo by the author, 2013.

Plate 17. Kirov District INKO-A type housing, Magnitogorsk, Russia, 1931–34. Architects: Standartgorproekt / Ernst May Brigade. Photo by the author, 2013.

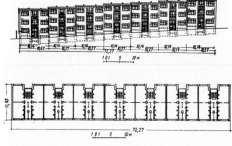

58. Жилые дома боковых зон квартала № 1 соцгорода. Внутриквартальный проезд, фасад и план типового этажа

Plate 18. Kirov District INKO-A type housing elevation (top) and plan (bottom), Magnitogorsk, Russia, 1931–34. Architects: Standartgorproekt / Ernst May Brigade. V.I. Kazarinova, *Magnitogorsk: Opyt sovetskoi arkhitektury* (Moscow: Gos. izd. lit. po stroitel'stvu, arkhitekture i stroit. materialam, 1961), 152.

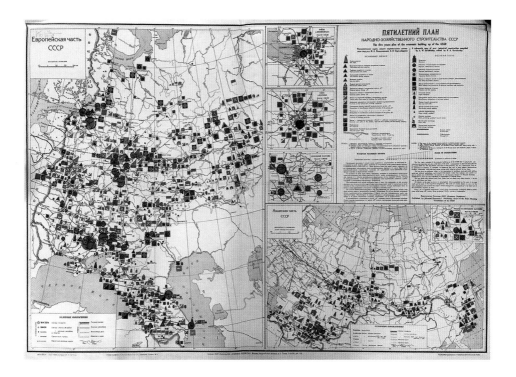

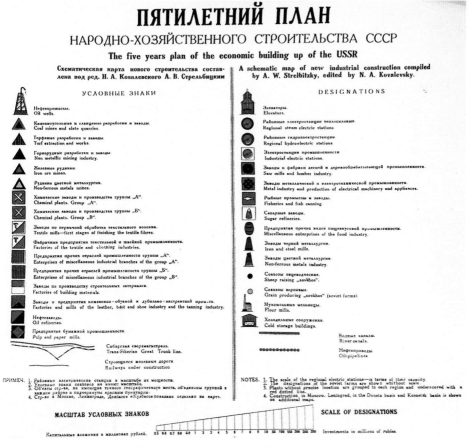

Plate 19. The Five-Year Plan of Economic Development of the USSR map (top) and key detail (bottom), 1930. Planners: Gosplan USSR (Moscow: Izdatel'stvo planovoe khozaistvo, 1930). RGB/KGR Ko 46/VII-37.

Plate 20. A plan of potential sites for the Kharkiv Tractor Factory, 1929. Report author: Ukrgipromez. The plan shows the city boundary of Kharkiv (hatched) plus major roads and rail lines radiating from the center. Ten potential factory sites are indicated by white rectangles. Losevo, a preexisting station stop on the southeast heavy rail line out of the city (far right), and largest site by far, was ultimately chosen. TsDAMLM Ukrainy, f. 8, po. 1, od. zb. 259, ark. 32.

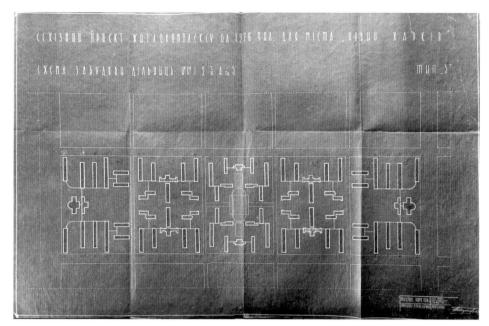

Plate 21. A draft site plan for residential complexes (*zhilkombinaty/zhilkompleksy*) for 1,276 people, New Kharkiv *sotsgorod*, Kharkiv, Ukraine, 1931. Architects: Pavel Aleshin, et al. TsDAMLM Ukrainy, f. 8, po. 1, od. zb. 260, ark. 166.

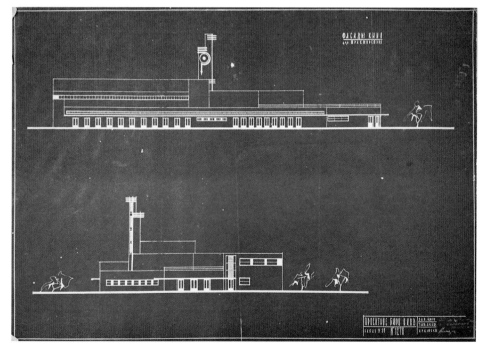

Plate 22. Cinema elevations, New Kharkiv *sotsgorod*, Kharkiv, Ukraine, 1931. Architects: NKVD Design Bureau, Ukraine. Derzhavna naukova arkitekturno-budivel'na biblioteka imeni V.G. Zabolotnogo.

Plate 23. Armenikend Test Block, Baku, Azerbaijan, in the bottom two images, compared to the prerevolutionary city, above. *USSR in Construction*, no. 12 (1931). Houghton Library, Harvard University.

Plate 24. Magnitogorsk issue, with Viktor Kalmykov, "young rural fellow" (*molodoi derevenskii paren'*), arriving to work on the factory's construction. *USSR in Construction*, no. 1 (1932). Magnitogorskii kraevedcheskii muzei.

residential construction, and trade union organizations were tasked "to take urgent measures to streamline and strengthen the financial restructuring of *byt*."[4] Lastly, the Central Committee proposed that Vesenkha immediately expand production of equipment for factory-kitchens, mechanized laundries, and so on, and consider increasing funding for *byt*-restructuring projects in the coming year.

Although ostensibly a resolution to support the restructuring of *byt*, the document reads as censure. After months of vigorous and wide-ranging discussions, the Central Committee intervened in the socialist urban debate to prohibit radical changes to the everyday life of workers and make clear that funding for the expensive undertaking was not forthcoming. What did this mean for Magnitogorsk? Just three days after *Pravda* published the resolution, 14,000 workers laid the foundation for the first blast furnace for the Magnitogorsk Iron and Steel Works.[5] The construction of the factory was underway, the first Five-Year Plan clock was ticking, and a city—visionary or not—still did not exist. The time had come to call in experienced planning experts who would blinker themselves to the chaos surrounding the socialist urbanism debate and simply produce housing.

German Housing: Standardization, Economization, and Efficiency

Back in the fall of 1927, a delegation of Soviet officials engaged in solving the housing crisis embarked on a month-long business trip to tour new worker housing settlements (*siedlungen*) in Germany.[6] Representatives from both Azneft and the Azerbaijani Vesenkha were among the group, traveling westward to see the fruits of German industrial housing construction at the same time Aleksandr Ivanitskii was completing the 1927 Baku Plan in his Moscow office. Thanks to Ivanitskii, Azneft representatives were uniquely positioned to advocate for architectural standardization. Less than two years before, hundreds of oil worker housing units were built in record time using a limited number of types in the garden-settlement of Stepan Razin. This mid-1920s success in Baku was an outlier in the Soviet sphere, however. The Germans were irrefutably ahead in the housing game in terms of quality and quantity of housing units produced thanks to industrialized construction techniques. Soviet housing officials on the 1927 tour were especially interested in how the Germans mass produced large architectural elements like pumice stone slabs and shipped them to building sites that were prepped to receive them. The report from the tour noted that "thanks to such slabs, construction [of the twenty-five-unit houses at Frankfurt am Main's Praunheim *siedlung*] takes just seventeen days and requires very few workers to complete."[7] The delegates concluded that in a command economy like the Soviet Union, architectural standardization would have an even greater reach and impact than in Germany. The group also toured the "Die Wohnung" Housing Exhibition (better known as the *Weißenhofsiedlung*) in Stuttgart, a full-scale experiment for prefabricated modern housing types. The Soviet delegation was photographed in front of architect Max Taut's round-edged housing prototype and Josef Frank's duplex, with Mies van der Rohe's multiunit apartment building in the deep background (figure 6.1).

The fact that many of the German settlements they toured were built under socialist administrations made the architectural ideas, forms, and techniques easier for Soviet officials to justify transferring. In Berlin-Britz, the delegation toured the Hufeisen Siedlung (1925–33), the so-called horseshoe settlement, designed by architects Bruno Taut and Martin Wagner. The project, still under construction during their visit, was developed by the "Gehag," Germany's largest building cooperative funded largely by socialist trade unions and run by a majority socialist administration. Walter Gropius's Siedlung Törten (1927), also visited, was built with the support of a Democratic Party mayor and Socialist Party officials of the city of Dessau.[8] Gropius gave the group a personal tour of Törten, the Bauhaus, and his private house. Members of the Soviet delegation were notably starstruck in the presence of the Bauhaus director, who was "well known to Soviet builders as an innovator-architect."[9]

The Soviet housing experts reserved their most effusive praise for the projects built in Frankfurt am Main under mayor Ludwig Landmann (a Democrat supported

Рис 1· Экскурсанты на выставке „Die Wohnung" в Штутгарте 18 сентября 1927 г.

Слева направо: Андреев, Н. В., Волков, Н. А., Саркисов, В. С., Герасев, А. Я., Гриссик, М. Я., Новак, А. О., Новиков, С. А., Виганд, К. П., Равлин, Д. П., Член Выставочного Управления арх. Schmidsrauter, член Штутгартского магистрата Müllerschon, Кулябко, В. Г., Суханов, Г. Н., Воробьев, Г. П., Управляющий выставкой „Die Wohnung" Carl Hagstotz и секретарь выставки.

Figure 6.1. Excursion of Soviet housing experts to the "Die Wohnung" Housing Exhibition (*Weißenhofsiedlung*). Stuttgart, Germany, September 18, 1927. S. N. Nakhmanson et al., *Sovremennoe stroitel'stvo Germanii: Pervaia zagranichnaia ekskursiia inzhenirov-stroitelei i arkhitektorov* (Moscow: Gostekhizdat, 1929), 10.

by the Socialist Party) and his chosen architect-planner, May. Landmann was a politician deeply invested in large-scale planning. In 1917, as an assemblyman, he advocated establishing a housing department in Frankfurt that would address "in a uniform way all questions of urban planning having regard for economic, legal, cultural, and artistic aspects within the framework of a major program."[10] When he became mayor of the city in 1924, he hired May to lead this comprehensive physical-economic-social planning effort. Landmann granted May extraordinary powers in the position of Frankfurt's Director of Municipal Planning from 1924 to 1930. In this period May created a general plan for the city that checked unruly growth and charted out future interventions; directed all municipal building projects; oversaw design of all new public housing; ran the city's largest building society; supervised building code officials; and adjudicated all applications for municipal and federal building loans.[11] May exerted such complete control over Frankfurt's built environment during his tenure that he was, effectively, overseer of a total planning effort on the municipal scale. His absolute administrative power did not translate to fiscal profligacy, however. From 1925 to 1928, May's office was the broker for approximately 26 million marks per year for settlement design and construction.[12] This fixed budget functioned similarly to early Soviet control figures, keeping expenditures for capital construction on a flat line and encouraging economization. Denser site planning, more efficient construction techniques, and ascetic architectural detailing yielded more housing units with the allotted funding. Increasingly, May's office practiced spatial economization within the unit designs as well, to build apartments that the workers could afford in a depressed economy. Between 1926 and 1929, the average new four-room apartment built in Frankfurt am Main shrank from ninety-four to seventy-five square meters.[13] Once his *siedlungen* were underway and deemed a success May went on a promotional speaking tour that included a lecture titled: "Oh! If I were in charge of town planning with an unlimited budget!!"[14] The lecture both highlighted his finished projects' frugality and imagined a future in which such penny-pinching would not be necessary.

May's work tacked between "establishment" planning and avant-garde architecture. He is like Ivanitskii and Pavel Aleshin (the architect featured in the Kharkiv story to come), a figure who defies easy categorization. According to Corinne Jaquand, May was the only active member of both IFHTP (The International Federation for Housing and Planning, founded in 1913 by the garden city theorist, Ebenezer Howard) and CIAM (Congrès Internationaux d'Architecture Moderne, the International Congresses of Modern Architecture, founded in 1928 by Le Corbusier, Sigfried Giedion, and others), two organizations that rarely saw eye to eye aesthetically or ideologically.[15] May's investment in the garden city movement stems from his 1910 apprenticeship to Raymond Unwin, whom he assisted with designs for Hampstead Garden Suburb, a satellite town north of London. Two particular recommendations from *Town Planning in Practice*, Unwin's book that May helped to translate into German in 1910, were taken by May into his Frankfurt projects: decentralization and cooperative service provision.[16] First, May located his new settlements outside of the city center in his plan for Frankfurt am Main, mobilizing the foundational garden city principle of decentralization in the industrial age. Second, May sought to install Unwin's neighborhood unit, a block that offers shared services in addition to residential programming. Unwin had written that it was possible, "and indeed easy, by co-operation to provide for all a reasonable *share* of these same conveniences and luxuries" like common rooms, baths, washhouses, recreation and reading rooms, and eventually common kitchens and dining halls.[17] In the planning stages for New Frankfurt, May followed Unwin's lead, setting aside land for robust community services in each *siedlung.* In the end, the Bruchfeldstrasse *siedlung* was the only settlement with a full-fledged community center akin to the Soviet workers' club, but Praunheim boasted an auditorium, club offices, and a branch library.[18] Much to May's disappointment, the New Frankfurt program for nurseries, daycare centers, and kindergartens in each *siedlung* was scrapped for lack of funding.[19]

Siting and programming commonalities aside, the spare architectural language of May's New Frankfurt housing had little in common with Hampstead's Arts and Crafts pitched-roofed bungalows. The largely orthogonal, flat-roofed, white-bodied multiunit housing complexes built under May's direction addressed functional needs and rejected historical allusions as a matter of principle, as he explained:

> The external form of the Frankfurt *Siedlungen* is developed from the situation of the internal structures and dispenses with representative gestures and decorative elements, both old and new. [We take] an approach to building that no longer sees the ultimate fulfilment of architectural aesthetics as lying in the so-called beautiful facade with a symmetrical composition animated by piers, cornices, and ornaments . . . By the repetition of numerous, similar elements and by harmoniously adapting the buildings to the landscape, [we] strive for architectural and urban design effects that are derived from our times.[20]

The goal for New Frankfurt's designers under May was no less than to channel the Weimar zeitgeist architecturally, permitting the appearance of the settlements' buildings to arise from the marriage of sensitive siting, functionality, and industrialized building methods. Unlike the jurors of the Magnitogorsk competition, May was unconcerned about architectural standardization's experiential monotony. "We are of the opinion," he explained in a 1929 lecture, "that the collective element in the life of people today, which so strongly influences work, sport, and politics, must logically be reflected in their housing . . . the *Siedlung* of our times will, like the honeycomb, be defined as the sum of similar housing elements."[21] May celebrated uniformity of architectural appearance as a means to dissolve corrosive individuality and encourage collectivity.

Two of the Frankfurt am Main settlements the Soviet housing delegation visited in 1927 were Praunheim and Westhausen (1925–29), located in the suburban Nidda Valley. In his general plan for Frankfurt, May pushed through zoning that designated previously unproductive swamp land for agricultural use, thereby reserving a perpetual green belt between the expanding urban center and his new settlements.[22] Praunheim was the first project built using the *Frankfurter Montageverfahren* (Frankfurt Assembly Method or, colloquially, the "May system"), in which prefabricated structural panels were tilted or hoisted up on the construction site. In the first phase at Praunheim, long rows of attached single family three-story houses were built along the east-west axis, following the preexisting roads that encompassed the site. In Westhausen, May and his staff experimented with a highly regimented site plan with a low-rise multifamily housing bar, or *zeilenbau*, arranged in parallel rows aligned on the north-south axis to maximize insolation along the broad east-west facades (figure 6.2).[23] Distance between the rows was determined by shadow studies, and each rowhouse was entered on the east side, with the west reserved for garden plots.[24] Because the *zeilenbau* projects were superblocks like the Armenikend test block in Baku, the Azerbaijani delegates would have recognized the cost-saving benefits of the pedestrian-friendly site planning strategy, namely economization on the hard infrastructure of roads and streetlights. Upon conclusion of their tour, the Soviet delegation enumerated four aspects of May's Frankfurt settlements that they proposed to emulate and turn into policy. Housing should be produced by "factory" rather than "handicraft" methods, meaning that construction elements should be prefabricated, shipped in, and installed on site, leading to

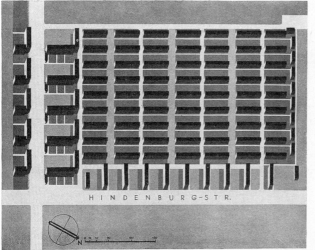

Figure 6.2. Siedlung Westhausen site plan, Frankfurt, Germany, 1929. Low-rise multifamily housing bars, *zeilenbauen*, sit in parallel rows aligned on the north-south axis to maximize insolation on the east-west facades. Planners: Ernst May et al. "Funf jahre wohnungsbautatigkeit in Frankfurt am Main," *Das Neue Frankfurt*, no. 2/3 (1930): 56.

a 30 percent reduction in project costs. Construction should be conducted year-round. Drawing sets should consist of both standardized designs and installation instructions, "similar to the drawings used for assembling cars." Finally, the whole project delivery system at all levels should be carefully organized and monitored to reduce construction costs.[25]

On May's recommendation, New Frankfurt was the site and focus of the second meeting of CIAM in 1929, which took as its theme *Existenzminimum* (the minimum subsistence dwelling). The two official Soviet delegates to the congress were Moisei Ginzburg and Nikolai Kolli, both members of OSA who knew Le Corbusier from his travels to the USSR beginning in 1928.[26] The journal *Das Neue Frankfurt* reported that another Soviet guest at the congress was the engineer German Krasin, at the time the chairman of the Commission for Housing Construction at the Central Scientific Research Institute of Building Construction (Gosudarstvennyi institut sooruzhenii or GIS), an organization under the umbrella of Vesenkha.[27] Krasin was later on the expert panel that selected May as the planner for Magnitogorsk, and he worked closely with May's design team in his role as head of the governmental commission on Magnitogorsk.

CIAM2 opened on October 24, 1929, the inauspicious date of the Wall Street stock market crash. Delegates and the public listened to lectures and debates, toured the New Frankfurt housing settlements, and visited the congress exhibition. Other active members of CIAM, like Walter Gropius, sought to maintain broad discussion of the theme, but the congress was undeniably a publicity juggernaut for May's New Frankfurt. "The Minimum Dwelling Unit" exhibition that opened at the end of the congress featured an international collection of 207 spatially economized housing floor plans, but the majority were German examples, and half of those were designed under May's supervision for Frankfurt.[28] Catherine Bauer, whose *Modern Housing* (1934) would introduce European housing innovations to a US audience, noted that the air of excitement at the conference was due in large part to the fact that May had one foot out the door. He was packed and ready to depart for a lecture tour in Leningrad.[29]

Ernst May, Soviet Planner

In March 1930, Tsekombank, the Central Bank for Municipal Economy and Housing, was named state financier for the construction of all socialist cities. Although thirty-eight cities were officially designated for construction during the first Five-Year Plan, once tabula rasa sites and interventions in existing cities were added up, the number of urban scale construction projects undertaken during the plan was more like 150–170.[30] Each project was run by a different constellation of administrators and designers, leading to mixed results. In an effort to install a measure of quality control, Tsekombank placed advertisements in Union-wide newspapers and journals, soliciting assistance from experienced architects for an in-house design office, an outreach that purportedly received little return.[31] As Evgeniia Konysheva and Mark Meerovich note, the decision of Tsekombank and other Soviet organizations to turn to foreign specialists in the early 1930s cannot be wholly explained by a shortage of local design talent. According to contemporary Soviet sources, in 1928–29 there were approximately 10,000 architects and civil engineers working in Moscow, another 9,000 in forty different design offices in Leningrad, and 5,500 in Kharkiv.[32] What foreign architects like May or Albert Kahn had to offer was cutting-edge expertise with architectural standardization.

May was invited back to the USSR in early 1930 to deliver lectures in Moscow, Leningrad, and Kharkiv that drew on his Frankfurt experience. Timely topics included "The New City," "The State of Residential Building in Germany," and "The Rationalization of Residential Construction." Upon request, May prepared an additional lecture for a select group of Soviet specialists entitled, "Organizational Proposals Concerning Russian City Planning and Residential Policies."[33] This lecture appears to have been an opportunity to vet the architect, and by all accounts May passed muster. Soon after this visit E. Luganovskii, the head of Tsekombank, traveled to Frankfurt am Main to hire May and his architectural brigade.[34] In a letter dated June 15, 1930, Tsekombank contracted May as its head design consultant for a period of five years. In this capacity May would 1) draft plans for new cities and settlements and replan old ones; 2) rationalize and standardize construction of residential buildings and civic structures and improve methods for construction of cities and settlements; 3) develop typical projects for residential buildings and civic buildings; and 4) develop projects for factories to produce standardized residential buildings.[35] May did not explicitly sign on with the Soviets to plan Magnitogorsk. Under his agreement with Tsekombank, May was responsible for urban design, housing typology design, and systems design throughout Soviet territories. He had ample experience with all three tasks, but the latter two, having to do with standardization, were of greatest interest to Tsekombank. At the start of 1929, Tsekombank had published—with parallel Russian and German texts—*Projects for Workers' Dwellings* (*Proekty rabochikh zhilishch*), an album of high-quality housing unit designs compiled from various Soviet projects. In the book's preface, Luganovskii lamented that "one of the main drawbacks of [Soviet housing] construction is that the design of residential buildings is inexpedient and extremely heterogeneous in nature and approach."[36] Type design, forwarded by the Tsekombank album and employed in May's work in Frankfurt, assumes replication. A single, well-resolved housing type could be tested and then deployed throughout Soviet space, saving time and money. In addition to developing standardized building types, May and his team would develop design and construction methods to rationalize the ragtag Soviet building industry and would design factories for manufacturing standardized building components. May signed the contract, agreed on an October departure date from Germany to the USSR, and went about gathering his brigade of experienced designers.[37]

It was not difficult to entice architects to leave Germany in the year after the international economic collapse. According to artist-architect Erich Borchert, "two years ago [in 1928], in the office of one of Berlin's best architects, there were 85 architects and specialists—now there are only 5."[38] In the lead up to his departure, May presented himself to the German press as a specialist-mercenary rather than a fellow traveler. "I am not interested in politics," he told the architectural journal *Bauwelt*. "I am a German architect fulfilling a contract with the Russian government in the hope of helping the German economy a little at the same time."[39] He even spun the consultancy as an opportunity to advance the international field of urban planning—again, without mention of politics. "Until now my activities, like those of almost all town planners in Western countries, has consisted largely of urban expansion, albeit on the new basis of satellite theory; but now I am to develop plans for new towns which are to be created from nothing as independent organisms."[40] Like his high-ranking clients plotting the Union's future from maps in Moscow, May ascribed to the tabula rasa myth of Soviet territorial expansion. Unlike many of his clients, however, he and his brigade would soon experience in person the contextual realities of those remote sites.

Meanwhile, the administration of Magnitostroi—without consulting its funder, Tsekombank—handed the general planning project over to the State Institute for City Planning for the Russian Republic (Rossiiskii institut gradostroitel'stva i intensivonnogo razvitiia or Giprogor) under the leadership of Chernyshev.[41] Despite intense pressure to complete the plan, the Giprogor team was plagued by delay. A month into the renewed design effort Chernyshev reported to the Communist Academy, citing a litany of reasons for his team's lack of progress. The factory production targets kept changing, which resulted in fluctuating territorial spread. Shifting decisions about the purifying-cleansing ponds and the location of the processing factory made spatial planning impossible. The population targets for the city were subject to constant change. The administration refused to resolve the size of the sanitary zone between the factory and the workers' settlement. Finally, as Ivanitskii had noted in Baku, the ambiguous general line on the planning and architecture of the ideal socialist city hindered real-time progress. By the fall of 1930, the planning and housing situation in Magnitogorsk was "catastrophic" and was even threatening the timely startup of the factory. Tsekombank decided it was time to intervene (or "meddle"—*vmeshivat'sia*) in the situation and called in May.[42]

Travel to Magnitogorsk

In October 1930, May left Berlin for Moscow with seventeen colleagues to begin his comprehensive design consultancy with the Soviet government.[43] Soon after they arrived in Moscow they were instructed, with just twenty-four hours' notice, of their departure for the Urals where they would act as planning consultants for the socialist city of Magnitogorsk.[44] Tsekombank representatives accompanied the May Brigade on their four-and-a-half-day train trip.[45] May had ample time traveling through the western Russian landscape to jot down observations that invariably tamed unfamiliar conditions. He noted that the peaks of the Urals recalled the Rhön Mountains and that the train coach outfitted for the foreign specialists was filled with the "special kind of good humor that often fills the long hours of wait in a dugout or the long evenings in an alpine ski hut."[46] The further the architects traveled from Moscow the more difficult analogical observations became. By the time May crossed the Ural Mountains and left behind Cheliabinsk, the capital of the Ural region, the unprecedented nature of this new context sank in. "We could immediately see by the faces of the native population that here was a different ethnic group. Their slanted eyes revealed that we were now dealing with Mongols . . . We did not see many villages," he wrote, "but flocks of horses of all colors roamed freely across the frozen soil."[47]

On November 2, 1930, May and his team reached the location for the future city of Magnitogorsk. May recalled his first view of the site:

> We reached our destination on a temporary rail spur. Fog gave way to clear skies, and our eyes beheld a fascinating spectacle. From the middle of the steppe arose a number of flat hills and among these, of larger size—a mountain of iron ore. One hundred and fifty million tons of rich iron-ore deposits are located in this area, ready to be surface mined. In order to exploit these deposits, the second largest industrial complex in the world has been planned here as part of the great Soviet plan of industrialization . . . Now 40,000 workers, living in temporary barracks, apply their labor to one the mightiest industrial ventures of our time. The innumerable blinking lights of the labor camp and the bright floodlights used for night work made an unforgettable impression on our minds.[48]

Though May's text amplifies the drama of this first encounter, his basic description matches other contemporary reports of the site. The architect finally stood on the steppe, took in the topography, and grasped the material implications of, and limitations on, the planning task. Chernyshev, who was already well acquainted with the site, had arrived in Magnitogorsk with his Giprogor design team a day before the Tsekombank-May group.

On the day of May's arrival, the two design teams met with local officials at the offices of Magnitostroi. The architects were presented with an exhaustive list of thirty-six items to consider when designing the city. Like the Magnitogorsk competition brief from which it undoubtedly was generated, this list encompassed all scales of urban intervention from regional infrastructure down to targeted living norms. The requirements foreclosed fantastical proposals like those submitted by the OSA and Stroikom competition teams. As in the brief, the average height of buildings in Magnitogorsk was to be four to five stories (no high-rises), and small-scale construction was discouraged (no izbas on chicken legs). Most surprisingly, however, the architects were instructed that "apartments for individual living [*individual'nogo zhil'ia*] will be constructed with two to three rooms, with a small percentage (no more than 5 percent) with four rooms."[49] Dormitories were requested but included as an afterthought, and the percentage of collective housing types was left to Magnitostroi and the local branch of Gosplan to determine. The typical residential commune, the fundamental building block of the All-Union competition, and the linchpin for sociospatial change in the 1929 urbanism debates, had disappeared altogether in keeping with the high-level ideological shift away from a radical reconfiguration of *byt*.

The May Brigade toured Magnitogorsk in Ford motorcars, met the Soviet, US, and German engineers in charge of factory construction, and collected information for four days. It was clear to the team from the outset that the site had serious contextual limitations. They concluded that "it was simply impossible to devise a solution based purely on desired relationships between industry and housing."[50] Hemmed in by the expanding production area to the north, and the river and topography to the west and south, a residential area would have to be wedged into the southeast. This was the area where, in the summer months before May's visit, residential foundations had already been laid. A photograph of the first foundation pit excavation provides a glimpse of the conditions May and his team likely witnessed that November (figure 6.3). With nothing but a horse, a pile of foundation stones, and the waving grass of the steppe in the background, workers (and one specialist in a suit) look down expectantly into the hand dug trench. May later lamented these buildings' existence specifically. "We were bound in our work by the fact that one of the project organizations designed a complex of 16 four-story buildings before our arrival. In parts the buildings' foundations had been laid, and in another the roofs were already in place . . . Numerous organizations working at increasingly accelerated rates were creating temporary or permanent buildings which were later a serious obstacle to crafting a clean plan of the city."[51] During their first visit May's team also saw that the vast majority of Magnitogorsk's 40,000 residents resided in the rows of wooden barracks between the factory site and the river (figure 6.4). The single men, women, and families slept alongside one another in beds lined on both sides of the open plan and ate together in common canteens (figure 6.5). The forced communality that had been written into the Magnitogorsk competition brief was already a condition of life on site.

Figure 6.3. Laying the first housing foundation, Pionerskaia Street, Magnitogorsk, Russia, summer 1930. Magnitogorskii kraevedcheskii muzei.

Figure 6.4. Aerial view of factory construction with rows of wooden barracks in the distance, Magnitogorsk, Russia, c. 1930. Magnitogorskii kraevedcheskii muzei.

Figure 6.5. Family barracks, Magnitogorsk, Russia, c. 1931. Magnitogorskii kraevedcheskii muzei.

Internal Competition

After site reconnaissance, a month-long internal design competition ensued. Chernyshev working for Giprogor, and May for Tsekombank, were ordered by the Magnitostroi administration to complete planning schemes for the city by November 25, 1930, less than a month into the future.[52] May's team, used to working quickly, immediately began sketching alternatives in Magnitogorsk, continued on the train journey, and finished in Moscow. They purportedly converted one of their train compartments into a drafting room and "using the charcoal supplied as fuel for the samovar as pencils and drafting boards made of plywood pieces as a drawing base" produced a draft of a general plan.[53] In another compartment colleagues typed up the explanatory texts for the project. The Tsekombank regional plan by the May team, dated November 1930, shows rectangular residential blocks originating at the southern end of the production zone and sweeping to the southeast (figure 6.6). The topographical model of this scheme explains the bowed shape of the housing region: it sits between the mine and industrial lake to the north, and a row of hills to the south, on the flattest land available close to the industrial zone (plate 14). The detailed site plan reveals that the Tsekombank scheme had much in common with the majority of the All-Union competition entries for Magnitogorsk, especially the "concentrated city planning" examples (figure 6.7). Repetitive residential communes fill in a wide band that wends its way in a southeasterly direction. May's standard residential building for Magnitogorsk is a *zeilenbau* of the Frankfurt type, a simple double exposure bar oriented along the north-south axis for maximal east-west insolation. In the bird's eye perspective, a drawing that uses perspectival drama to mask extreme regularity, blocks (*kvartaly*) for 8,000–10,000 residents extend into the distance in repeated rectangles; all buildings stand free, surrounded by green space (figure 6.8).[54]

Chernyshev was in the unenviable position of having to explain to his client that the project he had been working on for over a year was about to be snatched away. In a letter to the director of Giprogor, Chernyshev complained about chronic decision-making dysfunction on Magnitogorsk's fundamental planning questions. The very location of the city was still up for grabs. "We consider the choice of city's site to be the most critical task that stands before the State Commission," Chernyshev stressed.[55] Almost two weeks after receipt of the letter, someone at Giprogor scribbled an elliptical note at the top—"what should we do about this question?"—that confirms that Chernyshev was plagued by indecision on all sides. Nevertheless, he and his Giprogor team pushed through and finished their version of the Magnitogorsk general plan. In every planning scheme he devised for Magnitogorsk, Chernyshev utilized a fan-shaped organizational strategy that resembles a quarter of Moscow's historically radial plan, with a trident of radiating blocks reaching out from a plaza at the factory gates (figure 6.9).

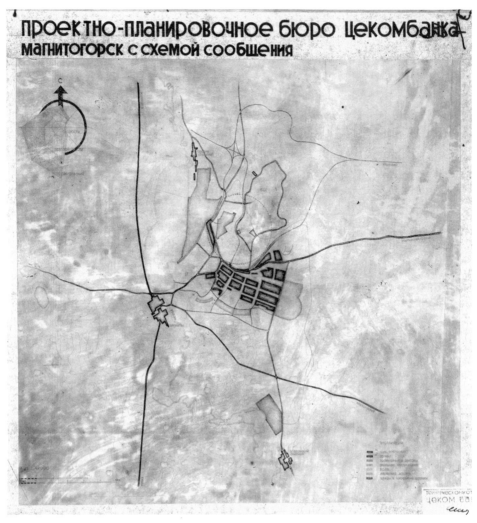

ПРОЕКТНО-ПЛАНИРОВОЧНОЕ БЮРО ЦЕКОМБАНКА
МАГНИТОГОРСК С СХЕМОЙ СООБЩЕНИЯ

Figure 6.6. Left Bank socialist settlement scheme within the regional context, Magnitogorsk, Russia, November 1930. Rectangular residential blocks originate at the southern end of the production zone and sweep to the southeast. Planners: Tsekombank / Ernst May Brigade. MUAR, Negative 07 569.

Experts, divided into two groups, met in Moscow in December 1930 to assess the May and Chernyshev schemes side by side.[56] Among the eminent architects and planners gathered to select a scheme for Magnitogorsk was Ivanitskii, CIAM2 participant German Krasin, and E. V. Luganovskii, head of Tsekombank. The two groups disagreed on the most basic issue: on which riverbank to place the socialist city. They also disagreed over which of the two schemes to support (Ivanitskii's group claimed May's scheme superior, but the majority of experts favored Chernyshev). Over a two week stretch, various tables and reports comparing the plans were made, meetings convened, and debates held over siting, density, and architectural volume. May and Chernyshev were called before the commission numerous times to weigh in on topics such as how to distinguish the socialist from the capitalist city.

Kirov District—the only portion of the
May Brigade socialist city to be built.

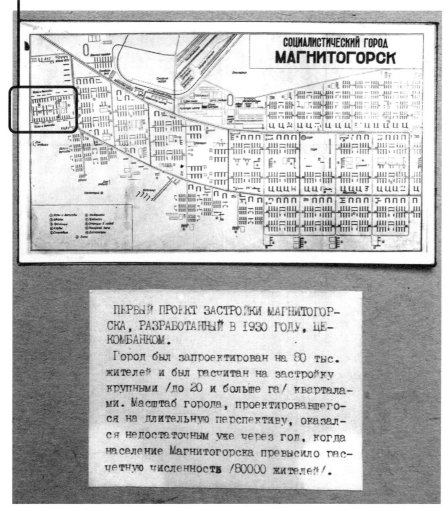

Figure 6.7. Left Bank socialist city, Magnitogorsk, Russia, 1930. The Kirov District, the only section of this scheme that was built, is located on the upper left-hand corner of the site plan. Planners: Tsekombank / Ernst May Brigade. Magnitogorskii kraevedcheskii muzei. Diagram by the author.

As May sat among the discussants, reliant on spot translation, he found his project maligned as a stereotypical example of capitalist urbanism. "But how do you understand *capitalist city*? Have you not read my explanatory text?" he asked exasperatedly through his interpreter.[57] To May, writing later in 1931, the difference between the two was straightforward.

The capitalist city has developed concentrically around the marketplace, and the rich, the middle classes, and the proletarians live in clearly separated districts of their own. This differentiation of class structure is recognizable from afar and defines the capitalist city's particular character and form. The city in the USSR knows only one class, the class of working people. Therefore, apart from the aforementioned requirement of locating people as close as possible to their respective places of work, the task consists of the equal distribution of all communal functions, for everybody's equal enjoyment.[58]

Chernyshev's project showed three parks for each lobe of his city; May's consolidated the citywide Park of Leisure and Culture in a single location. Which park configuration better represented the goals of socialist urbanism? A 4–2 vote on this point gave May the advantage, but again, no definitive consensus was reached.[59]

On December 10, 1930, May was declared the winner of the planning marathon, purportedly because his project was "worked out to a greater degree of detail, and because he has more organizational experience directing city construction."[60] In other words, the plan was good enough, and most important New Frankfurt, despite the taint of capitalism, was the ultimate proof that May could deliver an economical project quickly.[61] The May Brigade's first phase of work in 1931 was to

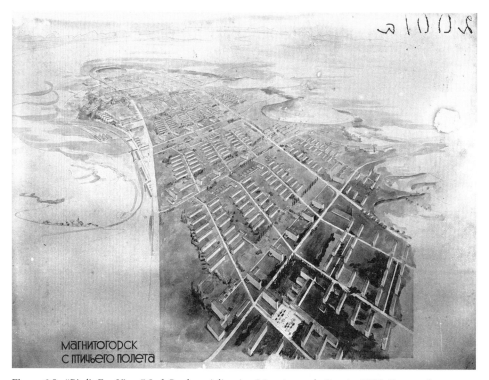

Figure 6.8. "Bird's Eye View," Left Bank socialist city, Magnitogorsk, Russia, 1930. Repeated rectangular blocks (*kvartaly*) for 8,000–10,000 residents extend into the distance. Planners: Tsekombank / Ernst May Brigade. MUAR, Negative VII-576.

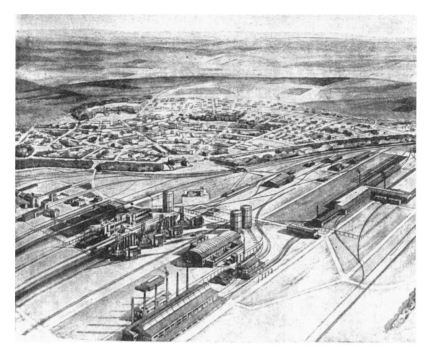

Figure 6.9. Widely published perspective of Chernyshev's fan-shaped city plan, Magnitogorsk, Russia, 1930. Planners: Giprogor / Sergei Chernyshev. M. Il'in, *Rasskaz o velikom plane*, 3rd ed. (Moscow: Ogiz—Molodaia gvardiia, 1931), 101.

design one test case *kvartal* (residential superblock) for 15,000 people to include a canteen, workers' club, stores, preschools, kindergartens, public baths, garages, fire stations, and ambulance facility, a factory bakery, open market, and other communal structures. In small consolation to the second-place architect, May was directed to use "a few solutions from Chernyshev's project," like a more westerly location for the Park of Leisure and Culture.[62]

Chernyshev may have lost in the short term, but he proved an astute player of the long game. From 1934 to 1941, he served as the Chief Architect of Moscow. Along with Vladimir Semenov, another prerevolutionary architect who waited out the avant-garde era, Chernyshev authored the 1935 General Plan for Moscow, an urban design—concentric, as was his penchant—that that was arguably more influential on Stalinist city planning than was May's Magnitogorsk intervention.[63]

Shifting Territories

As Chernyshev's letter of complaint to Giprogor suggested, managerial indecision plagued the Magnitogorsk city-building project. Most gravely, administrators could not agree *where* the city should be built. Convenience and cost savings determined the original left bank siting: housing proximate to the factory would result in less capital outlay for bridges over the Ural River to the right bank. The left bank location was justified further by a decade-old wind study that indicated a southwesterly wind pattern at the site. A month after the left bank-sited All-Union Design Competition was published, a commission of local construction administrators raised the possibility of building the city on the right bank of the Ural River, a change of tactic prompted by living experience.[64] Once factory construction began, administrators and residents alike noticed that industrial smoke blew most frequently in a southeasterly direction from the factory directly into the proposed residential site, proving the old wind study patently incorrect.[65]

With a new planning team at the helm, and despite the fact that all residential and administrative buildings were already located on the left bank, the question of the proper location for Magnitogorsk was posed anew. The most intense period of debate occurred between November 1930 and the end of May 1931. During those seven months the officially designated location of the city shifted from the left to the right bank and back seven times (plate 15).[66] In countless meetings on the topic in both Magnitogorsk and Moscow three options were considered: 1) continue to build the city on the left bank; 2) move all new city construction to the right bank; 3) follow a hybrid path and immediately construct a population-limited worker settlement (20,000–30,000 residents) on the left bank, while siting the future city on the right bank.[67]

In the absence of a clear locational directive, May's Tsekombank design team produced both left and right bank schemes for the city (figure 6.10).[68] Many of the architectural and planning issues that they resolved in this early period were, in fact, site-agnostic. Sitting in their rolling office on a rail spur outside of Novosibirsk, May's team typed out an explanatory text for their Magnitogorsk design that mentioned the siting briefly (at that point the primary scheme was for the left bank), but that more thoroughly concerned the housing types, construction technologies, and communal amenities for the new workers' settlement. The basic building block of the socialist city was the *kvartal* for 10,000–15,000 people. "The entire city will consist of the sum of these *kvartals*," and include clubs, canteens, a cinema, schools for children of a range of ages, shops, laundries, baths, ambulance service, and sports fields in addition to housing.[69] May's *kvartal* matches almost exactly Sabsovich's definition of the *zhilkombinat* requested in the All-Union competition, although it accommodates over five times the population. In each case, a single well-designed block type is repeated to reach the city's population goal, a strategy that assumes standardization not only of housing types but also urban units.

May and his brigade preferred the right bank scheme for Magnitogorsk for all of the reasons that it was eventually adopted in the postwar period. He explained that "it was quite clear to us that the right bank of the river, thanks to its uniform

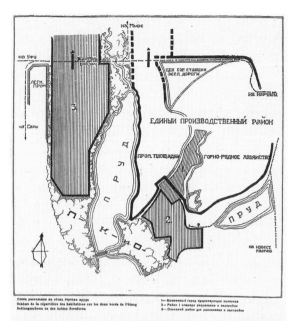

Right Bank Variant

1. Temporary existing settlement
2. Region for the first phase of development and construction.
3. Primary region for development and construction.

Left Bank Variant

1. Temporary existing settlement
2. South city
3. North city. Arrows indicate the direction of growth of the future city.

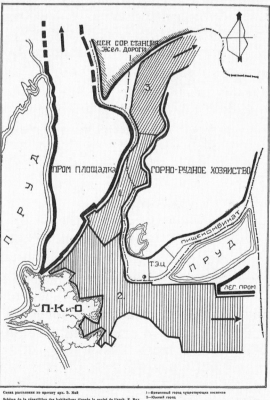

Figure 6.10. Left Bank (top) and Right Bank (bottom) variants for the socialist settlement, Magnitogorsk, Russia, 1933. Planners: Standartgorproekt / Ernst May Brigade. *Sovetskaia arkhitektura*, no. 3 (1933). Diagram by the author.

slope, is preferable for the organization of a residential town than the more difficult site located close to the factory on the left bank. We also have no doubt that
the right bank is an extremely convenient site for the construction of the railway
line that will connect the new city to the network of magistrals."[70] In addition to
right bank's gentle topography and convenient access to rail lines and future high-
ways, the location afforded both industrial and residential sectors room to expand
without conflict, and prevailing southeasterly winds would blow industrial smoke
away from right bank housing. May conceded, however, that the socialist city had
to be built on the left bank for three reasons out of his control. First, the dammed
and widened Ural River created a two-kilometer distance between the factory and
the nearest possible right bank settlement. Specialists determined that at least two
bridges would be needed to connect the riverbanks, a prospect that was fiscally
improbable in the near future. Second, left bank construction "provided a pedestrian connection between the residential and industrial areas for a very large part
of the industrial workers and miners who thus could live without mechanical transport."[71] The workers' ability to walk from left bank housing to the factory deferred
investment in costly transportation infrastructure. Lastly, a sizable number of temporary structures, roads, electrical wires, and other infrastructure already had been
installed on the left bank. Those settlements had to be incorporated into the general
plan so as not to squander the investment already expended. When May gave these
justifications for a left bank settlement in a 1932 article for *Sovetskaia arkhitektura*, almost a year had passed since the Sovnarkom of the Russian Republic issued
Protokol no. 405 in favor of the left. A definitive resolution by STO in August 1932
closed debate, and May was obliged to design a left bank general plan for Magnitogorsk that ran counter to his best planning instincts.

May's tactical retreat at the end of 1932 had much to do with his diminishing
status in the USSR. In September 1931, the Tsekombank planning office merged
with Gosproekt no. 2 (a planning office of the Vesenkha of the Russian Republic)
to create Standartgorproekt. May was designated chief engineer of the new design
organization and granted extraordinary powers in his position, but his upper
echelon location in the Soviet hierarchy was short-lived.[72] In Magnitogorsk, 80
percent of residential construction funding for 1931 (6.5 million of the 8 million
allocated) was siphoned away from housing to build the factory. Union-wide, the
astronomical targets set for new housing in 1932 were only 10 percent fulfilled.[73]
May was held personally accountable for these grim statistics as head of Standartgorproekt, the organization nominally responsible for meeting residential construction targets.

When May was granted an audience with Commissar of Heavy Industry Sergo
Ordzhonikidze in the fall of 1932, he tried to broach the subject of the city's
location in an amusing manner by presenting Ordzhonikidze a cardboard clock
with "left bank" and "right bank" printed on opposing sides of the circle. The
US engineer Zara Witkin, who befriended May in Moscow, recounted the interaction. When Ordzhonikidze asked May "on which side of the river is the housing of

Magnitogorsk to be?" May asked, "what month is this?" "Nettled, the commissar answered testily, 'March!' 'Ah,' said May, drawing the [clock] from his portfolio and turning its face to the commissar. Silently, he swung the arm around the dial . . . 'This month the housing will be on the left bank of the river, commissar!' he said."[74] "I had hoped to gaze into a smiling face," May wrote later of the ill-fated meeting. "Instead, O. looked at me with an earnest expression, put the clock face down on the table and finally told me that a decision would be made before long."[75] May later cited this encounter as the moment when he realized that he would have to leave the USSR.

The Magnitogorsk general plan completed by the May Brigade in 1933, as employees of Standartgorproekt on their way out the door, retained a left bank design (figure 6.11). This version shows two residential areas (the dark blocks) that flank the production area to the north and southeast. The northern sector is located to benefit from rail adjacency and proximity to the open steppe for future expansion northward. The southern sector is squeezed between the factory, the lake, and the mountains in the location utilized in the All-Union competition of 1929 and the May Brigade's first draft plan. The right bank of the Ural River is cut off from the drawing completely, as if to foreclose any future discussion on the matter.

This final published general plan is an almost unrecognizable sibling to the hyper-detailed plans of May's standard oeuvre, in which each individual *zeilenbau* building is carefully inked-in, no matter the drawing's scale. The Magnitogorsk general plan is a retreat from specificity to ambiguity. How is the abutting relationship between residential and industrial sectors handled? How are the *kvartals* organized? What are the residential building types? None of these questions is answered in this plan, which provides only a vague blueprint for future city-builders. May's accompanying text suggests that in the numbers-obsessed early Soviet context, withholding detail was his planning team's final subversive act:

> A far-sighted planned economy will admit the possibility that even the best organization of urban construction does not have at its disposal prophets capable of anticipating change with an accuracy up to 90 percent. Therefore, the master plan cannot be viewed as a complete, accurate picture of the city's development for ten or even twenty years ahead. It is rather a "desirable" plan; perhaps it would be more accurate to compare it to the plan of an army on the march. All military units and all types of weapons are distributed in certain places to ensure the attainment of a specific military goal. However, when the plan is launched a certain role belongs to the adversary who, through his movements, requires the commander to adapt his plan to the requirements of reality.
>
> As applied to urban construction, this means that the master plan cannot and should not represent a completely frozen condition but should, on the contrary, possess considerable elasticity, allowing it to be coordinated continuously with changing living conditions.[76]

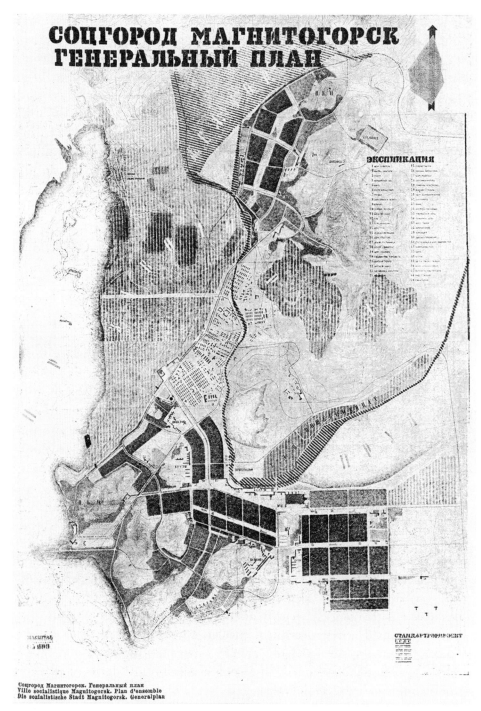

Figure 6.11. Sotsgorod General Plan, Magnitogorsk, Russia, 1933. Planners: Standartgorproekt / Ernst May Brigade. Ernst May, "K proekty general'nogo plana Magnitorgoska," *Sovetskaia arkhitektura*, May–June (1933): 19.

May's explanation for the plan's indeterminacy could be read as defensive. After all, the planner arrived in Magnitogorsk guns blazing (to continue his military metaphor), ready to install a rational Frankfurt-like plan with speed and efficiency. The so-called requirements of reality in the increasingly bureaucratic Soviet Union forced him to acknowledge that the project was out of his hands, and that he had accomplished little. Conflicting ideas about the proper form and location of the Magnitogorsk *sotsgorod* caused almost complete paralysis; the master plan could not be drawn when so many fundamental issues remained unresolved. May's vague plan is a white flag of surrender, a final concession to the complexity of Soviet conditions.

Frankfurt on the Steppe

The material legacy of the May Brigade in Magnitogorsk is found in a small section of the 1932 master plan constructed between 1931 and 1934 that still stands today. Called variously the Kirov District, the Socialist City, or *Kvartal* no. 1, this block that sits south of the factory on the left bank and is composed of freestanding housing bars aligned in parallel north-south rows: *zeilenbau* on the Soviet steppe (figure 6.12). As constructed, the neighborhood is an architectural hybrid. Pionerskaia Street, the central east-west axis of the plan, is flanked by six pairs of four-story buildings designed by Gosproekt and constructed before the May Brigade completed their housing designs. The Gosproekt buildings are 70-meter-long, 12-meter-wide brick apartment houses with shallow-hipped roofs, large windows, and balconies. In their original state, the spatially generous units ranged from three to five rooms, and each enjoyed its own kitchen, bath, and balcony. Three-story "sectional houses" (*sektsionnye doma*), designed by the May Brigade, sit at the north and south edges of the block (plate 16). Although the foreign architects designed a handful of housing types for Magnitogorsk, the majority constructed are the INKO-A type: 72-meter-long, 11.5-meter-wide row buildings (plates 17–18). The INKO-A is made up of seven standard ten-meter "sections" placed side to side, each of which holds a switchback stair and two two-room, double-exposure units per floor block. These modest units were designed without kitchens, on the architects' assumption of communal food provision within the *kvartal*, although the designers noted that one room could be converted to a kitchen later if the residents so desired.[77] The stucco exteriors of the INKO-A houses are devoid of ornamentation, but large windows and regular balconies provide volumetric relief on the simple, brightly painted facades. Open space between the east-west facades of the sectional house is at a width of 3–3.5 times the height of the buildings and was intended for passive recreation, gardens, storage sheds for fuel and preserves, and small communal buildings.

Figure 6.12. Kirov District after construction, Magnitogorsk, Russia, 1933–34. Architects / Planners: Gosproekt / Standartgorproekt / Ernst May Brigade. Magnitogorskii kraevedcheskii muzei.

The north-south orientation of the Kirov District's buildings, the green space between them, their narrow depth, and their austere character ally this project with May's New Frankfurt, especially the last phase at Praunheim. Despite the involvement of two different architectural teams—Gosproekt led by designers from within the Soviet system, and Standartgorproekt led by designers from a socialist municipality in the capitalist West—the overall scale and exterior character of the residential buildings in the Kirov District are markedly similar, making it all the more difficult to characterize these buildings as belonging to a specific economic or social system. Do any of these buildings communicate their affiliation to a specific ideology, as commentators on both sides claimed they did? Can a building look capitalist or socialist?

May broached the subject of socialist architectural expression when he wrote about the Magnitogorsk project for the Soviet press. "In view of the fact that the first socialist state in the world is relatively young, the architectural design of a socialist city has no firmly established image. We know only one thing: that in appearance, the socialist city will differ significantly from obsolete capitalist cities. New completely 'recrystallized' forms of human society should create an architectural image corresponding to a classless state."[78] Lest the reader of *Sovetskaia arkhitektura* be led to believe that May's evocation of "image" signaled a return to architectural design from the outside in, May clarified that it is the programmatic attributes of socialist housing that must determine its appearance. He explained:

> The basic requirement of planning and building a socialist city is to create for the entire population equally favorable living conditions with respect to the internal organization of the dwelling, its lighting, ventilation, social and cultural services, and communication amenities. The most radical implementation of this basic requirement is the "linear" (*strochnaia*) construction, which in recent years has increasingly spread in the modern architecture of Western Europe. We considered the shortcomings associated with the monotony of parallel blocks oriented at a slight angle to the north-south direction. But, in rejecting paper eclecticism, we give paramount importance, first and foremost, to providing the most essential elements without compromise.[79]

May justified the rational site plan and austere exterior expression at the Kirov District as the logical outcome of designing for a classless society. He argued that the point is not what the housing looks like but how it functions, an explanation already well practiced by Constructivist practitioners like Moisei Ginzburg. If the quintessential needs of each resident are met—light, fresh air, social, cultural, and technological amenities—then the architecture is suitably socialist. May acknowledged the critique of experiential monotony among the *zeilenbauen* at New Frankfurt and in his plan for the Kirov District, but he asserted that the careful siting of communal buildings at variegated heights and orientation "revitalized the architectural design of space" by providing massing contrast, and further, that "using the features of the terrain, the plan constantly seeks the most economical way to increase the impact of individual structures."[80] The INKO-A buildings on the southern edge of the *kvartal* climb a slight rise and stagger in elevation as they do so, rendering the standardized sections more lively, as May suggested.

The Moscow-based architect Dmitrii Shibaev wrote an immediate rebuttal to May's article in *Sovetskaia arkhitektura*, critiquing the architecture of Magnitogorsk's Kirov District and questioning whether a nonsocialist designer could properly address the needs of the Soviet populace. Shibaev used May's support for nonhierarchical, functional architecture against him. "The author [May] supports the planning of buildings in rows, stating that most progressive Western architects utilize it. This is despite the monotony of these structures, which they are compelled to put up in the name of advanced functional architecture. Such housing construction, which is natural for capitalist cities pursuing the goal of exploiting working people, creates a diminished quality of life for the individual due to the linear construction of such 'barracks.'"[81] Shibaev accused the INKO-A housing rows, although designed specifically for Magnitogorsk, of being Frankfurt *zeilenbauen* in disguise. Shibaev also argued against industrially standardized housing construction if the process resulted in long uniform lines of buildings that favored the needs of machines over humans. "For the convenience of the crane," Shibaev admonished May, "man is forced to live 'between the lines' that overwhelm his psyche."[82] Functionalism was no excuse for monotony which, to Shibaev, resulted in architecture that snuffed out the proletarian spirit. A July 14, 1932 resolution by Mossovet (the municipal administration of Moscow) stated that the preferred site planning strategy for Soviet housing going forward would be the perimeter block lined with "individual" variegated architecture. In no case would "the use of boring, monotonous facades" be permitted, Shibaev reported.

Despite their architectural similarities, the Kirov District differed from New Frankfurt in one significant respect: its modest impact. In Frankfurt, May oversaw the construction of 15,000 units in five years.[83] The May Brigade's contribution in Magnitogorsk, on the other hand, was approximately 1,050 units in 25 residential buildings, and the Kirov District as a whole accommodated just 4 percent of Magnitogorsk's population in November 1932.[84] While the neighborhood was planned to offer ample communal infrastructure in addition to housing, little was actually built. In 1933, one canteen and one food products store, a kindergarten for 160 children, a school for 640 students, and boiler room (*kotel'naia*) were completed, providing less than half of the promised services.[85]

At the end of 1933, Ernst May and most of his architectural brigade left the USSR. Their three-year design consultancy had limited material impact in Magnitogorsk. For all of the evocative drawings and models generated during their tenure as designers for the model steel city, just one small neighborhood was constructed based on their designs. This is not to say that their efforts were without long-term effect. In the years after the Kirov District was constructed on the left bank, state and local administrations finally conceded that the right bank was the best site for future residential growth. The Kirov District became detritus of an earlier era of the city, an island of the everyday in the heavily industrial territory of Magnitogorsk's left bank. May's urban planning position finally won the day, which meant that his architectural legacy in the city was left to languish.

Of the three sites linked in this narrative, Magnitogorsk was burdened with the highest expectations. Because of the city's importance to Soviet industrialization and the spotlight trained on it through pervasive publicity, the architects and physical planners who cycled through the design project from 1929 to 1932 were under pressure to satisfy a host of conflicting goals in their work. The designers were expected, first, to invent unprecedented urban forms based on theories of socialist city making unfolding in real time. Those who actually set foot in Magnitogorsk then had to modify their inventions to grapple with the complexities of a site that thwarted installation of prevailing urban theory at every turn. Because Magnitogorsk was a project in which design tasks and decisions came from the top down, both Chernyshev and May, the longest serving designers for the city, were heavily monitored by officials in Moscow and Magnitogorsk, and had scarce time or resources to engage in hands-on praxis to solve problems presented by industry and nature. They found themselves between a mountain of iron ore and a hard place, as it were.

Ernst May arrived in Magnitogorsk having proven his mettle through the delivery of workforce housing in Frankfurt am Main, and in both Germany and the USSR, May worked for socialist clients whose design tasks he embraced. In both contexts, he designed housing that shared architectural arrangement, form, and character. These narrow, spare, multiunit apartment buildings, placed in regular rows on a superblock, constituted the archetypal socialist housing solution, argued May. Homogeneity at the housing unit, building, and site planning scales visually communicated a flattening of class structure. But, most important, each citizen was provided "the most essential elements without compromise," which included access to natural light and ventilation inside the unit, and social, cultural, and communication amenities within close proximity to it.[86] Cooking, eating, recreating were deemed communal activities, and were extracted from the domestic unit and cast into the wider territory that, whether dubbed a *zhilkombinat* or *kvartal*, constituted an inherently socialist space. Once the design solution was resolved, May claimed, it could be replicated infinitely, ensuring fair and equal living conditions for all residents. The instaurational text of the All-Union competition brief—May's basic rules for operating in the Soviet condition—did result in constructed space, albeit significantly more modest in scale than projected or desired by the brief's drafters.

What, then, were the critical differences between the two scenarios, and why, in the end, was May unable to pull off a repeat of his Frankfurt success in Magnitogorsk or any other Soviet city on which he worked? There are myriad reasons why May's built footprint in the Soviet Union fell short, but five contextual conditions were irredeemable: project scope (continental), client-planner relationship (shifting, out of view), location (remote), program (much exceeding housing), and client priorities (industry first, all else afterward).

First, there was the matter of scope. May's work in Frankfurt was municipally scaled. The architects on his team designed for their local context and any bureaucratic or topographic conflicts that arose were addressed immediately. In the USSR, May's territory of responsibility was the entire Soviet Union. Magnitogorsk was just one project among many that May and his brigade tackled as planning consultants to the Soviet government. Their efforts were divided among many locations that were geographically, experientially, and culturally remote for the mostly German design teams who were spread too thin. Second, the client-planner relationship differed. As long as housing targets were met, May's client in Frankfurt, Mayor Landmann, did not meddle in questions of architectural and urban theory. Decentralization, heliotropism, functionalism, and industrialized construction were strategies proposed and ultimately implemented by May in Frankfurt. In the Soviet Union, May's client was a diffuse, multiscalar, mercurial entity, and he was a just a planner. His tasks were limited to solving design problems and taking ultimate responsibility for meeting housing targets. By 1930, the urban and social theory to be installed or avoided in a project like Magnitogorsk was dictated by the highest levels of Soviet power and May disregarded these directives at his own peril. Third, Magnitogorsk—and each city that the May team was tasked to design—was radically remote from existing infrastructure. It was not a blank site, but it was difficult to provision, staff, and ultimately build. Fourth, there was the question of the program. In designing the *siedlungen* in Frankfurt, May solved a housing problem. For his socialist municipal client, he included limited ancillary services like libraries and schools within the residential precinct at his own discretion. In Magnitogorsk, the program was much broader and included housing, social and commercial infrastructure, education, recreation, transportation, communications and hygienic infrastructure, and interface with industrial planning. Given the administrative dysfunction rampant in all of those realms in Magnitogorsk, any high-level attempt to solve them systemically was bound to fail.

Lastly, and perhaps most critically, with heavy industrial construction as his client's top priority, soft construction like the Kirov District was sorely undervalued and subsequently underfunded. Within the confines of Frankfurt's municipal socialism, and as director of municipal planning, May had complete juridical power over planning and architectural decisions. His budget to construct the *siedlungen* was tight, but a fixed capital funding cap was virtually the only limit with which he was faced. In Magnitogorsk, just 20 percent of funding allocated for housing construction in Magnitogorsk during May's tenure actually went to building housing.[87] Teleological planning permitted the abstract shift of numbers, and physical shift of building materials, from one site to another to ensure the success of the banner project: the factory. In short, May had to engage in total planning with a tiny budget and limited bureaucratic support. The gap between May's professional status in Frankfurt and the Soviet Union was ultimately unbridgeable.

Although it was beset with its own significant setbacks and missteps, the Magnitogorsk factory construction project did continue apace during the official dithering about the location and constitution of the socialist city.[88] The impossible industrial targets set by Moscow for Magnitostroi brought about a cognitive and logistical separation between production and reproduction, which proved devastating for the workers in the city. Using the design tool of architectural standardization, the Kharkiv Tractor Factory and its *sotsgorod* would be able to move interdependently, in lockstep.

PART III

MACHINE CITY

Kharkiv, 1930–1932

7

FROM TRACTORS TO TERRITORY

Kharkov starts with a year's experience gained at the expense of Stalingrad [and] shows the swift capacity of Soviet plants to learn from mistakes and improve . . . A year hence, and Kharkov in its turn will be, not the latest—but a landmark which other plants surpass. For so organization and technical skill forge ahead. Developments for which other countries require decades are accomplished in the Soviet Union in the course of a few years.

—Anna Louise Strong (1931)

The new Soviet-Ukrainian capital of Kharkiv / Kharkov was, in 1930, "alive, / laboring, / of reinforced concrete."[1] In his paean to the city, poet Vladimir Mayakovsky extolled Kharkiv as the materialization of the revolution's promise: it was a city that grew, buzzed, lived, and labored in a newly expanded environment purpose-built for the dictatorship of the proletariat. The copious construction projects rising in Kharkiv in the decade after 1922, when the capital was transferred eastward from Kyiv, included a new governmental complex, housing, and factories designed by architects who practiced according to Constructivist principles. Because of its political importance as the capital of the second largest Soviet republic, its architectural audaciousness, and its thriving intellectual scene, Kharkiv became a regular stop for foreign visitors to the USSR in the 1920s and 1930s. Ernst May, for one, visited just three cities in his 1930 Soviet lecture tour: Moscow, Leningrad, and Kharkiv.[2]

Kharkiv experienced a drastic increase in political importance from 1922, but its primary asset as a site for Soviet industry was its urbanity, which ensured preexisting transportation infrastructure, an educated managerial sector, and a skilled labor force, none of which Magnitogorsk benefitted from at its inception. The city of Kharkiv also adjoined the Soviet agricultural heartland that produced the grain that filled state coffers and fueled foreign trade. Kharkiv was in many ways a ready-made site, primed to accept a first Five-Year Plan tractor factory hastily added to the ledger a year into the plan's fulfillment. The Kharkiv Tractor Factory (Kharkivs'kyi traktornyi zavod or KhTZ) and "New Kharkiv," the *sotsgorod* to house its workers, was built ten kilometers outside of Kharkiv's urban center between 1930 and 1931 to manufacture tractors required for the headlong collectivization of Soviet agriculture.

Unlike the other chapters in this book, this one does not focus on socialist housing. A shift temporarily to the architectural program that has been hovering just out of sight throughout the narrative—the factory—sheds light on how the Soviet system of architectural standardization was established and laid the groundwork for mass socialist housing provision. Soviet centralized planning, stabilizing at the end of the first Five-Year Plan, permitted lessons from one construction site to be utilized immediately on the next. The US journalist Anna Louise Strong observed that the hand-over of construction expertise from the Stalingrad Tractor Factory to its near-twin in Kharkiv showed "the swift capacity of Soviet plants to learn from mistakes and improve."

The steep learning curve that Strong observed in successive Soviet construction projects demonstrated that industrial progress was not reliant on the secrecy and competition built into the capitalist system. Soviets learned about standardization, mass production, and industrial efficiency largely from technical consultants borrowed from the capitalist system, however. In June 1929, Detroit industrial architecture firm, Albert Kahn Inc., signed an agreement with the Soviet government to design and oversee the construction of a single tractor factory in Stalingrad. Six months later, the firm was promoted to become a consultant for all industrial construction in the USSR. The ambitious timetable set by Soviet state economic planners to meet first Five-Year Plan targets did not allow for a period of internal architectural research and development, nor were there experienced Soviet factory designers to lead the charge even if the timetable had been more leisurely. Pragmatism, forced by the schedule, led the Vesenkha to Kahn, Henry Ford's architect, just as it had led them to Henry Freyn and Co., Arthur McKee and Co., and the Ernst May Brigade to assist with factory and housing designs in Magnitogorsk.

It is Kahn's involvement with the factory design in Kharkiv—oblique and reliant on typological design—that makes this project critical in the history of socialist architecture and urbanism. The case of the factory and its *sotsgorod* demonstrates how Soviet planning and architecture were impacted by the "shock-work" culture of the first Five-Year Plan. The tempo of the plan forced Soviet economic and physical planners to devise a host of accelerating strategies; standardization was one that allowed the Kharkiv Tractor Factory to meet the unreasonable construction timetable set by Ukraine's State Institute for Metallurgical Factory Design, UkrGipromez. The relationship between the Stalingrad Tractor Factory and the one built immediately afterward in Kharkiv shows how the Fordist model of industrial standardization enabled and empowered the Soviets to settle territory quickly and diffusely, a hallmark of socialist spatial practice in the following decades. The near-impossible schedule of the first Five-Year Plan limited the options designers for both the tractor factory and the *sotsgorod* could pursue, which made easily replicable architectural types and models particularly attractive.

Priviazka (architectural adjustment) is the Russian term, still in use today, for the architectural practice of tweaking a standard design to meet the specific demands of a new site and also the result of that practice (it can be used as a verb and a noun).[3] In the 1920s and 1930s, the practice of adapting standard types to new circumstances was ascendant, even if the term *priviazka* remained in the realm of professional slang at that time. Texts published during the first Five-Year Plan on architectural standardization used terms and phrases like *popravka* (amendment), *prisposobit'* (to adapt), or *primeniat' tipovye proekty* (to apply typical/standard projects).[4] *Priviazka* is used here because it had staying power, both as a practice and a term. It became the prevailing mode of operation for Soviet architecture and planning professionals working in state-run design institutes in the following decades, yet it has its origin during the rapid capital development of the first Five-Year Plan.

The practice of *priviazka* was tested first on industrial architectural types, but it had a massive impact on socialist housing design and its delivery system in subsequent years. Once tested on an experimental site, a factory, residential block, or housing type deemed successful might join the ranks of those ready for slight adjustment and export to some far-flung site in the Soviet sphere. The logic of these last two chapters follows the scalar expansion of standardization from the object (tractor), to the building (tractor factory), to the socioresidential urban unit (*zhilkombinat*), to territory (Soviet space). Lessons learned about industrial standardization at the object scale ultimately led to the design of repeatable urban units, making *priviazka* the means by which heterogeneous Soviet territories were developed. Although not without its failures and drawbacks, standardization emerged from the Kharkiv experiment as one of the main strategies by which the Soviet Union was industrialized, settled, and housed.

Soviet Capital of Ukraine and Grain

The Bolsheviks claimed Kharkiv the capital of Soviet Ukraine as early as December 1917, while Kyiv, the former imperial-era capital, stood as the contesting administrative center of the Ukrainian People's Republic. When the dust settled in the aftermath of the Civil War, Kharkiv became the sole capital of Soviet Ukraine.[5] From 1922 to 1934, its twelve years as the capital, postrevolutionary Kharkiv proved an excellent site to test socialist space-making and iconography. The city had an expanded political role, and its population and industry increased precipitously. One 1932 chart plotted ten categories of growth in the city from 1913 to 1932 and projected their continued rise into the late 1940s (figure 7.1). Construction of new governmental buildings, housing, hospitals, schools, and modern infrastructure was needed, and the Soviet state seemed poised to provide them.[6]

State-building iconography was arguably most important, judging by capital project priorities. In 1925, an All-Union competition was held for the design of the first and most prominent governmental building in Kharkiv, the Derzhprom (*budynok derzkavnoi promyslovosty* or State Industry Building). A jury member later recalled that the winning design by Leningrad architects Samuil Kravets and Sergei Serafimov "looked without hesitation into the future . . . it was the only [submission] that broke with the eclecticism of the past . . . [its] selection is the victory of contemporary architecture in 1925." From afar, the complex resembles an "organized mountain," as Henri Barbusse, the French critic and visitor to Kharkiv, noted in 1930 (figure 7.2).[7] The building's compositional liveliness is due to its variable massing, from six to twelve stories. At the ground the building splits into three parts to allow two of the five radiocentric streets that spring from the foregrounding plaza to sneak under it. The buildings are then reconnected by skyways at various levels to visually represent cooperative collaboration in concrete and glass. Unlike most architectural competitions of the day, the winning Derzhprom entry was actually built; construction began immediately after working drawings were completed. The complex was under scaffolding from 1925 to 1929, four years fraught with great technical difficulty. Since reinforced concrete, the primary structural and finish material, was virtually unknown to the Ukrainian building trades, the building's constructional methods had to be learned from scratch. Completion of the complex was a Herculean feat intended to signal persistence and ultimately Ukraine's readiness for the world stage.

Kharkiv boasted qualities that made it an attractive choice for the new Ukrainian Bolshevik capital. The considerable population of Russian-speaking factory workers already living in the city offered culturally aligned support and immediate industrial potential. From the 1880s, Kharkiv had been the logistics center of mining in southern Russia, the control center of the southern railway, and the center for five regional factory districts.[8] The city stood to play an even more significant role in the early Soviet period as the transit and administrative center of the Donets'ko-Kryvoriz'ka industrial basin.[9] The official map of the first Five-Year Plan underscores the importance of the basin to the Soviet industrialization drive (plate 19). Only three sites merit inset maps at a larger scale: Leningrad, Moscow, and the Donets'k Basin, which was home to the raw materials of coal and iron ore needed to feed industry, and the plants to process them. Just to the west, and also within Kharkiv's sphere of influence, was the Dnipro Hydroelectric Station (DniproHES) at Zaporizhzhia, the largest infrastructural project to grow out of Lenin's GOELRO (State Commission for Electrification of Russia) Plan. Grain harvested in the agricultural heartland just beyond Kharkiv's borders funded these heavy industrial projects.

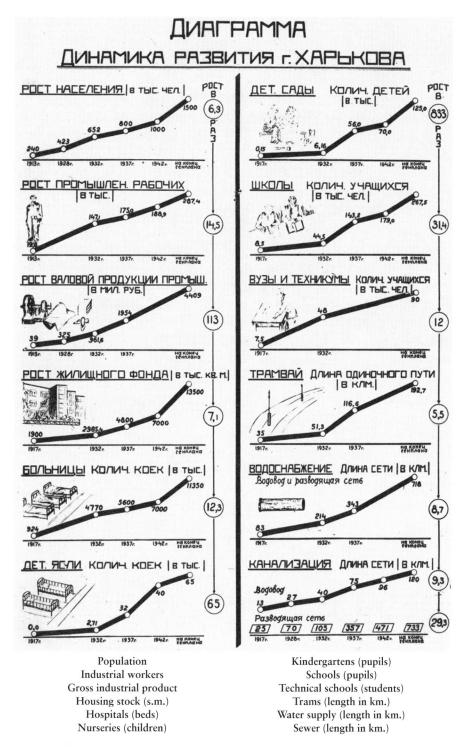

ДИАГРАММА

Динамика Развития г. ХАРЬКОВА

Population	Kindergartens (pupils)
Industrial workers	Schools (pupils)
Gross industrial product	Technical schools (students)
Housing stock (s.m.)	Trams (length in km.)
Hospitals (beds)	Water supply (length in km.)
Nurseries (children)	Sewer (length in km.)

Figure 7.1. Diagrams of dynamic growth, city of Kharkiv, c. 1932. Ten categories of growth are plotted from 1913 to 1932, and their continued rise is projected into the late 1940s. MUAR, 8-33295. Key translation and diagram by the author.

Figure 7.2. Derzhprom building, perspective (top) and aerial view (bottom). Kharkiv, Ukraine, c. 1929. Architects: S. Serafimov, S. Kravets, and M. Felger. El Lissitzky, *SSSR stroit sotsialism* (Moscow: IZO-GIZ, 1933), 267. © 2020 Artists Rights Society (ARS), New York.

Grain was a crucial raw material in the Soviet industrialization drive, as indispensable as Baku's oil and Magnitogorsk's iron ore. At the start of the first Five-Year Plan, the Soviet state established grain as the primary commodity to fund industrialization. It was a resource that the Soviet Union was capable of producing in excess, but it did not, administrators understood, "come by itself." It had to be extracted from peasant farmers, as the immediate postrevolutionary period had proven. To feed the Red Army and the starving Russian cities, armed Bolshevik units stormed Ukrainian villages in 1920–21 to forcibly requisition grain. In retaliation, peasants refused to grow crops; their dissent, coupled with a drought in 1921–22, brought famine to the region and economic collapse.[10] Peasant and worker uprisings followed, and while suppressed, mutual distrust between the rural population and perceived outsiders became the prevailing attitude that the Soviet government had to reckon with through the 1920s and 1930s. For a seven-year stretch during NEP, the Soviet state halted grain requisitioning in Ukraine, and peasants instead paid a moderate tax-in-cash to the government and were allowed to sell surplus crops at market value.

The era of self-organization and relative prosperity in the Ukrainian farmlands ended in the lead up to the first Five-Year Plan. At the Fifteenth Party Congress in December 1927, Soviet leadership codified a strategy that became known as *perekachka*—pumping agricultural resources into industrial projects.[11] Because the USSR was not in a diplomatic position to receive international credit (the US government, for instance, did not recognize the Soviet Union officially until 1933), Soviet grain was exported to provide capital funds for the purchase of foreign machinery and expertise necessary to meet the targets of the plan.

In November 1929, Stalin announced the kick-off of a comprehensive collectivization effort for Soviet agriculture. Mobilization crews conducted mass searches for hidden grain and livestock in the countryside and assessed stiff fines and issued arrests for peasants caught with concealed property. Many kulak (wealthy peasant) families were rounded up and deported to the Urals and Siberia, and their property assumed by the state. Small-scale family farms were assessed an unduly high percentage of their crops for requisition, which forced many of them into debt to the state and finally into collective farms (kolkhozy). The bumper grain crop in 1930/31 only caused the government to raise requisitioning totals, forcing more small landowners into poorly organized and inefficient kolkhozy. By 1931, so much grain was being utilized to feed the industrialization effort that there was not enough to sustain the agricultural effort. Preparation for the 1932 crop was stymied by insufficient seeds to sow and peasants who were, in any event, too hungry and exhausted to do so. Increasingly violent state-peasant interactions occurred in the immediate vicinity of the Kharkiv Tractor Factory, a plant built to manufacture agricultural machinery that many displaced and hungry peasants would not survive to use. At least 3.9 million Ukrainian peasants died in the Holodomor, or forced famine, of 1932–33.[12]

"To Common Work on Common Land! Integrally with Industry!"[13]

The interdependent economic relationship between industrializing Kharkiv and the Ukrainian countryside is illustrated through the tractor, an object coproduced and integral to the Sovietization of both territories. The tractor was among a small number of industrial products that carried specific objectives in the 1928 version of the first Five-Year Plan, even though its critical role in collectivization was not yet formulated.[14] Despite early distrust of mechanized horsepower (some peasants purportedly spat at the first tractors they saw), the tractor did become a coveted means to modernize Soviet farming life.[15] The most common and reliable model was the US Fordson tractor. Fanaticism for Detroit's agricultural machinery manifested in many ways, not least in Russified Ford-based baby names invented by Soviet peasant families.[16]

The tractor also became a powerful propagandizing tool in 1920s Soviet culture, as evidenced by its central role and frequent appearance in popular films released during the first Five-Year Plan. In *The General Line* (*Staroe i novoe*, director: Sergei Eisenstein, 1929) and *Earth* (*Zemlia*, director: Aleksandr Dovzhenko, 1930), the long-awaited tractor promises to enact transformation of *byt* and rural landscapes in particularly spatial ways. At the most intimate scale, the tractor lifts the former peasant, now collective farm worker, above the ground. In this elevated position, a new perspective emerges that focuses on the extended smooth horizon rather than the immediate tactile foreground. The tractor's efficient plows are capable of altering and inscribing the earth with the clean Euclidean geometries of mechanization, a purposeful conquering act of society over nature. Finally, and most important from

Figure 7.3. Tractor dance. As tractors altered the landscape beyond the frame, a new boundless scale was planted in the Soviet imagination, one that coincided with the diffuse patterns in the first Five-Year Plan's graphic representation. *The General Line*, 1929. Director: Sergei Eisenstein.

a planning perspective, the efficiency of the tractor drastically increases the productive range the agricultural worker can traverse in a day. The tractor-plowed landscape can be cognized as a vast territory of continuous fertile fields, commonly owned and worked without the historical divisions of contiguous family plots. All of these spatial repercussions are celebrated in the final minutes of *The General Line*. In shots montaged from various angles, the mass-produced steel wheels of a Fordson tractor approach, knock down, and snap the hand-hewn branches that formerly marked individual plots. Once the clearing is accomplished, a fleet of tractors engages in a remarkable choreographed dance (figure 7.3). They begin in a rigid line at the top of the shot, and then one by one they roll diagonally across the field joining rank to inscribe a perfectly plowed circle so large that it exceeds the limits of the camera's viewfinder by the end of the sequence. As tractors altered the landscape beyond the frame, a new boundless scale was planted in the Soviet imagination, one that coincided with the diffuse patterns in the Plan's graphic representation.

Assembling the Soviet Tractor Industry

In the common narratives of *The General Line* and *Earth*, small kolkhozy were able to usher themselves into agricultural modernization by acquiring a tractor for their collective farm. Tractor procurement for Soviet agricultural needs was more complex, and the tractor a less accessible object for individual kolkhozy, than these films suggest. Throughout the early and mid-1920s, tractors were few and far between in the Soviet Union. In 1922, the Soviet government repurposed their small store of wartime crawler tractors for agricultural use and organized state-run tractor columns, but the effort was patently unsuccessful. By the end of 1922, a mere 177 old and motley tractors existed in the entire Soviet Union, a fleet that could cover just 0.02 percent of arable land. By the end of the 1920s imports had increased the number of tractors on the ground, but these added machines did not change the complexion of Soviet agriculture appreciably. In 1928, only 1 percent of agricultural land in the Soviet Union was sown by tractor.[17]

Before 1929 the Soviet Union relied almost solely on imports of tractors from the United States. According to Anthony Sutton, the Ford Motor Company alone sold 20,000 tractors to the USSR between 1922 and 1926, and by 1927, 85 percent of all Soviet trucks and tractors had been built in Ford's Detroit factories.[18] Importation was so expensive—and the number of tractors so insufficient—that Soviet industrial planners recommended development of a Soviet-built version of the coveted agricultural machine. Charles Sorensen, one of Henry Ford's deputies, traveled to the USSR in 1928 to negotiate a contract for a new auto works. His host from the Vesenkha, vice chairman Valerii Mezhlauk, brought Sorensen to the famous Putilov Steel Works in Leningrad.[19] What the American saw on the factory floor was one of Ford's patented products. "We came right on into the assembly room and

I stopped in astonishment. There on the floor lines they were building the Fordson tractor . . . What the Russians had done was to dismantle one of our tractors in the Putilov works, and their own people made drawings of all the disassembled parts. [But] it was apparent that, while the Russians had stolen the Fordson tractor design, they did not have any of our specifications for the material that entered into the various parts. And you can't find that out merely by pulling the machine apart and studying the pieces."[20] The Soviet Fordzon-Putilovets tractors produced by this reverse engineering method were, simply, unusable. Because Soviet engineers could not recreate the precise forging process required for each steel component, the Putilov-made tractors fell apart as soon as they hit the fields. Sorensen's final assessment was that this "most ancient out-of-date plant" should be blown up with a barrel of dynamite.[21] After three years of trying and failing to replicate US technology through industrial espionage and literature review, the Soviet government brought US industrial specialists and their technology to the Soviet Union through aboveboard technical trade agreements.

A high-ranking delegation from Vesenkha visited the United States in 1928 and sought out architect Albert Kahn in his Detroit office.[22] Kahn's work for Henry Ford at the River Rouge auto plant was well known to Soviet development experts. The architecture and engineering firm had a reputation for designing flexible industrial complexes driven by the exigencies of assembly-line production. In the 1920s, Kahn's 400-person staff included architectural designers and draftsmen; structural, mechanical, electrical, and ventilation engineers; specification writers; estimators and expediters; field superintendents; and office workers.[23] In standard architectural practice at the time, coordination was sequential, meaning that architects developed a spatial scheme and then handed off drawings to outside technical specialists. Only after spatial or technical conflicts were flagged could negotiation between the architect and the engineers begin. By contrast, Kahn's office hosted all specialties under one roof and engaged in simultaneous design, touting itself as a streamlined one-stop project delivery shop. Once expedited bids for a project were in, Kahn's construction foremen could head directly to the field, and a completed factory could be up and running six months after the architect-client contract was signed. His firm's efficiency, coupled with technical know-how gleaned from his work for Ford, made Kahn an attractive consultant in the context of the breakneck pace set for Soviet industrialization.

Albert Kahn, Inc. was in an early group of US construction consultants to the Soviet Union that included specialists in auto, tractor, steel, hydroelectric power, chemical fertilizer, and baking plants.[24] The Detroit-based firm signed a $4 million contract in June 1929 to design a single tractor plant for the southern Russian city of Stalingrad (now Volgograd) to produce 40,000 tractors annually. In the same month, the *Economic Review of the Soviet Union* noted that in addition to the expected production in Stalingrad, other tractor plants would help reach a goal of 100,000 Soviet-made tractors by the end of the first Five-Year Plan. Kharkiv would produce 3,000 heavy tractors toward that goal, conceivably in the extant tractor shop at the Kharkiv Locomotive Factory, which turned out a small number of machines starting in 1924.[25] By October, the *Economic Review* reported that the Soviet Chief Machine Building Administration "had revised its program for the production of tractors and agricultural machinery during the remaining four years covered by the Five-Year Plan . . . based on the demand of the newly organized state and collective farms."[26] Due to the uptick in demand, the tempo of construction on tractor plants already under construction would increase. Additional factories would be swiftly built, preferably in the Central Black Soil region or the broadly defined "South." The tractor shop at the Kharkiv Locomotive Factory would be reconstructed to increase output from 5,000 (an inexplicable increase of 2,000 from the June numbers) to 10,000 tractors per year, and total tractor production in the USSR would reach 245,000 by the end of the Plan. This accounted for an overall 250 percent tractor production increase from estimates published just four months before (figure 7.4).

Concurrent events in the countryside just outside of Kharkiv put the astronomical tractor production increase in context. In October 1928, the Ukrainian Council of People's Commissars announced to the Council of Labor and Defense

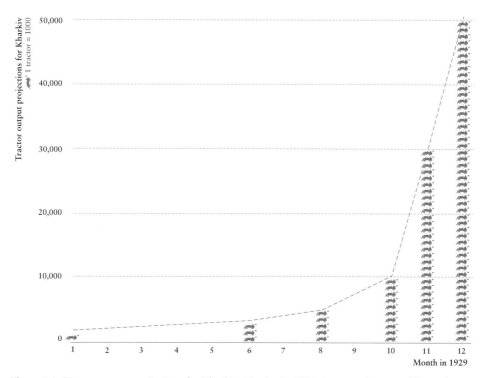

Figure 7.4. Tractor output projections for Kharkiv, Ukraine in 1929. Between August and December, the number of tractors projected for production at the future Kharkiv Tractor Factory increased from 5,000 to 50,000 units. Diagram by the author based on data from the *Economic Review of the Soviet Union*.

that new tractor allocation for the spring sowing season was insufficient simply to replace the hard used and poorly maintained tractors that had gone offline that year.[27] In October 1929, the month of these new projections, Stalin's announcement about increased agricultural collectivization was a month away. Yet not nearly enough tractors were in the fields to meet the state's escalating procurement demands. Soviet tractors needed to be produced en masse, which meant that Soviet tractor factories needed to be built, and quickly. A standard tractor factory model had to be found, one that could be as readily replicated as the Fordson tractor itself.

Standardization and Speed

Progress toward the first Five-Year Plan's ambitious capital construction goals was repeatedly thwarted by shortages. There were insufficient technical drawings, building materials, skilled foremen, and laborers to build the complexes already inscribed as active industrial sites on the plan's projective maps. In August 1929, the Building Committee of the USSR (Stroikom) issued a series of directives intended to usher the Soviet planning and construction industries into a new, more rationalized era.[28] The directives addressed settlement planning and building-scale design problems separately. Planning regulations for urban environments would be developed by the People's Commissariat for Internal Affairs (Narodnyi komissariat vnutrennikh del, NKVD), and regulations for agricultural stations would be handled by the newly established People's Commissariat for Agriculture and Food (Narodnyi komissariat zemeledeliia, NKZ). Each ministry would determine the amount and tempo of planning for its given sector, but all decisions were pegged to the timeline for national industrialization.

A separate section of the directive addressed "typification, normalization, and standardization of building design" through four requirements.[29] First, Stroikom required that each governmental department develop standard building types specific to its sector, draft measures to implement these types, and ensure their use in "real projects" by a set date. Second, building types critical to the first Five-Year Plan (especially industrial facilities) would be developed and put into use immediately. Third, nonindustrial programs such as housing and sociocultural facilities would be constructed based on only preapproved types by Stroikom. Fourth, building-related organizations would also be standardized, so that by the end of the plan all design would occur within state-run offices. Private design firms would no longer be permitted within the Soviet system. Solo practitioners like Aleksandr Ivanitskii would henceforth be subsumed into state-run design offices like Giprogor and Standartgorproekt.

Despite concerted internal efforts to satisfy the Stroikom conditions, design and construction standardization did not occur fast enough to meet the first Five-Year

Plan's schedule. On December 26, 1929, two concurrent decisions pushed the Soviet construction industry toward a model of internationally assisted national standardization. The Sovnarkom issued a decree "On measures to cure the ills of building affairs" that commanded immediate rationalization of professional practice and foundation of a special standardization institute that would develop, publish, and distribute albums of type-projects. Additionally, "foreign firms and specialists will be entrusted to the construction of individual factories," *Pravda* reported. "It is also considered expedient to attract a few engineering-construction firms to open branches to the USSR."[30] The same day, behind closed doors, the Sovnarkom signed off on a draft for an expanded contract with Albert Kahn, Inc. Under the new agreement, Kahn's firm would direct the design and supervise construction for all industrial projects in the USSR for a period of two years. In his previous contract with the Soviet government for the design of the Stalingrad Tractor Factory, Kahn had retained rights to the architect's instruments of service—drawings, specifications, and the intellectual property contained in the design—as is common practice in the United States. Under the new agreement with the Soviet government, Kahn's firm would provide its client, Vesenkha, "standard factory layouts, detailed drawings, specifications, and other technical documentation 'typical for architects working in America,'" all of which would become the lawful property of Vesenkha at the end of the term.[31]

The importance of this proviso that released Kahn's intellectual property to the Soviets, and the timing of the agreement, cannot be understated. When Kahn signed the expanded contract in January 1930, the Stalingrad Tractor Factory was nearing completion; the first Soviet-built "International" tractor rolled off the line six months later.[32] The Wall Street stock market crash just two months before contract signing also put the future of Kahn's work in the United States in question. Although the Stalingrad factory was designed under the restrictive US-style contract, once the client-favoring agreement was put in place, the Stalingrad blueprints fell under the new legal regime. On January 28, 1930, just nineteen days after the contract was inked, construction began on a new Soviet tractor factory outside Kharkiv, the capital of the Ukrainian Socialist Republic. It was to be an exact copy of Stalingrad.

Ukrainian Tractors and Stalinist Tempo: The Search for a Site

The Kharkiv Tractor Factory was not included in the original version of the first Five-Year Plan published in 1928; neither was industrialized agriculture, at least not on the scale instituted after 1929. The circumstances and the timeline of the factory's inclusion in the modified Plan are worth considering in some detail, for they reveal the mercurial and ultimately frantic nature of economic decision-making during the early stages of the plan's fulfillment. This single capital construction project also demonstrates how particular sites became implicated in the Union-wide race to Soviet industrialization and, further, how architectural strategies like standardization became invaluable in meeting the Plan's goals.

The Ukrainian branch of the State Institute for Metallurgical Factory Design (UkrGipromez) generated a feasibility and siting study in November 1929 to investigate possible Ukrainian Republic locations for a new tractor factory. It opened with a list of preconditions:

1. Guarantee of a fifteen-month construction period, in agreement with the directive provided by the highest economic bodies, such that the construction of the factory will be complete in the fall of 1931.
2. Guarantee that, even given this short period, full production will be met within a period of two years—that is, in 1931–32 the factory will turn out 30,000 units, and in 1932–33 50,000 units.
3. Achievement of a minimum cost.
4. Possible reduction of capital expenditures.[33]

The first precondition set the nearly impossible schedule. When one notes the published date of the feasibility study and calculates back fifteen months from the hard fall 1931 completion deadline, only seven months were allotted to prepare the drawings and site and gather the management and labor pool to construct the tractor factory. The second precondition stipulated that production targets be met in a timely fashion. This requirement attempted to head off a problem common to accelerated construction jobs in the first Five-Year Plan. Namely, that pressured officials would declare a factory complete before it was ready for production. The Stalingrad Tractor Factory, although still under construction at the time the report was filed, fell victim to this temptation. Leon Swajian, the US engineer and chief of construction from Detroit who oversaw Albert Kahn Inc's work on the Stalingrad, Cheliabinsk, and Kharkiv tractor factories, revealed this fact a year after Stalingrad was declared complete. "We learned a lesson from Stalingrad, which 'opened' more than a year ahead of schedule, but didn't make many tractors," Swajian noted in 1931. "At Kharkov we'll turn out a few tractors first, and then call her 'open.'"[34] The concern of the final two conditions was cost reduction, which was difficult to ensure given the expedited construction tempo. Architectural standardization was the only solution that could meet all four preconditions. The project could be either a kit, in which all components are factory fabricated and shipped to the site for rapid erection, like at Stalingrad, or a 1:1 copy of a preexisting factory, to forgo the design process altogether.

Three factors drove the tractor plant's siting. Local building materials had to be available and affordable. Quick, uninterrupted delivery of these materials had to be assured, and delivery costs minimized. Finally, the site had to be in a location from which ample construction workers could be drawn, up to 10,000 at the height of deployment (a number contingent on the requisite supply of food, medical, and cultural services). The report's authors quickly winnowed the list of possible sites down to "large industrial centers with the presence of a developed metal industry," and Kharkiv was ultimately selected because a new plant there could capitalize on a cadre of pretrained technical specialists from the small tractor shop embedded within the Kharkiv Locomotive Plant.[35]

The feasibility study's authors looked for a site no more than fifteen kilometers outside the city center of Kharkiv for a factory with an annual output of 5,000 tractors. They conducted reconnaissance on ten sites either on or adjacent to existing heavy rail lines, with areas ranging from 16 to 400 hectares. An exploratory extraurban plan shows the newly expanded Kharkiv city boundary (hatched) plus major roads and rail lines radiating from the urban center (plate 20). The ten potential sites are indicated by white rectangles coincident with their footprint; most read as tiny flecks within the greater Kharkiv region. Only one site, Losevo, a preexisting station stop on the southeast heavy rail line out of the city, could be construed as a city-sized parcel in its own right. When UkrGipromez received word that tractor output projections for the future factory would increase to 35,000 and finally to 50,000 units per year, "it became abundantly clear from the perspective of future expansion that the only site within the given radius that satisfied all requirements for such a powerful plant and factory village—really factory city— was Losevo."[36]

The Losevo siting would not have surprised the local planning community. In 1924, under the direction of local engineer A. F. Voitkevich and architect A. A. Main, Kharkiv city limits were expanded to accommodate industrial enterprise within municipal boundaries. Moskovskii Prospekt, running in a southeasterly direction from the center along the heavy rail line, was designated as an industrial growth zone where factories for machine tools, turbines, and tractors could be located.[37] Losevo was so far removed from Kharkiv city center and yet so rationally placed along the designated trajectory for future industrial growth that the site could have found support from both urbanist and disurbanist camps.

Documentary film footage of the Losevo site just prior to construction shows a snow-covered and windswept plain with a few structures in the far distance.[38] "Before" photographs show nothing more than a black strip of unoccupied land, topped by a slim strip of sky.[39] The territory was spoken for and controlled, nonetheless, by five local entities including the Stalin Kolkhoz.[40] UkrGipromez began negotiations in October with the People's Commissariat for Agriculture and Food to reassign existing tenants to parcels off the Losevo site.[41] It is no small paradox that a Ukrainian kolkhoz, undoubtedly under intense grain procurement pressure in late 1929, was uprooted to make way for a factory whose tractors were intended to bolster agricultural productivity.

The feasibility study concluded with a summary of why Losevo was the ideal site for the future tractor factory. The favorable natural conditions of the site included good local water supply; solid soil; flat topography; "healthy" qualities due to its distance from marshlands; local wind patterns that blew away from the site; and local stores of building material ingredients nearby like clay, sand, and stone. Equally important were the infrastructural and demographic resources of the site. National and local rail linkages permitted easy transportation of building materials. Proximity to Kharkiv was crucial, "so as to use all of the technical and scientific strength of the capital of Ukraine, and to rationally utilize local workforce to maximize cost reductions in the construction of the factory itself." Finally, the site benefitted from its location near the existing Kharkiv Locomotive Plant tractor shop and its cadre of experienced workers.[42]

Despite the fact that the socialist urbanism debate was at its peak when the Kharkiv Tractor Factory siting report was issued in late 1929, its authors only seriously considered sites in or adjacent to established urban nodes. The three main criteria for site selection—access to building materials, quick and inexpensive delivery of those materials, and proximity to a preexisting labor pool—are not explicitly socialist. No discussion took place about the importance of dissolving the urban-rural divide, expanding industrial efforts beyond existing urban centers, or creating a site where new socialist relations could be inculcated.[43] When UkrGipromez discussed the tractor plant's siting with the Land Department of the Regional Executive Committee and with US consultants, all parties agreed that Losevo was the ideal site.[44] The single most important factor that determined the site choice was speed. By jettisoning socialist settlement dispersal theory, UkrGipromez was able to site the factory based on project delivery criteria to meet the deadlines imposed on it.

From Stalingrad to Kharkiv: The Factories Compared

As the poor performance of the reverse engineered Fordzon-Putilovets tractors had proven, only an all-inclusive, vetted tractor production facility could ensure a faultless end product. As soon as Kharkiv was chosen as the site, negotiations began between Traktorstroi, the Kharkiv-based organization set up to oversee the construction project, and the US machine-building company Caterpillar to deliver full plans and construction support for the Kharkiv factory.[45] Talks broke down quickly over two crucial issues: cost and transparency. Traktorstroi's executives were affronted most by the US company's refusal to share industry secrets. A contemporary account followed the swift breakdown of negotiations:

> When a group of executives from Traktorstroi approached the owner of the US company "Caterpillar" with a proposal to order a project for the Kharkov Tractor Plant, the price quoted was 7 million rubles gold (!) and he agreed to develop and submit it to us only under the condition that Soviet representatives remain uninvolved in his enterprise, without the right to study the production or the machines (?!). These conditions were rejected, and technical

"aid" of US capitalists was replaced with the study of other tractor factories in the United States.[46]

The exclamatory punctuation interjected in this Soviet version of the story under-scores misaligned expectations between the two parties. The first point of friction was the price tag for the factory design. After the poor 1929 agricultural season, Soviet currency reserves could not satisfy Caterpillar's fee. Second, the US firm cor-rectly intuited that the Soviet objective in ordering the tractor plant was to possess a wholly replicable system of production. At such a price, the Soviet government expected nothing less than keys to the whole industrial process.

The expanded design consultancy contract with Albert Kahn, Inc. was solidified just before the Caterpillar talks collapsed. In mid-April 1930, the Council of Labor and Defense (STO) elected to change the tractor type at Kharkiv to the "Interna-tional," and to duplicate the plans from the Stalingrad tractor plant to speed up and reduce the cost of construction.[47] By the time this decision was made only eigh-teen months remained before tractors were expected to roll off the assembly line in Kharkiv. Even without clear planning direction, building materials were being "energetically" transported to the Losevo site in the dead of winter. A brick factory was also built three kilometers away from the future factory site, purportedly in a record eighty-two working days.[48] Ultimately, the decision to build the Kharkiv plant as a duplicate of Stalingrad came so quickly on the heels of Kahn's second con-tract that it seems likely that decision makers at Vesenkha and STO discussed the idea before the expanded agreement with Kahn was signed. Seen in this light, the accelerated completion schedule for the Kharkiv factory is the reflection of Soviet industrial planners' faith in architectural standardization.

Neither Soviet-era archives nor Kahn's Detroit office hold original Kharkiv Tractor Factory drawings. A comparison of the Stalingrad and Kharkiv Tractor Factory complexes emerges only through the aggregation of graphic, textual, and anecdotal evidence. But before comparing, it is important to invoke the difference between architectural type and model, which should not be conflated, as they work at different scales and require differing degrees of exactitude. A discrete tractor fac-tory structure (foundry, forge shop, assembly building) constitutes a type: each is a building so integrally designed to meet functional requirements that it asks to be copied near exactly. The factory site plan, on the other hand, is a model: a formal template that may be tweaked to respond to geographic, topographic, industrial, or social needs. Another way of articulating the difference is to insist that a type is tied to its plan and cannot deviate from it, whereas a model can be abstracted into a diagram that may generate any number of plans. The term "standardization" covers both: it is the practice by which a type or model is replicated and widely dissemi-nated. The Soviet-inflected standardization process of *priviazka* allowed for slight adjustment of both architectural types and models to meet the specific contours and needs of each site, and to respond to lessons learned from one installation of a proj-ect to the next, as the Stalingrad and Kharkiv pairing demonstrates. A methodical comparison of the factories in three registers—at the building scale, in terms of materiality, and as site plans—reveals that these projects were far from identical, and furthermore that 1:1 standardization of the tractor factory was not the goal of Soviet industrial planners; strategic use of US industrial types, and improvement of the factory model, was.

The Stalingrad Tractor Factory complex is composed of three large industrial buildings seen in a bird's eye perspective: a nearly square foundry at the upper right corner of the site, a large narrow rectangular assembly building stretching from the site's lower right edge, and a three-legged forge shop at the upper left (figure 7.5). To compare the plan, or type, of one individual building, it is instructive to consider the forge shop, which has the most distinctive footprint of the trio with a narrow rectangular bar for the first heat treatment and three slim legs attached perpendicularly to hold the heavy and light forge shops and die machining. Though the three-legged planometric idiosyncrasy of the forge shop is evident from the aerial, the rationality of the Albert Kahn Inc. design is revealed in the plan's structural grid (figure 7.6). The building's columnar organization, indicated by both horizontal and vertical dashed lines capped by circles, plats the site with a perfectly square six-meter grid. This neutral system, isometric in both directions, holds each leg of the building within strict structural logic and permits infinite expansion beyond the confines of the enclosed structure. The detached material storage building to the south of the forge shop, for instance, registers this infinite grid by snapping neatly into place. Kahn's outward architectural signature is in the myriad daylighting solutions illustrated in the building sections and elevations (figure 7.7). The butterfly trusses, popped monitors, and saw-tooth skylights—known in concert as the Kahn

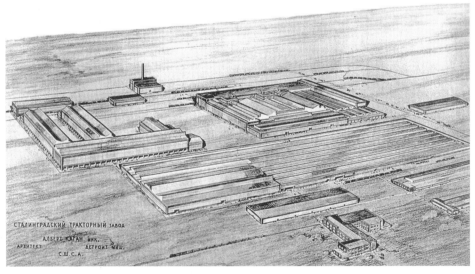

Figure 7.5. Bird's eye perspective, Stalingrad Tractor Factory, 1929. Included are the foundry building (upper right), assembly building (lower right), and forge shop (upper left). Architects: Albert Kahn, Inc. Albert Kahn Associates records, Bentley Historical Library, University of Michigan.

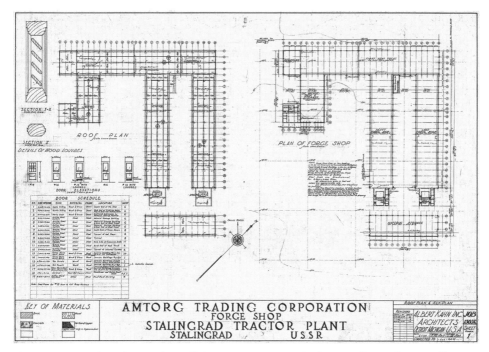

Figure 7.6. Forge shop plans, Stalingrad Tractor Factory, 1929. Architects: Albert Kahn, Inc. Albert Kahn Associates records, Bentley Historical Library, University of Michigan.

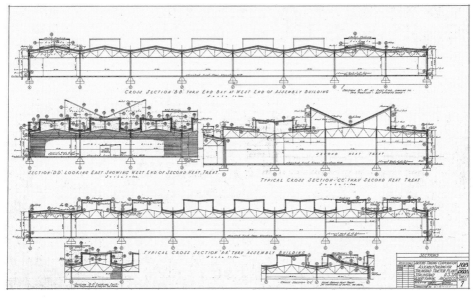

Figure 7.7. Forge shop sections, Stalingrad Tractor Factory, 1929. The Kahn Daylight System—butterfly trusses, popped monitors, saw-tooth skylights—and generously glazed elevations provide a working environment filled with natural light. Architects: Albert Kahn, Inc. Albert Kahn Associates records, Bentley Historical Library, University of Michigan.

Daylight System—work along with generously glazed elevations to provide a working environment filled with natural light from multiple directions.[49]

The dimensional precision and custom detailing promised by the drawings were quality-assured on the Stalingrad site by the project's material delivery system. The Stalingrad Tractor Factory was a fully imported artifact: a US-produced erector set constructed largely by US and German workers under the former's supervision in Stalingrad.[50] The structural columns—designed with US steel profiles—were manufactured in the United States and shipped to the USSR, as were the trusses, the door and window frames, and the technical equipment to run the factory such as steel presses imported from Toledo and Erie.[51] The construction process at Stalingrad should have been as straightforward as matching the pieces to the drawings, hoisting the members in place, and securing the joints. The relative chaos of the site and the lack of local skilled laborers to assist with construction were nonetheless stumbling blocks to the smooth and timely erection of imported pieces. Anna Louise Strong visited the Stalingrad Tractor Factory site in 1931 and noted that "around [the] finished buildings, to the north, south, east and west there is still the debris of construction, a year after the tractor works was formally declared open."[52]

The only architectural drawings of the Kharkiv Tractor Factory to have surfaced come from a 1932 pamphlet published at the completion of construction, and two later publications from 1962 and 1987 on the architecture of Soviet Ukraine. According to the 1987 book, four Soviet architects designed the "second phase" of the Kharkiv factory; Albert Kahn, Inc. is not mentioned (figure 7.8).[53] The three-legged forge shop is the sole building illustrated in the later books, and is well documented in a plan, long elevation, partial section, and axonometric projection. When this Kharkiv plan is placed on top of Kahn's Stalingrad forge shop plan, the building footprints perfectly align, down to the six-meter structural bays. Yet in a photograph, the Kharkiv factory buildings are notably heavier and more opaque than their Stalingrad siblings—thick-walled structures with punctured window openings, not the light steel-framed window walls of Stalingrad (figure 7.9).

Speed, cost, and labor supply pushed Soviet engineers and planners to differentiate the Kharkiv project materially. By April 1930 (the date of the STO resolution to produce "International" tractors at Kharkiv, which linked it to Stalingrad), imports from the United States had slowed. The tempo and economics of full factory importation were unsustainable in both the short and long term. As imported steel members slowly made their way from the United States to the USSR, tying the project schedule to foreign supply chains, on-site engineers used the downtime to rethink the structural constitution of the factory altogether.

Numerous texts confirm that significant material changes were made in the transformation from the first tractor factor complex to the second, namely from fully prefabricated steel structures at Stalingrad to hybrid steel and reinforced concrete structures at Kharkiv. Leon Swajian, the construction foreman from Kahn's office who was transferred to Kharkiv once Stalingrad was complete, noted in a 1931 interview that "Kharkov was supposed to follow the designs made for Stalingrad, but this

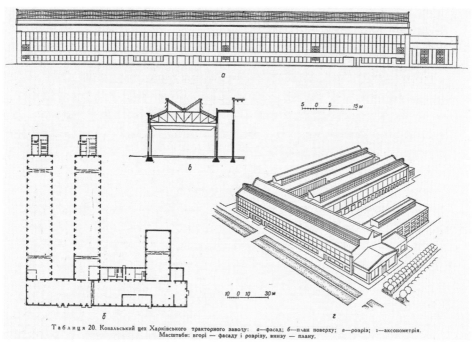

Табли ця 20. Ковальський цех Харківського тракторного заводу: *а—фасад; б—п\ан поверху; в—розріз; г—аксонометрія.*
Масштаби: вгорі — фасаду і розрізу, внизу — плану.

Figure 7.8. Forge shop elevation, section, plan, and axonometric projection, Kharkiv Tractor Factory, 1930. Architectural similarities render the Kharkiv factory a close sibling to the Stalingrad factory, although numerous material changes were made to the original (an enactment of *priviazka*). Architects: none cited. G. V. Golovko, ed., *Narysy istorii arkhitektury Ukrainskoi RSR (radianskyi period)* (Kyiv: Derzh. vyd. lit. z bud. i arkh., 1962), 2:70.

Figure 7.9. West entrance, with the forge shop's butterfly trusses visible in the background, Kharkiv Tractor Factory, Kharkiv, Ukraine, 1930s. Akademiia budivnytstva i arkhitektury URSR, *Ukraina: Arkhitektura mist i sil* (Kyiv: Derzh. vyd. lit. z bud. i arkh., 1959).

proved impossible. Imports of the steel had to be economized, so the Kharkov plant was built largely of reinforced concrete."[54] A Soviet engineer filled in the details:

> Initially, the project of the Kharkov tractor plant was fully purchased in the United States. The design department of "Indbudu" [Industrial Construction] developed only an adjustment (*priviazku*) to the overseas drawings to fit the site of the plant. But when the equipment and metalwork for workshops began to come from overseas, O. I. Nerovetsky [the Ukrainian head engineer] proposed for the first assembly plant, and then for all workshops of the plant, to replace the metal structures with reinforced concrete and to abandon the US project . . . Despite the large penalty paid for the refusal of the "US factory" due to the use of concrete on KhTZ, the country received savings of about five million rubles in gold.[55]

The Kharkiv Tractor Factory was intended to be Stalingrad's twin, an entire industrial installation preordered from US manufacturers. Ukrainian engineers in the local design bureau Indbudu were at first tasked only to tweak the project slightly to fit the Losevo site, but as the project progressed, the structural system at Kharkiv was more invasively redesigned by the Soviet technical team.

By that point, the nascent Soviet steel industry was able to produce the rough reinforcing bars for a concrete structure, which would be quicker and cheaper to build. In the final accounting, the Kharkiv factory was redesigned as a hybrid industrial complex that utilized three structural systems. The forge shop retained its full steel structure and became the only building on site that truly replicated its Stalingrad sibling; the mechanical assembly shop was redesigned as a reinforced concrete building; and the foundry was built as a concrete base topped by a steel frame. Some Kahn-like roof trusses in the complex were even redesigned by the Soviet engineers in wood. All remaining walls, and wall infill, were constructed of red brick produced at the new brick factory three kilometers from the tractor factory site.[56]

Labor diversity was a side benefit of the material changes, since "it helped with the lack of a good working cadre on site and the general deficit of qualified construction workers in the USSR," wrote one contemporary author.[57] The revised structural designs allowed Traktorstroi to employ construction workers from a number of different specialties: metal workers, stone workers, and those capable of doing the reinforcing and concrete work. Some newly skilled concrete workers were enticed to transfer their skills from Stalingrad to Kharkiv (figure 7.10). A comrade Marusin, who was "born and bred on a farm" but learned concrete-mixing at Stalingrad, became a shock brigade leader at Kharkiv, and later won the Order of Lenin for his work on both tractor factory sites. His fellow concrete-mixing colleague comrade Movlev "won fame and glory by establishing the record of 1,000 concrete mixings each day," claimed a Soviet pamphlet author.[58] It is also possible that some newly skilled local concrete specialists who had worked on the Derzhprom building (completed in 1929) came on to the project. Skilled laborers trained on one site were put into leadership positions on the next.

Figure 7.10. "Concrete-mixing brigade headed by comrades like MOVLEV and MARUSIN guarantee the rapid construction of the Kharkiv Tractor Factory." Fred E. Beal, *Foreign Workers in a Soviet Tractor Plant* (Moscow: Co-operative Publishing Society of Foreign Workers in the USSR, 1933), 12.

Although the building plans at the Kharkiv factory remained typologically related to Stalingrad's, the factory precinct's site plan changed by necessity, just as the construction materials had. Soviet chief engineer of construction, A. D. Bruskin (who also won the Order of Lenin for his work on the Kharkiv factory), oversaw both design and construction of the complex.[59] At the start of the project in April 1930, his construction management team was given a set of drawings similar to those provided by Albert Kahn, Inc. for the three main buildings at Stalingrad. "It is important to note," a contemporary account stressed, *"that the construction management did not have a definitively established final master plan at the beginning of actual construction* with the exception of the exact location of the three main shops and the repair shop, as well as the main office of the factory. The remaining parts of the general plan were worked out in detail almost over the whole length of the construction, and there were up to twelve variants of the general plan during that period." What was fixed on the Kharkiv site was the relationship between the three primary buildings, as a comparison of the site plans reveals (figure 7.11). All other planning decisions were left in the hands of the estimated 600+ local technical-engineering staff who participated in redesigning the project and drafting the working drawings needed by Traktorstroi.[60] Local designers determined the general plan of the entire factory territory, which included the organization of the support buildings, the location of underground tunnels and roads, and the placement of shops, canteens, and other social-service buildings that a socialist factory required. Planning decisions were made based on the particulars of the Losevo site, but also on lessons learned from Stalingrad. The tool and repair shops, located at the top of the Stalingrad site plan, were moved to more fitting locations within the assembly building and between the foundry and forge shops, respectively. Not only did these planning adjustments improve workflow, but they also opened up a more logical site for the main offices facing the future *sotsgorod* and tramline into Kharkiv. Smaller internal tweaks improved day-to-day working conditions. The wheel-room in the assembly shop in Kharkiv was placed not in the center of the open workspace with its deafening noise

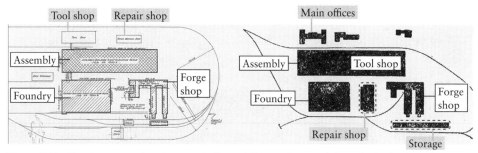

Figure 7.11. Site plan comparison between Stalingrad Tractor Factory (left) and Kharkiv Tractor Factory (right). Planning and logistical improvements were made on the Kharkiv site including moving the tool and repair shops to improve workflow and preserve a logical site for the main offices to face the future *sotsgorod* and tramline into Kharkiv. Diagram by the author based on materials from Albert Kahn Associates records, Bentley Historical Library, University of Michigan, and N. Baltuzevich, *Opyt i uroki stroitel'stva KhTZ* (Moscow: Gosstroiizdat, 1932), 34.

and combustible oil but in its own brick-walled chamber at the end of the building. Internal monorail lines and storage rooms were also adjusted and improved on the Kharkiv site to avoid the chaos and clutter that plagued Stalingrad.[61]

Priviazka, Brotherly Resemblance, and Tolerance

Given the significant differences between the factories at Stalingrad and Kharkiv, can the Kharkiv Tractor Factory be considered evidence of standardization? To answer this question requires carefully defining the term in the early Soviet context. Architectural standardization during the first Five-Year Plan was not a matter of identically duplicating a product; it required strategic reconfiguration of the original artifact to meet the conditions of a new site. At its core, the first Five-Year Plan was the accelerated effort to devise a distinctly Soviet version of standardization, one that mapped on to the realities of a transitional context. Soviet standardization may have originated with the direct importation of US industrial materials, systems, and management styles, but it morphed through trial and error into a set of practices applicable to wildly varied environments—from industrialized Ukraine to the Ural steppe.

Unlike the emphatically precise US version, the Soviet system of standardization was heuristic and flexible of necessity, forgiving of imperfect sites, supply chains, and labor conditions. Although these loosely standardized practices were appropriate for difficult circumstances, they were not without serious challenges.[62] In Swajian's opinion, Kharkiv's tractor factory was more difficult to build than Stalingrad's. Not only were the structural materials of the second factory changed for the reasons outlined above, but the success of any material request hinged on uncontrollable supply factors. As Swajian noted, US engineers were "accustomed to a country where you can order anything you like one day and get it the next," whereas in the Soviet context the construction manager either had to anticipate long lead times and make early material orders or, on a rushed project like Kharkiv, simply change tack. In the USSR, Swajian adopted a flexible management style to counter instability. "We must learn to take account of what material is available here, instead of imposing absolute standards," he concluded.[63] Swajian's comments refute the outdated but persistent narrative of unidirectional technology transfer between the United States and the USSR in the 1920s and 1930s. US efficiency and precision had to bend to Soviet contingency, and Swajian and other US experts acquired new skills of ingenuity and resilience during their Soviet tenure that they brought back to the United States and utilized on New Deal capital projects upon return. Turning out a successful project in the early USSR required more than competent administrative skills from the expert. Success hinged on the ability of the expert to solve problems on the fly, to use the materials and labor at hand, and to work toward acceptable tolerances, not perfection.

The long-term implications of the tractor factory standardization experiment become clearer at the Union scale. The Kharkiv Tractor Factory was a model project for the *priviazka* system of typological replication that continued well after

Kahn staff left the USSR in 1932. This Soviet version of standardized architectural production assumed that strategic adjustments to the original model would be necessary to permit the final product and its model to bear a family resemblance even if the material and labor conditions under which they were created differed drastically, as Yves Cohen aptly notes in his study comparing the US and Soviet versions of Ford tractors:

> Compared side by side, a *Fordson* and *Fordzon-Putilovets* resembled each other like brothers. At this level they were standard products; the artifact was well copied. At another level, the parts and the mechanical assemblies resembled each other, but there the resemblance ended. I do not at all mean to say that standardized products have to be identical. On the contrary: it is this very paradox of mass production that Henry Ford was the first to solve; to be identical at the level of the complete product, its constituent parts need to not be identical.[64]

What is important to control in the process of replication is not equivalence but tolerance, Cohen stresses, a reasonable distance between the original and its copy so that the two act satisfactorily alike. In the case of the Fordzon-Putilovets tractor, external tolerance was acceptable for propagandistic purposes. A photograph of a Soviet-made Fordzon-Putilovets plowing collectivized fields was good enough for Stalin to claim socialist cooptation of US technology. As Ford's colleague Sorenson found, however, poor manufacture of mechanical parts rendered the internal tolerance of the Fordzon-Putilovets unacceptable. The Soviet-made tractor could not perform its task; it disintegrated on the field. The Fordzon-Putilovets might have looked like a Fordson, but it did not act like a Fordson. Soviet standardization of the tractor was a failure.

Cohen's notion of tolerance is helpful to answer the question of whether the Stalingrad and Kharkiv tractor factories are early evidence of Soviet architectural standardization. If judged by external tolerance, Kharkiv was a poor copy of Stalingrad. The structural systems and material constitution of the two factories differed so greatly that the buildings could never be mistaken for one another. But the architectural DNA—the plans—reveal that the forge shops, at least, were typologically identical, as were the relationships between the three main factory buildings on the site plan. Since the task of the factories relied on spatial congruence, not appearance, internal tolerance was well within acceptable limits. The Kharkiv factory might not have looked like Stalingrad, but it acted the same. Soviet standardization of the tractor factory was a success.

Another way to assess whether the Kharkiv Tractor Factory was an example of architectural standardization is to pose the question to the architect of the original. Would Albert Kahn, well versed in Ford's philosophy of mass production, have considered Kharkiv his project, despite the copious material changes made to the copy?

In fact, he did. In a 1939 monograph, *Industrial Architecture of Albert Kahn, Inc.*, a two-page spread illustrates a map of the world peppered with cities in which Kahn architecture resides.[65] Kahn projects are found on all six habitable continents, with the United States and the USSR sharing the highest density of building. Stalingrad, Kharkiv, and Cheliabinsk are all indicated as Kahn sites, despite the fact that Soviet sources cited him as the architect of Stalingrad solely. In total, Kahn office records confirm that 531 factories based to some degree on the firm's drawings and specifications were completed in the USSR by the time the firm's two-year consultancy was over, and more than 4,000 Soviet technicians were trained by Kahn management in Detroit, Moscow, and in the satellite construction offices.[66] The number of unconfirmed facilities based on plans or details developed by Kahn's office, *priviazka* copies of brotherly resemblance, will probably never be known but is likely in the thousands.

Nearly a decade after the Soviet consultancy, Kahn noted that, in the firm, "all departments start work simultaneously instead of working in successive stages and this, in addition to speeding up the work of making the drawings, means that plans and specifications for all trades can be submitted for bids at one time. With this procedure, the drawings for a large factory can be completed in a week or ten days' time if necessary."[67] This speedy turn-around was bolstered by lessons Kahn's designers learned in the USSR. *Assembly Plant Plans* (1934), a booklet of automobile assembly building designs for numerous US sites, was compiled two years after Kahn's employees returned from the Soviet Union. It shows slightly tweaked versions of the same plan adjusted for site particularities, possibly inspired by the Soviets' practice of *priviazka*.[68]

Anna Louise Strong compared the two tractor factories in a 1931 article. "Poor Stalingrad," she lamented, "that had not only to start with a solid mass of unskilled labour, but to develop skill for itself and Kharkiv too! Shop by shop, the Americans [in Kharkiv] showed me improvements, made on the basis of Stalingrad experience." Her most poignant observation followed. "*Those who point to improvements made under capitalism through competition of opposing plants, overlook the improvements made in the USSR by passing on experience from one plant to another.*"[69] Within the confines of Soviet socialism, a new kind of architectural research and development process was invented. Each construction project presented an opportunity to learn from internal mistakes and improve on the model within the limits of a still-developing industrial complex. The Kharkiv Tractor Factory was not a mere copy of Stalingrad, or even a younger brother. It was its genetically superior offspring.

Two types of Western standardization—architectural and managerial—were assumed by the Soviets during and after the conclusion of the first Five-Year Plan. First, standard Western architectural details, plans, sections, and entire multibuilding projects were absorbed into everyday Soviet design practice. As promised by the Sovnarkom in 1929, "typification" was accelerated by the publication of books like *Modern Prefabricated-Factory Architecture* (*Sovremennaia fabrichno-zavodskaia arkhitektura*, 1933) by professor D. Tsvetaev (figure 7.12).[70] This manual, full of architectural details of the "American type," was pulled from the shelves in the later 1930s, when the story of US involvement in Soviet industrialization was no longer ideologically palatable, but the renamed details remained in circulation.[71] Second, centralized design organization, pioneered in Kahn's Detroit office, was quickly adopted as the Soviet managerial standard.[72] One Soviet example, the State Institute for City Planning (Gosudarstvennyi institut po proektirovaniiu gorodov or Giprogor), founded in 1929, employed architects, transportation engineers, and sanitation experts among other specialists within a single agency.

Most important, out of this period a distinctly Soviet version of architectural standardization emerged: *priviazka*. When the Kharkiv Tractor Factory was nearing completion in 1930, People's Commissar for External and Internal Trade, Anastas Mikoyan, laid out the official Soviet stance on standardization going forward. Mikoyan was well acquainted with US industrial practices but believed that only under a planned economy would standardization be optimized. "If we had such technology as America has, we would succeed fully in realizing a system of mass production and standardization and we would reduce wastefulness in the economy to nothing, for there are no such social barriers in our way," Mikoyan claimed.

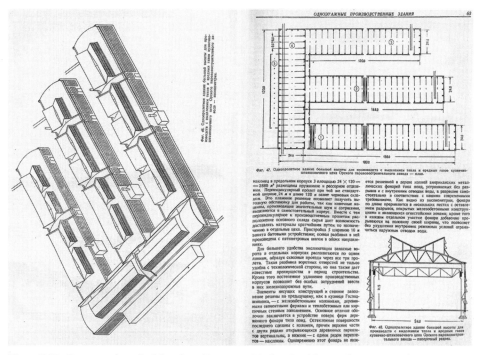

Figure 7.12. One-story forge building from Tsvetaev's *Modern Prefabricated-Factory Architecture*, a Soviet handbook for factory design. This spread shows the forge from the Orsk Locomotive Factory, although the building type is clearly emergent from earlier factories like Stalingrad and Kharkiv. Other spreads feature details of the "US type." V. D. Tsvetaev, *Sovremennaia fabrichno-zavodskaia arkhitektura*, 2nd ed. (Moscow: Gosstroiizdat, 1933), 62–63.

"When we overcome technical backwardness then doubtless we shall achieve colossal results. We will have a planned economy, high technology, mass production, standardization, and specialization of plants as well as regions."[73] In Mikoyan's view, once the planned economy and mass production were successfully combined, Soviet technology would leapfrog US technology. Mikoyan went so far as to implicate national space in his long-term standardization schema. He envisioned not only individual industrial installations like the Kharkiv Tractor Factory, but whole regions planned as standardized units. The diffuse settlement diagram justified by citations of Marx and Engels and forwarded by socialist urban theoreticians like Sabsovich and Okhitovich, could be instantiated by predesigned blocks colonizing the Soviet landscape. New Kharkiv, the name given to the *sotsgorod* constructed across the tram tracks from the Kharkiv Tractor Factory, was one of the first successful test cases of just such a standardized urban unit.

8

SOCIALIST URBANIZATION THROUGH STANDARDIZATION

The whole area was broken into functional zones, which, in their turn, were divided into thirty-six residential complexes. Each one of these complexes was composed of residential buildings and primary service buildings—schools, kindergartens and nurseries, clubs, canteens, and sports facilities . . . The design considered the construction experience from the residential area at the Stalingrad Tractor Factory and the Magnitogorsk Metallurgic Plant, where analogous complexes were calculated to hold 2,500 people.

The proposal at that time, on the development side, can be characterized as a kind of qualitative leap to a new kind of socialist city building. Despite the individual limitations of our project, practically all ideas and even aspects of the terminology became realized in contemporary architecture and city building.

—P. E. SHPARA (1998)

THE KHARKIV TRACTOR FACTORY WAS AN IMPROVEMENT ON ITS STALINGRAD predecessor in many ways, but none more so than in the residential sphere. Despite the fact that the Vesnin brothers had devised a general plan for the Stalingrad Tractor Factory *sotsgorod* in 1929, only half of that factory's workers were housed by 1931. The rest camped out on the plateau overlooking the factory or traveled to work on the crowded tram and bus lines from the city center of Stalingrad, about fifteen kilometers away.[1] Archival photographs show rows of pitched white tents on the Stalingrad site that recall those used to house workers at Magnitogorsk.

New Kharkiv, the exemplary *sotsgorod* designed and built for the Kharkiv Tractor Factory, by contrast, proved that the lessons of architectural standardization for industry could trickle down to Soviet housing. As for industry, standardization of residential design was a primary strategy for meeting the first Five-Year Plan's capital construction goals because time did not allow for design variance. At New Kharkiv, residential and sociocultural buildings organized in replicable blocks introduced a *sotsgorod* model that improved on previous attempts in Stalingrad and Magnitogorsk, such that it became exportable to other Soviet industrial sites.

Standardization was a central preoccupation of Soviet architects, economic planners, and government officials during the first Five-Year Plan, although for each of those groups the reasons for pursuing architectural standards sprung from differing concerns. For Soviet architects, to embrace standardization was to embrace rationality, new technology, and to assist in the construction of environments appropriate to the *novyi byt* (the new socialist way of life). Soviet economic planners' embrace of standardization was a matter of self-preservation in a society hell-bent on rapid industrialization, since the tempo of the plan accelerated project delivery. For government officials, first Five-Year Plan was a colonizing project—its elemental goal was to plot dots on the map and connect them into a productive web. Standardization was a way to speed up construction, ensure a degree of quality, and to conquer, through installation of industrial complexes continent-wide, the otherwise uncontrollable vastness of Soviet space.

Although the Kharkiv Tractor Factory design team (Traktorstroi) and New Kharkiv design teams worked primarily in their dashed boxes—factory to the north, *sotsgorod* to the south—the projects were integrally connected (figure 8.1).

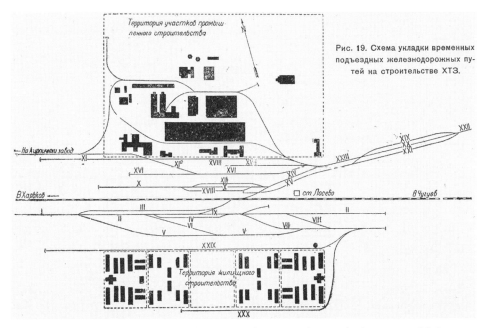

Figure 8.1. The separation of the tractor factory complex (top) and New Kharkiv *sotsgorod* (below) is stressed by individual dashed boxes around each project. The tram line that divides them leads into the city of Kharkiv to the west. N. Baltuzevich, *Opyt i uroki stroitel'stva KhTZ* (Moscow: Gosstroiizdat, 1932), 34.

Traktorstroi design engineers and New Kharkiv architects, the latter under the leadership of architect Pavel Aleshin, collaborated to ensure that their projects came online more or less simultaneously. Like Baku, Kharkiv offers a prime example of socialist urban praxis, although Aleshin was under more pressure than Ivanitskii had been in Baku to solve pragmatic problems quickly within a mercurial theoretical and political context. The socialist settlement debate was at its height during the same months in which the New Kharkiv *sotsgorod* architectural brief was being drafted. Aleshin noted that it was an "unnerving" time to be designing the very type of project that resisted clear definition.[2]

The ideological fog that surrounded the proper form for the *sotsgorod* unsettled the designers, but it was not the most distressing circumstance that they had to reckon with. In the immediate vicinity of the site, farming communities were being forcibly collectivized in a state-peasant struggle so violent that Lynne Viola has characterized it as a second civil war.[3] The early months of 1930, when the design team was frantically devising plans, were particularly brutal. De-kulakization (the stripping of property from wealthy peasants) was in full swing—twelve kulak farms were attacked and looted in one village near Kharkiv in a single outing.[4] On one March day in 1930, mass uprisings were reported in sixteen districts of Ukraine, with peasant groups of up to 500 people facing off against Soviet collectivizers with sawn-off shotguns, hunting rifles, and axes.[5] These episodes do not figure in the histories of the Kharkiv Tractor Factory written by Soviet authors, nor do they show up in archival materials related to the project, but they must undoubtedly have disquieted the designers in their work.

In Kharkiv, both the tractor factory and *sotsgorod* were *priviazki* (architectural adjustments), variations on architectural themes explored first elsewhere. Out of the spotlight, with comparatively low expectations compared to Magnitorgosk, the designers of New Kharkiv had the freedom to experiment with ideas explored in the 1929 Gosplan conference and journalistic debates, competition briefs, and designs for other sites. On this less prominent site, urban and architectural ideas floated for Magnitogorsk finally materialized.

Establishment of Socialist Housing Types

At the beginning of 1927, the architect Georgii Vegman focused on the critical relationship between the Soviet housing crisis and typological design in an essay published in *Sovremennaia arkhitektura* (SA).[6] The only way to improve the abysmal per capita living area allotted to each Soviet citizen, and solve the housing problem that was negatively impacting Soviet industrial growth, was to devise rational, replicable unit and building types, he argued. "The consolidation and concentration of construction organizations, and the establishment of types, are the essential prerequisites to reduce the cost of construction," Vegman insisted.[7] In direct response to his plea, SA launched the "Comradely Competition for Communal Housing" in late 1927 to brainstorm new standardized residential units within the socialist framework.[8] The eight published competition entries promoted the entire residential complex not as simply an agglomeration of individual units, but as a "social condenser," a collective space in which new social relations could be inculcated. At the same time, the entries capitalized on the designers' control of space, specifically the phenomenological asset of sectional generosity (expanded ceiling height) within the tiny footprint of the individual living cell. The promise of the competition entry designs prompted Stroikom RSFSR (the Building Committee of the Russian Republic) to tap the architect and SA editor Moisei Ginzburg to head a new Typification Section (Sektsiia tipizatsii) in 1928, to design experimental housing types, establish standards for future development, and draw up programs for the training and qualification of technical personnel.[9]

Over the next few months, the Stroikom Typification Section designed six standard residential unit types. When these units were first published in SA in early 1929, Ginzburg laid out an exhaustive list of social and technical criteria that the section's architects considered as they designed.[10] "The constructive study of housing should be based on the principle of maximum standardization of all elements, and should strive for the industrialization of building," Ginzburg insisted, meaning that Soviet architects engaged in housing design were beholden to use mass-produced elements to mass produce housing. But on a broader conceptual level, Ginzburg encouraged architects to think of standardization as a multiscalar design problem. "The design solution for the residential cell," he explained, "leads to the solution for the residential block and residential area."[11]

The most innovative unit designed by the Stroikom Typification Section, the Type F, successfully met the laundry list of criteria Ginzburg laid out (figures 8.2 and 8.3). The one-room twenty-seven-square-meter unit is accessed up or down a half flight of stairs from a skip-stop common corridor. The high-ceilinged living space, naturally lit by a wall of windows, was designed with only a "kitchen element"—a closet with shelves for dishes and a hotplate—to save space and encourage the occupant to dine in the communal canteen. Sleeping occurs in a low-ceilinged loft six steps up or down from the living space (squeezed above/below the skip-stop corridor) that serves as a secondary source of light and air from windows on the back wall of the building. Despite the significant press they received, however, only six projects that utilized Stroikom units were built, the most notable being the Narkomfin Communal House in Moscow, completed in 1929.[12]

Tsekombank, the Central Bank of Communal Services and Housing and the primary state construction funder, undertook its own housing typology research, yet it forwarded a more flexible procedure for housing standardization that encouraged local modification. From 1924 to 1928, Tsekombank gathered "a huge and diverse collection of materials, from almost all regions and districts of the Union." The bank published the materials in the album *Projects for Workers' Dwellings*

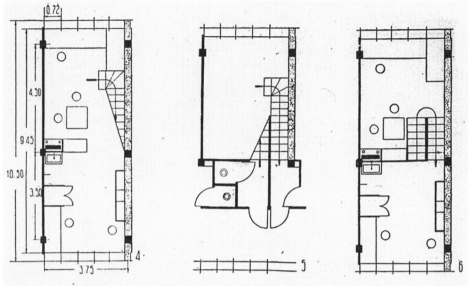

129. 2-й дом СНК. Планы квартиры—типа F. 4-й, 5-й и 6-й этажи

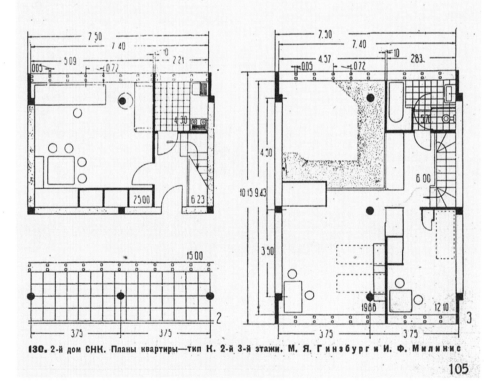

130. 2-й дом СНК. Планы квартиры—тип К. 2-й 3-й этажи. М. Я. Гинэбург и И. Ф. Милинис

105

Figure 8.2. Narkomfin F-type unit (top) and K-type unit (bottom) based on research by the Stroikom Typification Section. Architects: M. Ia. Ginzburg and I. F. Milinis. M. Ia. Ginzburg, *Zhilishche* (Moscow: Gosstroiizdat, 1934), 105.

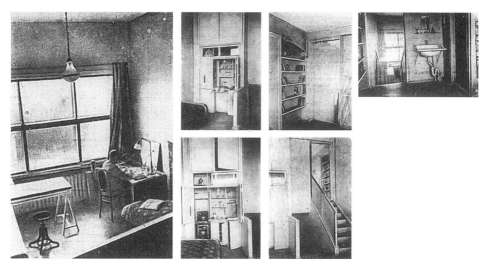

Figure 8.3. F-unit interiors, RZhSKT House, Saratov, Russia, 1930. Architect: S. A. Lisagor. M. Ia. Ginzburg, *Zhilishche* (Moscow: Gosstroiizdat, 1934), 127, 129.

(*Proekty rabochikh zhilishch*) that "summarized the accumulated experience and reflected existing achievements in the design of housing." The album, published in 1929, gestures at the practice of *priviazka*, though the text uses different terminology, including the term *popravka* (amendment) and *mestnyi programmnyi korrektiv* (local programmatic adjustment).[13]

E. Luganovskii, director of Tsekombank, noted in the album's preface that "given the extremely varied living and climatic conditions in each region of the USSR, it is obviously impossible to produce comprehensive solutions immediately."[14] The editors of the album also highlighted the Soviet Union's environmental heterogeneity, which precluded rigid typological replication:

> The variety of local conditions in both the center and on the edges of our Union make it impossible to identify a single solution to the housing question through developing type-projects. To produce the massive number of required types to meet all local requirements, considering all extremely diverse climatic, domestic, and technical conditions, would be an overly long and overwhelming task for a single publication. [We decided] that a more productive and urgent task was to publish only the technical, economic, and sanitary fundamentals of housing design, expressed through concrete examples, to provide a solid basis for local study and detailing . . . Changes in the building plot, orientation of the house, its number of stories, even the living area for specific units are achieved by minor amendments (*dostigaiutsia neznachitel'nymi popravkami*) to the original project or by choosing from several typical options.[15]

Most of the texts in Tsekombank's *Projects for Workers' Dwellings*, like the above, encourage architects to modify the types in the pages. The Tsekombank units are middle ground hybrids between type, which asks to be replicated near exactly, and model, which is a diagram that can absorb design changes. Although the designer is wise to start from a proven housing type, the editors note, nearly all unit characteristics are available for "minor amendments," including the building's solar orientation, its height, and the area of each unit. It is even possible to cherry-pick various typological options and create a new building form that is nonetheless related to the originals from which it was developed. This flexible process of architectural accommodation to a given context—the very definition of *priviazka*—does not map onto a Western conception of standardization but is logical given the diverse conditions for which Soviet architects were likely to be designing.

The Tsekombank album separates the types into four divisions: urban housing, rural housing, collective living buildings, and service buildings. The urban types are designed by section (*sektsiia*), a repeatable block of units that share stairwell access. The section, which might hold anywhere from two to four units, is repeated horizontally and stacked vertically until the desired site is filled or population met (figure 8.4). Rural types in the album include "paired" single-story houses like those built at Stepan Razin in Baku, and even wooden barracks like those occupied by Magnitogorsk's workers. The collective living types, like the dormitory seen in the illustration, are composed of individual sleeping cells supplemented by shared programs like canteens and reading rooms.

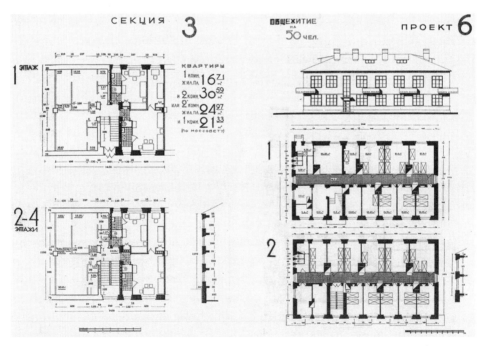

Figure 8.4. Worker housing types from Tsekombank, *Projects for Workers' Dwellings*. The multiunit apartment "section" (left) is a repeatable block of units that share stairwell access. The dormitory-style building (right) is composed of individual sleeping rooms and communal facilities. Tsentral'nyi bank kommunal'nogo khozaistva i zhilishchnogo stroitel'stva, *Proekty rabochikh zhilishch* (Moscow: Izdanie Tsekombanka, 1929), 27, 195.

Though these initiatives engaged typology at the discrete scale of the living cell and residential building, standardization of larger urban types and models—the entire factory complex, the neighborhood, the city—did not emerge until well into the first Five-Year Plan's crisis of manufactured deadlines. After the socialist settlement debate had died down, the Stroikom Typification Section was transformed into the Socialist Settlement Section of the Gosplan Building Division of the Russian Republic (Sektsiia sotsrasseleniia stroisektora gosplana RSFSR).[16] Among the experts working on new standardized settlement units were the architects Mikhail Barshch, Moisei Ginzburg, and Ivan Leonidov; sociologist Mikhail Okhitovich; and economist Genrikh Puzis. The Socialist Settlement Section's disurbanized, a-centralized, decentralized, and dispersed settlement diagrams skipped over the intermediate scale of the site plan, and instead jumped directly to the regional implications of disurbanization (figure 8.5). The dispersive process is clear in these diagrams, but the form of any given node is not.

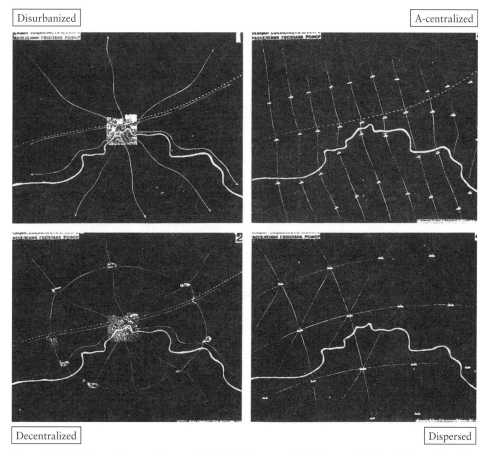

Figure 8.5. Socialist settlement schemes: disurbanized, a-centralized, decentralized, and dispersed settlement, 1930. Designers: Socialist Settlement Section of Gosplan RSFSR. Diagram by the author based on *Sovremennaia arkhitektura*, no. 6 (1930): 2.

Replicable urban units perform at the middle scale—what we now call urban design—where architecture and particularities of the site remain material and legible. This middle scale was where the New Kharkiv *sotsgorod* team worked—particularly with the design of the typical *zhilkombinat* (housing combine), the planned, standardized residential block that includes housing, educational institutions, social and commercial services, and local commercial programming for a population of 2,000–3,000, the building block of the *sotsgorod*.

Just as the tractor factory design team had learned from the mistakes at Stalingrad, the New Kharkiv team benefitted from housing research and development that preceded it in Moscow, Magnitogorsk, and elsewhere in the Soviet Union. Architectural and site planning criteria written into the Magnitogorsk competition brief, and well known to the head architect Pavel Aleshin, can be discerned at New Kharkiv, as can Stroikom Typification Section housing design criteria, and the Tsekombank housing type designs.

Actionable *Sotsgorod* Brief

Less than a month after Losevo was chosen as the Kharkiv Tractor Factory site, Traktorstroi, the entity overseeing project delivery, collaborated with the design-consulting arm of the Ukrainian branch of the People's Commissariat for Internal Affairs (NKVD) to divvy up and complete preliminary civil engineering tasks.[17] Local specialists prepared site-specific materials including two geological soil sections, a detailed site plan showing possible water supplies to the site, a "wind rose" diagram, and a topographical site plan (figure 8.6). The blueprints confirmed the Losevo site's assets; it was connected to heavy rail, was flat and on a solid geological base with good access to water, and had a regular wind profile. Logistics planning to ensure the timely arrival of building materials and workers to the site was also mobilized as part of this predesign effort.

In February 1930—after the publication of the Magnitogorsk All-Union competition brief, but before the publication of its entries—the NKVD Section for Rationalization, Standardization, and Reconstruction of the Communal Economy of the Ukrainian Republic, under which the New Kharkiv design team sat, submitted an initial *sotsgorod* brief.[18] It defined New Kharkiv as a "transitional" model socialist settlement, with three programmatic sectors—production, residential, and social-cultural—that together would support a *novyi byt*:

> The function of the production sector is to create real value for the livelihood of the workers. The function of the residential sector, influenced by centuries of tradition, is to serve workers' individual existence, their physical and biological needs, and to maintain their strength and health for human procreation, introspection, and education. All problems of *byt* are resolved

in this residential sector, making it more stable and causing its extraordinary transformation and consolidation. It is precisely here that the most painless and quick transition to complete socialization lies. The function of the socio-cultural sector, in direct connection with the residential sector, is to improve relationships between workers, and to develop a societal organization that serves the needs of the team.[19]

The New Kharkiv *sotsgorod* brief was more tempered in its approach to socialization than the Magnitogorsk competition brief had been, a fact that can be attributed to its precise temporal situation and obligation to buildability. By February 1930, the tide was turning against rapid, enforced socialization. Even Sabsovich was modifying his language, writing that "the definition of the socialist *byt* is far from being sufficiently developed . . . we do not yet have any experience in this matter. We have to feel and fumble in the dark to shape this new life. With that in mind, it is necessary to remember that while we build our cities, we are in a period transitioning towards socialism."[20] Although the Central Committee of the Communist Party had yet to issue its "Resolution on the work to restructure *byt*," which shut down "semi-fantastic" schemes like Sabsovich's, bureaucratic support was waning for radical cultural revolution because industrial demands eclipsed ideological imperatives as the first Five-Year Plan pushed into its second half.[21]

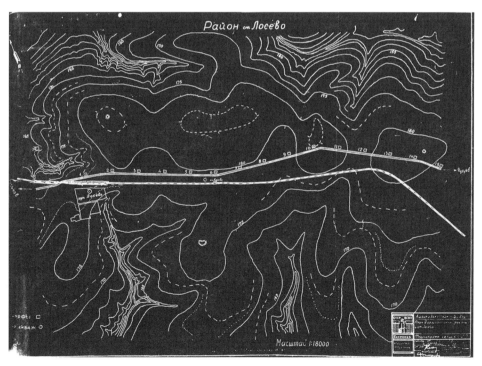

Figure 8.6. Topography at the Losevo site, chosen for the Kharkiv Tractor Factory, 1929. Report authors: Ukrgipromez. TsDAMLM Ukrainy, f. 8, po. 1, od. zb. 259, ark. 33.

The language of the New Kharkiv architectural brief registers its liminal status. Naming the project a "transitional socialist city" left the door open for the inclusion of certain traditional (i.e., prerevolutionary) architectural forms and cultural practices. The brief took a moderate stance on the controversial issue of familial structure, for instance, stipulating that "child-rearing will transition to become entirely socialized, such that children up to seventeen years of age will all be under socialized care in the near future . . . preschool and school-aged children up to ten years old will live with their parents with the exception of the daytime."[22] The New Kharkiv brief was, however, also laced with reference to a new socialist *byt* that would be constructed through interdependence of productive, residential, and sociocultural spheres.

The socialization of *byt* language in the New Kharkiv brief may well have been mandated by economic policy. In late 1929, the state banking system established strict borrowing preconditions for housing projects that were pegged to social transformation. In a Sovnarkom resolution attached to the New Kharkiv brief, Tsekombank requirements for residential construction lending in the 1929–30 building season are spelled out. "In the case of projects submitted by the borrower for house-communes, block developments, and villages, lending will be extended only to those that involve the following elements for the socialization of life: communal kitchens and dining / eliminating the kitchen in the individual apartments / nurseries, kindergartens with daycare for children, mechanized laundries, sports grounds and club facilities."[23] To receive capital funding for a housing project from Tsekombank, the borrower had no choice but to include robust communal services for the residents and refrain from including kitchens in the majority of the living units. But while this policy of Tsekombank's seems to have predetermined the constituent programs for New Kharkiv, the design of the site plan and buildings was a matter left to the New Kharkiv team. This process aligned with the bank's philosophy, which stated that typical plans "absolutely require local programmatic adjustments (*korrektivy*)."[24]

Linear City

Late 1929 to mid-1930, when the first site plans for New Kharkiv were being devised, was the most active period of the socialist settlement debate. Among the theoretical tracts published in just this small window of time were *Toward the Problem of Constructing the Socialist City* (Gosplan), *Sotsgorod* (Miliutin), *Cities of the Future* and *Socialist Cities* (Sabsovich), and the Magnitogorsk All-Union competition brief. All of these texts, and the vigorous public discussions that accompanied them, established the intellectual foundations for socialist space. More often than not, the authors sidestepped formal recommendations and stopped well short of nuts-and-bolts design detail. Stalingrad, Nizhnii Novgorod, Kharkiv, and a handful of other industrial settlements constructed during the first Five-Year Plan were the testing grounds.

The architect Pavel Aleshin was the head of the New Kharkiv design team. At that time, Aleshin was the chief architect of Giprograd, the State Institute for City Planning in the Ukrainian Republic, and at forty-nine an exact contemporary of Aleksandr Ivanitskii. Both architects were born in present-day Ukraine in 1881, attended the prestigious Institute of Civil Engineers in St. Petersburg, and graduated together in 1904.[25] Like Ivanitskii, Aleshin studied under notable Russian civil engineers at the institute, and he worked with one, G. D. Dubelir (author of the seminal book *City Planning* (*Planirovka gorodov*) from 1911), as chief city architect on a plan for Murmansk in 1918. Aleshin conducted the majority of his professional life in prerevolutionary and then Soviet Ukraine, but maintained contacts in Leningrad and Moscow, and kept abreast of architectural debates ongoing in the Soviet capital. Books from Aleshin's professional library that now reside at the Canadian Centre for Architecture include copiously annotated texts from the 1929–30 socialist urbanism debates. Aleshin's personal papers at the Central State Archives and Museum of Literature and Art of Ukraine (TsDAMLM), are also stocked with evidence of his engagement with socialist settlement issues. An original copy of the Magnitogorsk competition brief is clipped together with photographs of competition drawings and models, and materials from the Stalingrad *sotsgorod* competition are tucked in an envelope and annotated on the verso in Aleshin's hand, even though he did not enter either competition.[26]

In Aleshin's personal copy of the November 1929 Gosplan conference proceedings, the opening paper by architect A. Zelenko received the most readerly attention.[27] In it, Zelenko proposed a linear model for socialist settlement, and the passages that explain and justify this proposal are those most vigorously highlighted by Aleshin. The new socialist city, stated Zelenko, should be "built on the principles of production, expanded in a linear direction."[28] Zelenko described three zones in the linear city—manufacturing, green space, and residential— and articulated their relationships. "The manufacturing part of the city," he wrote, "should be separated from the residential area by a green boulevard or band on which internal transportation runs, and this is where the residential sector begins." The width of this green band is to provide a substantial buffer between the factory and housing but also be narrow enough to provide workers a walking commute. Zelenko continued, "the houses, which will accommodate 2,000–3,000 residents, can be called a block (*blok*), or a *zhilkombinat*. These residential blocks, separated from one another by a large green reserve and roads, can be placed in a chessboard grid, so that the whole city of 50,000 residents occupies 5–6 kilometers in length and 2–3 kilometers in width."[29] Zelenko included with his text diagrams of the linear organization of the industrial sector (diagram 1), and a single residential block bundled with nurseries and kindergartens (diagram 2) (figure 8.7).

Zelenko's ideas were foundational for the organization of the Kharkiv Tractor Factory and New Kharkiv. New Kharkiv's site plan, however, bears little resemblance to Zelenko's diagrams, and instead mimics the linear city proposed by Nikolai Miliutin for the Stalingrad Tractor Factory (figure 8.8).[30] Like Zelenko, Miliutin stressed that new socialist settlements must be organized according to industrial principles. "A flowing functional-assembly-line system is an absolutely necessary basis for the new planning," Miliutin wrote. "The residential sector of the settlement must be set up parallel to the productive zone and must be separated from it by a green belt (buffer zone). This protective strip must be no less than 500 meters wide."[31] Miliutin detailed more thoroughly than Zelenko the multiple social and economic benefits of a linear settlement scheme. First, the green strip acts as the "lungs" of the project to separate and filter any stray industrial particulates that might drift toward the residential zone. Second, the relative proximity between the factory and its *sotsgorod* cuts out the "superfluous expense for intersettlement transportation," since each worker has a short ten- to twenty-minute walk to work from his sleeping cell. Lastly, the green axis structures rational linear growth of the sectors in either direction along its length while maintaining the optimal distance between them.

Between Zelenko, Miliutin, Okhitovich, and others, the linear city concept was in the air at the start of 1930, when Aleshin and his team developed the first draft

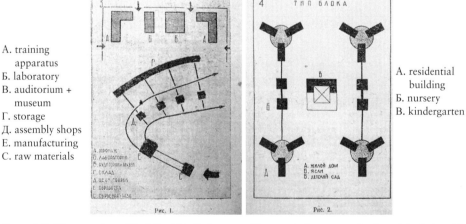

A. training
   apparatus
Б. laboratory
В. auditorium +
   museum
Г. storage
Д. assembly shops
Е. manufacturing
С. raw materials

A. residential
   building
Б. nursery
В. kindergarten

Figure 8.7. "Construction of Socialist Cities" diagrams. Diagram 1: linear organization of the industrial sector. Diagram 2: single combine-block residential cluster with common sociocultural amenities such as nurseries and kindergartens. A. U. Zelenko, "Stroitel'stvo sotsialisticheskikh gorodov," in *K probleme stroitel'stva sotsialisticheskogo goroda*, ed. Gosplan SSSR (Moscow: Izdatel'stvo "Planovoe Khoziastvo," 1930), 12, 15.

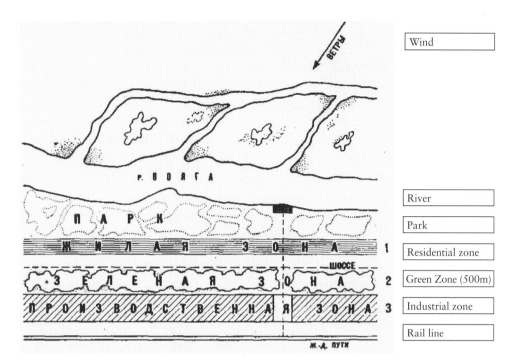

Wind

River
Park
Residential zone
Green Zone (500m)
Industrial zone
Rail line

Figure 8.8. Linear city scheme for Stalingrad, Nikolai Miliutin, 1930. N. A. Miliutin, *Sotstgorod: Problema stroitel'stva sotsialisticheskikh gorodov* (Moscow: Gosudarstvennoe izdatel'stvo, 1930), 29. Diagram by the author.

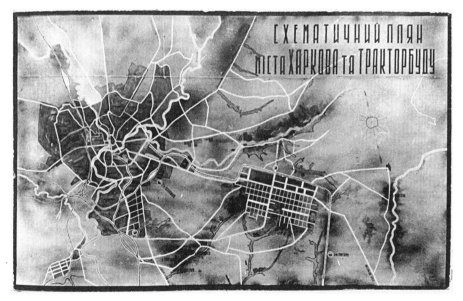

Figure 8.9. A schematic plan for the city of Kharkiv and its tractor factory, c. 1930s. The concentric prerevolutionary core of Kharkiv sits to the west, trailing a southeasterly transportation corridor on which a gridded urban rectangle, the future tractor factory and its *sotsgorod*, attaches. T. V. Tikhomirova, *Plany i vidy goroda Khar'kova: zastroika istoricheskogo tsentra* (Kharkiv: V.G. Korolenko State Scientific Library, 1989).

designs for New Kharkiv.[32] An early urban plan shows the concentric prerevolutionary core of Kharkiv to the west, trailing a southeasterly transportation corridor
on which a gridded urban rectangle, the future tractor factory and its *sotsgorod*,
attaches (figure 8.9). A concurrently drawn regional plan shows Kharkiv in the
center, encircled by a corona of linear cities, though New Kharkiv would be the sole
built example (figure 8.10).

A site plan and contemporary aerial photograph confirm that New Kharkiv
was constructed with exactly the programmatic layering recommended by Miliutin (flipped 180-degrees from his diagram) (figure 8.11). The heavy rail line that

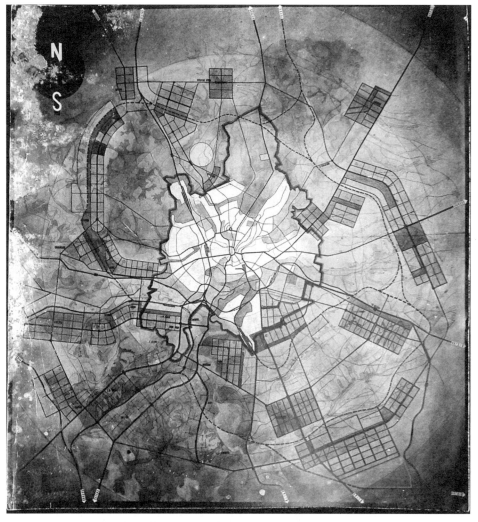

Figure 8.10. A schematic plan of linear cities. Kharkiv, Ukraine, 1929. This projective regional plan
shows prerevolutionary Kharkiv in the center, encircled by a corona of linear cities, although New
Kharkiv proved to be the sole built example. TsDAMLM Ukrainy, f. 8, po. 1, od. zb. 264, ark. 6.

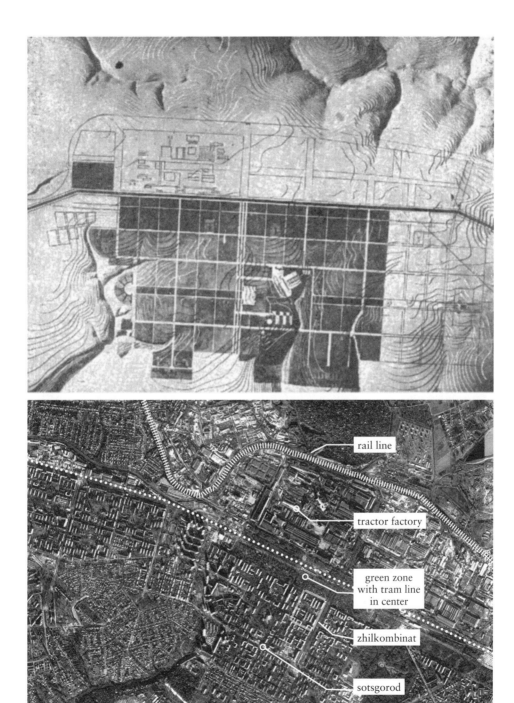

Figure 8.11. A linear city scheme for the Kharkiv Tractor Factory and the New Kharkiv *sotsgorod* (1930), and contemporary aerial photograph and diagram (2016). Note that the program layers at Kharkiv are 180° from Miliutin's model. Plan from N. Baltuzevich, *Opyt i uroki stroitel'stva KhTZ* (Moscow: Gosstroiizdat, 1932), 23. Diagram by the author based on Google Earth aerial.

connects Moscow to the Caucasus runs along the northeastern edge, below which lies the tractor factory precinct. Next, a green buffer—500 meters in width and carrying a tram line into the center of Kharkiv—separates the residential area of New Kharkiv from the factory zone. The diagram was built in Kharkiv, and the settlement structure remains unadulterated to this day, despite the fact that the interdependent relationship between the factory and residential area has been dissolved in the post-Soviet period.

The linear city model provided an additional logistical benefit in Kharkiv that was unarticulated by the theories of Zelenko or Miliutin but integral to meeting the fifteen-month construction deadline on an actual site. The green buffer was a construction expansion joint. The factory and *sotsgorod* projects could be built simultaneously but at different rates, sharing management, materials, and labor when convenient.

Demographically Closed System

Before an architectural scheme could be devised for New Kharkiv, Aleshin and his Giprograd colleagues needed the settlement's projected population subdivided by age, gender, and family structure to set the balance of residential unit types within the project. The tractor factory project's earliest demographic charts propose a final target population of 36,287. This emphatically precise number separates various demographic subgroups by livelihood including staff of the tractor factory; laborers at the factory; laborers in agriculture (to support the city); local and handicraft industry workers; commercial-sector employees (shop keepers, etc.); state catering employees; transportation workers; construction workers; employees of administrative organs; employees of municipal services; pensioners and nonworkers (*bezrabotnye*).[33] Additional demographic tables disaggregate the population further, dividing raw numbers into gendered percentages and age groups (men would ideally account for two-thirds of the total population). For each age, from under a year through sixty and over, an optimal percentage of the total population is given, again subdivided by gender. As in the idealized projections in the Magnitogorsk competition brief, the key demographic groups of optimal working age for the Kharkiv Tractor Factory project account for 65–70 percent of the settlement population. In this first round of demographic data, the familial composition of the settlement is also projected, with singleton "families" of one composing the largest demographic group.

Demographic charts proliferated in early project briefs for New Kharkiv, yet they rarely aligned. The categories and percentages articulated in February did not match up with March's projections. Why the numbers kept shifting is unclear, but there was certainly administrative purpose to these projections. James C. Scott proposes that the "continually frustrated goal of the modern state is to reduce the chaotic, disorderly, constantly changing social reality beneath it to something more closely resembling the administrative grid of its observations."[34] The State Institute for Metallurgical Factory Design in the Ukrainian Republic (UkrGipromez) and the Ukrainian NKVD, the de facto clients for the *sotsgorod*, desired for New Kharkiv to be a neatly closed system, "a terrain and a population with precisely those standardized characteristics that [would] be easiest to monitor, count, assess and manage."[35] By setting such precise demographic targets for the *sotsgorod* and making sure that the architects designed to those targets, UkrGipromez hoped to chart into being a perfectly circumscribed population to run the factory complex. No more, no less, and no differently composed.

Members of the design team "worked over" the UkrGipromez charts with data provided by the Central Statistical Administration (Tsentral'noe statisticheskoe upravlenoe or TsSU) to arrive at statistics better aligned with the socially transformative charge of the *sotsgorod*. "The age composition of the workers must consider the conditions for the planned new *byt*," the designers insisted.[36] Using a chart with revised demographic percentages, the designers homed in on spatial parameters for living units. They set areas for living cells (*zhiliachiki*) per familial group: a single person was allotted twelve square meters, a couple twenty square meters, and upward to the final six-person unit that was granted fifty-four square meters.[37] The team used the TsSU data to set the final unit mix. Singletons made up 23 percent of the population, and their living cells represented the most prevalent unit type.

The Architects Assemble

Petr Efimovich Shpara was a twenty-seven-year-old recent architecture school graduate and former student of Aleshin's from the Architectural Institute in Kyiv when he was tapped to participate on the New Kharkiv design team. It was a plum job in a burgeoning city. "Life in Kharkiv, the capital, was in full swing (*kipela*)," Shpara wrote in his autobiography. "The city was successfully transforming and had become a large socialist center with the lively rhythm of powerful industry. Kharkiv amazed us young architects with its dizzying creative energy. We understood how lucky we were, what a high honor it was, to join such a big creative collective engaged in designing and building such an enormous residential area immediately after graduating from the institute."[38]

By this time in 1930, Shpara, born in a rural village to two illiterate parents, had already rubbed shoulders with the brightest stars in the architectural firmament as part of the Ukrainian delegation to OSA's First All-Union Congress in Moscow in 1929. He and other young delegates "listened with excitement to the speeches of the famous Constructivists," like the Vesnin brothers, Moisei Ginzburg, and Ivan Leonidov. But Shpara's most vivid memory was of Le Corbusier, the congress's eminent foreign guest, who left an "enormous impression" on the auditorium by sketching live, in charcoal, a vision of modernist Paris on large sheets of paper tacked to the wall.[39] Shpara also commented on the theoretical difficulty of that historical moment for Soviet designers, young and old. "Socialist city-building . . . proceeded under seriously difficult conditions, in an atmosphere of perpetual collision of various directions and ideas. A number of architects defended superurbanism—calling for the creation of giant cities with skyscrapers. Others, on the contrary, proposed to redistribute the population in separate complexes with one-story cottage-houses, located with gaps along transportation magistrals."[40] Shpara's gloss of urbanist and disurbanist positions affirms that New Kharkiv head architect, Aleshin, was not the only designer at work on the *sotsgorod* well acquainted with contemporary design discourse in Moscow and beyond.

The New Kharkiv *sotsgorod* brief from February 1930, authored by the architectural team themselves, is a concise twenty-five-page instruction manual, filled only with information pertinent to design concerns.[41] Aleshin later stated that the design team's charge was "not only to study the materials available at the end of 1929 and early 1930, but also to develop new facilities regarding the *byt* in all of its manifestations: housing, child-rearing, education, nutrition, exercise, medical care, recreation, etc. in architectural design terms."[42] In line with this understanding, the architects' own brief is organized by building types: communal dining halls; childcare and educational facilities; *zhilkombinat*; "physical culture" and sports facilities; workers' clubs; food preparation facilities; mechanical laundries; and additional services (garages, shoe repair shops, etc.). Each of these categories is introduced with a short textual explanation of the general program, but the majority of the content is relayed in lists and charts that spell out the internal programmatic requirements for each type, their quantities, and areas. The structure of the New Kharkiv architects' brief mirrors the Magnitogorsk competition brief—it opens with information about demographics and territory then moves on to programmatic specifics—but it is exceedingly more detailed, as needed to generate constructible building types.

Armed with a clear set of instructions and target demographic numbers, the design team set feverishly to designing a standardized socialist urban model oriented to support the factory. The Giprograd design office's contract with Traktorstroi was signed on December 27, 1929. Draft designs of the *sotsgorod* and representative buildings of the residential sector were due March 1, 1930, working drawings for buildings in the residential sector were due April 20, and working drawings for the entire project were expected no more than sixty days later, on June 20.[43] To move from contract to construction drawings in less than six months, for a city of 36,287, was a design challenge of the highest order. Architectural standardization was a strategic imperative for the *sotsgorod* design team, just as it had been for the tractor factory design team.

The organization of the New Kharkiv brief suggests that the Giprograd design office was comprised of programmatically dedicated teams. Separated into small program-specific ateliers, the design groups could focus on a single new architectural type, whether a *byt*-transforming residential building, workers' club, live-in crèche, or factory kitchen. In January 1930, in his professorial role, Aleshin put out an open call to Kharkiv's third through fifth-year architecture students to assist with the New Kharkiv project.[44] These students were joined soon after by Shpara and other recent architecture school graduates.[45] Led by a limited number of seasoned designers, this small army of inexperienced but enthusiastic drafters cycled through numerous typological iterations.

While Shpara recalled the Kharkiv design effort with fondness, the stress imposed by the abbreviated timeline also comes through in his descriptions of that time:

> The collective was industrious and friendly. We worked with ambition and fire (*s pod"emom, s ogon'kom*), competing with one another. We paid no attention to time—it was all so new and interesting. Our supervisors were always nearby helping, making recommendations, supporting us. Thanks to them, and professor P. F. Aleshin in particular, the work was organized according to a regular rhythm. Despite the tight deadlines, we always provided the necessary construction documentation on schedule. The activities of our design bureau constituted not only a real school of creativity, but also a kind of scientific-research work, much of which was done for the first time.[46]

The youth and enthusiasm of the design team, as described by Shpara, certainly alleviated the pressure of tight deadlines, but even with dedicated type teams, and youthful energy to burn, the design schedule was near impossible. "Such a shock-work pace necessitated work not six-and-a-half hours a day, but often around the clock," Aleshin lamented after project completion.[47]

The divide and conquer typological method worked. According to Aleshin, the New Kharkiv design team met its obligations forty days before the contractual deadline, whereas the Traktorstroi factory design team did not. Despite having a construction-ready drawing set from which to work, the engineers at Traktorstroi were fifty-two days late in delivering their final draft of the factory design, a delay that caused coordination grief between the *sostgorod* and tractor factory projects.[48] The *sotsgorod* design team intended to take its dimensional cues from the factory so that the standard and repeatable *zhilkombinat* blocks might rationally connect across the green zone to production entrances. The size of the residential buildings, the smallest planning unit, was also pegged to and dependent on the elusive factory layout. Nonetheless, the tractor factory site plan lingered.[49]

Design of the Standardized Socialist City

In an early sketch of a prototypical *zhilkombinat* drawn by Aleshin, a superblock holds two smaller blocks that are mirrored on the centerline of a circle; a solo block variant sits off to the side (figure 8.12). Architectural standardization is already

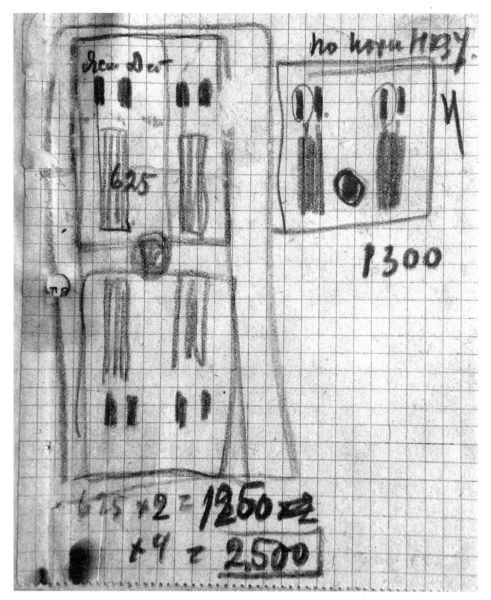

Figure 8.12. *Zhilkombinat* sketch for New Kharkiv, February 1930. Architects: Giprograd (Pavel Aleshin et al.). TsDAVO Ukrainy, f. 5, po. 3, od. zb. 2085, ark. 4.

evident in this first draft. Aleshin drew roughly the housing types (thin bars, each with a population of 625), school types (short nursery and kindergarten rectangles at the block edges), and a service building type (the circle) that would ultimately reach the project's demographic targets. Aleshin tallied accommodations at the building, block, and system level, to arrive at a total superblock population of 2,500. This was no arbitrary number. According to Shpara, the New Kharkiv *zhilkombinat* design "took into account the construction experience from the residential area at the Stalingrad Tractor Factory and the Magnitogorsk Metal-lurgic Plant, where analogous complexes were calculated to hold 2,500 people," though the constructed designs at New Kharkiv ultimately accommodated 2,730.[50]

An early rendered site plan shows the entire *sotsgorod* in a future build-out phase (figure 8.13).[51] The linear plan is divided into three horizontal zones: heavy rail to the north with the lightly penciled factory just below; local transportation corridor and 500-meter green band; and the residential *sotsgorod* made from stan-dardized *zhilkombinat* blocks that replicate insistently eastward in the promise of further colonization of the countryside. In this drawing, the factory precinct sets the block size: the factory zone's outside limits are carried down into the residential zone, and that total width is subdivided into six equal blocks. In the center of the six-block composition is a north-south road that leads directly to the factory's main gates; two minor block-dividing roads lead to minor factory entrances. There are just two prototypical *zhilkombinat* designs in use here, and they utilize the same few building types.

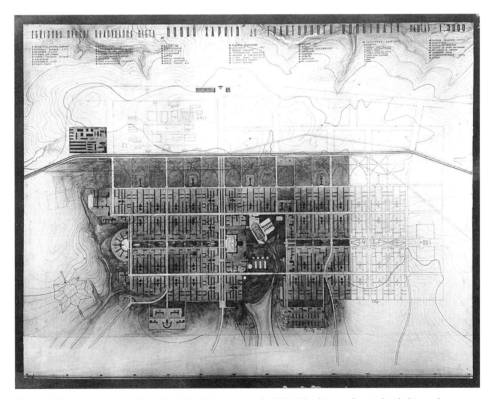

Figure 8.13. An early site plan, New Kharkiv *sotsgorod*, 1930. The linear plan is divided into three horizontal zones: heavy rail to the north with the factory just below; local transportation corridor and 500-meter green band; and the residential *sotsgorod* comprised of vertically rectangular repeated *zhilkombinat* blocks. Architects: Giprograd (Pavel Aleshin et al.). TsDAMLM Ukrainy, f. 8, po. 1, od. zb. 259, ark. 38.

The most prevalent building type in the New Kharkiv *sotsgorod* is the apartment house. As socialist housing evolved from Baku through Magnitogorsk, the typical apartment house became ever thinner and taller, so that by Kharkiv the unadorned freestanding bar building appears to be a preordained solution. This thin housing bar still had typological competition from the traditional perimeter block at New Kharkiv, however, due to mercurial theoretical directives in early 1930. "The difficulties [of schedule]," Shpara noted, "were compounded by the fact that in the field of architectural theory there was still no consensus, the struggle did not abate." He continued:

> Two generations of architects [at work on the *sotsgorod* design] were faced with the question of the planning structure of the new city. The older generation stayed on the side of the typical perimeter block structure with internal courtyards. We, the young generation, together with P.F. Aleshin, preferred the new type, the so-called line building (*strochnaia zastroika*), with the short ends of residential buildings facing the street, as the most appropriate to the conditions of socialist life. We put forth the following slogans: "Down with the old capitalist closed blocks! Give us linear buildings and through ventilation!" Of course, the new buildings were supposed to provide the most favorable lighting, maximum protection from noise, and surrounding green space. Sanitary doctors supported our position, and the project was built with linear buildings.[52]

According to Shpara, the health and hygiene argument that promoted buildings with maximum insolation, fresh air ventilation, and greenery won the day. Aleshin cited materials provided by Stroikom RSFSR and the Ukrainian NKVD in the New Kharkiv *sotsgorod* brief to set population, site coverage, and density rules to support mid-rise, freestanding housing types. He stated unequivocally that "new socialist cities should consist of a mixed generation population of 1,000–4,000 at a coverage of 20–25 percent and a density of 200–350 people per hectare. Once all of the facilities are installed to support the new socialist *byt*, and sanitary-technical and hygienic concerns addressed, it may be possible and desirable to increase density if the economic conditions allow."[53]

A later site plan shows *zhilkombinaty* at a closer scale and is evidence of lingering coordination troubles between the factory and *sotsgorod* design teams (plate 21). The tractor factory is off the sheet to the north, but its final adjusted width seems to have forced recalculation of the *zhilkombinat* block size, since this first residential phase consists of five blocks, not six as previously rendered. Compositional laws of symmetry drive the plan at multiple scales. In this revised *sotsgorod* plan, a north-south axis of symmetry runs through the center block; to either side are the other two block types, mirrored about this center axis. The interior logic of each of the five *zhilkombinat* blocks is also symmetrical about an implied east-west mirror line. Symmetry plays a pragmatic role here as a tactic to wrest variety from a limited number of standardized block types. A symmetrically composed plan is largely agnostic about situational particularities. If the goal of the New Kharkiv design team was to create model urban blocks deployable in myriad situations, an implicitly logical symmetrical composition makes good sense.

As at Magnitogorsk, the New Kharkiv brief exhaustively articulates the required sociocultural buildings programmatically and dimensionally. Among the additional building types described is a residential nursery for children up to age three; residential kindergarten for children ages four to seven; residential school for youth ages eight to fourteen; workers' club with auditorium, buffet, meeting rooms, library, and chess room; physical recreation facilities for both summer and winter sport; cafeteria and factory kitchen; mechanical laundry; shoe repair shop; garage for 100 cars; storage for 150 bicycles and 50 motorcycles; vehicular repair shop; telephone station; and infirmary and dispensary. Particularly important is the physical culture and sports facility associated with each residential corpus, "in order that the residents are able to go to that space after waking up to do their calisthenics before going to work."[54] The designs for the *sotsgorod* factory kitchen, built to provide 16,000 meals, the twenty-four-building hospital complex (with additional health amenities such as a running track), and a sizable cinema all demonstrate a notably Constructivist architectural aesthetic (plate 22).[55] Although only a portion of the settlement-wide sociocultural infrastructure was constructed, photographs taken immediately after the first phase confirm that the clubs, canteens, and schools designed into the first *zhilkombinat* block were built from the start.

Specific building types, largely constructed as they were rendered, come into clearer focus in an evocative aerial perspective drawing of the first *zhilkombinat* block (one of the outermost blocks on the blueprint) (figure 8.14). Two narrow six-story bars in the foreground hold dormitory-style living cells for singles. Six four-story bars behind hold multiroom family units. In the middle of the composition sits a round-nosed workers' club attached at the back to a communal dining hall and mechanized laundry. Four identical educational buildings—elementary schools, kindergartens and nurseries—line the back of the block. The project brief stipulates that "all rooms in the residential sector must be connected between themselves and the premises of the socialized sector by warm corridors."[56] These were included "so that children could walk to school without putting on outerwear, and could adults going to the store, canteen, or club."[57] The connecting skywalks are indicated on the blueprint by a single line to link the residential buildings and the social infrastructure together. In perspective, those lines become second floor glassed-in skyways sitting atop piloti (slim columns). The corridors' elevated position permits the ground plane to remain freely traversable between the residential bars.

The architects' creative aspirations are found in this aerial view. A three-propeller plane swoops into the upper right corner of the image to align the architectural project with its mechanized age. This drawing also highlights three architecturally

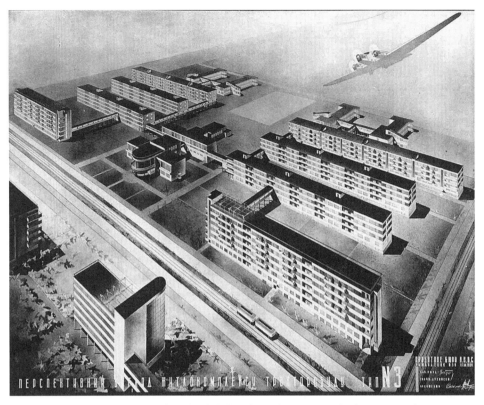

Figure 8.14. Bird's eye view of the first-phase *zhilkombinat* design, New Kharkiv *sotsgorod*, 1930. Architects: Giprograd (Pavel Aleshin et al.). TsDAMLM Ukrainy, f. 8, po. 1, od. zb. 259, ark. 389.

modernist details: flat roofs, narrow building widths, and broad functional facades. Each of these details, and the buildings' stripped aesthetic, align the New Kharkiv *sotsgorod* architecture not only with its Constructivist siblings in Moscow like the Narkomfin Building, but also New Frankfurt's *zeilenbau* (May's austere housing in Magnitogorsk had yet to be designed). The block reads as a perceptual whole due to consistent horizontal datum lines. Each story of each building is composed of a continuous opaque strip that conceals the floor slab and holds both the extended and inset balconies, alternating with a glazed strip of ribbon windows. Two additional *zhilkombinat* block prototypes, not rendered in the aerial but included on the blueprint, added a limited number of building types. In the first phase of construction seventy-eight buildings accommodating upwards of 7,500 residents were created from just ten building types.[58]

The most intimate architectural scale, the individual housing unit, was also designed for replication and for intense socialization. In a drawing of the single living cell (*zhiliachik*), the unit door opens onto a small foyer with a personal sink, then a second door leads into a narrow 2.86 meter (9.5-foot)-wide room with one generous window at the far end (figure 8.15). This unit was intended to enforce *byt* transformation of its occupant through economization (or elimination) of personal amenities. The architectural brief notes that "in the case where a unit is for one person, closets are not placed in the unit but in a convenient place so that one closet serves eight people, separated for men and women. Toilets for singles should be provided in common restrooms at a ratio of one toilet per fifteen people."[59] Two shared bathrooms off the main corridor hold a bathtub and two toilets for common use. Despite the inconvenience of shared toileting and washing, the twelve square meters of personal space in the single units was a significant spatial improvement on the Union-wide standard of nine square meters per person. Common gathering space and a shared balcony occur periodically in each corridor. From the exterior, the six-story buildings register as repetitive cells relieved at regular intervals by the small-windowed bathrooms and balconied social spaces.

Most controversially the lender, Tsekombank, required these units to be kitchen-less as a trade-off for common dining facilities. This decision generated conflict between funders and architects on the one side, and eventual residents on the other. The All-Union Population Census of 1926 found that 36.5 percent of families shared a kitchen with others, 22.3 percent had no kitchen facilities at all, and 4 percent were unknown.[60] Due to the acute housing crisis in the first decade of

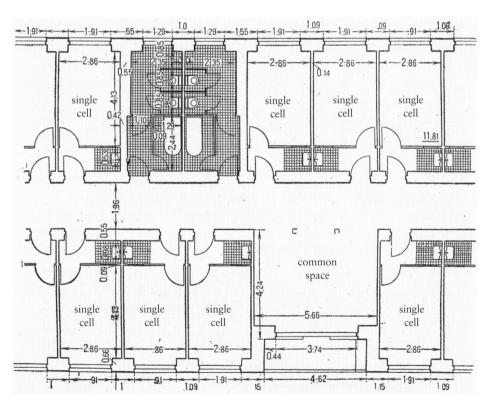

Figure 8.15. A plan for typical single living cells, New Kharkiv *sotsgorod*, Kharkiv, Ukraine, 1930. Architects: Giprograd (Pavel Aleshin et al.). Diagram by the author based on N. Baltuzevich, *Opyt i uroki stroitel'stva KhTZ* (Moscow: Gosstroiizdat, 1932), 23.

Soviet power, half of the Soviet population already lacked a private kitchen. As chief of Moscow housing, Nikolai Popov, noted in 1925, excision of such a crucial amenity in the unit was fine for citizens amenable to sharing communal facilities, but the majority instead clamored "let us die in our [private] kitchens."[61] To accommodate the transitional process of becoming fully socialist, Stroikom Typification Section units, like the Type F, provided small kitchen alcoves for reheating meals or making tea.[62] But because of Tsekombank's stringent borrowing rules, the single living cells at New Kharkiv were designed without such alcoves, never mind a full kitchen. Local anecdotes claim that residents swiftly smuggled hotplates into these units to avoid having to rely solely on the *zhilkombinat* canteen.[63]

There is more unit variety among the family apartments in the four-story walk-up buildings (figure 8.16). A partial floor plan shows four units clustered around a single shared stairwell. The standard elements of these units include foyer, closet, washbasin, and toilet. A minimal "transitional" galley kitchen lines the main living space of each type. Of the four units in evidence, there is one one-room example, two two-room types, and a single three-room version. In this representative foursome, half of the units enjoy a balcony, all facing one side of the building.

The New Kharkiv project required that the architects work at multiple scales and with a high degree of innovation and improvisation to ensure that the architecture

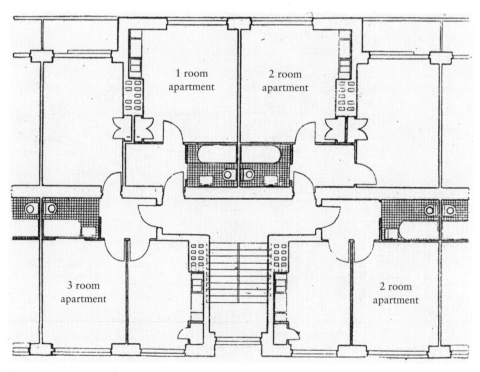

Figure 8.16. A plan for typical apartments in a house for families, New Kharkiv *sotsgorod*, Kharkiv, Ukraine, 1930. Architects: Giprograd (Pavel Aleshin et al.). Diagram by the author based on N. Baltuzevich, *Opyt i uroki stroitel'stva KhTZ* (Moscow: Gosstroiizdat, 1932), 24.

met the charge to socialize its residents. It was a discomfiting assignment almost impossible to get right. Aleshin lamented after the project was finished that over and above conflicts between the factory and *sotsgorod* design teams, the turbulent intellectual environment was ultimately most damaging to both project schedule and cost. In a formal memo written after project completion, Aleshin discussed the toll taken on his team (Giprograd) by the abbreviated timeline for completion paired with fluctuating theoretical imperatives:

> From the list of work completed by Giprograd on the tractor factory project, it should be evident that there was an extremely unclear sense of what the buildings should be, a lack of any material standards for designing the transitional [socialist] city and extremely diverse ideological positions in the various currents within Ukraine and all over the Union. Under these conditions, Giprograd engaged in a rather unexpected agreement not only to study the materials available at the end of 1929 and early 1930, but also to develop new facilities regarding the *byt* in all of its manifestations: housing, child-rearing, education, nutrition, exercise, medical care, recreation, etc., in terms of architectural design.
>
> Under shock-work construction conditions, Giprograd took full responsibility for the immediate fulfillment of its design obligations. Giprograd was forced to perform these tasks in the shortest possible time frame by going ahead of other similar construction projects, and without the benefit of other examples of *sotsgorod* construction.
>
> Moreover, all of the well-known discussions about the ideological establishment of the transitional *sotsgorod* were taking place during the design process. There were also numerous commissions constantly questioning the creativity of our youth, the very workforce creating the architectural objects for Traktorstroi. All of these conditions unnerved the work and led to repeated adjustments and improvements on already-completed designs. This resulted in increased labor and costs.
>
> For Giprograd, it was a great pleasure to read the decision by the TsK VKP(b) in the spring of 1930 on the left-wing distorter *(levozagibshchikakh)*, Sabsovich. By that time Giprograd had already finished the Traktorstroi project, which corresponded to the party line.
>
> This circumstance could only happen thanks to a deep exploration of the issues and through participation in discussions by professionals in Moscow, Kharkov, and Kiev. And through analysis by the whole Giprograd team of the conditions of construction and development for the transitional *sotsgorod* to reach the correct approach to solving the task.[64]

Aleshin claimed in his letter that there was no roadmap for the design work that Giprograd undertook at New Kharkiv. The terms for new architectural ensembles and objects—*sotsgorod, zhilkombinat, zhiliachik*—were coined but, as he noted, "there was an extremely unclear sense of what the buildings should be." What ensued was trial and error design "without the benefit of other examples of *sotsgorod* construction." Strictly speaking, this is true; no notably successful *sotsgorod* projects based on the sociospatial terms emerging from the debate had yet been built. To be conversant in the terms of the unfolding socialist urbanism debate, Aleshin and his team engaged in intense research. The vigorously annotated books on the debate in Aleshin's personal library testify to the architect's deep engagement with theoretical material, as do the copious and meticulously organized photographs of concurrent competition entries. He looked closely at the language and content of the Magnitogorsk brief and assessed the merits of the designs as he and his team crafted their own alternative. The Magnitogorsk competition brief acted, finally, as a true instaurational text for Aleshin and his Kharkiv team.

Because Aleshin became so well acquainted with the material from the socialist urbanism debate over such a short period of time—tracking the protagonists and their arguments, testing them against Giprograd's ongoing work to design a material environment—he was in a position to be critical of implausible recommendations. In what remains of Aleshin's personal library, there is only one Sabsovich book: *City of the Future and Organization of Socialist Byt* (*Goroda budushchego i organizatsiia sotsialisticheskogo byta*, 1929). It is not well annotated. Aleshin's pleasure at reading the Central Committee's "Resolution on the work to restructure *byt*," that admonished Sabsovich by name, was undoubtedly due to his team's difficulty satisfying terms that attempted "in 'one jump' to clear those obstacles to the socialist reconstruction of *byt*."[65] The theoretical ground was shifting, and yet for Aleshin and his team the deadlines were not.

Luckily for Giprograd, the New Kharkiv *sotsgorod* design was deemed a positive exemplar for future sites, in line with the new official position on socialist settlements. Ordzhonikidze, Politburo member and soon-to-be Commissar of Heavy Industry, reviewed the drawings for the project in 1931 and stated that New Kharkiv "fully meets the needs of the given period."[66]

Design Meets the Limits of Materials, Labor, and Force

For the New Kharkiv *sotsgorod* designers, standardization meant devising a limited number of replicable options, a strategy that ran from the scale of the residential unit, to the building type, to the *zhilkombinat* block. Standardization permitted the timely completion of working drawings despite hand-wringing setbacks wrought by theoretical inconstancy. But, as had been the case with the tractor factory, once the *sotsgorod* design came into contact with the actual construction site, the carefully crafted system of standardized parts had to adjust. Two on-site conditions impacted the Giprograd designs most drastically: material availability and the skill level of the construction workforce.

The aerial perspective of the first *zhilkombinat* block, the architectural team's wish image, shows smooth white volumes horizontally striated with flush ribbon windows and recessed balconies running in the same band across the facades. Materiality is merely implicit in this drawing, but monolithic effect suggests either reinforced concrete construction or parged masonry. In reality, there was only one material option for the buildings on the New Kharkiv site, and that was brick. In the frantic preparation for construction, a brick factory capable of producing 40 million red bricks a year was built nearby.[67] From the first through the subsequent construction phases, New Kharkiv was a brick complex.

The architects handled the material foisted on them with ingenuity. The narrow proportions of the housing were built as rendered, and from afar the signature horizontal striation also reads clearly (figure 8.17). Closer inspection reveals that the continuous ribbon window band is a *trompe l'oeil* (figure 8.18). The installed windows are not uninterrupted ribbon windows but are rectangular, mullioned, unmistakably punched openings that sit back from the building face to produce an undesirable shadow frame. The gridded effect of these openings is masked from afar with two simple additions: light-colored paint and finish tiles applied on top of the exterior brick. The dark bands that encircle the buildings are composed of windows, balconies, and dark bricks; the balance of the structure is painted or tiled in light yellow. The horizontally alternating result is, under the circumstances, in the same company as the rendered aspiration. The detail that most irrevocably divorces the rendering from the constructed condition, however, is the roof profile. All residential structures as built have traditional shallow-hipped roofs punctured by rows of chimneys that break aesthetic alliance with Constructivism. The shortage of steel on the tractor factory site, which caused significant material substitutions across the tracks, also affected the plans for the *sotsgorod*. The connecting heated skyways, reliant on long-span steel members, were left out of the initial construction phase, and they remained unbuilt in future phases.

New Kharkiv was a shock-work project not only for intellectual labor, as Aleshin claimed, but also for physical labor. Although some of the Stalingrad Tractor Factory leadership team and skilled workers were lured to continue at the Kharkiv project, the balance of the construction workforce was local, and the speed and simultaneity of tractor factory and *sotsgorod* construction impacted the allocation of that local workforce. Industrial construction was top priority, so skilled workers were pooled to complete the factory. A collection of barracks, like those seen at Magnitogorsk and Stalingrad, accommodated a small number of workers, but the site's relative proximity to Kharkiv meant that both construction and factory workers could commute from the city center or from local villages to the construction site in the short term.[68] The majority arrived on the Losevo site daily after an hour-long tram or forty-minute bus ride from the city center.

Figure 8.17. The first-phase *zhilkombinat*, with housing for singles in the foreground and the smoke-stacks of the factory in the distance, New Kharkiv *sotsgorod*, Kharkiv, Ukraine, c. 1932. Architects: Giprograd (Pavel Aleshin et al.). Derhzavna naukova arkitekturno-budivel'na biblioteka imeni V. G. Zabolotnogo.

Figure 8.18. The first-phase *zhilkombinat*, with houses for families in the foreground, New Kharkiv *sotsgorod*, Kharkiv, Ukraine, c. 1932. Architects: Giprograd (Pavel Aleshin et al.). RGAKFD, 1-18947.

According to accounts by Americans who lived at or visited the New Kharkiv site, a high percentage of construction work for the *sotsgorod* was completed by transient, unskilled, unpaid labor during *subbotniki,* or volunteer labor days.[69] The US reporter Anna Louise Strong—an avowed communist who positively spun her Soviet accounts—visited the *sotsgorod* construction site in August 1931 and recounted her interactions with the largely volunteer workforce, including a husky black-haired Ukrainian digger of ditches and a band of girls carting away the dirt. She was told that "perhaps half of all the unskilled labor at Tractorstroi [*sic*], the digging and loading of dirt, the cleaning of the yards, etc., had been done by these volunteers. This may be an exaggeration," she noted, "it is hard to estimate the amount. But it is known to all that the works could not have been finished this year if it had depended on the labour available for hire, in the present labour shortage." Strong added that she could immediately spot the volunteers "by a certain festivity, as of workers not on a regular routine."[70]

Fred Beal was an American communist labor organizer who fled to the USSR in 1930.[71] In 1931, he was sent to Kharkiv "to be in charge of propaganda and cultural relations, and serve as the contact man between the Soviet authorities and the foreigners."[72] In a Soviet-produced pamphlet, Beal reported much the same scene as Strong had. "As many as 17,000 workers shared in the construction of the plant. At least half of these workers came from the city of Kharkov and the surrounding small towns, giving their time voluntarily in what is called *subbotniks*," Beal explained. "One of the 'old timers' here told me that every morning a train and lorries loaded with workers came with bands playing and banners flying to do their share of work—usually unskilled, such as digging and loading dirt—to help the new plant in operation in record time. The Red Army men also did their share of this heavy initial work."[73]

Construction photographs show Red Army soldiers digging trenches, as Beal's excerpt notes (figure 8.19). They were not qualified to do much else on the site. The same held for the civilian volunteers who arrived "at half past six or seven" on a special train, according to Mrs. Raskin, one of the US housewives whom Strong interviewed. Like Beal, Raskin claimed that the volunteers came "with bands and banners; a different crowd each day, and always a jolly one."[74] The US engineer Leon Swajian, who oversaw the construction of the tractor factory, later also claimed collegiality and excitement in the volunteer workforce. "I don't think there was a man or woman in Kharkov who didn't come out to work on that plant," Swajian remembered. "Professors, women, girls, young bands of pioneers—they came every day in organized groups on 'subbotniki,' volunteering their free day to do unpaid work on their tractor plant. There were 400 to 500 of them every day, sometimes as many as 2,000. They came as if it was a good picnic. And why wasn't it? They wanted to see the big show and be in on it! Ten kilometers out from Kharkov they came, to where we were building not only the plant but the new workers' city."[75]

RED ARMY helps in construction

Figure 8.19. "Red Army helps in construction." Fred E. Beal, *Foreign Workers in a Soviet Tractor Plant* (Moscow: Co-operative Publishing Society of Foreign Workers in the USSR, 1933), 8.

Newsreel footage taken during construction provides a visual for this military and volunteer labor force on the New Kharkiv site (figure 8.20).[76] The flickering film pans slowly over a snow-covered plain, rendered desolate by the high ratio of sky to land in the frame.[77] This, the intertitles reveal, is the site designated for a Soviet tractor factory outside of Kharkiv, the new capital of Soviet Ukraine. In closer shots horses approach and pass the camera, drawing primitive carts loaded down with bricks and logs. The camera turns to an army of workers—shovels and *ushanka* earflaps flying—as they dig themselves deeper and deeper into the factory's foundation pit. Cut to black. The screen brightens once more on the plain—a steam train approaches. Young people standing in open doorways hop to the ground as a train slows in its passage across a barren landscape. They are there to "help speed construction" of the socialist city that will house tractor factory workers. A heavily scaffolded *zhilkombinat* building holds the background of the next shot in which three temporary workers stand, backs to the camera. The young woman in the center repeatedly turns her torso to the right, catches a brick, pivots, and slings it to the next volunteer in line to her left. Her body dips as the weight of each brick hits her hands. Extra hands would have been useful on simple tasks

Figure 8.20. Construction newsreels from the Kharkiv Tractor Factory *sotsgorod* site, 1930. Materials brought to the site by horse cart (top left), worker "volunteers" arrive by train from the city (top right), worker "volunteers" sling bricks (bottom). TsDKFFA Ukrainy, od. obl. 1429, 1447, 1469, 1483, 1486, 1516, 1517, 1529.

like moving bricks, or those that required brute force, like ditch digging. But organization of a job site staffed by transient unskilled workers was invariably a daily logistics challenge. Strong noted that each day New Kharkiv's chief of production faced the task of assigning jobs to yet another enthusiastic yet untrained group of volunteers.

Eve Garrette Grady, the wife of a US engineer at the tractor factory, questioned the picture of selfless volunteerism put forward by the above accounts, each released by a pro-Soviet media outlet. "Many times I have seen bookkeepers, clerks, stenographers, draftsmen—even professors from the University of Kharkov . . .—men and women who work every day in the week in an office, a schoolroom, or a factory, briskly laying bricks at Tractorstroy on their free day. Refuse to go, they dared not. But those whom I knew used to smile ruefully, albeit quite furtively, as I passed and hold up their white, office-worker or scholar's hands, all torn and scarred and bleeding."[78]

Whether the labor was volunteer or coerced (likely some combination thereof), the Kharkiv Tractor Factory was undoubtedly a site of local curiosity, removed from the established urban core and touted as one of Kharkiv's most significant contributions to the first Five-Year Plan. The *sotsgorod* was of particular interest. While there were many modern residential buildings constructed in Kharkiv city center during the late 1920s, New Kharkiv was the sole fully communalized complex. The *sotsgorod* was an important material touchstone for the new social order, one that even inner-city Kharkivites wished to have a hand in making, if not living in.

The largely unskilled workforce negatively affected the *sostgorod* project's quality of construction, however. Even if the architects had specified the most modern materials and processes, the composition of the labor pool on the construction site precluded complex assemblies. The US engineer Zara Witkin visited the tractor factory and *sotsgorod* in May 1932. By placing Kharkiv on his itinerary, Witkin noted that he had "one objective above all—the famous Kharkov Tractor Plant—and [I] insisted on seeing it, despite various objections which were raised."[79] After his visit, about a year after completion of the first *zhilkombinat* block, Witkin speculated why his guides sought to keep him away. "Near the factory a group of large apartment houses had been built to house the workers, engineers, foreign mechanics and consultants employed at the plant. We asked to see them," Witkin explained. "The recent rains had converted the dirt roads into mud, through which our car wallowed. This condition prevailed right up to the building. There had been no grading nor drainage around them. Mud and dirt had been tracked into the building. The staircases and walls were soiled. Though the houses had been 'completed' the previous year, rubbish and waste material remained in disorderly piles on the site."[80] Witkin was new to the Soviet Union, and this was his first trip outside of Moscow. He saw Soviet construction with fresh eyes, which lends his description immediacy. But the American also was unaware of the difficult material and labor conditions that conspired to set the disorderly scene he saw before him (he would learn this firsthand over time). Given the rotating cast of temporary workers, who ultimately carried the responsibility to clean up the rubbish and waste materials on the construction site? Postoccupancy plans are not among the texts that survive in the archive.

A contemporary Soviet assessment of the first phase of *sotsgorod* construction noted that "the projects of Giprograd, more than any other of the types carried out in the tractor factory complex, were the objects of public and architectural discussion, and severe criticism, mainly by the production-workers on the construction, which resulted in a lot of defects that had to be rectified."[81] Aleshin's Giprograd team was blamed for the so-called construction defects; however, it is more likely that the inexperienced workforce was the root of quality control problems.

Broadening the scope of inquiry beyond the immediate New Kharkiv design and construction project, to consider the *sotsgorod*'s lived experience after move-in, and the context outside of the enclave, reveals a seriously distressing picture. In *Proletarian Journey* (1937), a memoir written after his escape from the Soviet Union, Fred Beal enumerated the complaints logged by the foreign workers under his purview, the members of the "privileged upper class, divided by a chasm from the ten thousand Russian workers employed [at the Kharkiv Tractor Factory]."[82] The foreigners' grievances included 50 percent longer work hours than paid for; lack of wood and coal for stoves and freezing residential conditions; high prices for clothes and shoes at the state store when (infrequently) available; and insufficient food. Beal reminded his US readers to place these complaints in context, however. "The large colony of privileged foreign workers at the Kharkov Tractor Plant subsisted on a starvation diet. How then shall I adequately describe the condition of the Russian workers? Did the Russian workers have the barest of necessities of life? Did they have warm clothes? Were the barracks in which they were quartered warm? Was the factory heated?"[83] These difficulties were tolerated by Soviet workers because outside of the high brick wall that surrounded the factory, each entrance of which was guarded by a soldier with a loaded rifle and fixed bayonet, was manufactured famine and genocide of the Ukrainian peasantry.[84] Forced agricultural collectivization, directed from Moscow but undertaken by local actors, turned Kharkiv into a haunted city, overpopulated by peasants whose property was confiscated, and whose villages were subsumed in the now collective territory. They drifted into the center, hoping to secure food. Instead, many were rounded up by police and carted so far out of town that they could not return for exhaustion.[85]

Fred Beal devotes a chapter in his book to the enforced starvation that surrounded the tractor factory precinct. Because of the presence of armed guards, hungry peasants sought out other means of approaching better-provisioned workers on site. "Starving peasants and workers stormed the foreign colony at the Kharkov Tractor Plant every day," Beal explained. "With piteous cries for food, they went from house to house and from door to door whenever they could get past the guards stationed there. It was the only hope of getting bread. There was none on the land."[86] On a visit to a Ukrainian collective farm near the village of Chekhuyev in the spring of 1933, Beal and his companion saw "the worst of all possible sights." Only one live human remained, an old woman who spat at them as they approached. The rest of the collective had died of starvation. Their bodies, in various states of decomposition, were strewn throughout the village.[87]

The favorable outcome of New Kharkiv from an architecture and planning standpoint must be set against the horrific context in which it was created. From a systems perspective, the New Kharkiv *sotsgorod* project represents a successful installation of a replicable, and replicated, socialist urban block—the Armenikend superblock on a much larger scale—the benefits of which would be proven in time. Viewed in light of its local repercussions, the Kharkiv project suffers the taint of morally reprehensible political decisions made to install it.[88] Were the architects responsible for the famine occurring in their midst? Of course not. But the project's very being was contingent on myriad acts of violence incurred to clear the way for its success.

The New Kharkiv *sotsgorod* was one of the first ground-up, explicitly socialist urban projects conceived, designed, and constructed in Soviet space. Linked together, the *sotsgorod* projects at Magnitogorsk and Kharkiv can be understood as stand-ins for theory and practice. Socialist city theory was generated for Magnitogorsk and implemented in Kharkiv.

The architects for New Kharkiv did not have the benefit of a design development period before tackling the final version of the *sotsgorod* design. The shock-work tempo for completion meant that there would be no All-Union Design Competition for New Kharkiv. The project was simply assigned to a seasoned local architect who used both professional experience and research of prevailing trends to resolve the design problem as quickly as possible. Pavel Aleshin and his band of newly hatched Soviet-Ukrainian architects at Giprograd accomplished what Standartgorproekt, even under the seasoned leadership of Ernst May, could not. Namely, they created and installed a standardized unit of urban development, the replicable *zhilkombinat*, and provided a tested blueprint for future phases of build-out. Under much less scrutiny in Kharkiv than May suffered in Magnitogorsk, Aleshin was able to experiment in real time: drawing quickly, incorporating new theoretical precepts, and just building the thing. The first constructed *zhilkombinat* suffered from poor construction quality due to a host of material and labor factors, but architectural and planning standardization processes were launched that had an undeniable impact on subsequent settlements across Soviet territories.

By 1931, with a deeper collective understanding of large-scale planning issues, Giprogor (the State Institute for City Planning) began to work out the theoretical and methodological issues related to socialist settlement by applying the practice of architectural standardization to the problem of settlement types.[89] In the late 1980s, an elderly Petr Shpara, recalling his time working on the Giprograd team for New Kharkiv, made the intellectual connection between the New Kharkiv *zhilkombinat* unit and the Khrushchev-era *mikroraion* (microdistrict). "Such complexes for 2,730 people to a large extent correspond to the modern groups of houses for 2,000–3,000 inhabitants, located in the *mikroraion* . . . The foundational architectural-planning decisions made then have stood the test of time and served as a reliable basis for further future development."[90] Soviet residential design tested in the early 1930s, and picked up again after Stalin's death, relied wholly on standardization. State planners' desire to replicate industrial concerns and residential quarters quickly across vast territories met success, finally, through the interscalar standardization of architectural details, standard building types, and predesigned settlement modules, like those devised for the New Kharkiv *sotsgorod*.

CONCLUSION

The truth is that the economic and cultural reconstruction of all life in the USSR has no parallel in the history of mankind. *It is equally true that this reconstruction is being accomplished by a sober evaluation of all the realities, and it should be obvious to any observer that in each successive stage, matters recognized as desirable and ideal are being consciously subordinated to matters that are feasible and possible within the limitations of the present.*

—Ernst May (1931)

A year into his design consultancy with the Soviet government, the German architect Ernst May tempered his expectations of what he might accomplish in the USSR. May asserted that the first Five-Year Plan was a development project unparalleled "in the history of mankind," but he also understood that it was beset by severe limitations. Although the fiscal, material, and labor shortages that plagued Soviet construction projects were still in the future for May and his German brigade, they encountered stubborn topographies and client inconstancy within weeks of arrival. May concluded that desires and ideals became subordinate to reality under such difficult conditions.

The process of subordination that May described supports two readings of early Soviet architecture and planning, one negative and one positive. In the first—the failure narrative—the idealized vision of egalitarian socialist space was gradually erased by sober conditions in the here and now. This negative reading aligns with Manfredo Tafuri's assessment that once realism killed vision, avant-garde designers like Moisei Ginzburg simply disappeared into the "black fog" of anonymous state planning offices.[1] In the second, positive reading that has been forwarded here—the praxis narrative—improbable fantasy was vanquished by material fact. Iterative problem solving informed by interdisciplinary research, close observation, and haptic experience permitted the first Soviet architectural and urban plans to be built under extraordinarily difficult political and economic conditions. Design practitioners will read in May's assessment of the Soviet situation circa 1931 the evaluation of a seasoned pragmatist. He may have been blinded at the start of his work by the "magnitude of the task, and also the fact that nothing like it [had] ever been attempted before," but faced with facts on the ground, he and his team settled down to accomplish what was possible under the circumstances.[2] Under a Leninist definition of praxis, the success of a plan is gauged by its ability to engage the present as a means to effect change. For Aleksandr Ivanitskii, Ernst May, and Pavel Aleshin—the designer protagonists in Baku, Magnitogorsk, and Kharkiv— practical work prevailed over utopian dreaming. These practitioners approached the problem of the socialist environment and, most important, they intervened.

This book about three critical industrial sites distant from Moscow seeks to debunk the myth that Soviet planning was a centralized and totalized activity from the onset. Early Soviet spatial interventions were diverse and contingent on the particular geography, industry, and actors in play at specific sites. The designs for these sites spanned two distinct economic periods, each of which differently engaged the construction of socialist space. During NEP in Baku, the locally based oil company, Azneft, played a strong role in shaping the built environment because funding and direction from Moscow were not forthcoming. It took Azneft and the Baksovet some time and many false starts to recognize the importance of planning forward, but eventually they did, through a combination of imported, and increasingly local, expertise. During the start of the first Five-Year Plan, socialist spatial theory caught fire. The shift to a full command economy during the plan made large capital construction projects possible and imperative, and Magnitogorsk was held up as the site on which burgeoning theories of socialist space could be tested. The remoteness, difficulty of the site, and primacy of the industrial construction project limited the scope of experimental built housing and services in Magnitogorsk, but the ideas written into its design competition brief nonetheless circulated and in turn positively impacted the fates of other sites in the Union. By Kharkiv, a later first Five-Year Plan project, the socialist settlement debate took a backseat to frantic on-the-ground efforts to meet the plan's construction goals. The architectural strategy of standardization was harnessed to construct an integral, replicable model that bundled industrial, residential, and social spheres.

The standard history of early Soviet city planning holds that the experimental phase ended summarily with the "Resolution on the work to restructure *byt*" in May 1930, which denounced "utopian" spatial theories in favor of muted interventions into the domestic realm and replanning existing cities.[3] Just weeks after the resolution was published in *Pravda*, Lazar Kaganovich, Stalin's right hand, was appointed first secretary of the Moscow Committee. In a mid-1931 speech, later published as *Socialist Reconstruction in Moscow and Other Cities in the USSR*, Kaganovich held up Moscow as the sole model for all future Soviet spatial design.[4]

To do so, he had to elide the issue of urban form and assert that means of production alone made a context socialist: "There are at present many who decline in every possible declension the formula, 'we must build a socialist city.' They forget one little trifle: that the cities of the USSR are already socialist cities. Our cities became socialist from the very moment of the October Revolution."[5] The 1935 Moscow General Plan, conducted under Kaganovich, organized, modernized, and radically transformed the capital city. Urban movement was smoothed and quickened in Moscow through monumental boulevards widened for cars, waterways widened for boats, a new metro, and expanded surface transportation.[6]

The monumental Socialist Realist ensemble city of Kaganovich's Moscow did become a prevailing Soviet urban model. But the well-organized *zhilkombinat* (planned standardized residential block) tested at various scales in Baku's Armenikend neighborhood, Magnitogorsk's Kirov District, and at New Kharkiv, also persisted, rising again to prominence after World War II as the renamed *mikroraion* (microdistrict).[7] These two models for socialist urbanism coexisted. While monumental ensembles marked the central, representational spaces in Soviet cities from the mid-1930s and beyond, Soviet outskirts were ringed with dense quarters composed of freestanding housing and sociocultural support buildings sitting in common open space.

Living the Socialist City

How were these socialist settlement projects received in their day and lived in once completed? A conclusion begs at least glimpses, no matter how fleeting, after the last bricks were set.

No firsthand accounts of Baku's Stepan Razin or Armenikend settlements in the years immediately after their completion have surfaced, but issues of the multilingual journal *USSR in Construction* do provide a selective view of the lived condition.[8] Armenikend anchors a double-paged spread from a 1931 issue that employs the neighborhood's distinctively modern architectural language to draw a sharp distinction between pre- and postrevolutionary Baku (plate 23).[9] The issue, devoted to the Soviet petroleum industry, introduces English-language readers to "Baku, the pearl of Soviet Caucasia, the city of sunlight and oil, [that] has recently become a sunny place for the proletarians working on the oil fields." The text claims that the proletarian housing problem has been solved in Baku. "Before they lived in shattered dark huts. The Soviet power led the workers out of their filthy huts and built palace-like homes for them."[10] Running along the top of the pages is a wide panorama of *icheri sheher* with its historic granular buildings crowded against one another. The middle of the spread is dominated by a photo of ramshackle lean-tos constructed of stone and wood, sitting on the edge of the oilfields, remnants of the capitalist past. The bottom of the spread features two images of the Soviet solution: Armenikend, with its "palace-like" homes built for Baku's proletarian workers. Grinning strong limbed children run toward the photographer, with clean, rational three-story buildings—presumably their homes and schools—in the background. A cropped perspective of a typical Armenikend facade, to the right, highlights, as the eye moves up the building, greenery at the block's base, deep horizontal shaded balconies, open windows that invite fresh air into the units, and a lively profile against the sky created by the block's crenelated plan. These highly curated images give little sense of Baku's day-to-day *byt* at the start of the 1930s, however, and the voices of the thousands of worker-tenants are sorely missing. An interview with two families who coinhabited a Type B unit in Armenikend, on how and in what ways the design of the apartment and the socialized block impacted their daily lives, would be a treasure, indeed.

Magnitogorsk and Kharkiv, by contrast, are the settings for multiple firsthand accounts that abound in descriptions of everyday life in the 1930s.[11] The US writer John Scott lived in Magnitogorsk from 1933 through 1938 and published a memoir upon return. Scott's description of his neighborhood, the Kirov District (which he also refers to as the Socialist City), provides one view on how the May Brigade's sole built project in Magnitogorsk was perceived and occupied in the years immediately after its completion (figure C.1). The chapter opens with a shot across the bow, followed by a detailed illustration of the neighborhood:

> The Socialist City, renamed the Kirov District, because it was not really a very good example of a Socialist city to put before the population, was composed of some fifty large apartment houses, three, four, and five stories high, containing seventy-five to two hundred rooms each. The houses were of brick and stone, stuccoed and painted various colors, which looked very well against the white background in winter. They were arranged in long rows, like military barracks, and were all of the same matchbox-on-edge shape. The metal roofs were painted red and blue. There were balconies in all the houses. Between the rows of houses there were wide streets, with sidewalks, along which many trees had been planted. In the center of the development were two open squares, with fountains, benches, children's playground apparatus, flower gardens surrounded by neat green iron fences, and what would be shade trees in ten years . . .
>
> Particularly in the summer the Kirov District had definite charm; the fountains played, and innumerable little children, in bathing suits which left most of their sunburnt bodies open to the fresh air, splashed and splattered about. The walks were crowded with workers of all ages taking the air. Benches were occupied by men and women, young and old, reading and talking.[12]

Except for the note about the "military barracks" arrangement of the houses—a description that would have resonated with the vast majority of Magnitogorsk's

Figure C.1. Kirov District, Magnitogorsk, 1930s. Magnitogorskii kraevedcheskii muzei.

residents, who were still living in the temporary wooden structures—the remainder of Scott's portrayal conjures a neighborhood of neat, simple housing surrounded by green spaces that serve as magnets for communal conviviality. Scott did complain that the "one tremendous shortcoming was the fact that it was so crowded." Four to five people lived in each small room, at an average of 3.34 square meters of floor space per person—and these were the privileged few. The Kirov District was "inhabited principally by foremen, brigadiers, and skilled workers, as well as a scattering of teachers, doctors, and various city employees." The only residents of Magnitogorsk granted better accommodations were the high administrative technical and political personnel who took possession of a compound of single-family houses known as Berezki that had been built for departed foreign specialists. There, a young Russian architect had emulated designs from US architectural catalogs, with a result "very much approaching Mount Vernon, New York, or Germantown, Pennsylvania."[13] The Kirov District, while no ersatz US suburb, was nonetheless a significant improvement on flimsy temporary housing.

Daily life for the vast majority of Magnitogorsk's population living in barracks, tents, dugouts, and yurts was distinctly grimmer. In November 1932, a delegation of scientific-technical experts from Moscow visited Magnitogorsk to assess construction progress on the socialist city.[14] The architect I. M. Murev'ev, chief of the Residential Sector at the People's Commissariat of Heavy Industry (Narkomti-azhprom), jotted notes on the back of a topographical blueprint while his delegation toured the site. His raw shock comes through in these immediate recordings that communicate incredulity with frequent underlining.[15] The true population of Magnitogorsk stood at 230,000—a number already well in excess of the projected maximum population of 200,000—and these residents were allocated just 2 square meters of living space on average. Over half of the population lived in "temporary" settlements of wooden barracks and dugouts in the immediate vicinity of the industrial complex *that were constructed by 48 organizations*," Murev'ev wrote. Without one organization keeping track of the siting and quality of these makeshift structures they were built haphazardly, close together, and often on unsuitable soil. Obvious problems arose from the lack of oversight and planning of the settlements. First, "open fires, the constant, strong wind, and the absence of water together fail to protect against *a continuous threat of complete destruction by fire*." Second, the random placement of buildings and settlements precluded the installation of a rational road network so that "automobiles, trucks, and pedestrians move in a completely disorderly fashion." Finally, and most critically from the standpoint of labor reproduction, basic hygienic services were lacking, as Murev'ev scribbled with intensity:

> The population of the socialist *city is without drinking water* . . . it was put too shallowly in the ground, and *is not filtered* . . . *The sewage system is completely absent* (with the exception of Berezki), and the large-scale build-ings of the industrial site and the community buildings of the settlement have *cesspools* in the place of internal plumbing . . . None of the other residential buildings in the settlement have any kind of municipal improvements and the residential sites with remote latrines are completely anti-sanitary—muddy in the spring and summer which leads to a high degree of epidemics.[16]

Even before the scientific-technical experts toured the worker settlements, a local newspaper reported a fact that all residents of Magnitogorsk already knew: "the growth of the [typhus] epidemic is due to the anti-sanitary conditions in the bar-racks and the generally poor living provisions."[17] In 1931 alone, there were 1,989 reports of typhoid fever in Magnitogorsk.[18]

Murev'ev's field notes from 1932 illuminate the uncomfortable and even dan-gerous environment that early settlers in Magnitogorsk tolerated each day. In *Magnetic Mountain*, Stephen Kotkin also enumerates the many challenges faced by the typical resident to accomplish even the simplest tasks. Both of these texts act as important correctives to the selective narrative of the model steel city crafted by Soviet media outlets. Publications like *USSR in Construction*, designed for foreign audiences, presented the tribulations of the site's workers only insofar as they pushed forward a story about strength of will, perseverance, and ultimately victory over adversity (plate 24). The protagonist of the journal's Magnitogorsk narrative, Viktor Kalmykov, enters wearing the homemade bark and rope shoes of a peasant (*lapti*) and is sent to live in a tent with other new arrivals. By the end of the issue Kalmykov has proven his worth as a shock-worker on and in the steel mill, and exits the tale wearing the jacket, white button-up shirt, and tie of a bureaucrat.[19]

In between these two poles of representation—complete dysfunction and triumph of socialist resolve—was a Magnitogorsk that slowly moved in the direction of quiescent normalcy. "Speaking Bolshevik" is the term Kotkin coined to explain popular support for the Soviet status quo that emerged at Magnitogorsk. Through "little tactics of the habitat," workers learned to situate themselves within the system that they were building.[20] Miscellaneous candid photographs from the local history museum provide views of this shift to regularity in the 1930s (figure C.2). In the maternity ward of the hospital, tightly wrapped first-generation Magnitogorskans sleep in makeshift baby cots created by sheets stretched along the sides of steel frame beds. A wooden kiosk selling "sanitary and hygienic" goods sits on the bare steppe. Men dressed in work clothes and caps—some barefoot, akin to a Repin painting—crowd the left side of the shop while out of the nineteenth-century scrum strides a pair of modern young women in white, one carrying books, the other her own coat. A crowd gathers around the water station to watch a swimmer arcing backward from the rickety high dive into the pool below. A black bear and suited man stand at the entrance to a circus tent that advertises a "Soviet Attraction: Motorcycle racers on vertical walls." These are all unremarkable snapshots of prosaic events that took place in a context of material provisionality. The structures are temporary, like the barracks, but their transient nature does not preclude the construction of social life inside, outside, and around them.

Kharkiv is, in many ways, the architectural and urban success story among these three sites. The tractor factory and its *sotsgorod* were built quickly, largely according to plan, utilizing new iterations of standardization—*priviazka* at the urban and architectural scale—that drove Soviet design practice for the next sixty years. Photos taken soon after construction completion at the New Kharkiv *sotsgorod* feature the six-story dormitory-type buildings and the shared open spaces between them (figures C.3–C.4). Newly planted trees register as light-colored wisps against dark swaths of grass and garden. Solid wooden benches for community socializing are in place, facing the center of the open space. Well-bundled children shuffle through the eerily still landscape, and a cyclist in a worker's jumpsuit glides by. These carefully posed images register Euclidean order and architectonic firmness that contrast mightily with "before" photos of the relentlessly horizontal farmland. This city of repeated housing blocks and supporting social infrastructure stands at the ready to receive the tractor factory population.

There is an ethics of architecture that shifts and adjusts as society does.[21] But what is architectural history's ethical responsibility? Recent scholarship insists

Figure C.2. Miscellaneous candid photographs provide views of a shift to normalcy in Magnitogorsk in the 1930s. Read clockwise from the upper left: children's and maternity section, Magnitogorsk hospital; sanitary and hygienic goods kiosk; diving platform at the water station; "Soviet Attraction: Motorcycle racers on vertical walls." Magnitogorskii kraevedcheskii muzei.

Figure C.3. First-phase *zhilkombinat*, with houses for singles in the background, New Kharkiv *sotsgorod*, Kharkiv, Ukraine, c. 1931. Architects: Giprograd (Pavel Aleshin et al.). RGAKFD, 0-59662a.

Figure C.4. Phase I *zhilkombinat*, with houses for singles in the background, New Kharkiv sotsgorod, Kharkiv, Ukraine, c. 1931. Architects: Giprograd (Pavel Aleshin et al.). RGAKFD, 0-55676a, MUAR, 11-5407.

that we cannot study architecture, contemporary or historical, without addressing labor.[22] In that spirit, this book has attempted to widen the field of view to include not only the intellectual labor of the architects and spatial planners designing social-ist spaces, but also that of experts from other disciplines, and the physical labor of workers who mixed the concrete and carried the bricks. How and in what ways did projects like the Kharkiv Tractor Factory become implicated in campaigns of political terror in the years immediately after the project's completion? Fred Beal's horrific firsthand account of the 1932–34 *Holodomor* in the Ukrainian countryside has nothing, ostensibly, to do with the 1929–30 design for a tractor factory some two-hour train ride from the starved village. But, if a history of early Soviet archi-tectural process and product widens to include the economic, political, and social milieu, it would be irresponsible, if not unethical, to elide the fatal effects of those political forces that conspired to build the factory.

These projects were designed and built with transformation as the signal goal: transformation of rural landscapes into industrial landscapes and transformation of peasants into socialist workers. Individual Soviet citizens, both the designers chronicled here and young Communists like Lev Kopelev, became embroiled and ultimately implicated in effecting these changes. Kopelev wrote:

I was convinced that I was accomplishing the great and necessary transforma-tion of the countryside; that in the days to come the people who lived there would be better off for it; that their distress and suffering were a result of their own ignorance or the machinations of the class enemy; that those who sent me—and I myself—knew better than the peasants how they should live . . . In the terrible spring of 1933 I saw people dying from hunger. I saw women and children with distended bellies, turning blue, still breathing but with vacant, lifeless eyes. And corpses—corpses in ragged sheep-skin coats and cheap felt boots; corpses in peasant huts, in the melting snow of old Vologda, under the bridges of Kharkov . . . I saw all this and did not go out of my mind or commit suicide.[23]

Creating socialist spaces required destroying the preexisting built environment and its occupants to accomplish the "great and necessary transformation" of which Kopelev wrote. The first Five-Year Plan was a spatial revolution, to be sure, accompanied by all of the violence that revolution entails.

If architecture's ethical dimension lies in understanding, channeling, and providing for dwelling, as Martin Heidegger—and Karsten Harries after him—claims, then the minimal living cells of New Kharkiv are also problematic, as is the practice of removing children from their parents in the name of freedom from filial ties and labor efficiency. This mother, for one, cannot imagine handing over her children to be raised by the state. Incidentally, neither could Kharkiv's mothers. The present principal of the school in the New Kharkiv district (now simply referred to as KhTZ, shorthand for the Kharkiv Tractor Factory district) shared anecdotally that the school originally designed in 1930 as a dormitory for older children had almost immediately to be adapted as a normative day school when not a single mother offered up a single child to live in separate quarters.

Postwar Soviet Architectural Theory and Practice

Stalin's death in 1953 marked a new chapter in the Soviet pursuit of socialist spatial models and specifically socialist housing. Cities like Leningrad and Kyiv suffered massive destruction during World War II that only compounded the systemic housing shortage, which is to say that housing experiments in the 1920s and 1950s shared an unenviable backlog of need. In a 1954 speech to the National Conference of Builders and Architects, Nikita Khrushchev demanded industrial standardization for housing to "significantly speed up, improve the quality of, and reduce the cost of construction," with a goal to supply each Soviet family with its own, separate apartment in the course of three Five-Year Plans.[24] Soviet architects of the 1950s dusted off architectural and urban models from the 1920s. Natan Osterman, the lead architect of the experimental Moscow *mikroraion* Novye Cheremushki (completed in 1958), collaborated both as a student and young practitioner with architects active in the 1920s, like Mikhail Barshch and Andrei Burov, forging a link between avant-garde and postwar Soviet housing efforts.[25]

On Khrushchev's command, designers worked on interdisciplinary teams to devise new standardized residential buildings filled with minimized apartments. In the 1960s, the architect A. Gegello described the typical process by which a standard design (*tipovoi proekt*) was developed, codified, and then adjusted through the practice of *priviazka*:

> Mass construction is carried out mainly according to standard designs (*po typovym proektam*). This, today, is the only sure way to meet the needs of a socialist society quickly. . .
>
> First of all, the architect-author of a standard design, and the team participating in its development, must take an active part in the implementation of initial buildings built from this type. This is the stage of experimental construction, on the basis of which all necessary improvements must be made to the standard design. Close involvement by the architect at the experimental stage should be mandatory for all typical designs.
>
> In further implementation of the type-project in various locations throughout the country, the creative authorship of the project should be taken up by that architect on site who enacts the *"priviazka"* of the project to the local conditions. No one would claim that the work done by an actor or musician is uncreative, or that creative expression is absent in the work of the symphony conductor or theater director who brings to life the creative output of the composer or playwright. It is equally obvious that the process of *priviazka*, while slightly different in nature, is also a creative process.[26]

Gegello was at pains to explain that *priviazka* was an act of design, not mere copying, because it entailed interpretation and improvisation. Using this process, Soviet architects designed and adjusted components at expanding scales from concrete panels to plug-in kitchen and bath modules; from apartments to buildings; from discrete block plans to sprawling neighborhoods.[27] As the architectural and planning professions matured in the Soviet Union, state design offices intensely researched the various climatic zones in the country, articulating more fully local differentiation. *Priviazka* became a more sophisticated and creative process as more variables entered the equation.

Two decades after the completion of New Kharkiv, and upon the rediscovery of earlier models in the wake of Khrushchev's housing campaign, a group of young Moscow-based architects who came to be known as the NER Group developed an articulate socialist spatial theory that connected the early works chronicled in this book and postwar Soviet design practices.[28] A diagram in *The Ideal Communist City*, the English translation of the NER Group's manifesto, shows the system of relationships in communism (figure C.5). Read from left to right, the diagram introduces man connected first to forms of social relations, including familial, educational, productive (work), recreational, and consumer realms. A web of lines

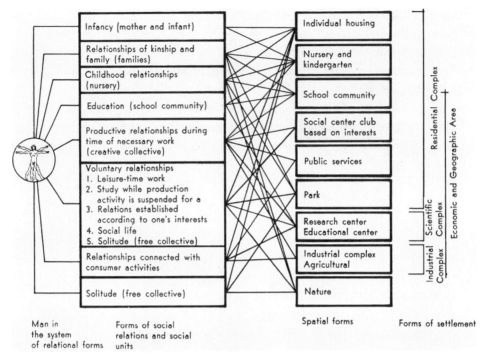

Figure C.5. "The system of relationships in communism determines the functional structure of the environment. Each type of construction is imagined as an element of the unified structure." Diagram by the author based on A. Baburov and A. Gutnov, *The Ideal Communist City*, I Press Series on the Human Environment (New York: G. Braziller, 1971), 27.

connects these social realms to spatial forms. Individual housing, for instance, is linked to infancy, family, leisure, consumer activities, and solitude. Spatial forms are then gathered into forms of settlement in a "unified structure."[29]

What is at stake in this diagram? The authors explain that "a total unified space must be designed by using a system in which single buildings make up a variable spatial field and form a total community."[30] According to the NER Group, architects traditionally design stand-alone buildings because under capitalism the private parcel is the physical limit of the architect's purview. The architect's task is completely transformed under the socialist property regime. Because all space is collective, the designer may consider social, spatial, and settlement forms to be codependent in a "variable spatial field," more commonly referred to in the book as a "unified space." The authors define the New Unit of Settlement (NUS) thus: "the unified space of the NUS is a gigantic room under the open sky. You feel your own presence in the NUS, whether looking out the window of your apartment, leaving a residential unit, going to work, or traveling to the sociocultural center."[31] The mental image summoned here is a powerful one that recalls the complete territorial freedom promised by Okhitovich's disurbanism. But instead of individual structures being strung together along transportation lines as Okhitovich imagined, The NER

Group proposes that the socialist settlement is no longer composed of a collection of object-buildings at all; it is a single shared living room in which all human activities occur under the dome of the sky.

The theory presented in *The Ideal Communist City* proposes that under socialism the built and unbuilt are mutually constitutive and wrapped together in common space. Interior and exterior spaces can engage in a complex and fluid game of give and take, as they exist within the same sociospatial bubble. When designing a standardized residential unit, the architect can, and should, consider it to be a node in a complex web of relations that extends far beyond the vertical walls that enclose it.

The New Unit of Settlement, and its actual built sibling, the *mikroraion*, are riffs on the *zhilkombinat*, but without tethering to the factory. The *mikroraion* accommodates just two spheres of everyday life—the residential and sociocultural—and the productive sphere is accessible only by commute. Nevertheless, the equitable provision of social and cultural programming for residents, robust transportation, and abiding faith in architectural and planning standardization are distinct through lines in the Soviet spatial experience.

Living the Postsocialist City

While nearly a century has passed, and the system under which they were designed and constructed has been superseded, the built environments at the heart of this book persist. Armenikend, the socialist settlement at the edge of Baku, is nearly subsumed by the oil boom city of the present. A handful of the original Constructivist buildings remain, but they are under constant threat of demolition to make way for new high-rises that mimic their dynamic volumetric massing in metal panels and reflective glass. The Kirov District in Magnitogorsk ceased to play an important role in the city once residential construction moved definitively to the right bank of the Ural River in the late 1930s. Some of the May Brigade's housing has been left to ruin, and the green spaces described by John Scott are overgrown, but much of the neighborhood is still, improbably, occupied. The New Kharkiv *sotsgorod* also remains populated, but it is no longer a celebrated site in the former Ukrainian Soviet capital. In spring 2011, a future resident of Kharkiv posted a question on a local web forum: "Which region of Kharkov would you recommend for someone relocating to the city?" The first respondent replied definitively: "*tol'ko ne KhTZ*"—*anywhere* but KhTZ.[32] The reciprocal relationship between the tractor factory and the residential community is broken. A local architectural historian, well versed in spatial politics, has noted that "KhTZ is completely its own world. [The residents there] are somehow mentally, and even arrogantly, isolated. They have their own special psychological complexes, mixed with bravado. Psychologists and reform are what is needed there."[33]

Negative local perceptions of this experimental site of socialist space-making are difficult to disentangle from pervasive disappointment with the collapse of Soviet socialism. A visit to the former tractor factory settlement on a beautiful summer day refutes these blanket claims of dysfunctionality. The open green spaces between residential buildings are filled with tended flowerbeds. Newly painted wooden play structures see heavy use by the children of the neighborhood, whose parents and grandparents sit on nearby benches under the shade of now mature trees. Pedestrians moving through the residential precinct, though now joined by vehicles, still enjoy the spatial liberation planned into the settlement by architects and planners at the start of the 1930s. A cyclist glides by—in jeans rather than jumpsuit—on his way, perhaps, to the coffee roasting company that has set up shop in a disused wing of the old tractor factory.

Contemporary visits to these heroic industrial installations of the early Soviet period are deeply affecting; it is difficult to "unsee" the sites' current conditions. A scholar's struggle with presentism is compounded by local presentism. In the post-Soviet states of Azerbaijan, Russia, and Ukraine, the material legacy of socialism is viewed as detritus of a failed experiment. In attempting to permit the past its due, the archival meeting minutes, memos, briefs, and drawings produced in the months leading up to the planning and construction of these sites help immeasurably. The settlements' import in their time, and the designers' and administrators' seriousness of purpose to create new environments for a new way of life, emerges from the bound sheaves of typing paper and stiff blueprints.

Lessons from the Socialist Spatial Experiment

Soviet architectural and urban experiments were well known outside of the Soviet Union in the 1930s. The Soviets published and distributed information about Baku, Magnitogorsk, and Kharkiv internationally.[34] Foreign architects and engineers working on these sites also directed public attention from the capitalist world in the direction of the Soviet Union. Although Soviet theorists like Sabsovich and Okhitovich took pains to conceptualize socialist spatial difference, US housing specialists, for instance, seriously interrogated the Soviet case for architectural forms and programs that could be utilized to solve the housing problem in the Depression-stricken United States.

In 1934, after spearheading a successful federal grant for slum clearance and low-cost housing construction in Atlanta, Georgia, the US real estate developer Charles F. Palmer took a European housing grand tour to visit projects worthy of possible emulation.[35] The sites he visited were interwar nodes of social housing experimentation that spanned economic and political regimes. Palmer visited first recently constructed *case populari* (people's houses) in Fascist Naples and Rome; he swung through Red Vienna to tour the *gemeindbauten* (communal housing blocks) built by the municipal socialist government; he made a quick stop in Warsaw, and then spent a number of days in Moscow. Palmer presented his Soviet hosts with a question-naire that revealed the for-profit real estate magnate's curiosity about development in a socialist context. He asked about land costs (none, his Soviet respondent explained), construction costs per square meter (250 rubles), and interest and amortization rates for the housing cooperatives (1 percent per annum for both). Palmer also, however, wished to know about the inclusion of common laundries, kitchens, and childcare in the housing complexes, like the ones he had seen in Rome and Vienna, and about the "average percent of land covered by structure, [with the] balance left for parks and playgrounds."[36] The first federally-funded public housing projects completed in the US—Techwood Homes for white families (1936) and University Homes for Black families (1937), both in Atlanta—were superblock projects of freestanding mid-rise housing bars set in shared green space with common laundries, playgrounds, and tenant meeting spaces. Were they socialist? Well, in many ways, yes, or at least the policies enacted to install them were socialist in spirit. The large amount of land cleared for the Techwood and University Homes sites in the center of a capitalist city was only possible through strong central governmental actions. The supplemental social programming for the residents was, for all intents and purposes, inspired by what Palmer saw in Rome, Vienna, and Moscow. But these projects sat in the heart of a business-focused, capitalist US city. This closing example confirms that the socialist spatial project had influence that well exceeded political borders and that snippets of socialist space are embedded worldwide.

The elements universally agreed-on to compose the "good city" were in the 1930s, and remain today, largely the same in socialist and capitalist contexts. They include housing (ideally close to the workplace), reliable transportation, convenient social and commercial services, educational and cultural infrastructure, green space, and recreational opportunities. What differs in socialist and capitalist city making efforts are the funding and delivery methods. Under socialism, the state is responsible for providing all elements—an expensive and logistically complex undertaking. Many socialist and postsocialist cities do have extraordinary public transportation, ample green space, and excellent cultural amenities; but inadequate housing is also a significant legacy of socialism. Architectural standardization and mass production did not fully solve the Soviet housing delivery problem. Post-Soviet cities are plagued by repetitive and disintegrating *mikroraiony* in dire need of maintenance.

Yet in staging interventions in either the postsocialist or the neoliberal condi-tion, contemporary planners will benefit from looking back to the intense debates, experiments, foundational theories, and projects of the early Soviet period. Seeds of solutions for how to plan and build with equity as a principal concern remain in these spatial experiments that still stand, waiting to be discovered again.

APPENDIX

MAGNITOGORSK COMPETITION BRIEF

TsDAMLM Ukrainy, f. 8, po. 1, od. zb. 431, ark. 1.
Translation: Christina E. Crawford

MAGNITOSTROI MANAGEMENT ANNOUNCES
ALL-UNION OPEN COMPETITION
For the drafting of:

A. Planning and construction for the socialist city of Magnitogorsk in the Urals, next to the metallurgical plant
B. Typical residential communes

(All interested parties are free to participate in the competition)
NKVD Publications
Moscow—1929

————

Program.
The main provisions.

The newly planned industrial city of the Magnitogorsk metallurgical plant is to be erected in the Urals, 260 kilometers southwest of the town of Troitsk.

The city is planned based on complete socialization of cultural, educational, and everyday life of all workers, namely:

a. All of the adult population (men and women), except for the elderly, the disabled, and the sick, are involved in productive labor and of various kinds of social work.

b. The life of the workers, aside from production work and engagement with city institutions, is concentrated in the housing commune and its environment, liberating the working people from the worries of maintaining individual farms, but with the active participation of the working people in all kinds of collective economy and way of life of their commune.

c. Children under sixteen years of age live under socialized care in closed nurseries, kindergartens, and boarding schools, located near adult dwellings. They are not, however, isolated in children's campuses and schools.

   Note 1: Space for children is not provided in the living quarters for married couples.

   Note 2: For handicapped children, special centralized institutions will be provided.

d. Meal preparation for the entire population of the city is carried out by a centralized organization in food processing plants that deliver all types of food to all manufacturing facilities, public agencies, and residential communes.

e. Supplies for the entire population—items of general and individual consumption—will be taken care of by a department store as well as a commodity supply network organized by the residential communes.

f. Transportation for the workers in more remote manufacturing locations and institutions will be provided by autobus and automobile transport, which will also be used to provide the population with countryside excursions.

   It is necessary to consider the construction of a tramway on one of the magistrals that heads in the direction of possible further development of a city with over 50,000 residents.

g. Residential communes may be built by the state similarly to a housing cooperative.

h. There is no land provided for individual builders.

i. The premises must be oriented with regard to the most favorable sunlight conditions.

A. Background information for the preparation of preliminary planning and construction of the city of Magnitogorsk

I. The entire population of the city at the full development of the mining plant, including the silicate factories and mines, is determined to be 50,000 residents.

Note: 1. The planning layout of the city should provide roads in the direction of the silica factories and mines to connect workers living in the city with these operations.

II. The city's population distributed by age:

Able-bodied adult population, including men and women ... 34,000 people

Children under 16 years of age 12,000

   from 0–4 3,500

   from 4–8 3,000

   from 8–16 5,500

Elderly and disabled 4,000

III. All construction of the city should be completed over two Five-Year Plans. 30,000 residents should be accommodated in the first Five-Year Plan, with subsequent expansion of 20,000 in the second Five-Year Plan. The city should be planned to accommodate further expansion in future, after the first two Five-Year Plans.

IV. The city will provide the most modern scientific municipal improvements including district heating, water supply, sewage, electrification, and gasification provided by the combined factory installations.

Note 1. The city's water supply is provided from groundwater aquifers on the floodplain of the Urals, and intake wells are located on the banks of flood plains.

Note 2. Release of sewage after biological treatment is planned for the Ural River below the dam, in the direction of the "Magnitkoi" station.

V. The open steppe nature of the city calls for tree planting, especially in the area that separates the factory enterprises from the city.

VI. Data that describes the topography of the city, the location of the individual parts of the mining plant, railway lines to populated areas nearby, and more, are outlined in the attached master plan, presented at a scale of 1/5000.

The above note should be considered when designing the street network.

VII. The planning and development of the city includes: *)

1. Residential communes
2. Palace of Labor and Culture with a library / reading room and meeting rooms for trade unions and health education

3. House of Soviets
4. House of the protection of public order [local security]
5. Theater and cinema
6. Kindergartens and a day nursery for disabled children
7. Educational institutions with no more than 800 children of different ages in any given complex

   Note: Schools should be located so as to provide the opportunity for sufficient land for planting crops and raising animals.
8. VTUZ [*Vyshee tekhnicheskoe uchebnoe zavedenie* or higher technical school] with metallurgical, chemical, and mining departments, all located on a single site near the factory grounds
9. Central clinic and two regional branches in locations convenient to the industrial complex and the residential part of the city
10. Hospital with 400 beds in the first phase, followed by a second phase expansion of 100 beds, consisting of departments for:

    a. Maternity
    b. Gynecology
    c. Surgery
    d. Therapy
    e. Ear, nose, and throat
    f. Eye
    g. Venereal skin disease
    h. Childhood disease
    i. Nervous system
    j. Infectious disease
    k. Pathological wing with morgue
    l. Pharmacy
    m. Administrative wing with a kitchen
    n. Chronic disease

11. Disinfection station
12. Isolation unit for 100 people
13. Sanitary hygienic and clinical laboratory
14. Tuberculosis sanatorium (for children)
15. House for mothers and children [birthing facility]

    Note: When locating the health and sanatorium facilities, one must consider their distance from noise, and their proximity to green areas, in addition to the Commissariat of Health's rules for the location of hospitals.
16. Central children's house and club

17. Food processing plant, consisting of:

   a. Factory kitchen
   b. Baking factory
   c. Production facilities for sausage- and cheese-making, confectionery products, kefir, and various drinks
   d. Slaughterhouses
   e. Refrigerators and warehouses
   f. Disposal plants

   Note: 1. The factory kitchen, bread factory, and other such production facilities should feed a population of 30,000 people, with the subsequent expansion of the facility to serve the entire population of 50,000.
   Note 2. Food processing plants should be located near railway tracks.
18. Department store
19. Mail, telegraph, and telephone building
20. Radio broadcasting center
21. Central mechanical laundry
22. Banya [bathhouse] with pool for swimming
23. Garage
24. Central incineration plant
25. Fire station
26. Material warehouses and repair shops serving the city
27. Park of Culture and Leisure with a stadium and other sporting institutions, as well as fields for the youth of premilitary age
28. Municipal nurseries and greenhouses
29. Crematorium
30. Squares, boulevards, and other tree-planted places

The size of plots allocated for public buildings should be of a width to permit future expansion.

*) The buildings of the Main Administration of the mining plant factory and the hotel are already built, and their locations are indicated on the master plan.

B. **Background information for the preparation of a conceptual design for the residential commune.**

I. The housing commune (complex of buildings) is designed for a capacity of 1,500–3,000 people of all ages who will occupy their own respective sectors of the commune.

II. Sleeping accommodation for adults can be designed for both single capacity and for two or three people.

In order to obtain a variety of solutions, the authors have complete freedom to choose the number of each type of residential room. When calculating the area of rooms, utilize 9 square meters for singles, and 7.5 square meters per person for other types.

Note: For elderly workers sleeping accommodations are located in a quieter part of the building.

III. Service spaces should be designed with each group of sleeping rooms, such as a pantry with a gas stove for heating food, social room (for greeting guests), bathroom, showers, washroom, toilet, laundry basin, and common balcony.

IV. The sleeping quarters should be provided with furniture in the form of folding beds, sofa chairs, cupboards, and so on.

V. The common areas for the adult population are made up of:

   a. Central vestibule with cloakroom, or a series of individual cloak-rooms organized by section
   b. Dining room for 25 percent of the adult population to eat at the same time, with an area near the buffet for snacks and individual meals, a kitchen that allows for partial cooking of food, cooler, pantry, washing, laundry, etc.
   c. Club facilities, consisting of a common room for meetings, movies, and so on with a capacity for 20–30 percent of the adult population of the commune; red corner; library reading room; room for music, study circles, and sports with showers and toilets
   d. Small commercial area with a hairdressing salon
   e. Laundry with dryer and ironing (for small washables) and toilet
   f. Solarium and sports playing fields

Note 1. Common-use areas associated with the housing may be mixed in with the housing or separated, but in any case, they must be connected by heated passageways.

Note 2: The total floor area for public use programs, not counting auxiliary areas (lobby, hallway, stairs, bathrooms, showers, toilets), should be calculated at 2–3 square meters per adult.

VI. Nursery for children from 0–4 years of age.

VII. Kindergarten for children aged 4 to 8 years.

Note: Nurseries and kindergartens must meet all requirements set by the People's Commissariats Health and Education with regard to the size of each respective age group and the spatial norms for each type.

VIII. Play yards should be provided near all nurseries and kindergartens.

IX. Boarding schools for school-aged children should consist of:

    a. Dormitory rooms with a capacity of up to ten children each, with bathrooms, showers, toilets, linen closet, and bathrooms near the sleeping area

    b. Common areas, composed of: dining room that can accommodate half of the children at one time, with service areas included; red corner; classrooms with a library-reading room; room for different kinds of entertainment and sports, with shower and toilets

    c. Lobby with cloakroom.

  X. The spaces of the nurseries, kindergarten, and boarding schools must be connected with the rest of the commune by heated passageways.

 XI. Buildings within the residential commune are allowed to be no more than 4 stories. The ceiling height of the residential spaces should be 2.8 meters and the common areas from 2.8–4 meters. The exception is a large hall (theatre) space, which should have the ceiling height of no less than 4 meters.

The composition of the preliminary designs

The submitted projects must consist of:

1. General plan of the city at the scale of 1/5000 with indication on the plan of residential, public, and administrative structures, their plots, as well various types of green spaces and schematic locations of water and sewer mains
2. Cross sections of streets
3. General plan of a typical residential commune at the scale 1/500
4. Plans of each unrepeated floor of the residential commune at the scale of 1/200, with the typical residential cells at the scale 1/100
5. Sections of the commune buildings that clarify the general construction of the buildings and the height of the most important spaces, at a scale of 1/100
6. Main facade at the scale of 1/200
7. Axonometric or perspective views of one or a few of the buildings of the residential commune
8. Explanatory notes that outline the basic information about the total composition, containing estimates with formulas

On the layout of the city

a. Area of the entire territory of the city
b. % of area occupied by public and administrative buildings

c. % of area occupied by residential communes
d. % of area occupied by all residential and public buildings
e. % of area occupied by green spaces (parks, squares and green buffer zones)
f. % of area occupied by streets, trains, public squares, etc.

On the project of the residential communes

g. Volume of the residential commune buildings (volumes calculated from the sidewalk to the attic floor)
  Note: When a basement is to be constructed, volume is calculated from the basement floor to the attic floor.
h. For each age group, determine: 1) living area (bedrooms); 2) the public area; 3) service area (corridors, passages, toilets, bathrooms, washrooms, etc., with the exception of stairs)
i. Relationship between cubic capacity of the residential buildings of the commune and total area for all population groups
j. Volume of the buildings of the residential commune assigned to each resident, including children
  Note: Schematic drawings indicating the calculations and estimates should be attached; drawings and calculations must be in meters. On the plans, areas and dimensions should be indicated, as well as height in the sections. How the drawings are organized is up to the author but must clearly express the construction of the buildings and their external materiality.

No drawings other than those indicated above will be allowed in the competition submission, and if included will not be considered by the Members of the Jury, nor will they be included in the exhibition.

General terms and schedule for the Members of the Jury

December 22, 1929 at 10 am: competition programs will be issued.
  Competition programs will be distributed by the Magnitostroi Administration (Moscow, at the corner of Nikolskaya Street and Bol. Bogoyalavlenskogo Lane, 1/8) and the Moscow Architectural Society (Ermolaevsky Pereulok, 17).
  January 5, 1930 at 4 pm: the deadline for submission of questions about the competition program to the jury.
  January 7, 1930 at 4 pm: the jury issues answers to the competition questions via the Magnitostroi Administration and the Moscow Architectural Society. Nonresident answers may be communicated by mail on request.
  February 2, 1930 at 8 pm: projects must be deposited at the Magnitostroi Office at the above address with a receipt noting the day and hour of the project submission.

Projects must be submitted under a slogan/motto (verbal or graphic), with the author's name and address in a sealed envelope with the same slogan.

Projects not submitted under a slogan/motto, or in which the name of the author is provided, are disqualified.

Projects submitted by mail are considered to have met the deadline if they were mailed no later than the date of the competition deadline. Out-of-town competitors must send a telegram announcing their submission at the same time that they send the project and must secure documentation that certifies the mailing (postal receipt, etc.). If a project has not been received seven days after the deadline noted in the program, out-of-town competitors lose the right to participate in the competition.

March 2, 1930 completion of the jury deliberations and award of prizes.

For the best projects, the following prizes will be given:

1st Prize	5,000 rubles
2nd Prize	4,000 rubles
3rd Prize	3,000 rubles
4th Prize	2,000 rubles
TOTAL	14,000 rubles

From the nonprize-winning projects, the Administration of Magnitostroi retains the right to acquire projects of their own selection at the price of the last award.

February 28—March 1, 1930: comprehensive public exhibition before the award of prizes.

March 3–4, 1930: comprehensive public exhibition after the award of prizes.

Prize-winning and "acquired" projects become the property of Magnitostroi.

The remaining projects that are not retrieved by their authors before April 1, 1930 become the property of Magnitostroi, although the sealed envelope with slogan will be destroyed, unopened.

The surnames of the prize-winning projects' authors will be published in the same press outlets that the competition itself was published in; the names of the authors of the "acquired" projects will likewise be published.

Magnitostroi retains the right to publish the competition projects.

The Members of the Jury may not participate in the development of competition projects and will not give any clarifying information about the competition program except for the official question-and-answer from the jury included in the program to this competition.

Members of the Jury

1. Lunacharskii, A. V.—Chair
2. Miliutin, N. A. (Chairman of the Lesser Council of People's Commissars (Malyi Sovnarkom))

Participants:

    3. Magnitostroi

    4. Uraloblast' (Ural Regional Government)

    5. NKVD (People's Commissariat for Internal Affairs)

    6. Narkompros (People's Commissariat for Education)

    7. Narkomzdrav (People's Commissariat for Health)

    8. Stroikom RSFSR (Construction Committee of the Russian Republic)

    9. VTsSPS (All-Union Central Soviet of Trade Unions / 4 participants)

  10. TsK VLKSM (Central Committee of the Young Communist League)

  11. Zhenotdel TsK (Women's Department of the Central Committee)

  12. Vesnin, V. A., civil engineer

  13. Mashkov, I. O., architect

  14. Ivanov, A. K., architect-artist

Upon publication of this program the composition of the Members of the Jury shall not be altered.

Mosoblit no. 184   Order no. 1076   Circulation 400 copies

NKVD Publishing House, 16 Mal. Kamenshchiki

NOTES

Introduction

1. Philip A. Adler, "Russia Arming with Tractor: Part Three," *Detroit News*, December 22, 1929. "A series telling the truth about conditions in Russia today as observed by Mr. Adler, Detroit News reporter who traveled several thousand miles through that country last summer." This and other articles on technical exchanges between Detroit and the USSR in the late 1920s and early 1930s are found in Albert Kahn Associates scrapbooks held at the Bentley Historical Library, University of Michigan, Albert Kahn Associates records.

2. Incredible speed and immense scale are just two of six points Gerschenkron makes to characterize industrialization in a "backward" country. Russia's backwardness can be debated, but Gerschenkron's *rash speed* and *large-scale* points do map on to the transformation of the built environment under the first Five-Year Plan. Alexander Gerschenkron, "Economic Backwardness in Economic Perspective," in *Economic Backwardness in Economic Perspective: A Book of Essays* (New York: Praeger, 1962), 27.

3. Researching the gap between projections and reality—telling the nonofficial history of Soviet spatial planning—now occupies post-Soviet architectural and planning historians like Mark Meerovich, Dmitrii Khmelnitskii, and Evgeniia Konysheva. See, e.g., M. G. Meerovich, "Neoffitsial'noe gradostroitel'stvo: Tainyi aspekt sovetskoi industrializatsii (1928–1932)," in *Problemy otchestvennoi istorii: Istochniki, istoriografiia, issledovaniia*, ed. M. V. Drusin (St. Petersburg: Sankt Peterburgskii institut istorii RAN, 2008), 395.

4. Anna Louise Strong, *From Stalingrad to Kuzbas* (New York: International Pamphlets, 1932), 33.

5. Catherine Cooke, *Russian Avant-Garde Theories of Art, Architecture and the City* (London: Academy Editions, 1995); S. Khan-Magomedov and Catherine Cooke, *Pioneers of*

Soviet Architecture: The Search for New Solutions in the 1920s and 1930s (New York: Rizzoli, 1987); S. O. Khan-Magomedov, *Arkhitektura sovetskogo avangarda* (Moscow: Stroiizdat, 1996); Anatole Kopp, *Town and Revolution: Soviet Architecture and City Planning, 1917–1935* (New York: G. Braziller, 1970); Manfredo Tafuri, "Toward the Socialist City," in *The Sphere and the Labyrinth* (Cambridge: MIT Press, 1990), 149–70.

6. While he was at the Harvard Graduate School of Design (GSD), Professor Neil Brenner's concept of "planetary urbanization," indebted to early Soviet urban theory, generated among his GSD students latter-day urban diagrams that riffed on disurbanism in particular.

7. A thorough discussion of the pervasiveness of the failure narrative for socialist architecture and construction scholarship can be found in Michal Murawski, "Actually-Existing Success: Economics, Aesthetics, and the Specificity of (Still-) Socialist Urbanism," *Comparative Studies in Society and History* 60, no. 4 (2018): 907–37. A notable exception is Milka Bliznakov, "Urban Planning in the USSR: Integrative Theories," in *The City in Russian History*, ed. Michael F. Hamm (Lexington: University Press of Kentucky, 1976).

8. For the year 1925 as a "start date" for Soviet architecture, see Kopp, chap. 5: "1925–32: An Architecture for the New Times," in *Town and Revolution*.

9. See, for example, the assessment of the "disturbing degree of realism" in Soviet-built architecture in Tafuri, *The Sphere and the Labyrinth*, 164.

10. Cohen insisted that "circulation does not imply detachment from the ground," and further that to understand the global, one must remain tethered to the local. Yves Cohen, "Circulatory Localities: The Example of Stalinism in the 1930s," *Kritika: Explorations in Russian and Eurasian History* 11, no. 1, Winter (2010): 17. Unlike actor-network theory, nodal history is interested in the handoffs or translations of design ideas from one node to the next rather than the things that move. Nodal history also differs from Deleuze and Guattari's rhizomatic theoretical model, which insists that the system can be entered from any point, "has no beginning or end; it is always in the middle, between things, interbeing, intermezzo." Nodal history is unabashedly narrative and historically grounded. See Bruno Latour, *Reassembling the Social: An Introduction to Actor-Network-Theory*, Clarendon Lectures in Management Studies (Oxford: Oxford University Press, 2005); Gilles Deleuze, and Félix Guattari, *A Thousand Plateaus: Capitalism and Schizophrenia* (Minneapolis: University of Minnesota Press, 1987), 25.

11. Aristotle makes a distinction between poiesis (making) and praxis (acting). In this book, I conflate the two into praxis, following Hannah Arendt's claim that Aristotle's examples show "that he thinks of acting in terms of making . . . (his emphatic attempts to distinguish between action and fabrication, praxis and poiesis, notwithstanding.)" Hannah Arendt, *The Human Condition*, 2nd ed. (Chicago: University of Chicago Press, 1958), 196.

12. Amanda Reeser and Ashley Schafer, "Defining Praxis," *Praxis: Journal of Writing + Building* 0, no. 1 (1999): 7. Other authors also stress the importance of flexibility, tactic-switching, and compromise in Marxist-oriented physical planning. See Norman Fainstein and Susan Fainstein, "New Debates in Urban Planning: The Impact of Marxist Theory in the United States," *International Journal of Urban and Regional Research* 3, no. 3 (1979): 387.

13. Karl Marx, "Theses on Feuerbach," in *Marx/Engels Selected Works*, vol. 1 (Moscow: Progress Publishers, 1969), XI. https://www.marxists.org/archive/marx/works/1845/theses/theses.htm.

14. Marx, "Theses on Feuerbach," I.

15. Roger Paden, "Marxism, Utopianism, and Modern Urban Planning," *Utopian Studies* 14, no. 1 (2003): 93–95.

16. Martin Buber, *Paths in Utopia* (New York: Macmillan, 1950), 99.

17. Buber, *Paths in Utopia*, 7.

18. Heather D. DeHaan, *Stalinist City Planning: Professionals, Performance, and Power* (Toronto: University of Toronto Press, 2013), 64–65, 75.

19. Vladimir Ilich Lenin, "The New Economic Policy and the Tasks of the Political Education Departments," in *Report to the Second All-Russia Congress of Political Education Departments* (October 17, 1921). https://www.marxists.org/archive/lenin/works/1921/oct/17.htm.

20. The first paragraph proclaims that "landed proprietorship is abolished forthwith without any compensation," and the second extends appropriation to church and monastic holdings, country estates, and so on, transferring all above-noted property into the hands of local government organs. This decree did not appropriate the land of ordinary peasants. "Decree on Land," October 26 (November 8), 1917, published on the front page of *Izvestiia*. https://www.marxists.org/archive/lenin/works/1917/oct/25-26/26d.htm.

21. This plan to "overtake and outstrip" capitalist countries—a phrase originally used by Lenin—took on heightened meaning at the start of the first Five-Year Plan. In a November 1928 speech at the Plenum of the Communist Party of the Soviet Union (Bolsheviks), Stalin said, "we have overtaken and outstripped the advanced capitalist countries in the sense of establishing a new political system, the Soviet system. That is good. But it is not enough. In order to secure the final victory of socialism in our country, we must also overtake and outstrip these countries technically and economically. Either we do this, or we shall be forced to the wall." J. V. Stalin, "Industrialisation of the Country and the Right Deviation in the C.P.S.U.(B.)," November 19, 1928. https://www.marxists.org/reference/archive/stalin/works/1928/11/19.htm.

22. Stephen J. Collier, *Post-Soviet Social: Neoliberalism, Social Modernity, Biopolitics* (Princeton: Princeton University Press, 2011), 57.

23. According to the early Soviet historian E. H. Carr, "the word 'planning' is held merely to mean the exercise of state authority to regulate the economy," a definition that skips over spatial planning activities altogether. Edward Hallett Carr, *Foundations of a Planned Economy, 1926–1929*, ed. R. W. Davies (London: Macmillan, 1969), 787.

24. The conflation of economic and spatial planning leaked into Soviet historical scholarship. In his seminal history on the construction of Stalinist culture, Stephen Kotkin uses the term "planner" to refer to a range of expert types, but his damning commentary on the state of urban affairs in Magnitogorsk elides which type of planner was to blame for Magnitogorsk's dysfunction. See Stephen Kotkin, *Magnetic Mountain: Stalinism as a Civilization* (Berkeley: University of California Press, 1995), 144.

25. Konysheva and Meerovich dispute this claim, noting that in 1928–29 approximately 24,500 Soviet architects and civil engineers were working between Moscow, Leningrad, and Kharkiv. Speech given by the NKVD representative B. S. Gurevich at the Gosplan conference on November 26, 1929. Gosplan-SSSR, *K probleme stroitel'stva sotsialisticheskogo goroda* (Moscow: Izd-vo planovoe khoziaistvo, 1930), 28. For a counterargument see Konysheva, Meerovich, and Thomas Flierl, "Ernst May v istorii sovetskoi industrializatsii," *Project baikal* 8, no. 27 (2011): 137.

26. Although he was educated as a civil engineer in St. Petersburg before the revolution, Ivanitskii sought to establish Soviet city-building as a discipline distinct from architecture or engineering. DeHaan, *Stalinist City Planning*, 3.

27. Cohen notes that "as for the relationship between invention and borrowing, the ethnologist André Leroi-Gourhan has convincingly shown that 'the example of an invention wholly linked to a local milieu can only be identified somewhat arbitrarily.' Invention supposes borrowing, and vice versa." Cohen, "Circulatory Localities," 16.

28. L. M. Sabsovich, "Problema goroda," *Planovoe khoziaistvo*, no. 7 (1929): 31.

29. Sabsovich, "Problema goroda," 34–35.

30. Chapter 4 of this book covers this debate in detail. See also S. Frederick Starr, "Visionary Town Planning during the Cultural Revolution," in *Cultural Revolution in Russia, 1928–1931*, ed. Sheila Fitzpatrick (Bloomington: Indiana University Press, 1978), 207–40.

31. M. Okhitovich, "Ne gorod, a novyi tip rasseleniia," in *Goroda sotsializma i sotsialisticheskaia rekonstruktsiia byta*, ed. B. Lunin (Moscow: Tip. Mospoligrafa "Iskra Revoliutsii," 1930), 153–55.

32. Antonio Gramsci, *Prison Notebooks*, trans. J. A. Buttigieg (New York: Columbia University Press, 2007), 3:168–69.

33. Fredric Jameson, "Architecture and the Critique of Ideology," in *The Ideologies of Theory* (New York: Verso, 2008), 359.

34. Although the NKVD is best known historically as the seat of political terror (the secret political police—the OGPU, KGB—both emerge from it after 1934), in the 1920s it was involved in construction. The quote comes from an architectural brief authored by the Higher Technical-Construction Committee of the NKVD of the Ukrainian Soviet Socialist Republic. TsDAVO, f.5, o.3, d.1877, ll. 1–2.

35. Although Lefebvre acknowledged "prodigious creative ferment in Soviet Russia between 1920 and 1930," he concluded that "those fertile years were followed by years of sterility." Henri Lefebvre, *The Production of Space* (Oxford: Blackwell, 1991), 54.

36. The quote continues, "whereas a single building was once perceived as a unique spatial composition, we are now ready to conceive a unified spatial field, which includes the whole community." A. Baburov and A. Gutnov, *The Ideal Communist City*, I Press Series on the Human Environment (New York: G. Braziller, 1971), 164.

37. Kimberly Elman Zarecor's two conditions of "infrastructural thinking" and "socialist scaffold" are also useful concepts to define socialist space. Infrastructural thinking is akin to my assertion that socialist space is massive in scale and coordinated, qualities present in a

fully state-owned property regime. The socialist scaffold is the totalized material systems that work together, composed of transport, road and rail, public utilities, green space, cultural programming, housing and services. Kimberly Elman Zarecor, "What Was So Socialist about the Socialist City? Second World Urbanity in Europe," *Journal of Urban History* 44, no. 1 (2018): 95, 99–100.

38. Kotkin concluded that the "superblocks, now called microregions, remained the dominant planning units" throughout the Soviet era. Stephen Kotkin, "The Search for the Socialist City," *Russian History / Histoire Russe* 23, no. 1–4 (1996): 245.

39. El Lissitzky, *Russia: An Architecture for World Revolution* (London: Lund Humphries, 1970), 27.

40. Experimental director Dziga Vertov released a film-length travelogue of the Soviet Union in 1926 entitled *Shetaia chast' mira* (One-Sixth of the World) that lodged this notion in Soviet consciousness.

41. Stuart Chase, *A New Deal* (New York: Macmillan, 1932), 153–54.

42. Adler, "Russia Arming with Tractor."

43. Moshe Lewin, *The Making of the Soviet System: Essays in the Social History of Interwar Russia* (London: Methuen, 1985), 144.

44. Lev Kopelev, *To Be Preserved Forever*, ed. and trans. Anthony Austin (Philadelphia: Lippincott, 1977), 11–12.

45. Kopelev, *The Education of a True Believer* (New York: Harper & Row, 1980), 249–50.

46. Oleh Wolowyna, et al., "Regional Variations of 1932–34 Famine Losses in Ukraine," *Canadian Studies in Population* 43, no. 3–4 (2016): 175. For spatial mapping of the effects of the Holodomor, visit the Harvard Ukrainian Research Institute site at http://gis.huri.harvard.edu/.

47. The Aggregate Architectural History Collaborative uses the framing mechanism of events, defined as "moments when architecture and design participated integrally in managing the changes associated with modernization." Ten years after he dismissed microhistory as a mere "history of events," Fernand Braudel, founder of the Annales School and proponent of the longue durée, conceded that: "The incident (if not the event, the socio-drama) exists in repetition, regularity, multitude, and there is no way of saying absolutely whether its level is quite without fertility or scientific value. It must be given closer examination." Aggregate Architectural History Collaborative, *Governing by Design: Architecture, Economy, and Politics in the Twentieth Century* (Pittsburgh: University of Pittsburgh Press, 2012), ix. See also Carlo Ginzburg, "Microhistory: Two or Three Things That I Know about It," *Critical Inquiry* 20 (Autumn 1993): 13.

48. Elena Korotkova, "Planning Maps in Russia: From State Secrecy towards World Openness" (Fellows Seminar, Davis Center for Russian and Eurasian Studies, Harvard University, October 14, 2014). https://daviscenter.fas.harvard.edu/events/planning-maps-russia-state-secrecy-towards-world-openness. The state is not the only body afflicted with cartographic paranoia; MMK, the private company that owns the Magnitogorsk Iron and Steel Works, refused access to their historical planning materials.

49. The book Aleshin authored in 1911 on school architecture is illustrated with examples from abroad. P. F. Aleshin, *O sovremennoi shkol'noi arkhitekture: Otdel'nyi ottisk doklada avtora 4-mu s''iezdu Russkikh zodchikh* (St. Petersburg: Gos. tipografiia, 1911).

50. Aleshin made an appeal to Soviet officials for extra living space in 1918. "I affirm that my library, collected with great difficulty over the course of my whole life, constitutes my scientific, artistic and societal work. It is a crucial productive tool used every day, and it cannot fit in other extremely small rooms of the apartment." Alena Mokrousova, "Biblioteka Pavla Aleshina," *Antikvar* 101, no. March–April (2017), https://antikvar.ua/biblioteka-pavla-alyoshina/.

51. An example of a technical text from the Aleshin library at the CCA in Montréal is G. B. Barkhin, *Sovremennye rabochie zhilishcha* (Moscow: Voprosy truda, 1925). Examples of socialist city theory texts include Lunin, *Goroda sotsializma i sotsialisticheskaia rekonstruktsiia byta* and Gosplan-SSSR, *K probleme stroitel'stva sotsialisticheskogo goroda*.

52. Or, per the Beckettian injunction, "Ever tried. Ever failed. No matter. Try again. Fail again. Fail better." Samuel Beckett and Raymond Danowski, *Worstward Ho* (London: John Calder, 1983), 7. Thank you to an anonymous reader at Cornell University Press for this allied philosophy.

Chapter 1. Socialism Means Housing

Epigraph: Azneft, *Obzor Azerbaidzhanskoi neftianoi promyshlennosti za piat' let nationalizatsii: 1920–1925* (Baku: Azneft, 1925), 67–68.

1. Eve Blau claims for Baku the title of the "original oil city: a cosmopolis built on and with oil." During and after the 1870s oil boom, Baku's population grew precipitously, as did the physical fabric of the city. Local oil barons plowed their earnings back into the public life of the city through institution building and representational construction projects. Eve Blau, Ivan Rupnik, and Iwan Baan, *Baku: Oil and Urbanism* (Zurich: Park Books, 2018), 15, 70–73.

2. Azneft, *Obzor Azerbaidzhanskoi neftianoi promyshlennosti za piat' let nationalizatsii*, 67.

3. General plans were developed for Baku in 1807, 1810, 1822, 1833, 1835, 1842, 1855, 1864, 1876, 1878, and 1898. See Sh. S. Fatullaev-Figarov, *Arkhitekturnaia entsiklopediia Baku* (Baku: Mezhdunrodnaia akademiia arkhitektury stran vostoka, 1998), chap. 2: "Gradostroitel'stvo Baku XIX–nachala XX vekov."

4. In effect, 1872 marked the end of the traditional *otkupshchina* system of tsarist landownership, in place since 1806, when Russia took control of the Baku khanate. Rovshan Ibrahimov, "Azerbaijan's Energy History and Policy," in *Energy and Azerbaijan: History, Strategy and Cooperation* (Baku: SAM, 2013), 8.

5. Audrey Altstadt-Mirhadi, "Baku: Transformation of a Muslim Town," in *City in Late Imperial Russia*, ed. Michael F. Hamm (Bloomington: Indiana University Press, 1983), 288.

6. Fatullaev-Figarov, *Arkhitekturnaia entsiklopediia Baku*, 31.

7. Fatullaev-Figarov, *Arkhitekturnaia entsiklopediia Baku*, 43.

8. Fatullaev-Figarov, *Arkhitekturnaia entsiklopediia Baku*, 52.

9. The seaside esplanade and boulevard were ultimately installed under the Soviets in 1937. For an image of the completed project, see Blau, *Baku*, 92.

10. Altstadt-Mirhadi, "Baku," 302–3.

11. "The Baku Oilfields: Great Fires Will Cripple Russia's Oil Trade," *New York Times*, September 10, 1905, 13.

12. *Mineral Resources of the United States, Calendar Year 1905*. Department of the Interior, United States Geological Survey (Washington, DC: Government Printing Office, 1906), 896.

13. Ronald Grigor Suny, "A Journeyman for the Revolution: Stalin and the Labour Movement in Baku, June 1907–May 1908," *Soviet Studies* 23, no. 3 (1972): 383.

14. Quoted in Suny, "A Journeyman for the Revolution," 373.

15. Audrey L. Altstadt, *The Azerbaijani Turks: Power and Identity under Russian Rule* (Stanford: Hoover Institution Press, 1992), 45–46.

16. Tadeusz Swietochowski, *Russian Azerbaijan, 1905–1920: The Shaping of National Identity in a Muslim Community* (Cambridge: Cambridge University Press, 1985), 135. For an account of the first nationalization of the oil industry after the October Revolution and under the Baku Commune, see Suny, *Baku*, 237–50.

17. Ronald Grigor Suny, *The Baku Commune, 1917–1918: Class and Nationality in the Russian Revolution* (Princeton: Princeton University Press, 1972), 238.

18. Françoise Companjen, László Marácz, and Lia Versteegh, *Exploring the Caucasus in the 21st Century: Essays on Culture, History and Politics in a Dynamic Context* (Amsterdam: Amsterdam University Press, 2012), 119.

19. Both Altstadt and Swietochowski agree on a three-phase characterization of the ADR period: 1) ADR with Ganja as capital, 2) Unified ADR with Baku as capital, under British occupation, and 3) Unoccupied and independent ADR. See Altstadt, *The Azerbaijani Turks*, 89–90, and Tadeusz Swietochowski and Brian C. Collins, eds., *Historical Dictionary of Azerbaijan* (Lanham, MD: Scarecrow Press, 1999), 6.

20. Nasib Nassibli, "Azerbaijan: Oil and Politics in the Country's Future," in *Oil and Geopolitics in the Caspian Sea Region*, ed. Michael P. Croissant and Bülent Aras (Westport, CT: Praeger, 2000), 103.

21. For extraction data, see A. P. Ivanitskii, "'Planirovka G. Baku': Poiasnitel'naia zapiska k proektu. Chast'1–4," RGALI, f. 2991, op. 1, 1928, diagram 1. See also Edgar Wesley Owen, *Trek of the Oil Finders: A History of Exploration for Petroleum*, vol. 6 (Tulsa, OK: American Association of Petroleum Geologists, 1975), 1356.

22. Similar consolidations were undertaken in the other two significant oil-producing regions now under Soviet control, Grozny-Kuban (Grozneft) and the Ural Emba district (Embaneft). Vladimir Mishin, "Breaking through the Oil Blockade," *Oil of Russia*, no. 3 (2005).

23. Glavneftkom of the VSNKh of the RSFSR, ARDA, f. 2548, o. 2, d. 3, l. 18.

24. S. Aslanov, *Aleksandr Serebrovskii: Biograficheskii ocherk* (Baku: Azerbaidzhanskoe gos. izd-vo, 1974).

25. Sara G. Brinegar, "Baku at All Costs: The Politics of Oil in the New Soviet State" (PhD diss., University of Wisconsin, 2014), 9.

26. Kirov, Russian by birth, was present in Baku as a Communist Party organizer as early as 1910 and had a hand in the Red Army's takeover of the Apsheron Peninsula in 1920. In 1939, a large statue to Kirov was installed at the apex of Baku's Dagustu (Highland) Park and stood as a landmark over the city until 1992.

27. In 1904, Kirov earned a degree in engineering from the Kazan Technical School. In his party biography from 1923, Kirov noted that he then moved to Siberia to work as a municipal draftsman while studying for the entrance exams to the Tomsk Technological Institute, an extension to his education that he did not finish. Matthew E. Lenoe, *The Kirov Murder and Soviet History*, Annals of Communism Series (New Haven: Yale University Press, 2010).

28. Despite the success their tenure in Baku brought to the new Soviet oil industry, neither Kirov nor Serebrovskii survived the Stalinist terror of the 1930s. Kirov was shot under mysterious circumstances in 1934, Serebrovskii was arrested in 1937 and killed in 1938.

29. Sara Brinegar offers a useful distinction between Azerbaijani and standard Soviet chronologies. The period between Red Army occupation of the territory and NEP she calls "Revolutionary Communism" (as opposed to "War Communism"). "Revolutionary Communism was characterized by the same ideological militancy and harsh punishments as War Communism but allowed trade and did not requisition foodstuffs from the peasantry, two fundamental differences." Brinegar, "Baku at All Costs," 4.

30. The economy of the new Soviet Union had already passed through one disastrous stage, War Communism (1917–20), which attempted rapid nationalization. The state assumed control of all means of production, exchange, and communication, and all land was declared nationalized by the 1917 Decree on Land.

31. Amtorg Trading Corporation, *Soviet Oil Industry: A Compilation of Statements Regarding Purchases of Soviet Oil by the Standard Oil Company of New York and the Vacuum Oil Co.: Statistics of the Oil Industry of the U.S.S.R.* (New York: Amtorg Trading Corporation, 1928), 26.

32. Yakov A. Gelfgat, Mikhail Y. Gelfgat, and Yuri S. Lopatin, *Advanced Drilling Solutions. Volume 1: Lessons from the FSU* (Tulsa, OK: PennWell Books, 2003), 7–8.

33. Antony C. Sutton, *Western Technology and Soviet Economic Development, 1917 to 1930* (Stanford, CA: Hoover Institution on War, Revolution and Peace, 1968), 18.

34. "Electric power is widely applied in the Soviet oil industry. The oil wells in Baku are at present electrified to the extent of 93 per cent. This compares with 30 per cent in 1913." Amtorg Trading Corporation, *Soviet Oil Industry*, 28.

35. Michael P. Croissant and Bülent Aras, *Oil and Geopolitics in the Caspian Sea Region* (Westport, CT.: Praeger, 2000), 11–12.

36. Sutton, *Western Technology and Soviet Economic Development*, 43. Amtorg clarified in 1925 how the Soviet state would utilize oil from various regions. Oil from three primary sites—Baku among them—was for foreign export, to be exchanged for hard currency to feed other branches of the economy. From the establishment of Soviet control in Azerbaijan, Baku's oil was pooled and controlled by the central authorities. "All the trusts are subordinated to

the Supreme Economic Council of the Soviet Union, which is the equivalent to a Ministry of Industry. The trusts do not sell their product to the consumer directly. All sales are conducted by the Soviet Naphtha (Oil) Syndicate, which handles the output of the three trusts." Coal, by contrast, was to be the preferred fossil fuel for Soviet domestic use. See Amtorg Trading Corporation, *Soviet Oil Industry*, 26.

37. For an extended discussion of *circulation des saviors* in the Soviet context, see Yves Cohen, "Circulatory Localities: The Example of Stalinism in the 1930s," *Kritika: Explorations in Russian and Eurasian History* 11, no. 1 (2010).

38. "Former Mines Professor Tells about Russia," *Colorado School of Mines Magazine*, March (1930), 28–29.

39. Charles van der Leeuw, *Oil and Gas in the Caucasus & Caspian: A History* (Richmond, UK: Curzon, 2000), 108–10.

40. See Suny, *The Baku Commune*, chap. 2: "Social Democracy and the Labor Movement in Baku, 1898–1917; Altstadt, *The Azerbaijani Turks*, chap. 3: "Industrialization, Conflict, and Social Change.

41. Suny, "A Journeyman for the Revolution," 377. Both the Nobels and local industrialist Zeynalabdin Taghiyev built some worker housing in the late nineteenth century. The Nobel housing was largely for foreign specialists in the White Town near the grounds of Villa Petrolia, and Taghiyev's housing and support services were for the workers of his textile factory on the Caspian coast east of Baku, not for oil workers. Taghiyev divested of his oil property by 1897, before he constructed the textile workers' settlement.

42. Suny, *The Baku Commune*, 54–57.

43. ARDA f. 2548, o. 2, d. 3, l. 18.

44. The survey was to be at the scale of fifty sazhens, to include contours every two sazhens. A sazhen is the equivalent of seven feet. ARDA f. 1114, o. 1, d. 515, ll. 59–61.

45. Azneft, *Obzor Azerbaidzhanskoi neftianoi promyshlennosti za dva goda nationalizatsii: 1920–1922* (Baku: Azneft, 1922), 262.

46. "On the location for the construction of houses: In Ramani, Zarbat, Black Town, Bingadi, Shubani and Bibi-Eibat construction will occur in the assigned locations. In Surakhani, we charge V.N. DELOV, together the geologists and the administration of the regions, to choose a location that does not conflict with oil-producing land." ARDA, f. 2940, o. 1, d. 12, l. 53, rev.

47. Azneft, *Obzor Azerbaidzhanskoi neftianoi promyshlennosti za dva goda nationalizatsii*, 261.

48. Brinegar, "Baku at All Costs," 25.

49. Azneft, *Obzor Azerbaidzhanskoi neftianoi promyshlennosti za dva goda nationalizatsii*, 74, 32.

50. Brinegar, "Baku at All Costs," 20.

51. Azneft, *Obzor Azerbaidzhanskoi neftianoi promyshlennosti za dva goda nationalizatsii*, 76.

52. Azneft, *Obzor Azerbaidzhanskoi neftianoi promyshlennosti za dva goda nationalizatsii*, 262.

53. Azneft, *Obzor Azerbaidzhanskoi neftianoi promyshlennosti za dva goda national-izatsii*, 263–64.

54. Azneft, *Obzor Azerbaidzhanskoi neftianoi promyshlennosti za piat' let nationalizat-sii*, 67.

55. Azneft claimed to have renovated 8,000 housing units through 1923 in their 1925 overview. In archival documentation, this count jumped to 12,000. See ARDA, f. 1610, o. 4, d. 22, ll. 9–11

56. Azneft, *Obzor Azerbaidzhanskoi neftianoi promyshlennosti za piat' let nationalizat-sii*, 67.

57. M. Astafieva-Dlugach, "Proekt raionnoi planirovki Apsheronskogo Poluostrova," *Arkhitektura SSSR*, no. 10 (1971).

58. ARDA, f. 1114, o. 1, d. 24, l. 28.

59. Azneft, *Obzor Azerbaidzhanskoi neftianoi promyshlennosti za piat' let nationalizat-sii*, 67–68.

60. Continual use of a bed by succeeding shift workers—called "hot-bedding" in con-temporary parlance—is a problem without geographical or temporal boundaries. See, for example, hot-bedding in a global context in the 1960s in Bruce E. Newling, "Geographical Record: Urban Population Densities and Intra-Urban Growth," *Geographical Review* 54, no. 3 (1964): 440–42; or among African American workers in Los Angeles in the 1940s in Don Parson and Kevin Starr, "Homes for Heroes: Public Housing during World War II," in *Making a Better World* (Minneapolis: University of Minnesota Press, 2005), 56.

61. ARDA, f. 2940, o. 1, d. 12, l. 12, October 24, 1923.

62. ARDA, f. 2940, o. 1, d. 12, l. 12.

63. Gosplan was established as the RSFSR State Planning Commission to deal only with the Russian Federation, but GOELRO and other Union-wide plans shifted Gosplan's role to oversee planning for all Soviet territories.

64. Formally, Gosplan sat under the Sovnarkom and STO, but Gosplan economic advisers served the Politburo directly. R. W. Davies and O. Khlevnyuk, "Gosplan," in *Decision-Mak-ing in the Stalinist Command Economy, 1932–37*, ed. E. A. Rees, *Studies in Russian and East European History and Society* (Basingstoke: Macmillan, 1997), 32.

65. Davies and Khlevnyuk, "Gosplan," 37.

66. ARDA, f. 2940, o. 1, d. 12, l. 7.

67. The total of new apartments built in 1923–24 and their per unit cost come from a December 9, 1924 report by the head engineer of the Azneft Building Committee A. P. Sido-renko. In ARDA, f. 2940, o. 1, d. 12, l. 8.

68. Azneft, *Obzor Azerbaidzhanskoi neftianoi promyshlennosti za piat' let nationalizat-sii*, 68.

69. ARDA, f. 2940, o. 1, d. 12, ll. 9–10.

70. Modern planning in the Soviet territories did not begin abruptly in 1917, nor was there a seamless continuation with Russian imperial practices. For a full discussion, see S. Frederick Starr, "The Revival and Schism of Urban Planning in Twentieth-Century Russia," in *The City in Russian History*, ed. Michael F. Hamm (Lexington: University Press of Kentucky, 1976).

71. ARDA, f. 1933, o. 1, d. 222, l. 19.

72. The UK worker settlements Ivanitskii showed in slides were in Birmingham, Bournville (the Cadbury-built worker village), Cardiff, Bristol, Liverpool, Leeds, Manchester, Nestingham, Port Sunlight (the Lever-built worker village), and Sheffield. ARDA, f. 1933, o. 1, d. 222, l. 19.

73. ARDA, f. 1933, o. 1, d. 222, l. 20.

74. ARDA, f. 1933, o. 1, d. 222, l. 20.

75. ARDA, f. 1933, o. 1, d. 222, l. 20.

76. ARDA, f. 1933, o. 1, d. 222, l. 22.

77. RGALI, f. 2991, o. 1, ed. kh. 1, l. 29.

78. Ivanitksii is one of the chief protagonists in Heather D. DeHaan, *Stalinist City Planning: Professionals, Performance, and Power* (Toronto: University of Toronto Press, 2013). DeHaan focuses on Ivanitskii's tenure as planner of Nizhnii Novgorod (1928–35) but also thoroughly unpacks his biography and professional preoccupations.

79. V. G. Davidovich and Tatiana Aleksandrovna Chizhikova, *Aleksandr Ivanitskii*, Mastera arkhitektury (Moscow: Stroiizdat, 1973), 18.

80. Among the texts Ivanitskii translated into Russian were "Regulations for the 1911 Expansion Plan of Lausanne" (from French) and "Saxon Building Laws, 1900" (from German). Davidovich and Chizhikova, *Aleksandr Ivanitskii*, 20n6.

81. A. P. Ivanitskii, "O ratsional'noi planirovke gorodov," *Stroitel'naia promyshlennost'*, no. 4 (1926): 298.

82. Ivanitskii, "O ratsional'noi planirovke gorodov," 298.

83. Ivanitskii, "O ratsional'noi planirovke gorodov," 301.

84. A. P. Serebrovskii, *Neftianaia i gazovaia promyshlennost' v Amerike. Chast' pervaia* (Moscow: Tsentral'noe upravlenie pechati VSNKh, 1925), 5.

85. B. M. Shpotov, *Amerikanskii biznes i sovetskii soiuz v 1920–1930-e gody: Labirinty ekonomicheskogo sotrudnichestva* (Moscow: URSS, 2013), 143.

86. Vagit Alekperov, *Oil of Russia: Past, Present and Future*, trans. Paul B. Gallager and Thomas D. Hedden (Minneapolis: EastView Press, 2011), 113.

87. Alekperov, *Oil of Russia*, 113.

88. "USSR Oil Head Here to Study US Production," *Daily Worker*, November 17, 1927, 3.

89. A. P. Serebrovskii, *Neftianaia i gazovaia promyshlennost' v Amerike. Chast' vtoraia* (Moscow: Tsentral'noe upravlenie pechati VSNKh, 1925), 8.

90. Alekperov, *Oil of Russia*, 115.

91. Bethlehem Steel also utilized prefabricated Sears houses for its workers in Hellertown, Pennsylvania. Katherine H. Stevenson and H. Ward Jandl, *Houses by Mail: A Guide to Houses from Sears, Roebuck and Company* (Washington, DC: Preservation Press, 1986), 21; "Aladdin Company of Bay City: Other Commercial Ventures," Clarke Historical Library, Mount Pleasant, MI, 2001, https://www.cmich.edu/library/clarke/ResearchResources/Michigan_Material_Local/Bay_City_Aladdin_Co/OtherCommercialVentures/Pages/default.aspx#commericalsales.

92. Azneft, *Obzor Azerbaidzhanskoi neftianoi promyshlennosti za piat' let nationalizat-sii*, 69.

93. Azneft, *Obzor Azerbaidzhanskoi neftianoi promyshlennosti za piat' let nationalizat-sii*, 69.

94. The US engineer William Chamberlin, a fan of Serebrovskii's, noted that the Azneft offices in Baku were "the only place in Russia where I have seen such [sanitary paper] cups." William Henry Chamberlin, "Missionaries of American Technique in Russia," *Asia* 32, no. July–August (1932): 422. A package of soccer balls sent from the US led to the establishment of Azerbaijan's first soccer team, the Azneft "Neftchi" (Oilers). Shpotov, *Amerikanskii biznes i sovetskii soiuz*, 148.

95. Azneft, *Obzor Azerbaidzhanskoi neftianoi promyshlennosti za piat' let nationalizat-sii*, 70.

96. The Russian, then Soviet, fascination with the United States was widespread among politicians and intellectuals. See, for example, Jean-Louis Cohen, *Building a New New World: Amerikanizm in Russian Architecture* (New Haven: Yale University Press, 2020).

Chapter 2. From Garden Cities to Urban Superblocks

Epigraph: Maksim Gorkii, "Po soiuzu sovetov," in *Polnoe sobranie sochinenii: Khudozhest-vennye proizvedeniia v dvadtsati piati tomakh* (Moscow: Izd-vo "Nauka," 1974), 121–22.

1. ARDA, f. 2983, o. 1, d. 38, l. 133, rev., for instance.

2. Ebenezer Howard, *To-Morrow: A Peaceful Path to Real Reform*, ed. Dennis Hardy and Colin Ward (London: Routledge, 2003), 7–8.

3. The first article dedicated to the English Garden City in Russian was published in the journal *Zodchii* (*Architect*) in 1904. See also Mark Meerovich, *Gradostroitel'naia poli-tika v SSSR (1917–1929). Ot goroda-sada k vedomstvennomu rabochemu poselku* (Moscow: Novoe literaturnoe obozrenie, 2017), 43.

4. S. Frederick Starr, "The Revival and Schism of Urban Planning in Twentieth-Century Russia," in *The City in Russian History*, ed. Michael F. Hamm (Lexington: University Press of Kentucky, 1976), 232.

5. Meerovich enumerates many architects and planners interested in, writing about, and designing Soviet versions of the English Garden City in the immediate postrevolutionary period in his book on Russian garden cities. Ivanitskii and the Vesnins make his list. See Meerovich, *Gradostroitel'naia politika*, chap. 2.1, "Poselki-sady v poslerevoliutsionnyi period."

6. P. Kozhanyi, *Rabochee zhilishche i byt* (Moscow: Izdanie VTsSPS, 1924), 48.

7. Kozhanyi, *Rabochee zhilishche i byt*, 50.

8. Letchworth was incorporated in 1903 by Howard. Raymond Unwin and Barry Parker won the competition for the town's design, based on Howard's garden city principles.

9. ARDA, f. 1933, o. 1, d. 222, l. 19.

10. Mark B. Smith, *Property of Communists: The Urban Housing Program from Stalin to Khrushchev* (DeKalb: Northern Illinois University Press, 2010), 8.

11. ARDA, f. 1933, o. 1, d. 256, l. 13.

12. ARDA, f. 1933, o. 1, d. 256, l. 13.

13. The settlement name Belogorod suggests a connection with *belyi gorod* (White Town), the name used to refer to Nobel land holdings just to the south of this area, though no archival documentation confirms this affiliation.

14. Phillip Wagner, who has written extensively on interwar international planning conferences, found no mention of Ivanitskii in the attendees of the International Federation for Housing and Town Planning (IFHTP) conferences but notes that there were numerous "anonymous" Russian members of the IFHTP in the early 1920s. The International Federation for Town & Country Planning and Garden Cities conference in 1924, the year Ivanitskii was in London, was held in Amsterdam. Phillip Wagner, "Facilitating Planning Communication across Borders: The International Federation for Housing and Town Planning in the Interwar Period," *Planning Perspectives* 31, no. 2 (2016): 304. The Soviet-era citation about the meeting is in V. G. Davidovich and Tatiana Aleksandrovna Chizhikova, *Aleksandr Ivanitskii* (Moscow: Stroiizdat, 1973), 21.

15. A memoir by Unwin's distant cousin, Frieda White, provides sketchy notes on this meeting. She writes that the "chief commissaire [*sic*] for housing of Soviet Russia" visited Unwin to study working-class English housing sometime in the 1920s. Frieda White, "Raymond Unwin," Unwin Collection, John Ryland Library, Manchester University, September 8, 1962, box 1, folder 3, 4–5. Source courtesy of Phillip Wagner.

16. Unwin's arrival in Manchester, then a hotbed of socialist recruitment, was a mere forty years after the young Friedrich Engels walked the streets of the city and recorded his findings in *The Conditions of the Working Class in England*. The Fabian Society, the socialist organization in which Unwin was active, advocates work from within, meaning that members seek economic parity through dedicated incremental work. In early articles published in the Socialist League's *Commonweal*, Unwin advocated "the abolition of private property in the means of production," but, like his mentor William Morris, he stopped short of a call to revolution. See also Mervyn Miller, *Raymond Unwin: Garden Cities and Town Planning* (Leicester: Leicester University Press, 1992), 14, 17.

17. From the chapter titled "Of Cooperation in Site Planning, and How Common Enjoyment Benefits the Individual," in Sir Raymond Unwin, *Town Planning in Practice: An Introduction to the Art of Designing Cities and Suburbs* (London: T. F. Unwin, 1909), 375–76, 381.

18. Unwin's garden city planning paradigms were picked up not only in the socialist Soviet Union but also in locally socialist contexts, like Frankfurt, Germany, where Unwin's former draftsman, Ernst May, installed thousands of municipally funded worker housing units. For more on Unwin's influence in Europe in the 1920s, see Mark Swenarton, "Rationality and Rationalism: The Theory and Practice of Site Planning in Modern Architecture 1905–1930," *AA Files*, no. 4 (July 1983): 49–59.

19. From the chapter titled "Of Centres and Enclosed Places," in Unwin, *Town Planning in Practice*, 187.

20. Originally published in 1889, Sitte's "City Planning According to Artistic Principles" (Der Städtebau nach seinen künstlerischen Grundsätzen) made a plea for planners to design

cities according to best practices of urban history, most important through the insertion of urban rooms. Camillo Sitte, "City Planning According to Artistic Principles," in *Camillo Sitte: The Birth of Modern City Planning*, ed. George R. Collins and Christiane Crasemann Collins (New York: Rizzoli, 1986).

21. The editorial board of *Architecture* (1922–1924), the short-lived journal of the Moscow Architectural Society (MAO), included Leonid Vesnin and Ginzburg. Ginzburg's 1924 book *Style and Epoch* crystallized definitions of the architect's role under socialism that were tested in the pages of *Architecture* and among his colleagues at MAO.

22. Anatole Kopp proposes 1923 as the beginning of architectural Constructivism, a year when several architects, (including Aleskandr Vesnin and Ginzburg), joined the Left Front of the Arts (*Levy front iskusstv* or LEF). The announcement of the first-round winners of the Palace of the Soviets competition in 1932 is its most logical endpoint. Danilo Udovicki-Selb argues for a more attenuated chronology for Soviet architectural modernism—to 1938—although the later projects are increasingly exceptions to the general trend toward Socialist Realist monumentality in Soviet architecture. Anatole Kopp, *Constructivist Architecture in the USSR* (London: Academy Editions, 1985), 22. Danilo Udovicki-Selb, *Soviet Architectural Avant-Gardes: Architecture and Stalin's Revolution from Above, 1928–1938* (London: Bloomsbury, 2020) and Udovicki-Selb, "Between Modernism and Socialist Realism: Soviet Architectural Culture under Stalin's Revolution from Above, 1928–1938," *Journal of the Society of Architectural Historians* 68, no. 4 (2009): 467–95.

23. Ginzburg, *Style and Epoch* (Moscow: Fontanka, 2019), 140–41. For an additional discussion of Constructivist architectural practice, see M. Ia. Ginzburg, "Novye metody arkhitekturnogo myshleniia," *Sovremennaia arkhitektura*, no. 1 (1926): 1–4. Translated in Catherine Cooke, *Russian Avant-Garde Theories of Art, Architecture and the City* (London: Academy Editions, 1995), 129.

24. Ginzburg, *Style and Epoch*, 142, 146, 148.

25. From *Arkhitektura SSSR*, no.7, 1934, as translated in S. O. Khan-Magomedov and Aleksandr Aleksandrovich Vesnin, *Alexander Vesnin and Russian Constructivism* (London: Lund Humphries, 1986).

26. El Lissitzky, *Russia: An Architecture for World Revolution* (London: Lund Humphries, 1970), 32–33.

27. Fili, first a Russo-Balt automobile factory, was subsumed into the boundaries of Moscow in 1931. Davidovich and Chizhikova, *Aleksandr Ivanitskii*, 20.

28. Davidovich and Chizhikova, *Aleksandr Ivanitskii*, 11–12.

29. For more detail on the how architecture was impacted by the ongoing sociopolitical debate about the *novyi byt*, or new way of living under socialism, turn to chapter 4 of this book.

30. M. Ia Ginzburg, *Zhilishche* (Moscow: Gosstroiizdat, 1934), 68.

31. Audrey Altstadt-Mirhadi, "Baku: Transformation of a Muslim Town," in *City in Late Imperial Russia*, ed. Michael F. Hamm (Bloomington: Indiana University Press, 1983), 295.

32. James Dodds Henry, a British oil executive who lived and worked in Baku in the late nineteenth century, noted that the old Tartar portion of Baku was "intersected by winding

alleys, with curious, flat-roofed, windowless houses." James Dodds Henry, *Baku: An Eventful History* (London: A. Constable & Co., 1905), 15.

33. The Vesnin houses closely match the requirements written into the brief for a late 1924 Azneft housing competition. While the winning competition types were constructed in Montina and other Azneft settlements, the first development phase for Stepan Razin appears to have been constructed solely of the Vesnin versions.

34. Stepan Razin housing Types II and III made up almost three-quarters of the units built in the easternmost sector of Phase I construction, according to the Vesnin blueprint from late 1925.

35. The blueprint from 1925 indicates that seventeen Type V houses were planned for the western side of Phase I. These were interspersed among the smaller two-unit types. See "Layout of 142 houses: Settlement S.T. Razin, "Azneft" (*razbivka 142x domov: Poselok S.T. Razina, "Azneft"*), 1925." RGALI, f. 2991, o. 1, d. 17, l. 10.

36. Gorky, "Po soiuzu sovetov," 121–22.

37. The timeline for Stepan Razin is impressive by any measure. Relying only on the artifacts at hand, a drawing for the Type II house dated May 1, 1925, marks a possible (though unlikely) project start date, and a cache of postconstruction photographs dated November 22, 1925, marks its end. These traces of process reveal that less than seven months separated architectural concept from completed settlement. The 110 additional houses built were identified as "American" types. Azneft, *Obzor Azerbaidzhanskoi neftianoi promyshlennosti za piat' let nationalizatsii, 1920–1925* (Baku: Azneft, 1925), 69.

38. V. Kuz'min, "O rabochem zhilishchnom stroitel'stve," *Sovremennaia arkhitektura*, no. 3 (1928): 82 and note 1. On Azneft's switch to more dense housing types, Kuz'min cited the newspaper "Izvestiia VTsIK" from August 4, 1927.

39. S. Khan-Magomedov and Catherine Cooke, *Pioneers of Soviet Architecture: The Search for New Solutions in the 1920s and 1930s* (New York: Rizzoli, 1987), 276.

40. Armenikend (Armenian Town) was officially renamed "Shaumian" in the 1920s, after the Armenian Bolshevik leader Stepan Shaumian. Colloquially, and in the 1927 Baku Plan documentation, it retained its original name. RGALI, f. 2991, o. 1, ed. kh. 1, l. 113.

41. RGALI, f. 2991, o. 1, ed. kh. 1, l. 34.

42. All of the buildings on Armenikend test block no. 171 were three-story, with a unit mix as follows: Type A (3-room/2-family, 27.5 percent): 48 units. Types Б (2-room/2-family, 45 percent): 78 units. Type Г (1-room/1-family, 27.5 percent): 48 units. The average cost of one apartment was 3,824 rubles (based on the Building Committee's estimate of sixteen rubles/square meter). Taking that number to a single family, they arrived at the cost of 2,224 rubles/family. ARDA, f. 1933, o. 1, d. 353, ll. 30, 32.

43. There is no text on the plan to confirm the service building's use, but these programs were referred to in various texts on Armenikend.

44. N. Kolli, "Pamiati Anatoliia Vasil'evicha Samoilova" *Arkhitektura SSSR*, no. 12 (1954): 37.

45. Timothy Sosnovy, "The Soviet Housing Situation Today," *Soviet Studies* 11, no. 1 (July 1959): 3.

46. ARDA, f. 1933, o. 1, d. 353, l. 25, rev.

47. Generosity was cited because each apartment enjoyed double exposure, ample natural ventilation, and light. ARDA, f. 1933, o. 1, d. 353, l. 35.

48. Sosnovy, "The Soviet Housing Situation Today," 4. The legal minimum per capita living area in the Russian Republic was set at a (rarely met) nine square meters in 1929. Steven E. Harris, *Communism on Tomorrow Street: Mass Housing and Everyday Life after Stalin* (Washington, DC: Woodrow Wilson Center Press and The Johns Hopkins University Press, 2013), 50–51.

49. ARDA, f. 1933, o. 1, d. 353, l. 35.

50. ARDA, f. 1933, o. 1, d. 353, l. 37.

51. The inaugural editorial stated that although *Sovremennaia arkhitektura* was "primarily the result of the work of members of the Association of Contemporary Architects (OSA) . . . the editorial board seeks in every way to systematically reflect on all issues of architectural modernity . . . not only within the USSR, but globally." By the fall of 1926, OSA was granted official status as an architectural organization, and its members began to move into positions of officialdom. "Ot redaktsii," *Sovremennaia arkhitektura*, no. 1 (1926): frontispiece.

52. For a full discussion of *SA*'s housing competition, see Christina E. Crawford, "The Innovative Potential of Scarcity in SA's Comradely Competition for Communal Housing, 1927," *ArchiDOCT* 1, no. 2 (2014): 32–65.

53. The "red line" in Russian planning and construction denotes the possible building envelope and distinguishes boundaries of common / public areas from building plots. While this term originates from a prerevolutionary capitalist context of private land ownership, it persisted in the Soviet era to designate the build-to line at the sidewalk.

54. One of the only remaining architectural details drawn by the architects shows the condition at this turn. A minimal square masonry pier holds the corner but immediately recedes to make way for a window on each facade, which is as close to the modernist glass corner that this economical project can afford.

55. RGALI, f. 2991, o. 1, ed. kh. 89, l. 8.

56. ARDA, f. 1114, o. 1, d. 7246, l. 22.

57. ARDA, f. 2983, o. 1, d. 38, ll. 146, + rev.

58. ARDA, f. 2983, o. 1, d. 38, l. 153.

59. The 1938 book was designed by the married avant-garde artists Aleksandr Rodchenko and Varvara Stepanova, and the text was written by the Formalist literary critic Viktor Shklovsky. V. M. Gorfunkel', Aleksandr Mikhailovich Rodchenko, and Varvara Fedorovna Stepanova, *Moskva rekonstruiruetsia* (Moscow: IZOSTAT, 1938).

Chapter 3. A Plan for the Proletariat

Epigraph: ARDA, f. 2983, o. 1, d. 38, l. 133, January 11, 1930.

1. Two other items—limited city size and urban symbolism as an integral part of national planning—are more hallmarks of socialist realist planning and not as operative in the 1927

Baku Plan. See James H. Bater, *The Soviet City: Ideal and Reality*, vol. 2: *Explorations in Urban Analysis* (Beverly Hills: Sage, 1980), 27.

2. Bater, *The Soviet City*, 27–30.

3. ARDA, f. 1933, o. 1, d. 145, l. 167.

4. In *The Twelve Chairs*, a classic satire of the first decade of the Soviet period, the authors Ilya Ilf and Evgeny Petrov offered a glimpse into the politics and financing structure of a NEP-era capital campaign. In the provincial town of Stargorod, underemployed engineer Treukhov plans a streetcar system in his spare time that will transform his hometown backwater into a well-oiled modern urban center. Stargorod's streetcar system is finally built by tapping into local trade organizations that will directly benefit from its arrival. The Food Trust, Central Butter, and cable factory workers pay out of their own pockets for local transportation to be modernized, but only on the promise that their investment will be amortized in less than a decade. "It has to pay for itself," Treukhov is overheard muttering as he wanders the construction site. Ilya Ilf and Evgeny Petrov, *The Twelve Chairs: A Novel*, trans. Anne O. Fisher, Northwestern World Classics (Evanston: Northwestern University Press, 2011), 159–60.

5. ARDA, f. 1933, o. 1, d. 145, l. 167.

6. ARDA, f. 1933, o. 1, d. 302, l. 15.

7. Transliterated from Russian, the French garbage incineration firm is "Sud Komters." ARDA, f. 1933, o. 1, d. 306, l. 6.

8. ARDA, f. 1933, o. 1, d. 306, l. 6.

9. V. G. Davidovich and Tatiana Aleksandrovna Chizhikova, *Aleksandr Ivanitskii*, Mastera Arkhitektury (Moscow: Stroiizdat, 1973), 19.

10. Davidovich and Chizhikova, *Aleksandr Ivanitskii*, 21.

11. ARDA, f. 2983, o. 1, d. 38, l. 133.

12. ARDA, f. 2983, o. 1, d. 38, l. 133.

13. "The level of data completion [for the municipal surveys] was far from sufficient. This, however, is the general condition for the vast majority, if not all, of the cities in the Soviet Union," claimed Ivanitskii. RGALI, f. 2991, o. 1, ed. kh. 4, ll. 270–73.

14. Ivanitskii cited "administrative obscurity" for this omission from the plan. RGALI, f. 2991, o. 1, ed. kh. 1, l. 18.

15. Corner elaborates on the categories of tracing and mapping first established by Gilles Deleuze and Félix Guattari. James Corner, "The Agency of Mapping: Speculation, Critique and Invention," in *Mappings*, ed. Denis Cosgrove (London: Reaktion Books, 1999), 214.

16. These cartograms align with Deleuze and Guattari's definition of "map," insofar as "what distinguishes the map from the tracing is that it is entirely oriented toward an experimentation in contact with the real . . . the map has to do with *performance*, whereas the tracing always involves an alleged 'competence.'" Gilles Deleuze and Félix Guattari, *A Thousand Plateaus: Capitalism and Schizophrenia* (Minneapolis: University of Minnesota Press, 1987), 12–13.

17. The invention of the cartogram reaches back to the eighteenth century, though the term was not in regular use until the 1860s. H. Gray Funkhouser, "Historical Development of the Graphical Representation of Statistical Data," *Osiris* 3 (1937): 299–301, 364–65. For

additional examples, see Etienne-Jules Marey, *La Méthode Graphique Dans Les Sciences Expérimentales et Principalement en Physiologie et en Médecine* (Paris: G. Masson, 1885).

18. Funkhouser, "Historical Development of the Graphical Representation of Statistical Data," 364–65. Thank you to Anna Vallye for directing me to this source.

19. In 1872, St. Petersburg hosted the Eighth International Statistical Congress, a historical event that places the Russian Empire as a center of quantitative-graphic experimentation in the nineteenth century. According to the historian of statistical graphics Funkhouser, two important papers were presented at the St. Petersburg congress, one that argued for a common set of graphic conventions for statistical graphics (such as scale, color, grouping), and the other that countered by advocating "the greatest freedom of the imagination and of the mind." The author of the second position, Adolf Fiker, director of administrative statistics in Vienna, highlighted the Russians in his speech for their particularly creative combinations of geographic and graphic methods. Ivanitskii, a graduate of the Institute for Civil Engineering in St. Petersburg, would have been well versed in Russian and European cartogrammatic examples and techniques. Funkhouser, "Historical Development of the Graphical Representation of Statistical Data," 317.

20. Corner, "The Agency of Mapping: Speculation, Critique and Invention," 216.

21. Corner, "The Agency of Mapping: Speculation, Critique and Invention," 214.

22. F. E. Enakiev, *Zadachi preobrazovaniia S.-Peterburga* (St. Petersburg, 1912). For full discussion, see S. Frederick Starr, "The Revival and Schism of Urban Planning in Twentieth-Century Russia," in *The City in Russian History*, ed. Michael F. Hamm (Lexington: University Press of Kentucky, 1976), 222–42.

23. A high, salty water table and chronic outbreaks of water-borne disease instigated construction of a modern pipeline of clean water from Shollar in the Caucasus Mountains to Baku starting in 1899. Baku's parliament obtained technical assistance for the project from William Lindley, an experienced British civil engineer with water systems in thirty-five cities to his credit. Stalled repeatedly by war, the 110-mile porcelain pipeline—the longest in Europe or Russia at that time—was finally completed in 1917, although it did not tamp out disease, as the cartogram shows. Ryszard Zelichowski, "Water—Not a Drop to Drink: How Baku Got Its Water—the British Link—William H. Lindley," *Azerbaijan International* 10, no. 2 (2002): 53.

24. A. P. Ivanitskii, "Planirovka goroda Baku," *Gigiena i epidemiologiia*, no. 4 (1925): 95.

25. To limit the population growth of major cities, every Soviet citizen was required to have a residence permit, or *propiska*, in their internal passport, indicating their legal residence and allowing housing and work within the city. The internal passport system was instituted on December 27, 1932.

26. Ivanitskii read to the group the short presentation he had given at the conference on their behalf. ARDA, f. 1933, o. 1, d. 322, l. 11.

27. Davidovich and Chizhikova, *Aleksandr Ivanitskii*, 24–26.

28. A. P. Ivanitskii, "O ratsional'noi planirovke gorodov," *Stroitel'naia promyshlennost'*, no. 4 (1926): 298–99.

29. ARDA, f. 1933, o. 1, d. 322, ll. 8–9.

30. ARDA, f. 1933, o. 1, d. 322, l. 9.

31. ARDA, f. 1933, o. 1, d. 345, l. 2 (Bakispolkom); ARDA, f. 1933, o. 1, d. 350, l. 12 (enlarged meeting of the Baksovet Planning Commission together with the Financial Budgeting and Local Maintenance Sections and specialists). The resolution also specified priority projects that would be completed in the coming five years.

32. RGALI, f. 2991, o. 1, ed. kh. 89, l. 7.

33. RGALI, f. 2991, o. 1, ed. kh. 89, l. 8.

34. RGALI, f. 2991, o. 1, ed. kh. 89, ll. 8–9

35. RGALI, f. 2991, o. 1, ed. kh. 89, l. 9.

36. The final published plan indicates the boulevard in Ivanitskii's desired location, and later photographs confirm that it was built as the planner recommended.

37. RGALI, f. 2991, o. 1, ed. kh. 2, l. 34.

38. RGALI, f. 2991, o. 1, ed. kh. 2, l. 8.

39. ARDA, f. 2983, o. 1, d. 38, l. 135.

40. ARDA, f. 2983, o. 1, d. 38, ll. 139, 140, rev.

41. ARDA, f. 2983, o. 1, d. 38, l. 135.

42. The street width was noted in sazhens by Ivanitskii. Torgovaia Street began at 12 sazhens wide in the east and progressively narrowed as it moved westward to 10, 8, 5, and finally just 4 sazhens wide when it ended as Torgovaia Lane. ARDA, f. 2983, o. 1, d. 38, l. 135.

43. Per Ivanitskii's presentation in 1930, the six magistrals designed in detail were the seafront boulevard; an inland magistral parallel to the shore that linked the Nagornoe Plateau and the Black Town; Balakhanskoe shosse (now Heydar Aliyev prospekti); the exit from Kishli to Baku-1 rail station; from the ninth parallel to the Black Town; from the seminary/nursery to the Sarainskoe Shosse in the industrial region (through Bingady). ARDA, f. 2983, o. 1, d. 38, l. 136.

44. Iur'evskaia was renamed Sovetskaia, c. 1929 and Narimen Narimenov pr., c. 1991.

45. The 710 impacted structures accounted for just 6.5 percent of the 11,000 structures in the city circa 1926. The typical area of the dwarf plots was noted by Ivanitskii as 6–8 square sazhens. ARDA, f. 2983, o. 1, d. 38, ll. 136–37.

46. It is unclear who hired Bregadze, a self-proclaimed artist-photographer, but copious—and often identical—photographs from his Iur'evskaia expeditions sit in both Ivanitskii's personal archive and the Azerbaijan State Archive.

47. ARDA, f. 2983, o. 1, d. 38, ll. 136–37.

48. Ivantiskii wrote in his final report on the 1927 Baku Plan, "According to US data that were collected based on knowledge of directing traffic, ten feet are needed for each lane on streets with large traffic volume; for parking lanes, eight feet are needed. For a street with a lower traffic volume nine or eight-and-a-half feet are needed. I propose to try this scale here [in Baku]." ARDA, f. 2983, o. 1, d. 38, l. 147, rev.

49. According to Ivanitskii, "the width of Iur'evskaia is taken at fifty-six feet, so that in the future it can handle three-story structures along its edge, and at the corners with transverse streets it can even handle four-story buildings." ARDA, f. 2991, o. 1, d. 89, l. 4, rev.

50. ARDA, f. 2983, o. 1, d. 38, l. 137.

51. RGALI, f. 2991, o. 1, ed. kh. 2, ll. 298–99.

52. ARDA, f. 2983, o. 1, d. 38, ll. 138–39.

53. ARDA, f. 2983, o. 1, d. 38, ll. 138–39.

54. RGALI, f. 2991, o.1, ed. kh. 2, l. 244–49.

55. R.M. Efendizade, *Planirovka i zastroika zhilykh raionov Baku (1920–1967 gg.)* (Baku: Elm, 1971), 13.

56. The entire US classification system of open spaces was as follows, in RGALI, f. 2991, o.1, ed. kh. 2, l. 253. 1) Reserves; 2) City parks; 3) Suburban parks; 4) Regional sports complexes for children and adults, for a larger radius of use; 5) Schoolyards, for children, local radius of use; 6) Playgrounds for children under five years, placed in each residential quarter; 7) Parkways and boulevards that connect the parks together as well as the center with its regions.

57. RGALI, f. 2991, o. 1, ed. kh. 2, l. 253.

58. RGALI, f. 2991, o. 1, ed. kh. 2, l. 300.

59. ARDA, f. 2983, o. 1, d. 38, ll. 138–39.

60. RGALI, f. 2991, o. 1, ed. kh. 90, l. 3. The letter from the Baku Department of Communal Services requests their professional opinion on the 1927 Baku Plan, to be submitted no later than November 1928 (a month from the date of the letter).

61. From Frenkel's book: "There was an extremely successful system of daily garbage collection in 1924–25 by the Baksovet. Until 1924 garbage was put in the courtyard in wooden barrels, usually open to the air . . . Now it is collected in covered metal cans and is collected by a light Ford truck . . . For the whole city 31 trucks and 40 horses with a workforce of 150 people have completely changed the 'sanitary conditions' of the city of Baku for the collection of garbage, in the place of 200 horses and 300 workers. For now, the garbage is collected in Baku center city. The city hauls it to a barge and sends it far into the sea, and the rest is sent to a landfill, where they bury it deeply. A small amount of garbage is set aside to feed hundreds of pigs. A garbage incinerator is still not planned for Baku, but it is expected that it will be necessary in the future for such a large amount of trash." Z. G. Frenkel', *Osnovy obshchego gorodskogo blagoustroistva* (Moscow: Glavnogo upravleniia komnal'nogo khoziaistva NKVD, 1926), 144.

62. See L.A. Il'in, ed., *Arkhitekturnye problemy planirovki Baku*, t. 2, kn. 1: *Problemy arkhitektury* (Moscow: Izdatel'stvo vsesoiuznoi akademii arkhitektury, 1937).

63. RGALI, f. 2991, o. 1, ed. kh. 107, ll. 1–6.

64. RGALI, f. 2991, o. 1, ed. kh. 107, ll. 1–6.

65. ARDA, f. 2983, o. 1, d. 38, l. 133.

66. ARDA, f. 2983, o. 1, d. 38, l. 134, rev.

67. ARDA, f. 2983, o. 1, d. 38, l. 154.

68. ARDA, f. 2983, o. 1, d. 38, l. 142–43.

69. ARDA, f. 2983, o. 1, d. 38, ll. 145–46.

70. ARDA, f. 1933, o. 1, d. 752, l. 5.

71. ARDA, f. 2983, o. 1, d. 38, l. 151.

72. Chapter 4 of this volume covers the 1929 socialist city debate at length.

73. ARDA, f. 2983, o. 1, d. 38, l. 152.

74. ARDA, f. 2983, o. 1, d. 38, l. 152.

75. ARDA, f. 2983, o. 1, d. 38, l. 153.

76. ARDA, f. 2983, o. 1, d. 38, l. 152, rev.

Chapter 4. The Great Debate

Epigraph: From a Soviet children's book on the first Five-Year Plan. M. Ilin, *New Russia's Primer: The Story of the Five-Year Plan*, trans. George S. Counts and Nucia P. Lodge (Boston: Houghton Mifflin, 1931), 76. Original: M. Il'in, *Rasskaz o velikom plane*, 3rd ed. (Moscow: Ogiz—molodaia gvardiia, 1931).

1. ARDA, f. 2983, o. 1, d. 752, l. 132.

2. "Magnitogorsk: Gigant vtoroi metallurgicheskoi bazy," *SSSR na stroike*, no. 1 (1932): 3.

3. See Ilin, *New Russia's Primer*; Joris Ivens, dir., *Song of Heroes* (Mezhrabpomfilm, 1932).

4. The author noted that Magnitogorsk "is the forerunner of even more grandiose construction projects. Therefore, its practical experience, which will serve as a school for builders, is especially valuable." R. Roman, *Krokodil v Magnitogorske* (Sverdlovsk: OGIZ, 1931), 3.

5. David L. Hoffmann, *Peasant Metropolis: Social Identities in Moscow, 1929–1941*, Studies of the Harriman Institute (Ithaca: Cornell University Press, 1994), chap. 2: "The Process of In-Migration."

6. Stephen Kotkin, *Magnetic Mountain: Stalinism as a Civilization* (Berkeley: University of California Press, 1995), 81.

7. The first department dedicated to construction under Soviet rule was the Central Commission of National Construction Planning (Tsentral'naia komissiia obshchegosudarst-vennogo plana stroitel'stva or TsGOLS) under Glavkomgosoor and directly subordinate to STO, which was established on March 17, 1921. TsGOLS was disbanded in early 1922, and its staff scattered among other Gosplan departments. On February 15, 1922, a Building Section (stroisektsiia) was established in the Transportation Section of Gosplan (since most of the questions of construction fell to them), and on March 30, 1922 the Building Section of Gosplan became independent under Bernatskii's leadership. Most of the employees were carryovers from TsGOLS, and the work remained largely the same. L. N. Bernatskii, "Kratkii obzor deiatel'nosti stroisektsii Gosplana," *Planovoe khoziaistvo (Biulleteni gosplana)*, no. 3 (1923): 56.

8. Bernatskii, "Kratkii obzor," 56.

9. "Osnovy planirovaniia stroitel'stva," *Planovoe khoziaistvo*, no. 1–2 (1924): 3.

10. G. T. Grinko, *The Five-Year Plan of the Soviet Union, a Political Interpretation* (New York: International Publishers, 1930), 22–23.

11. Edward Hallett Carr, *Foundations of a Planned Economy, 1926–1929*, ed. R. W. Davies (London: Macmillan, 1969), 809.

12. L. N. Bernatskii, "Zhilishchnyi krizis i zhilishchnoe stroitel'stvo," *Planovoe khoziaistvo*, no. 6 (1925): 36, 42.

13. A. Gordon, "Problema plana i kapital'noe stroitel'stvo," *Planovoe khoziaistvo*, no. 2 (1928): 68.

14. *Materialy osobogo soveshchaniia po vosstanovleniiu osnovogo kapitala pri Presidiume VSNKh SSSR*, Seriia II, I (1926), 4, as quoted and translated in Carr, *Foundations of a Planned Economy*, 792.

15. S. G. Strumilin, *Ocherki sovetskoi ekonomiki: Resursy i perspektivy* (Moscow: Gosudarstvennoe izdatel'stvo, 1928), 422.

16. Carr, *Foundations of a Planned Economy*, 789–90.

17. G. Krzhizhanovskii, "Zametki o planirovanii," *Revoliutsiia i kul'tura*, no. 8 (1929).

18. Grinko, *The Five-Year Plan of the Soviet Union*, 23–24.

19. Expansion went from 26.5 to 64.6 billion rubles overall expenditure, and from 4.4 to 16.4 billion rubles in industry alone. Grinko, *The Five-Year Plan of the Soviet Union*, 58.

20. R. W. Davies and O. Khlevnyuk, "Gosplan," in *Decision-Making in the Stalinist Command Economy, 1932–37*, ed. E. A. Rees, Studies in Russian and East European History and Society (Basingstoke: Macmillan, 1997), 36.

21. The electricity and transportation infrastructure required to serve industry were separate line items in the budget.

22. S. A. Bessonov, "Problemy prostranstva v perspektivnom plane," *Planovoe khoziaistvo*, no. 6 (1928): 77.

23. Although he was well published, and his ideas had remarkable traction for three to four years, Sabsovich's biography both before and after this period of intense public exposure remains vague. A book devoted to the Sabsovich family tree could not confirm his dates of birth or death, or locate a photograph of Leonid Moiseevich. The authors did manage to ascertain that he was arrested on Trotskyist charges (likely in the late 1930s) and died in a gulag camp. See V. Ia. and S. V. Vershinin Fain, *Taganrogskie Sabsovichi i ikh potomki* (Moscow: Izdatel'stvo Triumf, 2013), 169. Some information about Sabsovich's professional timeline can also be found in D. M. Khmel'nitskii, "Leonid Sabsovich ili kto pridumal obobshchestvlenie byta?," in *Sem'ia v traditsionnoi kul'ture i sovremennom mire*, ed. Iu. M. Smirnov (Vladimir: Transit IKS, 2011), https://archi.ru/lib/publication.html?id=1850569891.

24. His first article appeared in *Commerce and Industry* newspaper (*Torgovo-promyshlennaia gazeta*) on August 19, 1928; follow-ups were published on November 7 and 29. These and other articles were republished as *SSSR cherez 15 let* (USSR in 15 years) in March 1929.

25. L. M. Sabsovich, *SSSR cherez 15 let: Gipoteza general'nogo plana, kak plana postroeniia sotsializma v SSSR* (Moscow: "Planovoe khoziastvo", 1929), 2, 8, 13.

26. Nikolai Miliutin's *Sotsgorod* (1930), in comparison, was given a single 7,000-copy run. Khmel'nitskii, "Leonid Sabsovich ili kto pridumal obobshchestvlenie byta?"

27. Sabsovich, *SSSR cherez 15 let*, 156.

28. Sabsovich, *SSSR cherez 15 let*, 154. For a fuller discussion of *byt* versus *bytie*, see Svetlana Boym, *Common Places: Mythologies of Everyday Life in Russia* (Cambridge: Harvard University Press, 1994), chap. 1: "Mythologies of Everyday Life."

29. "The mode of production of material life conditions the general process of social, political and intellectual life. It is not the consciousness of men that determines their existence, but their social existence that determines their consciousness." Karl Marx, *A Contribution to the Critique of Political Economy* (Moscow: Progress Publishers, 1977), preface.

30. L. Trotskii, "Chtoby perestroit′ byt, nado poznat′ ego," *Pravda*, July 11, 1923.

31. L. Trotskii, "Ot staroi sem′i—k novoi)," *Pravda*, July 13, 1923.

32. Katerina Clark, *Petersburg: Crucible of Cultural Revolution* (Cambridge: Harvard University Press, 1995), 251.

33. Alexandra Kollontai, "Communism and the Family (1920)," in *Selected Writings of Alexandra Kollontai* (London: Allison & Busby, 1977), 258–59.

34. V. Kuz′min, "O rabochem zhilishchnom stroitel′stve," *Sovremennaia arkhitektura*, no. 3 (1928): 82. This speech is also discussed in Anatole Kopp, *Town and Revolution; Soviet Architecture and City Planning, 1917–1935* (New York: G. Braziller, 1970), 145.

35. Hoffmann, *Peasant Metropolis*, 1.

36. Hoffmann, *Peasant Metropolis*, 138.

37. For discussion of the sociology and psychology of the Soviet-era communal apartment, see Boym, *Common Places*, chap. 2: "Living in Common Places: The Communal Apartment."

38. Moshe Lewin, *The Making of the Soviet System: Essays in the Social History of Interwar Russia* (London: Methuen, 1985), 220. See also Hoffmann, *Peasant Metropolis*, chap. 6: "Official Culture and Peasant Culture."

39. Catherine Ann Chichester Cooke, "The Town of Socialism" (PhD diss., University of Cambridge, 1974), 110.

40. L. M. Sabsovich, *Goroda budushchego i organizatsiia sotsialisticheskogo byta* (Moscow: Gosudarstvennoe tekhnicheskoe izdatel′′stvo, 1929), 9–10.

41. Sovnarkom had established VARNITSO in February 1928 as a political organization for scientific and technical workers. Their opening resolution stated that "the intelligentsia should not be neutral but should participate actively in the planning and of the capital construction of the whole industry of the country." "The Problem of the City" / *Cities of the Future* was the first well-disseminated text on socialist space. On VARNITSO, see Carr, *Foundations of a Planned Economy*, 620–21.

42. Sabsovich, *Goroda budushchego*, 11.

43. Sabsovich, *Goroda budushchego*, 12.

44. Sabsovich, *Goroda budushchego*, 11–12, 13–15.

45. The German economist Alfred Weber's law of agglomeration states that industry tends to cluster to take advantage of the cheaper production, transportation, and marketing costs resulting from concentration. See Claude Ponsard, *History of Spatial Economic Theory* (Berlin: Springer-Verlag, 1983), 27–29.

46. Sabsovich, *Goroda budushchego*, 14–15.

47. Sabsovich, *Goroda budushchego*, 60.

48. Vladimir Il'ich Lenin, "Karl Marx: A Brief Biographical Sketch with an Exposition of Marxism," in *Collected Works* (Moscow: Progress Publishers, 1974), 21: 43–91, https://www.marxists.org/archive/lenin/works/1914/granat/ch04.htm. Used as the opening epigraph in Sabsovich, *Goroda budushchego*.

49. Sabsovich, *Goroda budushchego*, 15–18.

50. GOELRO has been cited by Richard Stites, among others, as the single most utopian project Lenin—a vehement critic of utopian projects—supported. In a 1920 speech to the Moscow Committee of the Russian Communist Party of Bolsheviks (R.C.P.(B.)), Lenin famously quipped: "communism is Soviet power plus the electrification of the whole country," which laid the theoretical groundwork for the GOELRO Plan. V. I. Lenin, "Our Foreign and Domestic Position and Party Tasks," Speech Delivered on November 21, 1920 to the Moscow Gubernia Conference of the R.C.P.(B.), published in *Collected Works*, 4th English ed., vol. 31 (Moscow: Progress Publishers, 1965), 408–26. https://www.marxists.org/archive/lenin/works/1920/nov/21.htm. An excellent discussion of Lenin's dreams for the GOERLO Plan can be found in Richard Stites, *Revolutionary Dreams: Utopian Vision and Experimental Life in the Russian Revolution* (New York: Oxford University Press, 1989), 48.

51. "In socialist conditions, in the socialization of education, children will no longer be the 'property' of their parents: they are the 'property' of the state, which will take over all the tasks and care for the education of children." Sabsovich, *Goroda budushchego*, 37.

52. Sabsovich, *Goroda budushchego*, 52, 54.

53. Okhitovich, the son of a tsarist bureaucrat, joined the party in 1917, served in the Red Army from 1918 to 1925, and was expelled from the party on Trotskyist charges in 1928. When he visited Ginzburg in 1929, he had recently been absolved of those charges. The meeting story, recounted by the architect and OSA member Mikhail Barshch in his autobiography, was quoted in S. O. Khan-Magomedov, *Mikhail Okhitovich*, Tvortsy avangarda (Moscow: Russkii avangard, 2009), 37. Okhitovich's biographical information from Hugh D. Hudson, "Terror in Soviet Architecture: The Murder of Mikhail Okhitovich," *Slavic Review* 51, no. 3 (1992): 453.

54. Khan-Magomedov, *Mikhail Okhitovich*, 36.

55. Khan-Magomedov, *Mikhail Okhitovich*, 39.

56. For a full discussion of OSA's functional method, see Catherine Cooke, *Russian Avant-Garde Theories of Art, Architecture and the City* (London: Academy Editions, 1995), chap. 5: "Constructivism: From Tatlin and Rodchenko to a 'Functional Method' for Building Design."

57. M. Okhitovich, "K probleme goroda," *Sovremennaia arkhitektura*, no. 4 (1929): 130–34.

58. In Russian these terms are also twinned: *kapital / Kapital*. Okhitovich, "K probleme goroda," 131.

59. Okhitovich, "K probleme goroda," 131, 132–33.

60. Okhitovich claimed that there was simply no need for concentrated settlement since "the whole world is at our service, transportation first of all." The autonomous automobile,

more than fixed rail, made spatial dispersal possible and desirable. Okhitovich, "K probleme goroda," 132–33.

61. Okhitovich, "K probleme goroda," 134.

62. Okhitovich, "K probleme goroda." 134.

63. Lewis Mumford, "Regions—to Live In," *The Survey* 54 (1925): 151.

64. Regional plans require significant state interference into the private land ownership regime. As Peter Hall noted, the high degree of state intervention proposed by the RPAA was impractical in the United States in the 1920s, since even the constitutionality of zoning was in question until a definitive 1926 Supreme Court decision. Peter Hall, *Cities of Tomorrow: An Intellectual History of Urban Planning and Design in the Twentieth Century*, 3rd ed. (Oxford: Blackwell, 2002), 161.

65. Frank Lloyd Wright, "Broadacre City: A New Community Plan," *Architectural Record*, April (1935): 244.

66. Wright had public contact with Soviet popular and architectural press from 1932 on, and visited Moscow in 1937 to participate in the First All-Union Congress of Soviet Architects. Donald Leslie Johnson, "Frank Lloyd Wright in Moscow: June 1937," *Journal of the Society of Architectural Historians* 46, no. 1 (1987): 69.

67. Wright, "Broadacre City," 254.

68. Okhitovich, "K probleme goroda," 134.

69. Okhitovich did not have access to high officialdom like Sabsovich, and thus had more difficulty spreading his views to larger audiences. On October 1, 1929, he gave a speech at the Cooperative section of the Communist Academy that elicited three sessions worth of discussion on the presentation's implications. By December parts of that speech, accompanied by commentary, were published in *Ekonomicheskaia zhizn'*, the daily newspaper of the STO, as a kick-off to their regular series on socialist city-building. "Problema sotsialisticheskogo rasseleniia," *Ekonomicheskaia zhizn'*, December 5, 1929, 3.

70. B. Rev, "Besplanovost' i anarkhiia v stroitel'stve gorodov," *Pravda*, November 4, 1929.

71. N. A. Paskutskii, "Vstupitel'noe slovo," in *K probleme stroitel'stva sotsialisticheskogo goroda*, ed. Gosplan SSSR (Moscow: Izd-vo planovoe khoziastvo, 1930), 6.

72. The full names of the commissariats represented at the Gosplan conference are: the People's Commissariat for Trade (Narodnyi komissariat torgovli or Narkomtorg), the People's Commissariat for Health (Narodnyi komissariat zdravo-okhraneniia or Narkomzdrav), the People's Commissariat for Railways (Narodnyi komissariat putei soobshcheniia or NKPS), the People's Commissariat for Internal Affairs (Narodnyi komissariat vnutrennikh del or NKVD), and the People's Commissariat for Education (Narodnyi komissariat prosveshcheniia or Narkompros).

73. Strumilin summarily dismissed the urbanism/disurbanism debate in his speech, calling both schemes unnecessarily extreme. Gosplan-SSSR, *K probleme stroitel'stva sotsialisticheskogo goroda*, 72.

74. Gosplan-SSSR, *K probleme stroitel'stva sotsialisticheskogo goroda*, 39.

75. Gosplan-SSSR, *K probleme stroitel'stva sotsialisticheskogo goroda*, 71.

76. Because he both opened and closed the conference (with N. A. Paskutskii from Gosplan), Aleksandr Zelenko was likely a key organizer behind the event. Like Aleksandr Ivanitskii and Pavel Aleshin (the architect for the New Kharkiv *sotsgorod*, covered in chapter 8 of this book), Zelenko graduated from the Institute for Civil Engineering in St. Petersburg and had a robust Moscow architectural practice before the revolution. During the early Soviet period he worked as an architect at Narkompros (People's Commissariat for Education) under the leadership of Nadezhda Krupskaia. Zelenko visited the United States three times—before and after the revolution—and was well acquainted with US architecture and planning precedents. See http://www.spbgasu.ru/Vypusknikam/Stud_Vip_Prep/ZELENKO_Aleksandr_Ustinovich/.

77. Zelenko used similar data to that cited by Bessonov in *Planovoe khoziaistvo* a year before. A. U. Zelenko, "Stroitel'stvo sotsialisticheskikh gorodov," in *K probleme stroitel'stva sotsialisticheskogo goroda*, 7–8. This speech was also published as A. Zelenko, "Problema stroitel'stva sotsialisticheskikh gorodov," *Planovoe khoziaistvo*, no. 12 (1929): 16–31.

78. Zelenko, "Stroitel'stvo sotsialisticheskikh gorodov," 25–26.

79. Gosplan-SSSR, *K probleme stroitel'stva sotsialisticheskogo goroda*, 71.

80. Gosplan-SSSR, *K probleme stroitel'stva sotsialisticheskogo goroda*, 64.

81. The first Russian-language review of *Vers Une Architecture* was published in September 1924 in the journal *Pechat' i revoliutsiia* (Press and revolution) 4, no. 55, and an entire debate on the merits of the book soon followed in *Stroitel'naia promyshlennost'*, no. 12, 1924. Jean-Louis Cohen, *Le Corbusier and the Mystique of the USSR: Theories and Projects for Moscow, 1928–1936* (Princeton: Princeton University Press, 1992), 22.

82. Cohen, *Le Corbusier and the Mystique of the USSR*, chap. 6: "Response to Moscow and the Origins of the 'Ville Radieuse.'"

83. M. G. Meerovich, "Neoffitsial'noe gradostroitel'stvo: Tainyi aspekt sovetskoi industrializatsii (1928–1932)," in *Problemy otchestvennoi istorii: Istochniki, istoriografiia, issledovaniia*, ed. M. V. Drusin, Istoriia rossiia (St. Petersburg: Sankt Peterburgskii institut istorii RAN, 2008), 396. *Revoliutsiia i kul'tura*, 1930, no. 13–14, had a whole section on socialist cities.

84. Even citizens in a far-flung republic like Azerbaijan were following the thorough journalistic coverage of the socialist city debate in *Ekonomicheskaia zhizn'*. That this publication of STO took on the issue with such aplomb is not surprising: Gosplan was the permanent advisory subcommittee on economic issues within the STO hierarchy.

85. Two of the series' installments commenced with the same neutral title: "Novye goroda, rasselenie, zhilishche. Materialy dlia diskussii, praktika i obmen opytom" (New cities, settlement and housing. Materials for discussion, practice and experience-sharing), *Ekonomicheskaia zhizn'*, December 7, 1929; December 20, 1929. The socialist city articles in *Ekonomicheskaia zhizn'* were typically at the front of the paper.

86. "Komissiia po bytu pri NK RKI pristupila k rabote," *Ekonomicheskaia zhizn'*, December 7, 1929.

87. Commission on the Question of Socialist *byt* under NK RKI and the editors of *Ekonomicheskaia zhizn'*, "Sotsialisticheskaia peredelka byta—real'naia problema segodniashnego dnia," *Ekonomicheskaia zhizn'*, December 7, 1929.

88. V. A. Vesnin and A. A. Vesnin, "Predposylki stroitel'stva novykh gorodov," *Ekonomicheskaia zhizn'*, December 6, 1929.

89. L. Sabsovich, "'Vzbesivshiisia melkii burzhua' ili kommivoiazher avtomobil'noi firmy," *Ekonomicheskaia zhizn'*, December 20, 1929.

90. M. Okhitovich, "Ne gorod, a novyi tip rasseneniia," *Ekonomicheskaia zhizn'*, December 7, 1929.

91. Okhitovich, "Ne gorod, a novyi tip rasseneniia."

92. M. Ia. Ginzburg, "Sotsialisticheskoe rasselenie: Detsentralizatsiia krupneishikh gorodov," *Ekonomicheskaia zhizn'*, December 7, 1929.

93. Groundbreaking for the Stalingrad "Avtostroi" factory took place on June 12, 1926, although the project long stalled and did not begin producing tractors until the late spring of 1930. Kurt Stephen Schultz, "The American Factor in Soviet Industrialization: Fordism and the First Five-Year Plan, 1928–1932" (PhD diss., Ohio State University, 1992), 100–106. The construction of the socialist city at Nizhnii Novgorod had siting and design problems similar to those that plagued Magnitogorsk. Groundbreaking for this project occurred on April 11, 1930. Lewis H. Siegelbaum, *Cars for Comrades: The Life of the Soviet Automobile* (Ithaca: Cornell University Press, 2008), chap. 2: "GAZ, Nizhnii Novogorod-Gorkii-Nizhnii Novogorod." Additional information on this project can be found in Heather D. DeHaan, *Stalinist City Planning: Professionals, Performance, and Power* (Toronto: University of Toronto Press, 2013); Richard Cartwright Austin, *Building Utopia: Erecting Russia's First Modern City, 1930* (Kent, OH: Kent State University Press, 2004).

94. "Kak budet postroen Magnitogorsk," *Ekonomicheskaia zhizn'*, December 15, 1929.

95. Gosproekt was a factory design bureau within the Vesenkha of the Russian Republic, set up in August 1928. Chernyshev would go on to become the chief architect of the city of Moscow from 1934 to 1941, and one of the primary authors of the 1935 General Plan for Moscow. I. A. Kazus', *Sovetskaia arkhitektura 1920-kh godov: Organizatsiia proektirovaniia* (Moscow: Progress-Traditsiia, 2009), 227.

96. The population stipulated in the 1929/30 competition was 50,000 residents. See chapter 5 in this book. Evgeniia Vladimirovna Konysheva and M. G. Meerovich, *Ernst Mai: Proektirovanie sotsgorodov v gody pervykh piatiletok (na primere Magnitogorska)* (Moscow: URSS, 2012), 29.

97. Miliutin was chair of the State Commission on the Construction of Socialist Cities in 1929. Dmitrii Khmel'nitskii and Ekaterina Miliutina, *Arkhitektor Nikolai Miliutin* (Moscow: Novoe literaturnoe obozrenie, 2013), 497.

98. N. Miliutin, "Bor'ba za novyi byt i sovetskii urbanizm," *Izvestiia*, October 29, 1929.

99. Oblastnoi ispolnitel'nyi komitet–arkhivnyi otdel Cheliabinsk, "Iz postanovleniia sovnarkoma RSFSR o stroitel'stve Magnitogorskogo kombinata i g. Magnitogorsk (November 11, 1929)," *Iz istorii Magnitogorskogo metallurgicheskogo kombinata i goroda*

Magnitogorska, 1929–1941 gg.; Sbornik dokumentov i materialov (Cheliabinskaia oblast': Iuzhno-Ural'skoe knizhnoe izd-vo, 1965), 219. See also "Sotsialisticheskie goroda v sovnarkome RSFSR," *Pravda*, November 12, 1929.

100. Cheliabinsk, *Iz istorii Magnitogorskogo metallurgicheskogo kombinata i goroda Magnitogorska*, 220.

Chapter 5. Competition and Visions

Epigraph: Gosplan-SSSR, *K probleme stroitel'stva sotsialisticheskogo goroda* (Moscow: Izd-vo planovoe khoziaistvo, 1930), 39. G. V. Puzis became a strong advocate of disurbanism. In 1930, he joined Barshch, Ginzburg, and others at the newly founded section for Socialist Settlement in the Construction Department at Gosplan RSFSR.

1. Looking closely at the founding of Magnitogorsk requires acknowledging that this time and place have been investigated closely before. A second look might seem unnecessary in the face of the archival depth and scholarly importance of Kotkin's *Magnetic Mountain*, a book that located the establishment of everyday Stalinist culture in this single site. The chapter titled "The Idiocy of Urban Life" brings forward a litany of details that emphasize the incompetence of the planners entrusted to bring the socialist city to life. The "planners" to which Kotkin repeatedly refers in the text are left unqualified, however, prompting the question of whether, in his view, the failure to construct a visionary Magnitogorsk was the result of poor economic or spatial decisions—or both. Stephen Kotkin, *Magnetic Mountain: Stalinism as a Civilization* (Berkeley: University of California Press, 1995).

2. Works of both fiction and nonfiction are devoted to the mythic construction effort at the Magnitogorsk Steel and Iron Works. The one that best captures day-to-day life under "Stalinist tempo" is Valentin Kataev, *Time, Forward!* (Bloomington: Indiana University Press, 1976). The film *Pesn' o geroiakh* (Song of Heroes) by Joris Ivens (1932) also conveys the importance of the plant's construction in its time.

3. Françoise Choay, *The Rule and the Model: On the Theory of Architecture and Urbanism*, ed. Denise Bratton (Cambridge: MIT Press, 1997), 6.

4. V. S. Fedosikhin and V. V. Khoroshanskii, *Magnitogorsk—Klassika sovetskoi sotsialisticheskoi arkhitektury 1918–1991* (Magnitogorsk: Magnitogorskii gosudarstvennyi tekhnicheskii universitet, 1999), 24.

5. Kotkin, *Magnetic Mountain*, 37.

6. Henry Freyn and Co. first arrived in the USSR to provide technical assistance in reconstructing existing plants, as well as new plants like the Kuznetz Iron and Steel Plant. Their involvement with Magnitogorsk began only in 1928. Antony C. Sutton, *Western Technology and Soviet Economic Development 1917 to 1930* (Stanford: Hoover Institution on War, Revolution and Peace, 1968), 3:74.

7. Fedosikhin, *Magnitogorsk*, 40.

8. Kotkin's chapter 2, "Peopling a Shock Construction Site" outlines the various bureaucratic means by which Magnitogorsk was populated. The technical elite, higher

administrators, and foreign experts were "mobilized," or ordered to the site by the party; regular workers were recruited with promises of good pay; and kulaks, among other undesirable class categories, were deported there forcibly. Kotkin, *Magnetic Mountain*, 81.

9. GARF, f. P-7952, o. 5, d. 354, l. 1.

10. GARF, f. P-7952, o. 5, d. 354, l. 3.

11. Kotkin, *Magnetic Mountain*, 40.

12. Gosproekt Magnitostroi, the primary planning team for Magnitogorsk, sent around its version of the brief on December 10, 1929, asking key organizations to review and approve the document for public release within the week. The competition draft in the archive was sent to the Central Organization of Trade Unions (VTsSPS), although the follow-up discussions imply that it was sent to a number of relevant organizations. Three days later the NKVD's General Administration of Communal Services (GUKh)—copying Stroikom representative/disurbanist theorist Okhitovich, among others—wrote a strongly worded memo that branded the Magnitostroi brief unacceptable. They then sent their own version of the brief around. Finalization occurred at an interdepartmental meeting on December 17, 1929. GARF, f. 5451, o. 13, d. 225, l. 1 and GARF, f. 5451, o. 13, d. 225, l. 16.

13. GARF, f. P-7952, o. 5, d. 179, l. 40.

14. GARF, f. P-7952, o. 5, d. 179, l. 41.

15. The Sovnarkom decree held six specific mandates for the future Magnitogorsk *sotsgorod* that drove the brief's language: 1) all services and cultural programs will be communalized; 2) child-rearing will be state run; 3) medical services will be fully provided; 4) the most modern sanitary-technical systems will be used; 5) population estimates for the settlement will account for all people of working age; and 6) buildings will be designed according to modern architectural standards. GARF, f. P-7952, o. 5, d. 178, l. 4. See also Oblastnoi ispolnitel'nyi komitet–arkhivnyi otdel Cheliabinsk, "Iz postanovleniia sovnarkoma RSFSR o stroitel'stve Magnitogorskogo kombinata i g. Magnitogorsk (November 11, 1929)," *Iz istorii Magnitogorskogo metallurgicheskogo kombinata i goroda Magnitogorska, 1929–1941 gg.; Sbornik dokumentov i materialov* (Cheliabinskaia oblast': Iuzhno-Ural'skoe knizhnoe izd-vo, 1965), 219–20.

16. All projects had to be deposited at the Moscow office of Magnitostroi by 8 am on February 2, 1930.

17. Choay, *The Rule and the Model*, 6.

18. Martin Buber, *Paths in Utopia* (New York: Macmillan, 1950), 115.

19. Buber, *Paths in Utopia*, 7.

20. TsDAMLM, f. 8, o.1, d.431, ll. 1–3. All direct quotes in this section come from the competition brief, unless otherwise indicated.

21. The original discussion and definition of these terms can be found in L.M. Sabsovich, *Sotsialisticheskie goroda* (Moscow: Gosizdat RSFSR "Moskovskii rabochii," 1930). For *sotsgorod*, see chap. 4: "Dal'neishie puti razvitiia nashikh promyshlennikh gorodov," (Future development of our industrial cities) and for *zhilkombinat*, see chap. 11: "Kakie doma dolzhny my stroit' v sotsialisticheskikh gorodakh" (What type of houses should we build in socialist cities?).

22. This point prescribes fully state-run provisioning of the sort that Sabsovich advanced in his 1929 *Planovoe khoziaistva* article, which stated that "the economic apparatus for the individual distribution of manufactured products will have no place in socialist settlements." "Problema goroda," *Planovoe khoziaistvo*, no. 7 (1929): 49. An entire chapter devoted to the problematic installation of communal provisioning in Magnitogorsk can be found in Kotkin, *Magnetic Mountain*, chap. 6: "Bread and Circus."

23. Sabsovich, *Sotsialisticheskie goroda*, 61.

24. Sabsovich, *Sotsialisticheskie goroda*, 43.

25. ARDA, f. 2983, o. 1, d. 38, l. 152.

26. This four-story (maximum five-story) limit was imposed in Sabsovich's original definition of the *zhilkombinat*. Sabsovich, *Sotsialisticheskie goroda*, 46.

27. Sabsovich, *Sotsialisticheskie goroda*, 46.

28. The brief further stipulates that auxiliary areas such as lobbies, hallways, stairs, bathrooms, showers, and toilets do not count toward the total floor area of the public use programs.

29. This number assumes a full residential commune population of 3,000 people, with adults accounting for 76 percent of that population.

30. Sabsovich, *Sotsialisticheskie goroda*, 46–47.

31. Sabsovich, *Sotsialisticheskie goroda*, 49.

32. N.A. Miliutin, *Sotsgorod: The Problem of Building Socialist Cities* (Cambridge: MIT Press, 1974), 75.

33. N. Krupskaia, "Goroda budushchego," in *Goroda sotsializma i sotsialisticheskaia rekonstruktsiia byta*, ed. B. Lunin (Moscow: Tip. Mospoligrafa "Iskra Revoliutsii," 1930), 11.

34. Gosplan-SSSR, *K probleme stroitel'stva sotsialisticheskogo goroda*, 116–17.

35. Sabsovich, *Sotsialisticheskie goroda*, 48–49.

36. N. Dokuchaev, "Konkurs na planirovku Magnitogorska," *Stroitel'stvo Moskvy*, no. 4 (1930): 25.

37. Specifically, the jury had representatives from Magnitostroi, the Ural oblast' (region); the NKVD, Narkompros, and Narkomzdrav; Stroikom RSFSR; the Central Committee of the Komsomol (Vsesoiuznyi leninskii kommunisticheskii soiuz molodezhi or TsK VLKSM); the Women's Department of the Central Committee (Zhenotdel TsK); four representatives from the All-Union Central Council of Trade Unions (Vsesoiuznyi tsentral'nyi sovet prefossional'nykh soiuzov or VTsSPS); and the individuals V. A. Vesnin, civil engineer; I. O. Mashkov, architect; A. K. Ivanov, architect-artist. TsDAMLM, f. 8, o.1, d.431, l. 3. Viktor Vesnin was a member of MAO and OSA and a noted Constructivist architect. Ivan O. Mashkov was a prerevolutionary Art Nouveau architect turned deputy city architect for Moscow after the revolution. Andrei K. Ivanov was involved in numerous state architectural bureaus in Moscow such as Arkhistroi. I. A. Kazus', *Sovetskaia arkhitektura 1920-kh godov: Organizatsiia proektirovaniia* (Moscow: Progress-Traditsiia, 2009).

38. Dokuchaev, "Konkurs na planirovku Magnitogorska," 25.

39. "Sotsialisticheskii gorod Magnitogorsk," *Stroitel'naia promyshlennost'*, no. 3 (1930): 197, 198.

40. Dokuchaev, "Konkurs na planirovku Magnitogorska," 25.

41. A. Gozak, *Ivan Leonidov: The Complete Works*, ed. Andrei Leonidov, Catherine Cooke, and Igor Palmin (New York: Rizzoli, 1988).

42. Dokuchaev, "Konkurs na planirovku Magnitogorska," 28.

43. The Stroikom scheme referred to the future site as "Magnitogor'e," and not "Magnitogorsk," likely to erase all indication of urbanity from their submission.

44. M. Barshch, V. Vladimirov, M. Okhitovich, and N. Solnikov, "Magnitogor'e," *Sovremennaia arkhitektura* no. 1–2 (1930): 44, 41.

45. Dokuchaev, "Konkurs na planirovku Magnitogorska," 28.

46. M. Okhitovich, "Ne gorod, a novyi tip rasseneniia," *Ekonomicheskaia zhizn'*, December 7, 1929.

47. An *izba* is a traditional one-room peasant house, and one on chicken legs would have been known to all readers as the folkloric home of the witch, Baba Yaga. L. Sabsovich, "'Vzbesivshiisia melkii burzhua' ili kommivoiazher avtomobil'noi firmy" ('Rabid petty bourgeois' or the car salesman) *Ekonomicheskaia zhizn'*, December 20, 1929.

48. Dokuchaev, "Konkurs na planirovku Magnitogorska," 25.

49. Dokuchaev, "Konkurs na planirovku Magnitogorska," 25.

50. Dokuchaev, "Konkurs na planirovku Magnitogorska," 25.

51. Miliutin's Linear City should not be confused with the similarly named model proposed by Arturo Soria y Mata in late nineteenth-century Spain, which was, in effect, a streetcar suburb for Madrid, and did not accommodate industry.

52. Miliutin, *Sotsgorod*, 70.

53. "Members of the Jury may not participate in the development of competition projects and will not give any clarifying information about the competition program except for the official question-and-answer from the Jury that is included in the program to this competition." TsDAMLM, f. 8, o.1, d.431, l. 3.

54. Ernst May, "City Building in the USSR," *Das Neue Rußland*, 8–9 (1931). Translated in El Lissitzky, *Russia: An Architecture for World Revolution* (London: Lund Humphries, 1970), 192.

Chapter 6. Frankfurt on the Steppe

Epigraph: Anna Louise Strong, "Magnet Mountain," *From Stalingrad to Kuzbas* (New York: International Pamphlets, 1932), 66.

1. This decision was dated April 2, 1930. Oblastnoi ispolnitel'nyi komitet–arkhivnyi otdel Cheliabinsk (Cheliabinsk Ispolkom), *Iz istorii Magnitogorskogo metallurgicheskogo kombinata i goroda Magnitogorska, 1929–1941 gg.; Sbornik dokumentov i materialov* (Cheliabinskaia oblast': Iuzhno-Ural'skoe knizhnoe izd-vo, 1965), 270.

2. GARF, f. P-7952, o. 5, d. 354, l. 2.

3. "O rabote po perestroike byta (Postanovlenie TsK Rkp(B) ot 16 Maia 1930 goda)," *Pravda*, May 29, 1930.

4. "O rabote po perestroike byta."

5. "Akt zakladki fundamenta 1-i domny Magnitorgoskogo kombinata," June 1, 1930, in Cheliabinsk Ispolkom, *Iz istorii*, 62.

6. The tour extended from September 1 to October 1, 1927, and the delegation included representatives from Building Committee of the Vesenkha RFSFR, Stroikonventsii, Mosstroi, Gospromstroi, Tekstilstroi, the Third State Cotton Trust, Glavenergo, Iugostal', Industroi, Vesenkha Azerbaijan, Azneft, NIGRES, and the Krasnoe Sormovo Factory. S. N. Nakhmanson et al., *Sovremennoe stroitel'stvo Germanii: Pervaia zagranichnaia ekskursiia inzhenirov-stroitelei i arkhitektorov* (Moscow: Gostekhizdat, 1929), 9. My knowledge of this book comes from Evgeniia Konysheva, Mark Meerovich, and Thomas Flierl, "Ernst May v istorii sovetskoi industrializatsii," *Project baikal* 8, no. 27 (2011).

7. Nakhmanson, *Sovremennoe stroitel'stvo Germanii*, 89.

8. Barbara Miller Lane, *Architecture and Politics in Germany, 1918–1945* (Cambridge: Harvard University Press, 1985), 104, 117–19.

9. Nakhmanson, *Sovremennoe stroitel'stvo Germanii*, 97.

10. Claudia Quiring et al., eds., *Ernst May, 1886–1970* (Munich: Prestel, 2011), 51.

11. Lane, *Architecture and Politics in Germany*, 90–91.

12. For the first three years of the housing program (1925–28), May and his team received 16 million marks per year from the Hauszinssteuer (a new 15 percent tax on rents of existing buildings), 5 million from municipal grants, and another 5 million from loans. John Robert Mullin, "City Planning in Frankfurt, Germany, 1925–1932. A Study in Practical Utopianism," *Journal of Urban History* 4, no. 1 (1977): 9.

13. Mullin, "City Planning in Frankfurt," 20.

14. This lecture was given on November 8, 1928, and was also broadcast to a wider audience by radio. Quiring et al., *Ernst May*, 136.

15. Corinne Jaquand, "The Town Planning Congresses at the Paris Universal Exhibition of 1937. Ultimate Encounters," paper presented at the *International Planning History Society (IPHS) Conference*, Yokohama, Japan 2018.

16. May maintained a close personal relationship with Unwin and his family throughout his life. Quiring et al., *Ernst May*, 19.

17. Raymond Sir Unwin, *Town Planning in Practice: An Introduction to the Art of Designing Cities and Suburbs* (London: T. F. Unwin, 1909), 382.

18. Susan R. Henderson, *Building Culture: Ernst May and the Frankfurt Initiative, 1926–1931* (Bern: Peter Lang, 2013), 209.

19. Henderson, *Building Culture*, 339–42.

20. Christoph Mohr, "The New Frankfurt: Housing and Construction in the City 1925–1930," in Quiring et al., *Ernst May*, 60–61.

21. Mohr, "The New Frankfurt," 65.

22. Mullin, "City Planning in Frankfurt," 10.

23. An extensive discussion on the birth of *zeilenbau* planning is in Henderson, *Building Culture*, chap. 7, "Rationalization Takes Command: *Zeilenbau* and the Politics of CIAM." For a thorough analysis of Frankfurt interwar housing typologies see Alessandro Porotto,

L'intelligence Des Formes: Le Projet de Logements Collectifs à Vienne et Francfort (Geneva: Mētispresses, 2019).

24. Research conducted by Walter Schwagenscheidt—who traveled to the Soviet Union as part of May's Brigade—determined that the optimal orientation for residential insolation occurred at an angle 22½° from true north-south. Mark Swenarton, "Rationality and Rationalism: The Theory and Practice of Site Planning in Modern Architecture 1905–1930," *AA Files*, no. 4 (1983): 55–56.

25. Konysheva, "Ernst May v istorii sovetskoi industrializatsii," 139.

26. In the published proceedings of CIAM2, the "Russian" delegates are noted as "Ginsbourg" and "Colly." CIAM, *Die Wohnung für das Existenzminimum*, Documents of Modern Architecture (Nendeln: Kraus Reprint, 1979). Moisei Ginzburg and El Lissitzky were invited to the first meeting of CIAM in La Sarraz, Switzerland, held in June 1928, but were denied visas by the Swiss authorities. Eric Paul Mumford, *The CIAM Discourse on Urbanism, 1928–1960* (Cambridge: MIT Press, 2000), 18, 42.

27. German Krasin was the brother of Leonid Krasin, a close Bolshevik associate of Lenin's, member of the Presidium of the Vesenkha, and the first commissar for foreign trade of the USSR, among other positions. Thomas Flierl, "'Possibly the Greatest Task an Architect Ever Faced': Ernst May in the Soviet Union (1930–1933)," in Quiring et al., *Ernst May*, 193n14. For more on GIS, see I. A. Kazus', *Sovetskaia arkhitektura 1920-kh godov: Organizatsiia proektirovaniia* (Moscow: Progress-Traditsiia, 2009), 116.

28. The first CIAM book, *Die Wohnung für das Existenzminimum* was published in 1930 and included papers by Gropius, Hans Schmidt, and Le Corbusier, all of whom would produce designs for Soviet sites in the following two years. Mumford, *The CIAM Discourse on Urbanism*, 42.

29. Henderson, *Building Culture*, 427.

30. Evgeniia Vladimirovna Konysheva and M. G. Meerovich, *Ernst Mai: Proektirovanie sotsgorodov v gody pervykh piatiletok (na primere Magnitogorska)* (Moscow: URSS, 2012), 42–43.

31. Kazus', *Sovetskaia arkhitektura*, 151.

32. Konysheva, "Ernst May v istorii sovetskoi industrializatsii," 137.

33. "City Councillor May's Russian Plans," *Bauwelt*, no. 36 (1930): 1156. Translated in El Lissitzky, *Russia: An Architecture for World Revolution* (London: Lund Humphries, 1970), 173.

34. Kazus', *Sovetskaia arkhitektura*, 151.

35. Konysheva and Meerovich, *Ernst Mai*, 44.

36. Tsentral'nyi bank kommunal'nogo khozaistva i zhilishchnogo stroitel'stva, *Proekty rabochikh zhilishch* (Moscow: Izdanie tsekombanka, 1929), 7.

37. Evgeniia Konysheva and Mark Meerovich, "Bereg levyi, bereg pravyi: Ernst Mai i otkrytye voprosy istorii sovetskoi arkhitektury," *Arkhitekton: Izvestiia vuzov*, no. 30 (2010).

38. Borchert claimed that 90 percent of German architects were unemployed in the years immediately after the 1929 economic crash. Kazus', *Sovetskaia arkhitektura*, 152.

39. "City Councillor May's Russian Plans," 174.

40. Flierl, "'Possibly the Greatest Task an Architect Ever Faced,'" 159.

41. The branch of Giprogor that Chernyshev led to design Magnitogorsk was administratively beholden to the People's Commissariat for Internal Affairs of the Russian Republic (NKVD RSFSR).

42. The date of Chernyshev's reinstatement was September 17, 1930, and his speech to the Komacademy took place on October 19. Konysheva and Meerovich, *Ernst Mai*, 41–42.

43. Flierl, "'Possibly the Greatest Task an Architect Ever Faced,'" 157.

44. Ernst May, "From Frankfurt to the New Russia," *Frankfurter Zeitung*, November 30, 1930. Translated in Lissitzky, *Russia: An Architecture for World Revolution*, 176.

45. The May Brigade's itinerary ran from October 26 to November 8, 1930. Moscow to Magnitogorsk: 4.5 days; Magnitogorsk: 4.5 days; Magnitogorsk to Moscow: 4 days. Evgenija Konyseva, Thomas Flierl, and Mark G. Meerovic, *Linkes Ufer, rechtes Ufer: Ernst May und die Planungsgeschichte von Magnitogorsk (1930–1933)* (Berlin: Theater Der Zeit, 2014), 206.

46. May, "From Frankfurt to the New Russia," 176–77.

47. May, "From Frankfurt to the New Russia," 177.

48. May, "From Frankfurt to the New Russia," 175–76.

49. GARF, f. A-314, o. 1, d. 7667, ll. 1–2.

50. Ernst May, "K proekty general'nogo plana Magnitorgoska," *Sovetskaia arkhitektura*, May–June (1933): 17.

51. May, "K proekty," 18.

52. An architect referred to as Davidovich (first name unnoted), working for an organization called Uralgiev, was also ordered to develop a scheme. He remained involved in the discussions about Magnitogorsk planning through December 1930, and may have been retained solely as a planning researcher; the documents make his position difficult to ascertain. GARF, f. A-314, o. 1, d. 7667, l. 3.

53. Lissitzky, *Russia: An Architecture for World Revolution*, 179.

54. Ernst May, "City Building in the USSR," *Das Neue Rußland*, 8–9 (1931). Translated in Lissitzky, *Russia*, 199.

55. GARF, f. A-314, o. 1, d. 7667, l. 4

56. The expert panel consisted of the most eminent Moscow architects of the day: G. B. Krasin, Ginzburg, A. P. Ivanitskii, V. N. Semenov, N. P. Makarov, Davidovich, O. A. Vutke, Afanas'ev, N. I. Gundorov, Vesnin, Ivanov, V. Voeikov, I. Zholtovskii, Rukavishnikov, Shchusev, Frolov and K. I. Dzhus. As Konysheva and Meerovich note, the inconsistent degree of naming specificity on this list is simply reflective of inconsistency in the original documentation. Konysheva and Meerovich, *Ernst Mai*, 49.

57. GARF, f. P-7952, o. 5, d. 178, ll. 17–19.

58. May, "City Building in the USSR," 198.

59. GARF, f. A-314, o. 1, d. 7668, ll. 8–9.

60. GARF, f. A-314, o. 1, d. 7668, ll. 8–9.

61. Konysheva and Meerovich propose that the results of the internal competition were preordained: Politburo member Ordzhonikidze, Tsekombank director Luganovskii, and Magnitostroi director Iakov Shmidt favored May and were able to override any objections from

experts and officials further down the chain of power. Konysheva and Meerovich, "Bereg levyi, bereg pravyi," 17.

62. Construction for this model residential area was completed under Luganovskii's direction, costing 40 million rubles, and May's group was paid 34,154 rubles. GARF, f. A-314, o. 1, d. 7668, ll. 8–9 and Irina Cheredina, "Stroitel'stvo goroda Magnitogorska 1930-e gody. K istorii voprosa," *Budownictwo*, no. 17 (2011): 34.

63. The Moscow 1935 General Plan is here cited as a model for "Stalinist" planning because the site plans of post-Stalinist, Khrushchev-era *mikroraiony* (microregions) in fact bear striking similarity May's plan for Magnitogorsk.

64. The administrators represented Magnitostroi, Stal'stroi, and Vodokanalstroi. Cheliabinsk Ispolkom, *Iz istorii*, 270–71.

65. Stephen Kotkin, *Magnetic Mountain: Stalinism as a Civilization* (Berkeley: University of California Press, 1995), 111.

66. Konysheva and Meerovich recount in great detail the locational indecision for Magnitogorsk from 1929 until after World War II. Konysheva and Meerovich, *Ernst Mai*, chap. 4: "Bereg levyi, bereg pravyi . . .".

67. The timeline and details about the locational changes for Magnitorgosk from 1929 to 1932 come from GARF, f. A-314, o. 1, d. 7667, ll. 184–92.

68. Kotkin, *Magnetic Mountain*, 113.

69. May took another reconnaissance trip to Magnitogorsk in February 1931, and this explanatory text likely was formulated after that trip. GARF, f.A-314, o. 1, d. 7667, ll. 17. "Ob"asnitel'naia zapiska k proektu Tsekombanka goroda Magnitogorska. 14 February 1931, pered Novosibirskom."

70. May, "K proekty general'nogo plana Magnitorgoska," 17.

71. May, "K proekty general'nogo plana Magnitorgoska," 17.

72. Kazus', *Sovetskaia arkhitektura*, 158–59.

73. Kotkin, *Magnetic Mountain*, 117–18.

74. Zara Witkin and Michael Gelb, *An American Engineer in Stalin's Russia: The Memoirs of Zara Witkin, 1932–1934* (Berkeley: University of California Press, 1991), 233.

75. Flierl, "'Possibly the Greatest Task an Architect Ever Faced,'" 187.

76. May, "K proekty general'nogo plana Magnitorgoska," 20.

77. Konysheva and Meerovich, *Ernst Mai*, 184. An version of the INKO-A section plan with modest galley kitchens included can be found in M. G. Meerovich, "Razdroblennoe proektirovanie (pismo Ernsta Maia Iosifu Stalinu)," *Arkhitekton: Izvestiia vuzov*, no. 38 (2012): 120.

78. May, "K proekty general'nogo plana Magnitorgoska," 22.

79. May, "K proekty general'nogo plana Magnitorgoska," 22.

80. May, "K proekty general'nogo plana Magnitorgoska," 24.

81. D.E. Shibaev, "Za sotsialisticheskii gorod Magnitorgosk," in *Sovetskaia arkhitektura*, May–June (1933): 30.

82. Shibaev, "Za sotsialisticheskii gorod Magnitorgosk," 30.

83. Lane, *Architecture and Politics in Germany*, 102.

84. Between the Standartgorproekt and Gosproekt apartments, Kvartal no. 1 accommodated 9,600 residents. The number of units is calculated from the typical INKO-A type, with 42 units each. The 1932 population estimate of 230,000 residents is from "CONCLUSIONS of the representatives of the STROINTS NKTP, who took part in the works of the Brigade of NKKKh on the issue of residential construction of Magnitogorsk from 12–18 November 1932." GARF, f. A-314, o. 1, d. 7674, l. 95.

85. The school was designed by Wilhelm Schutte, husband of Margarete Schutte-Lihotzky, the designer of the Frankfurt kitchen. The couple lived and worked for May in the USSR from 1930 to 1937. Konysheva and Meerovich, *Ernst Mai*, 185.

86. May, "K proekty general'nogo plana Magnitorgoska," 22.

87. Kotkin, *Magnetic Mountain*, 117–18.

88. The fraught narrative of the Magnitogorsk metallurgical factory's design, construction, and in some cases reconstruction, is masterfully told in Kotkin, *Magnetic Mountain*, chap. 1: "On the March for Metal."

Chapter 7. From Tractors to Territory

Epigraph: Anna Louise Strong, *From Stalingrad to Kuzbas* (New York: International Pamphlets, 1932), "Kharkov Learns from Stalingrad Pioneers," *Moscow News*, August 1931, 35. The current Ukrainian spelling of *Kharkiv* is used throughout this text, although the name of the city is *Kharkov* in Russian, and *Khar'kov* as transliterated with the Library of Congress standard. The exceptions are in direct quotes from original/archival sources in which the original document's spelling is retained.

1. "And I see— / from the capital a capital / There it grows / from the immense power of the Union; Where crows / hovering over carrion caw, / Completely / with railways / wrapped, / The capital / buzzes /Ukrainian Khar'kov, / Alive, / laboring, / of reinforced concrete." Mayakovsky's poem as cited in Nikolai Timofeevich D'iachenko, *Ulitsy i ploshchadi Khar'kova*, 3rd ed. (Khar'kov: Prapor, 1974), 14.

2. May returned to Kharkiv in 1931 and snapped an artful worm's eye photo of the Derzhprom building. Thomas Flierl, "'Possibly the Greatest Task an Architect Ever Faced': Ernst May in the Soviet Union (1930–1933)," in Quiring et al., *Ernst May*, 150.

3. The term *priviazka* was brought into English-language scholarship by Sonia Melnikova-Raich, whose two articles on Kahn's involvement in Soviet industrialization bring much new archival material to bear. See Sonia Melnikova-Raich, "The Soviet Problem with Two 'Unknowns': How an American Architect and a Soviet Negotiator Jump-Started the Industrialization of Russia, Part I: Albert Kahn," *IA: The Journal of the Society for Industrial Archeology* 36, no. 2 (2010); "The Soviet Problem with Two 'Unknowns': How an American Architect and a Soviet Negotiator Jump-Started the Industrialization of Russia, Part II: Saul Bron," *IA: The Journal of the Society for Industrial Archeology* 37, no. 1–2 (2011).

4. Thank you to Evgeniia Konysheva, who helped pinpoint terminology utilized by architectural practitioners in both the first Five-Year Plan period and in the 1950s. See, for

instance, the album of typical workers' housing projects published by the Central Commercial Bank of the USSR (Tsekombank) at the start of 1929, which uses the term *popravka*. Tsentral'nyi bank kommunal'nogo khozaistva i zhilishchnogo stroitel'stva, *Proekty rabochikh zhilishch* (Moscow: Izdanie tsekombanka, 1929), 15.

5. The capital of Soviet Ukraine was transferred back to Kyiv in 1934.

6. In 1923–24, a newly established municipal technical bureau initiated Kharkiv's first socialist planning effort to address four major issues: modernization of municipal systems, industrialization, state-building, and worker housing.

7. Titus Hewryk, "Planning of the Capital in Kharkiv," *Harvard Ukrainian Studies* 16, no. 3/4 (1992): 332, 333.

8. The Ukrainian factory districts are in Kharkiv, Poltava, Ekaterinoslav, Chernihov, and Don. E. T. Cherkasova, "Idei i realiztsiia plana sotsialisticheskoi rekonstruktsii Khar'kova," in *Sovetskoe gradstroitel'stvo 1920–1930kh godov: Novye issledovaniia i materialy*, ed. Yu. L. Kosenkova (Moscow: Librokom, 2010), 130.

9. Volodymyr Kravchenko, *Khar'kov—Kharkiv: Stolitsa pogranich'ia* (Vilnius: Evropeiskii gumanitarnyi universitet, 2010), 242.

10. Orest Subtelny, *Ukraine: A History*, 3rd ed. (Toronto: University of Toronto Press, 2000), 381.

11. The Fifteenth Congress was concerned with the impending agricultural procurement "grain crisis" that led in 1928 and 1929 to forced collectivization. Even members of the more conservative right faction, such as Aleksei Rykov, agreed that *perekachka*, the practice of pumping agricultural resources into industrial projects, was necessary, but they split on the degree of violence with which agricultural extraction should be enacted. Moshe Lewin, *The Making of the Soviet System: Essays in the Social History of Interwar Russia* (London: Methuen, 1985), 95.

12. Anne Applebaum, *Red Famine: Stalin's War on Ukraine* (New York: Doubleday, 2017), xxvi. Fred Beal's chapter "Famine" is devoted to the enforced starvation that surrounded the Kharkov Tractor Plant. Fred E. Beal, *Proletarian Journey: New England, Gastonia, Moscow* (New York: Hillman-Curl, 1937).

13. "To common work on common land! Integrally with industry!" is an intertitle in Sergei Eisenstein's film *The General Line*, 1929.

14. Forty-four industrial products carried specific objectives in the first Five-Year Plan, but only eight were mechanical products, a category into which the tractor fell. Yves Cohen, "The Soviet Fordson. Between the Politics of Stalin and the Philosophy of Ford, 1924–1932," in *Ford, 1903–2003, the European History*, ed. Hubert Bonin et al. (Paris: Plage, 2003), 539.

15. Maurice Hindus, "Henry Ford Conquers Russia," *The Outlook*, no. 29 (1927): 282.

16. Richard Stites, *Revolutionary Dreams: Utopian Vision and Experimental Life in the Russian Revolution* (New York: Oxford University Press, 1989), 149. Kendall E. Bailes, "The American Connection: Ideology and the Transfer of American Technology to the Soviet Union, 1917–1941," *Comparative Studies in Society and History* 23, no. 3 (1981): 436.

17. Chizuko Takao, "The Origin of the Machine Tractor Station in the USSR: A New Perspective," *Acta Slavica Iaponica* 19 (2002): 122, 118.

18. Antony C. Sutton, *Western Technology and Soviet Economic Development 1917 to 1930* (Stanford: Hoover Institution on War, Revolution and Peace, 1968), 1:140.

19. Valerii Mezhlauk and Amtorg's Saul Bron brokered the agreement with the Ford Motor Company to assist in constructing the auto factory in Nizhnii Novgorod.

20. Charles E. Sorensen, *My Forty Years with Ford* (Detroit: Wayne State University Press, 2006), 202–3.

21. In his study of US-Soviet technical exchange, Bailes noted that there were five main channels for Russians, then Soviets, to gain access to US technology and methods of industrial organization. The first two, trade and direct ownership/concessions/enterprises operated by Americans within Russia, were used primarily in the nineteenth century. The postrevolutionary period saw the rise of the last three: "industrial espionage," or the unauthorized replication of US technology without the aid of licensing agreements like Sorensen witnessed; importation of American technical literature, as Serebrovskii had recommended in Baku; and technical trade agreements. Bailes, "The American Connection," 432.

22. Melnikova-Raich, "The Soviet Problem with Two 'Unknowns,'" 60. See also Bay Brown, "Albert Kahn: The Russian Legacy," *Proekt Rossiia = Project Russia* 7b (1997).

23. "Producer of Production Lines," *Architectural Record*, June (1942): 40.

24. The twelve companies that signed contracts with the Soviet government in June 1929 were Ford ($30 million for manufacturing Ford trucks and for the construction of an auto plant); Hugh L. Cooper (for engineering consultation on the DniproHES hydroelectric station); Stuart James and Cooke (engineering consultation for the coal mining industry); H. J. Freyn Engineering (consultation on steel mills); Radio Corporation of America and International General Electric (exchange of patents and technical assistance); Nitrogen Engineering (technical assistance to build a nitrogen fertilizer factory; DuPont de Nemours (technical assistance to build ammonia fertilizer factories); Longacre Engineering & Construction (technical assistance and supervision on apartment building construction in Moscow); Arthur Davis (chief consulting engineer in irrigation projects in Soviet Central Asia); McCormick company (design of a large baking plant in Moscow); and Albert Kahn, Inc. (design of the Stalingrad Tractor Factory). From "Soviet Closes Big U.S. Deals," *Detroit Free Press*, June 4, 1929.

25. TsDAMLM, f. 8, po. 1, od. zb. 259, ark. 2–31.

26. "Tractor Plants Speed up Production," *Economic Review of the Soviet Union*, October 1 (1929): 329.

27. Takao, "The Origin of the Machine Tractor Station in the USSR," 135.

28. The Stroikom directives date from August 15, 1929. "Iz direktiva Stroikoma RSFSR vedomstvam i ucherezhdeniiam po prorabotke konkretnogo piatiletnego plana organizatsii stroitel'nogo dela," *Nashe stroitel'stvo*, no. 12–13 (1929). Partially reprinted in I. A. Kazus', *Sovetskaia arkhitektura 1920-kh godov: Organizatsiia proektirovaniia* (Moscow: Progress-Traditsiia, 2009), 414–15.

29. "Iz direktiva Stroikoma RSFSR."

30. The decree was summarized in *Pravda* on December 29, 1929, in an article titled "The Reorganization and Improvement of Construction." The decree required mechanization

of construction work; standardization; industrialization of building materials; skilled work cadres; professional exchanges with other industrialized nations; use of foreign technical expertise; the organization of manufacturing in construction work; establishment of construction firms and branches; management and planning of the construction industry; and decrease of construction costs.

31. Milka Bliznakov, "The Realization of Utopia: Western Technology and Soviet Avant-Garde Architecture," in *Reshaping Russian Architecture: Western Technology, Utopian Dreams*, ed. William C. Brumfield (New York: Cambridge University Press, 1990), 157; Melnikova-Raich, "The Soviet Problem with Two 'Unknowns,'" 62.

32. "$1,9000,000 Building by the Soviet in 1930: Albert Kahn, Inc., Get Contract as Consulting Architects in Five-Year Program," *New York Times*, January 11, 1930.

33. TsDAMLM, f. 8, po. 1, od. zb. 259, ark. 1.

34. Leon A. Swajian, "Building the Kharkov Tractor Plant," *Economic Review of the Soviet Union* 6 (1931): 413.

35. Kharkiv, Dnipropetrovs'k, Zaporizhzhia, Kyiv, Mykolaiv, and Odesa were the sites considered. Kharkiv and Dnipropetrovs'k were deemed finalist sites. TsDAMLM, f. 8, po. 1, od. zb. 259, ark. 29–31.

36. TsDAMLM, f. 8, po. 1, od. zb. 259, ark. 19.

37. Five years later, at the time of Kharkiv Tractor Factory site selection, the same A. A. Main established a planning bureau on Moskovskii Prospekt to study how Kharkiv's future expansion might play out along disurbanist lines. Cherkasova, "Idei i realiztsiia plana," 133–35.

38. Odes'ka kinofabryka VUFKU, *Priskorennia buduvannia traktorobudu—Veletens'ka peremoha sotsialistychno budivnytstva* (1930), no. 14/180, Apx. no.1447. Documentary film footage on KhTZ can be found at VUKFU Newsreels, TsDKFFA, archive numbers 1429, 1447, 1469, 1483, 1486, 1516, 1517, 1529.

39. I.N. Baltuzevich, *Opyt i uroki stroitel'stva KhTZ* (Moscow: Gosstroiizdat, 1932), 31.

40. TsDAMLM, f. 8, po. 1, od. zb. 259, ark. 29.

41. DAKhO, f. r-5652, po. 1, od. zb. 2861.

42. TsDAMLM, f. 8, po. 1, od. zb. 259, ark. 29–31.

43. The Gosplan conference took place on November 26 and 29, 1929; the KhTZ siting report was filed on November 29. Although the Moscow debates could not have made a material difference in KhTZ's site selection, socialist urban theories were well publicized in *Ekonomicheskaia zhizn'* and elsewhere when the report was being compiled.

44. TsDAMLM, f. 8, po. 1, od. zb. 259, ark. 19.

45. The Soviets focused their first tractor collaboration effort on Caterpillar because the firm's tractor chassis could be adapted to tank production, like the Caterpillar-Holt transformed for the German A74 tank in World War I. Melnikova-Raich, "The Soviet Problem with Two 'Unknowns,'" 80n81.

46. Baltuzevich, *Opyt i uroki stroitel'stva KhTZ*, 8.

47. Baltuzevich, *Opyt i uroki stroitel'stva KhTZ*, 9.

48. Baltuzevich, *Opyt i uroki stroitel'stva KhTZ*, 8.

49. Melnikova-Raich, "The Soviet Problem with Two 'Unknowns,'" 66.

50. According to Sutton, a cadre of 570 Americans and 50 Germans reassembled the factory in Stalingrad. For a full accounting of US companies involved in operation and supply delivery for the plant, see table 11-2 in Sutton, *Western Technology and Soviet Economic Development*, 2:186.

51. Swajian, "Building the Kharkov Tractor Plant," 414.

52. Strong, *From Stalingrad to Kuzbas*, 18.

53. The architects are V. Bogomolov, I. Vinograd, A. Goncharuk, and D. Shirokograd. I. N. Sedak, *Arkhitektura sovetskoi Ukrainy = Architecture of the Soviet Ukraine* (Moscow: Stroizdat, 1987).

54. Swajian, "Building the Kharkov Tractor Plant," 414.

55. D. Ia. Frolov, *Inzhener O.I. Nerovets'kii* (Kyiv: Budivel'nik, 1967); as quoted in Halyna Mykhailenko, "Diial'nist' O.I. Nerovets'koho v haluzi promyslovnoho ta tsivil'noho budivnitstva v Ukraini v 1922–1936 rokakh," *Doslidzheniia z istorii tekhniki* 22 (2016): 6–7.

56. Baltuzevich, *Opyt i uroki stroitel'stva KhTZ*, 10–11.

57. Baltuzevich, *Opyt i uroki stroitel'stva KhTZ*, 11.

58. Fred E. Beal, *Foreign Workers in a Soviet Tractor Plant* (Moscow: Co-operative Publishing Society of Foreign Workers in the USSR, 1933), 8.

59. Beal, *Foreign Workers*, 9.

60. Baltuzevich, *Opyt i uroki stroitel'stva KhTZ*, 10.

61. Strong, *From Stalingrad to Kuzbas*, 33.

62. The substitution of too many variables from one project to the next resulted in dysfunctional construction sites or unusable end products, as purportedly was the case in Cheliabinsk, the next tractor factory built after Kharkiv. Sutton, *Western Technology and Soviet Economic Development*, 188–89.

63. Swajian, "Building the Kharkov Tractor Plant," 414.

64. Cohen, "The Soviet Fordson," 553.

65. George Nelson, *Industrial Architecture of Albert Kahn, Inc.* (New York: Architectural Book Publishing Company, 1939), 22–23.

66. Anatole Senkevich Jr., "Albert Kahn's Great Soviet Adventure," *Dimensions* 10 (1996): 48.

67. Nelson, *Industrial Architecture of Albert Kahn, Inc.*, 19.

68. "Assembly Plant Plans," 1934, Albert Kahn Papers, Bentley Historical Library, University of Michigan. Two prominent members of the firm leadership in 1942, George Scrymgeour (secretary) and Robert Linto (vice president) were "head men" during the Soviet consultancy. "Louis Kahn Heads Firm of Architects," *Detroit Free Press*, January 7, 1943, 1. Thank you to Claire Zimmerman for this observation.

69. Strong, *From Stalingrad to Kuzbas*, 33; emphasis added.

70. V. D. Tsvetaev, *Sovremennaia fabrichno-zavodskaia arkhitektura*, 2nd ed. (Moscow: Gosstroiizdat, 1933).

71. Meerovich, M. G. "Al'bert Kan v istorii sovetskoi industrializatsii." *Proekt Baikal*, no. 20 (2009). https://archi.ru/lib/publication.html?id=1850569787.

72. The comprehensive organizational model was also utilized in the Kahn Moscow out-post of Gosproektstroi. Nelson, *Industrial Architecture of Albert Kahn, Inc.*, 19.

73. Bailes, "The American Connection," 444.

Chapter 8. Socialist Urbanization through Standardization

Epigraph: P. E. Shpara, *Zapiski arkhitektora* (Kyiv: Budivel'nyk, 1988), 24. When he was a young architect, Shpara worked on the New Kharkiv *sotsgorod* design team.

1. Anna Louise Strong, *From Stalingrad to Kuzbas* (New York: International Pamphlets, 1932), 18–19.

2. TsDAMLM, f. 8, po. 1, od. zb. 265, ark. 4–5.

3. Lynne Viola, *Peasant Rebels under Stalin: Collectivization and the Culture of Peasant Resistance* (Oxford: Oxford University Press, 1996), 14.

4. Anne Applebaum, *Red Famine: Stalin's War on Ukraine* (New York: Doubleday, 2017), 127.

5. Applebaum, *Red Famine*, 151.

6. Georgii Gustavovich Vegman was a collaborator of the Vesnins and a regular con-tributor to SA. He designed the "Red Ray" residential district in Kharkiv while KhTZ was being designed, and lived and worked in Kharkiv from the mid-1940s until his death in 1973. I. V. Utkin and I. V. Chepkunova, *Arkhitkektor Vegman* (Ekaterinburg: Tatlin Pub-lishers, 2008).

7. G. Vegman, "Ukrupnennoe zhil'e 2," *Sovremennaia arkhitektura*, no. 1 (1927): 20.

8. The *dom-kommuna* competition was announced in *Sovremennaia arkhitektura*, no. 5–6 (1926), and the competition entries were published mid-1927. For a discussion of their merits, see A. Pasternak, "Novye formy sovremennogo zhil'ia," *Sovremennaia arkhitektura*, no. 4–5 (1927). For a full discussion of SA's competition for communal housing and its after-math, see Christina E. Crawford, "The Innovative Potential of Scarcity in SA's Comradely Competition for Communal Housing, 1927," *archiDOCT* 1, no. 2 (2014): 32–53.

9. The first issue of SA in 1929 focused on the Stroikom Typification Section. Work-ing alongside Ginzburg were fellow OSA members Mikhail Barshch, V. Vladimirov, Alek-sandr Pasternak, and G. R. Sum-Shik, "Stroikom RSFSR," *Sovremennaia arkhitektura*, no. 1 (1929): 8–22.

10. The nine main criteria for standard Soviet housing designs set out by Ginzburg were as follows:

1. In a country constructing socialism the economics and improved quality of hous-ing are inextricably linked to raising labor productivity, supporting cultural revo-lution, and transitioning to new socially higher forms of everyday life.

2. Thorough rationalization of an old prerevolutionary apartment type plan, which analyzes and studies the household and labor processes in the rooms, particularly in the kitchen, can lead to 10 percent savings.

3. Using the excessive height of ancillary rooms (foyer, bathroom, toilet, kitchen) can significantly increase the economic efficiency of old-type apartments. In apartments with less than fifty square meters of living space, economic efficiency forces us to replace the kitchen with a "kitchen element," and to combine the bathrooms and showers of multiple apartments into a shared one.

4. The economically advantageous small apartment (*melkaia kvartira*) is brought to the fore by our social conditions in the first Five-Year Plan.

5. An apartment with twenty-seven square meters of living space can be designed to the same coefficient as an apartment with fifty-four square meters of living space. Analysis of the curves of our diagram shows that we can push even further in this direction. To do this, we must move toward new methods of housing solutions.

6. Type F represents an important transition to communal housing, as it responds to the social process of family differentiation and encourages the use of collective premises.

7. The design solution for the residential cell (*tipa zhiloi iacheki*) leads to the solution for the residential block and residential area.

8. We strive to achieve the following qualities in housing:

    1. Light in all areas
    2. Through ventilation—two exposures
    3. Orientation of all bedrooms to one side of the building
    4. Size of the rooms according to the number of people living in them
    5. Size and shape of rooms from accurate accounting of household and labor processes
    6. Equipment of the highest possible quality
    7. Ideal room proportions
    8. Rational color scheme for all surfaces

9. The constructive study of housing should be based on the principle of maximum standardization of all elements and should strive for the industrialization of the building industry. Lightweight elements, possibly manufactured in a factory during winter, should be able to be installed on site with unskilled labor."

In the full article, each of these nine points is followed by a more robust explanation of the criteria in question. M. Ia. Ginzburg, "Problemy tipizatsii zhil'ia RSFSR," *Sovremennaia arkhitektura*, no. 1 (1929): 4–6.

11. Ginzburg, "Problemy tipizatsii zhil'ia RSFSR," 6.

12. The celebrated Narkomfin (Commissariat of Finance) Communal House, with its innovative skip-stop section, combined Stroikom's tiny Type F units with the larger Type K that had two bedrooms and a full kitchen, making it capable of accommodating families. The anthropologist Victor Buchli has written extensively about the Narkomfin Building in Victor Buchli, "Moisei Ginzburg's Narkomfin Communal House in Moscow: Contesting the Social and Material World," *Journal of the Society of Architectural Historians* 57, no. 2 (1998):

160–81; and Victor Buchli, *An Archaeology of Socialism* (Oxford: Berg, 1999). A recent renovation of the Narkomfin Building led by Moisei Ginzburg's grandson, architect Alexey Ginzburg, is chronicled in Alexey Ginzburg, *Dom narkomfina restavratsiia, 2016–2020* (Moscow: Departament kul'turnogo naslediia goroda Moskvy, 2020). https://www.mos.ru/upload/documents/files/3458/Narkomphin.pdf?fbclid=IwAR2VKSV1wjZ4U6a9CAYlc6vzjc6q-gDuW8eyFbCnHBDmsxoQZgpgj40e3M8.

13. Tsentral'nyi bank kommunal'nogo khozaistva i zhilishchnogo stroitel'stva, *Proekty rabochikh zhilishch* (Moscow: Izdanie tsekombanka, 1929), 7, 12.

14. Tsentral'nyi bank kommunal'nogo khozaistva, 8.

15. Tsentral'nyi bank kommunal'nogo khozaistva, 9, 12.

16. The Socialist Resettlement Section, founded in September 1930, was made up of K. N. Afanasev, M. O. Barshch, V. N. Vladimirov, M. Ia. Ginzburg, G. A. Zundblat, I. I. Leonidov, I. F. Milinis, A. L. Pasternak, G. G. Savinov, N. B. Sokolov, designer S. V. Orlovskii, sociologist M. A. Okhitovich, economist G. B. Puzis, and transportation expert Iu. N. Loran. I. A. Kazus', *Sovetskaia arkhitektura 1920-kh godov: Organizatsiia proektirovaniia* (Moscow: Progress-Traditsiia, 2009), 275.

17. TsDAMLM, f. 8, po. 1, od. zb. 260, ark. 2–5.

18. TsDAVO, f. 5, po. 3, od. zb. 2085, ark. 13–25.

19. TsDAVO, f. 5, po. 3, od. zb. 2085, ark. 13.

20. L. M. Sabsovich, *Sotsialisticheskie goroda* (Moscow: Gosizdat RSFSR "Moskovskii rabochii," 1930), 39.

21. "O rabote po perestroike byta (Postanovlenie TsK RKP(b) ot 16 Maia 1930 goda)," *Pravda*, May 29, 1930.

22. TsDAVO, f. 5, po. 3, od. zb. 2085, ark. 13, rev.

23. TsDAVO, f. 5, po. 3, od. zb. 2085, ark. 27.

24. Tsentral'nyi bank kommunal'nogo khozaistva, 15.

25. Aleshin was born in Kyiv, Ivanitskii in Chernihiv. Ivanitskii graduated from technical high school (*real'noe uchilishche*) in Kharkiv in 1898, before matriculating at the Institute of Civil Engineers in St. Petersburg.

26. Aleshin did not enter either of these competitions. Magnitogorsk competition materials are at TsDAMLM, f. 8, po. 1, od. zb. 431, while TsDAMLM, f. 8, po. 1, od. zb. 421 holds the Stalingrad Competition entries.

27. Pavel Aleshin's copy of into *K probleme stroitel'stva sotsialisticheskogo goroda* is signed by him on the flyleaf and hand dated March 7, 1930, marking overlap with the KhTZ design process.

28. A. U. Zelenko, "Stroitel'stvo sotsialisticheskikh gorodov," in *K probleme stroitel'stva sotsialisticheskogo goroda*, ed. Gosplan SSSR (Moscow: Izdatel'stvo "Planovoe Khoziaistvo," 1930), 10.

29. Zelenko, "Stroitel'stvo sotsialisticheskikh gorodov," 14–15.

30. N. A. Miliutin, *Sotsgorod: The Problem of Building Socialist Cities* (Cambridge: MIT Press, 1974), 71.

31. Miliutin, *Sotsgorod*, 65.

32. The origins of the Linear City are in Madrid, where the idea was first diagrammed by the urban planner Arturo Soria y Mata in 1882. In Soria y Mata's scheme, however, the linear city did not replace the urban center but rather provided a way for industrial and residential satellites to be rationally extended and contained.

33. TsDAMLM, f. 8, po. 1, od. zb. 260, ark. 13–16.

34. James C. Scott, *Seeing Like a State: How Certain Schemes to Improve the Human Condition Have Failed*, Yale Agrarian Studies (New Haven: Yale University Press, 1998), 82.

35. Scott, *Seeing Like a State*, 82.

36. TsDAVO, f. 5, po. 3, od. zb. 2085, ark. 16.

37. These area targets were set in February 1930. TsDAVO, f. 5, po. 3, od. zb. 2085, ark. 17.

38. Shpara, *Zapiski arkhitektora*, 22.

39. Shpara, *Zapiski arkhitektora*, 20. Around the time that the first Stroikom unit designs were being rolled out, in May 1928, the Constructivists, under the aegis of OSA, held their first congress. Reportage about the larger and more geographically heterogeneous First All-Union Congress of OSA in Moscow in 1929 that Shpara attended can be found in "Pervyi s''ezd OSA," *Sovremennaia arkhitektura*, no. 1 (1929): 38.

40. Shpara, *Zapiski arkhitektora*, 20.

41. The concision of the architects' brief stands in contrast to most of the voluminous official documents prepared in advance of the New Kharkiv *sotsgorod* design that tally, on average, one hundred or more pages of exhaustive text, worked and reworked demographics, justifications, and charts. UkrGirpomez, NKVD UkrSSR, and Giprograd were some of the parties engaged in defining New Kharkiv, but often the project briefs found in the archives are devoid of identifying information, including dates, signatories or the organizations involved in their formulation.

42. TsDAMLM, f. 8, po. 1, od. zb. 265, ark. 4.

43. TsDAMLM, f. 8, po. 1, od. zb. 265, ark. 3.

44. TsDAMLM, f. 8, po. 1, od. zb. 261, ark. 62.

45. Shpara, Zapiski *arkhitektora*, 22.

46. Shpara, Zapiski *arkhitektora*, 22.

47. TsDAMLM, f. 8, po. 1, od. zb. 265, ark. 5.

48. TsDAMLM, f. 8, po. 1, od. zb. 265, ark. 5.

49. I. N. Baltuzevich, *Opyt i uroki stroitel'stva KhTZ* (Moscow: Gosstroiizdat, 1932), 10.

50. Shpara, *Zapiski arkhitektora*, 24.

51. There are roughly thirty-eight *zhilkombinat* blocks in this site plan. If each held 1,500 residents, this plan would support a *sotsgorod* population of 57,000, a number well in excess of the original demographic target of 36,500.

52. Shpara, *Zapiski arkhitektora*, 24.

53. TsDAVO, f.5, o.3, d.2085, l.16.

54. TsDAVO, f.5, o.3, d.2085, l.20.

55. Another design from 1934 shows a settlement-wide House of Culture (*dvorets kul'tury*) with stripped neoclassical ornamentation that marks it as belonging to early Socialist Realism.

56. TsDAVO, f.5, o.3, d.2085, l. 25.

57. Shpara noted that "the project was envisioned with enclosed glass passageways between buildings on the second floor, arranged so that children could walk to school without putting on outerwear, as could adults going to the store, canteen, or club. Unfortunately, that idea was not realized in the built project." Shpara, *Zapiski arkhitektora*, 24.

58. This data is derived from the blueprint. Blocks 1 and 5 each had fourteen buildings; blocks 2 and 4 had sixteen buildings; and block 3 had eighteen, adding up to a total of seventy-eight buildings. Each *zhilkombinat* (residential block) was intended to serve 1,500 residents.

59. TsDAVO, f. 5, o. 3, d. 2085, l. 17 verso.

60. Timothy Sosnovy, "The Soviet Housing Situation Today," *Soviet Studies* 11, no. 1 (1959): 3.

61. Timothy J. Colton, *Moscow: Governing the Socialist Metropolis*, Russian Research Center Studies (Cambridge: Belknap Press of Harvard University Press, 1995), 222.

62. Buchli, *An Archaeology of Socialism*, 67.

63. Eventually, residents also knocked down walls to make larger units and build the desired kitchens. From an anecdote shared in 2012 by the architectural historian Jenia Gubkina, whose grandmother lived at New Kharkiv.

64. TsDAMLM, f. 8, po. 1, od. zb. 265, ark. 4–5.

65. "O rabote po perestroike byta (Postanovlenie TsK RKP(b) ot 16 Maia 1930 goda)."

66. TsDAMLM, f. 8, po. 1, od. zb. 265, ark. 4–5.

67. Baltuzevich, *Opyt i uroki stroitel'stva KhTZ*, 11.

68. The original siting document notes that the workforce would come largely from the city and local villages. TsDAMLM, f. 8, po. 1, od. zb. 265. See also V. Vol's'kyi and B. Borfin, *Kharkivskii traktornyi zavod i novyi Kharkiv* (Kharkiv: Vydnavnytsvo mis'krady, 1930).

69. The term is taken from the Russian word for Saturday, *subbota*, when these efforts first took place in 1919. The history of the first *subbotnik* can be found in William Chase, "Voluntarism, Mobilisation and Coercion: Subbotniki 1919–1921," *Soviet Studies* 41, no. 1 (1989): 111–28. *Subbotniki* and *vosresniki* (Sunday workdays) were often required of workers on projects for the so-called social good.

70. Strong, *From Stalingrad to Kuzbas*, 30–31.

71. Beal was a communist and National Textile Workers Union organizer who was convicted (along with three others) for the death of the Gastonia, North Carolina, police chief, who was killed breaking a picket line organized by Beal. Beal fled to the Soviet Union in 1930, and returned to the United States in 1933. He served his jail time starting in 1938, and was pardoned in 1942. From the Guide to the State of North Carolina vs. Fred Erwin Beal et al. (1929), http://n2t.net/ark:/99166/w6qv4r7q. See also "All Convicted at Gastonia Trail," *New York Times*, October 22, 1929.

72. Fred E. Beal, *Proletarian Journey: New England, Gastonia, Moscow* (New York: Hillman-Curl 1937), 280.

73. *Foreign Workers in a Soviet Tractor Plant* (Moscow: Co-operative Publishing Society of Foreign Workers in the USSR, 1933), 8.

74. Strong, *From Stalingrad to Kuzbas*, 30.

75. Leon A. Swajian, "Building the Kharkov Tractor Plant," *Economic Review of the Soviet Union* 6, September 15 (1931): 414.

76. Odes′ka kinofabryka VUFKU, *Priskorennia buduvannia traktorobudu—Veletens′ka peremoha sotsialistychno budivnytstva* (1930), no. 14/180. TsDKFFA, Archive numbers 1429, 1447, 1469, 1483, 1486, 1516, 1517, 1529.

77. The "large sky" shot of the Ukrainian countryside, then in the throes of agricultural collectivization, is a framing hallmark of the film director Oleksandr Dovzhenko's *Earth* (*Zemlia*), also from 1930.

78. Eve Garrette Grady, *Seeing Red* (New York: Brewer, Warren & Putnam, 1931), 46–47.

79. Zara Witkin and Michael Gelb, *An American Engineer in Stalin's Russia: The Memoirs of Zara Witkin, 1932–1934* (Berkeley: University of California Press, 1991), 53.

80. Witkin and Michael Gelb, *An American Engineer in Stalin's Russia*, 53–54.

81. Baltuzevich, *Opyt i uroki stroitel′stva KhTZ*, 23.

82. Beal, *Proletarian Journey*, 283.

83. Beal, *Proletarian Journey*, 287.

84. Beal, *Proletarian Journey*, 294.

85. Applebaum, *Red Famine*, 204.

86. Beal, *Proletarian Journey*, 296.

87. Beal, *Proletarian Journey*, 305–8.

88. The site was commandeered from a collective farm. The funding was forcibly extracted from the surrounding countryside. The peasants for whom the tractors were purportedly being assembled were being starved in a power play from the top of the Soviet hierarchy.

89. Mark Meerovich, "Giprogor: Organizatsiia i Liudi," *Archi.Ru*, 2014, https://archi.ru/russia/54884/istoriya-otechestvennogo-gradostroitelstva-giprogor-1929-1932-gg.

90. Shpara, *Zapiski arkhitektora*, 24–25.

Conclusion

Epigraph: Ernst May, "City Building in the USSR," *Das Neue Rußland* 8–9 (1931). Translated by Eric Dluhosch in El Lissitzky, *Russia: An Architecture for World Revolution* (Cambridge: MIT Press, 1984), 190.

1. Recent Russian scholarship on this early period of Soviet urban planning, like the exemplary work produced by Mark Meerovich, Dmitrii Khmelnitskii, and Evgeniia Konysheva, arrives at similar conclusions. Manfredo Tafuri, *Modern Architecture*, ed. Francesco Dal Co (New York: Electa/Rizzoli, 1986), 190.

2. "City Councillor May's Russian Plans," *Bauwelt*, no. 36 (1930): 174.

3. "O rabote po perestroike byta (Postanovlenie TsK RKP(b) ot 16 Maia 1930 goda)," *Pravda*, May 29, 1930. Danilo Udovicki-Selb also challenges the conventionally accepted narrative of the "death of the Soviet avant-garde" in 1932, arguing that certain architects continued working experimentally in the USSR until 1938. Danilo Udovicki-Selb, *Soviet Architectural Avant-Gardes: Architecture and Stalin's Revolution from Above, 1928–1938* (London: Bloomsbury, 2020).

4. "By means of the concrete experience in Moscow we shall solve problems of city development for the whole of the Soviet Union." L. M. Kaganovich, *Socialist Reconstruction of Moscow and Other Cities in the U.S.S.R.*, no. 159 (New York: International Publishers, 1931), 61.

5. Kaganovich, *Socialist Reconstruction of Moscow*, 83.

6. An overview of the 1935 General Plan for Moscow can be found in Katherine Zubovich, *Moscow Monumental: Soviet Skyscrapers and Urban Life under High Stalinism* (Princeton: Princeton University Press, 2020), 22–27. Also see Koos Bosma and Helma Hellinga, eds., *Mastering the City: North European City Planning, 1900–2000* (Rotterdam: NAI Publishers, 1998), 2:232–34.

7. For more on *mikroraiony*, see Blair A. Ruble, "From Khruchsheby to Korobki," in *Russian Housing in the Modern Age*, ed. William Craft Brumfield (Washington, DC: Woodrow Wilson Center Press, 1993); and Philipp Meuser and Dmiitrij Zadorin, *Towards a Typology of Soviet Mass Housing: Prefabrication in the USSR 1955–1991* (Berlin: DOM Publishers, 2015).

8. There is repeated mention of "American colonies" in Baku similar to those found in Moscow, Leningrad, and Kharkiv, but no memoirs of Bakuvian expats have been found to date. Eve Garrette Grady, *Seeing Red* (New York: Brewer, Warren & Putnam, 1931), e.g., 171.

9. For an extended discussion of this issue, see Maria Gough, "John Heartfield's Biography of Soviet Petroleum," in *Magazines, Modernity and War*, ed. Jordana Mendelson (Madrid: Ministerio de Cultura, Museo Nacional Centro de Arte Reina Sofía, 2008).

10. "Dedicated to Soviet Petroleum Industry," *USSR in Construction*, no. 12 (1931).

11. Just as we should be circumspect about the transparency of Soviet publications, the motives of disillusioned communist fellow-travelers must also be considered when assessing the efficacy of memoirs by these foreigners who returned home.

12. John Scott and Stephen Kotkin, *Behind the Urals: An American Worker in Russia's City of Steel* (Bloomington: Indiana University Press, 1989), 209–10.

13. Scott and Stephen Kotkin, *Behind the Urals*.

14. The "brigade" of technical experts from Moscow to Magnitogorsk consisted of delegates from Narkomkhoz RSFSR (People's Commissariat of Municipal Services of the Russian Republic), Narkomtiazhprom SSSR (People's Commissariat of Heavy Industry of the USSR), and Narkomzdrav RSFSR (People's Commissariat of Health Protection of the Russian Republic).

15. GARF, f. A-314, o. 1, d. 7674, l. 95.

16. GARF, f. A-314, o. 1, d. 7674, l. 95.

17. The archival newspaper clipping indicates only the year, 1931. GARF, f. P-7952, o. 5, d. 178, l. 92.

18. There were also 1,174 reports of spotted fever in 1931. Stephen Kotkin, *Magnetic Mountain: Stalinism as a Civilization* (Berkeley: University of California Press, 1995), 464n177.

19. Kalmykov was an actual peasant turned Soviet worker at Magnitogorsk, who met and married a German woman there. Stephen Kotkin discovered that Kalmykov—despite his heroic-worker status—did not survive the Stalinist purges. He was arrested in 1938 and shot as a German spy. Kotkin, *Magnetic Mountain*, 433n43.

20. Kotkin, *Magnetic Mountain*, chap. 5: "Speaking Bolshevik."

21. Karsten Harries, *The Ethical Function of Architecture* (Cambridge: MIT Press, 1998); Thomas Fisher, *The Architecture of Ethics* (London: Routledge, 2019); Tom Spector, *The Ethical Architect* (New York: Princeton Architectural Press, 2001).

22. Peggy Deamer, and Phillip Bernstein, eds., *Building (in) the Future: Recasting Labor in Architecture* (New Haven: Yale School of Architecture, 2010). Katie Lloyd Thomas, Tilo Amhoff, and Nick Beech, eds., *Industries of Architecture*, vol. 11, Critiques (Abingdon: Routledge, 2016).

23. Lev Kopelev, *To Be Preserved Forever*, ed. and trans. Anthony Austin (Philadelphia: Lippincott, 1977), 11–12.

24. Nikita Khrushchev, "On the Extensive Introduction of Industrial Methods, Improving the Quality and Reducing the Cost of Construction (December 7, 1954)," *Volume* 21, no. 3 (2009): 26. See also Ruble, "From Khruchsheby to Korobki," 235.

25. Daria Bocharnikova, "Inventing Socialist Modern: A History of the Architectural Profession in the USSR, 1932–1971" (PhD diss., European University Institute, 2014), 125.

26. A.I. Gegello, *Iz tvoricheskogo opyta: Vozniknovennie i razvitie arkhitekturnogo zamysla* (Leningrad: Gosudarstvennoe izd. literatury po stroitel'stvu, arkhitekture i stroitel'nym materialam, 1962), http://ussr.totalarch.com/from_creative_experience_alexander_gegello.

27. In their typological catalog of Soviet mass housing built between 1955 and 1991, Philipp Meuser and Dimitrij Zadorin track and enumerate the downsizing of Stalinist era design standards to achieve Khrushchev's goals. In 1955, the minimum clear ceiling height for Soviet housing was reduced from 3 meters to 2.5 meters, and the minimum kitchen area was slashed from 7.5 square meters to 4.5 square meters. Meuser, *Towards a Typology of Soviet Mass Housing*, 21.

28. NER is an acronym taken from *Novyi element rasselenia*, or New Unit of Settlement, the original urban concept developed by the group.

29. A. Baburov and A. Gutnov, *The Ideal Communist City*, I Press Series on the Human Environment (New York: G. Braziller, 1971), 27. The original book, published in Russian, is Andrey Baburov, Alexey Gutnov, Georgiy Dumenton, I. Lezhava, S. Sadovskiy, and Z. Kharitonova, *Noviy element rasselenia: Na puti k novomu gorodu* (Moscow: Stroiizdat, 1966). For an extensive discussion of the book, see Bocharnikova, "Inventing Socialist Modern," 214–40.

30. The quote continues, "whereas a single building was once perceived as a unique spatial composition, we are now ready to conceive a unified spatial field, which includes the whole community." Baburov and Gutnov, *The Ideal Communist City*, 164.

31. Baburov and Gutnov, *The Ideal Communist City*, 154.

32. "Kakoi raion posovetuete priezzhaiushchemu zhit v Khar'kov?," https://www.kharkovforum.com/archive/index.php/t-1564096.html. A 2010 national newspaper poll cited KhTZ as one of the ten most dysfunctional and dangerous residential communities in all of Ukraine. "Korrespondent sostavil top-10 samikh neblagopoluchnykh zhilmassiv v Ukraine," http://korrespondent.net/ukraine/events/1058465-korrespondent-sostavil-top-10-samyh-neblagopoluchnyh-zhilmassivov-v-ukraine2010.

33. Jenia Gubkina, Facebook thread on KhTZ, February 25, 2014, https://www.facebook.com/jenia.gubkina/posts/475306642595275.

34. In the United States, for instance, publications like *USSR in Construction*, the *International Pamphlets* series, and *Co-operative Publishing Society of Foreign Workers in the USSR* spread news of the first Five-Year Plan construction projects.

35. Charles Palmer's autobiography, written twenty years after the trip, is useful for a broad sense of his 1934 European housing tour itinerary. Charles F. Palmer, *Adventures of a Slum Fighter* (Atlanta: Tupper and Love, 1955).

36. Charles Palmer, "Questionnaire Regarding Low-Cost Housing in Moscow," in *Charles F. Palmer Papers, 1903–1973*, Emory University, Stuart A. Rose Manuscript, Archives & Rare Book Library, 1934, Box 35, Folder 1.

BIBLIOGRAPHY

Primary Sources

Archives and Research Libraries

Azerbaijan State Film and Photo Documents Archive

Bentley Historical Library, University of Michigan, Albert Kahn Associates records

Canadian Centre for Architecture

Central State Archives and Museum of Literature and Art of Ukraine

Central State Archives of Supreme Bodies of Power and Government of Ukraine

Central State Cine-Photo-Phono Archives of Ukraine, named after G. S. Pshenychnyi

Central State Scientific and Technical Archives of Ukraine

Central State Scientific Architectural and Construction Library of Ukraine, named after V. G. Zabolotnyi

Gipromez Metallurgic Design Institute of Magnitogorsk Archive

Kharkiv State Scientific Library, named after V. G. Korolenko

Magnitogorsk Local History Museum

N. A. Nekrasov Library

Russian State Archive of Economics

Russian State Archive of Literature and Art

Russian State Archive of Documentary Films and Photographs

Russian State Library, Division of Cartographical Publications

Scientific Technical Library of the Magnitogorsk Metallurgic Factory

State Archive of the Azerbaijan Republic

State Archive of the Kharkiv Oblast

State Archive of the Russian Federation

State Museum of Architecture, named after A. V. Shchusev

Newspapers, Periodicals, and Magazines

Arkhitektura SSSR

Das Neue Frankfurt

Detroit Free Press

Detroit News

Economic Review of the Soviet Union

Ekonomicheskaia zhizn'

Ezhegodnik MAO

Izvestiia

Nashe stroitel'stvo

New York Times

Planovoe khoziaistvo

Pravda

Sotsialisticheskuiu rekonstrukstiiu gorodov (SoReGor)

Sovetskaia arkhitektura

Sovremennaia arkhitektura

SSSR na stroike / USSR in Construction

Stroitel'stvo Moskvy

Stroitel'naia promyshlennost'

Stroitel'stvo i akhitektura (Ukraine)

Books, Pamphlets, and Articles

Aleshin, P. F. *O sovremennoi shkol'noi arkhitekture: Otdel'nyi ottisk doklada avtora 4-mu s"iezdu Russ-kikh zodchikh*. St. Petersburg: Gos. tipografiia, 1911.

Amtorg Trading Corporation. *Soviet Oil Industry: A Compilation of Statements Regarding Purchases of Soviet Oil by the Standard Oil Company of New York and the Vacuum Oil Co.: Statistics of the Oil Industry of the U.S.S.R.* New York: The Corporation, 1928.

Azneft. *Obzor Azerbaidzhanskoi neftianoi promyshlennosti za dva goda nationalizatsii: 1920–1922*. Baku: Azneft, 1922.

———. *Obzor Azerbaidzhanskoi neftianoi promyshlennosti za piat' let nationalizatsii: 1920–1925*. Baku: Azneft, 1925.

Baburov, A., and A. Gutnov. *The Ideal Communist City*. I Press Series on the Human Environment. New York: G. Braziller, 1971.

Baburov, Andrey, Alexey Gutnov, Georgiy Dumenton, I. Lezhava, S. Sadovskiy, and Z. Kharitonova. *Noviy element rasseleniia: Na puti k novomu gorodu*. Moscow: Stroiizdat, 1966.

Baltuzevich, I. N. *Opyt i uroki stroitel'stva KhTZ*. Moscow: Gosstroiizdat, 1932.

Barkhin, G. B. *Sovremennye rabochie zhilishcha*. Moscow: Voprosy truda, 1925.

Barshch, M., V. Vladimirov, M. Okhitovich, and N. Solnikov. "Magnitogor'e." *Sovremennaia arkhitektura* no. 1–2 (1930): 38–57.

Beal, Fred E. *Foreign Workers in a Soviet Tractor Plant*. Moscow: Co-operative Publishing Society of Foreign Workers in the USSR, 1933.

——. *Proletarian Journey: New England, Gastonia, Moscow*. New York: Hillman-Curl 1937.

Benjamin, Walter, and Gary Smith. *Moscow Diary*. Cambridge: Harvard University Press, 1986.

Bernatskii, L. N. "Kratkii obzor deiatel'nosti stroisektsii Gosplana." *Planovoe khoziaistvo*, no. 3 (1923): 56–58.

——. "Osnovy planirovaniia stroitel'stva." *Planovoe khoziaistvo*, no. 1–2 (1924): 3–9.

——. "Sovremennoe polozhenie zhilishchnogo voprosa." *Planovoe khoziaistvo*, no. 9 (1926): 76–87.

——. "Stroitel'noe proizvodstvo i promyshlennost' stroitel'nykh materialov v piatiletnom plane." *Planovoe khoziaistvo*, no. 3 (1929): 214–22.

——. "Zhilishchnyi krizis i zhilishchnoe stroitel'stvo." *Planovoe khoziaistvo*, no. 6 (1925): 36–55.

Bessonov, S. A. "Problemy prostranstva v perspektivnom plane." *Planovoe khoziaistvo*, no. 6 (1928): 63–89.

Block, Alexander. "Land Problems and Town-Planning in Soviet Russia." *Garden Cities* 17, no. 3 (1927): 82–84.

Blokhin, P. "Planirovka zhilykh kvartalov sotsgoroda. Opyt chetyrekhletnei raboty standartproekta." *Arkhitektura SSSR* no. 5 (1933): 4–8.

Borovoi, A. A. *Planirovochnaia set' bol'shoi Moskvy*. Moscow: Izdatel'stvo Mosoblispolkoma, 1930.

Chase, Stuart. *A New Deal*. New York: Macmillan, 1932.

CIAM. *Die Wohnung Für das Existenzminimum*. Documents of Modern Architecture. Nendeln: Kraus Reprint, 1979.

Dikanskii, M. G. *Postroika gorodov: Ikh plan i krasota*. Petrograd: Izd. N.P. Karbasnikova, 1915.

Dokuchaev, N. "Konkurs na planirovku Magnitogorska." *Stroitel'stvo Moskvy*, no. 4 (1930): 25–28.

Eingorn, A. L. *Ekonomia zhilishchnogo stroitel'stva*. Khar'kov: Gosizdat "Khoziiastvo Ukrainy," 1930.

——. "Pereplanirovka i arkhitekturnaia rekonstruktsiia Khar'kova." *Arkhitektura SSSR*, no. 2 (1934): 38–51.

——. "Skhema pereplanirovki Khar'kova." *Arkhitektura SSSR*, no. 6 (1933): 12–14.

Enakiev, F. E. *Zadachi preobrazovaniia S. Peterburga*. St. Petersburg, 1912.

Engels, Friedrich. *Anti-Dühring. Herr Eugen Dühring's Revolution in Science*. Leipzig, 1878, https://www.marxists.org/archive/marx/works/1877/anti-duhring/.

——. *The Condition of the Working Class in England*. Leipzig, 1845, https://www.marxists.org/archive/marx/works/1845/condition-working-class/.

——. *The Housing Question*. Leipzig, 1872, https://www.marxists.org/archive/marx/works/1872/housing-question/.

——. *The Origin of the Family, Private Property and the State*. Hottingen-Zurich, 1884, https://www.marxists.org/archive/marx/works/1884/origin-family/.

Ensh, Arnol'd Karlovich. *Plan i zastroika gorodov*. St. Petersburg: Tipografiia SPB gradonachal'stva, 1914.

Evseev, M. *Kodeks pravil planirovki naselennykh punktov*. Khar'kov: Gosudarstvennoe izdatel'stvo Ukrainy, 1930.

Fidrovskii. "Zhytlove budivnytstvo KhTZ na pershomu ioho etapi." *Budivnytstvo*, no. 6 (1932): 200–204.

Frenkel', Z. G. *Osnovy obshchego gorodskogo blagoustroistva*. Moscow: Glavnoe upravlenie komnal'nogo khoziaistva NKVD, 1926.

Fülöp-Miller, Rene. *The Mind and Face of Bolshevism: An Examination of Cultural Life in Soviet Russia*. London: G.P. Putnam's Sons, 1927.

Funkhouser, H. Gray. "Historical Development of the Graphical Representation of Statistical Data." *Osiris* 3 (1937): 269–404.

Gan, A. "Kommunisticheskii gorod (v planovykh razrabotkakh konstruktivistov)." *Teatral'naia Moskva*, no. 40 (1922): 5–6.

Ginzburg, M. Ia. "Novye metody arkhitekturnogo myshleniia." *Sovremennaia arkhitektura*, no. 1 (1926): 1–4.

——. "Problemy tipizatsii zhil'ia RFSFR." *Sovremennaia arkhitektura*, no. 1 (1929): 4–6.

——. *Ritm v arkhitekture*. Moscow: Izd-vo "Sredi kollektsionerov," 1923.

——. "Sotsialisticheskoe rasselenie: Detsentralizatsiia krupneishikh gorodov." *Ekonomicheskaia zhizn'*, December 7, 1929, 3.

——. *Style and Epoch*. Moscow: Fontanka, 2019.

——. "Tselevaia ustanovka v sovremennoi arkhitekture." *Sovremennaia arkhitektura*, no. 1 (1927): 4–10.

——. *Zhilishche*. Moscow: Gosstroiizdat, 1934.

Gordon, A. "Problema plana i kapital'noe stroitel'stvo." *Planovoe khoziaistvo*, no. 2 (1928): 64–78.

Gorfunkel', V. M., Aleksandr Mikhailovich Rodchenko, and Varvara Fedorovna Stepanova. *Moskva rekonstruiruetsia*. Moscow: Izostat, 1938.

Gorky, Maksim. "Po soiuzu sovetov." In *Polnoe sobranie sochinenii: Khudozhestvennye proizvedeniia v dvadtsati piati tomakh*. Moscow: Izd-vo "Nauka," 1974.

Gorskii, I. E. "Organizatsiia zhilishchnogo stroitel'stva i raboshii biudzhet." *Planovoe khoziaistvo*, no. 10 (1927): 100–21.

Gosplan-SSSR. *K probleme stroitel'stva sotsialisticheskogo goroda*. Moscow: Izd-vo planovoe khoziaistvo, 1930.

Gosplan RSFSR. *Rekonstruktsiia gorodov SSSR, 1933–1937*. Moscow: Izd-vo standartizatsii i ratsionalizatsiia, 1933.

Grady, Eve Garrette. *Seeing Red*. New York: Brewer, Warren & Putnam, 1931.

Gramsci, Antonio. *Prison Notebooks*. Translated by J. A. Buttigieg. New York: Columbia University Press, 2007.

Grinko, G. T. *The Five-Year Plan of the Soviet Union, a Political Interpretation*. New York: International Publishers, 1930.

Gurevich, A. I. "Bolezni kapital'nogo stroitel'stva." *Planovoe khoziaistvo*, no. 12 (1928): 17–33.

Gvakhariia, G. "Bol'nye voprosy kapital'nogo stroitel'stva." *Planovoe khoziaistvo*, no. 7 (1928): 86–100.

Henry, James Dodds. *Baku: An Eventful History*. London: A. Constable & Co., 1905.

Hindus, Maurice. "Henry Ford Conquers Russia." *The Outlook*, no. 29 June (1927): 282.

——. "Pinch Hitter for the Soviets." *American Magazine*, no. April (1932): 31–33, 134–36.

Howard, Ebenezer. *To-Morrow: A Peaceful Path to Real Reform*. Edited by Dennis Hardy and Colin Ward. London: Routledge, 2003.

Ilf, Ilya, and Evgeny Petrov. *The Twelve Chairs: A Novel*. Translated by Anne O. Fisher. Northwestern World Classics. Evanston, IL: Northwestern University Press, 2011.

Ilin, M. *New Russia's Primer: The Story of the Five-Year Plan*. Translated by George S. Counts and Nucia P. Lodge. Boston: Houghton Mifflin, 1931.

Il'in, L. A., ed. *Arkhitekturnye problemy planirovki Baku*. Moscow: Izdatel'stvo vsesoyuznoi akademii arkhitektury, 1937.

Il'in, M. *Rasskaz o velikom plane*. 3rd ed. Moscow: Ogiz—molodaia gvardiia, 1931.

Ivanitskii, A. P. "O ratsional'noi planirovke gorodov." *Stroitel'naia promyshlennost'*, no. 4 (1926): 298–302.

———. "O razmerakh kvartalov v novykh planirovkakh." *Stroitel'naia promyshlennost'*, no. 12 (1929): 1064–68.

———. "Planirovka goroda Baku." *Gigiena i epidemiologiia*, no. 4 (1925): 93–95.

Ivanitsky, A. "The Development of City Planning in the Soviet Union." *American City* 66, August (1941): 44–47, 81.

Ivanov, V. F. *Goroda-sady i poselki dlia rabochikh: Planirovka, vodosnabzhenie, kanalizatsiia*. Leningrad: Akademicheskoe izdatel'stvo, 1925.

Kaganovich, L. M. *Socialist Reconstruction of Moscow and Other Cities in the U.S.S.R.* Williams College Propaganda Pamphlet Series. New York: International Publishers, 1931.

Karpov, A. M. "Stroitel'stvo v perspektivnom plane." *Planovoe khoziaistvo*, no. 1 (1928): 104–11.

Kas'yanov, O. "Rekonstruktsiya tsentra Khar'kova." *Arkhitektura SSSR*, no. 2 (1934): 52–59.

Kataev, Valentin. *Time, Forward!* Bloomington: Indiana University Press, 1976.

Kollontai, Alexandra. "Communism and the Family." Translated by Alix Holt. In *Selected Writings of Alexandra Kollontai*. London: Allison & Busby, 1977.

———. *Love of Worker Bees*. Translated by Cathy Porter. Chicago: Academy Press, 1978.

Kozhanyi, P. *Rabochee zhilishche i byt*. Moscow: Izdanie VTsSPS, 1924.

Krasil'nokov, N. "Problemy sovremennoi arkhitektury." *Sovremennaia arkhitektura*, no. 6 (1928): 170–76.

Krugliakov, Yu. G. *Rekonstruktsiia zhilikh kvartalov*. Edited by N. M. Ushakova. Leningrad: Gosudarstvennoe izdatel'stvo standardizatsiia i ratsionalizatsiia, 1933.

Krzhizhanovskii, G. "Zametki o planirovanii." *Revoliutsiia i kul'tura*, no. 8 (1929): 27–33.

Kuz'min, V. "O rabochem zhilishchnom stroitel'stve." *Sovremennaia arkhitektura*, no. 3 (1928): 82–83.

Kviring, E. I. "Osnovy voprosy plana kapital'nogo stroitel'stva na 1928/29." *Planovoe khoziaistvo*, no. 10, 11 (1928): 7–27, 18–37.

Larin, Yu. "Pokazatel'naia rol' Magnitogorska v kommunal'nom i zhilishchnom khoziaistve." *SoReGor*, no. 1 (1932): 33–36.

Lenin, Vladimir Il'ich. "Karl Marx: A Brief Biographical Sketch with an Exposition of Marxism." In *Collected Works*, vol. 21, 43–91. Moscow: Progress Publishers, 1974. https://www.marxists.org/archive/lenin/works/1914/granat/index.htm.

———. "The New Economic Policy and the Tasks of the Political Education Departments." *Report to The Second All-Russia Congress of Political Education Departments*, October 17, 1921. In *Collected Works*, vol. 33, 60–79. Moscow: Progress Publishers, 1965. https://www.marxists.org/archive/lenin/works/1921/oct/17.htm.

Lezhava, A. "Postanovlenie soveta narodnykh komissarov RSFSR: Po dokladu o stroitel'stve Magnitgorskogo kombinata i rabochego poselka pri nem." *Pravda*, November 11, 1929.

Lissitzky, El. *Russia: An Architecture for World Revolution*. Translated by Eric Dluhosch. Cambridge: MIT Press, 1984.

Lunin, B. *Goroda sotsializma i sotsialisticheskaia rekonstruktsiia byta*. Moscow: Tip. Mospoligrafa "Iskra Revoliutsii," 1930.

Marey, Etienne-Jules. *La Méthode Graphique Dans Les Sciences Expérimentales Et Principalement En Physiologie Et En Médecine*. Paris: G. Masson, 1885.

Markovnikov, N. V. *Zhilishchnoe stroitel'stvo za granitsei i v SSSR*. Biblioteka zhilkooperatora. Edited by V. Ia. Belousova. Vol. IV. Moscow: Tsentrozhilsoiuz, 1928.

Marx, Karl. "Theses on Feuerbach." In *Marx/Engels Selected Works*, vol. 1, 13–15. Moscow: Progress Publishers, 1969. https://www.marxists.org/archive/marx/works/1845/theses/theses.htm.

May, Ernst. "K proekty general'nogo plana Magnitorgoska." *Sovetskaia arkhitektura*, May–June (1933): 17–25.

Miliutin, N. A. "Bor'ba za novyi byt i sovetskii urbanizm." *Izvestiia*, October 29, 1929, 5.

——. *Sotsgorod: Problema stroitel'stva sotsialisticheskikh gorodov*. Moscow: Gosudarstvennoe izdatel'stvo, 1930.

——. *Sotsgorod: The Problem of Building Socialist Cities*. Cambridge: MIT Press, 1974.

Mumford, Lewis. "Regions—to Live In." *The Survey* 54 (1925): 151–52.

Nakhmanson, S. N., N. A. Volkov, M. Ia. Grissikom, D. I. Ravdinym, and A. N. Rozhanovich. *Sovremennoe stroitel'stvo Germanii. Pervaia zagranichnaia ekskursiia inzhenirov-stroitelei i arkhitektorov*. Moscow: Gostekhizdat, 1929.

Nelson, George. *Industrial Architecture of Albert Kahn, Inc.* New York: Architectural Book Publishing, 1939.

Okhitovich, M. "K probleme goroda." *Sovremennaia arkhitektura*, no. 4 (1929): 130–34.

——. "Ne gorod, a novyi tip rasseneniia." *Ekonomicheskaia zhizn'*, December 7, 1929, 3.

——. "Otchego gibnet gorod?" *Stroitel'stvo Moskvy*, no. 1 (1930): 9–11.

——. "Zametki po teorii rasseleniia." *Sovremennaia arkhitektura*, no. 1–2 (1930): 7–16.

Ostrovskii, Z. "Doma, ulitsy, bol'nitsy, transport, byt' Magnitogorska (zapisi velikikh stroek)." *SoRe-Gor*, no. 1 (1932): 53–56.

Pasternak, A. "Novye formy sovremennogo zhil'ya." *Sovremennaia arkhitektura*, no. 4–5 (1927): 125–29.

Petrov, N. N. "Amerikanskoe stroitel'stvo." *Planovoe khoziaistvo*, no. 6 (1929): 225–40.

Pokshishevskii, S. N. *Promyshlennyi gorod: Ego raschet i proektirovanie*. Leningrad: Gosudarstvennoe nauchno-tekhnicheskoe izdatel'stvo stroitel'noi industrii i sudostroeniia, 1932.

Rev, B. "Besplanovost' i anarkhiia v stroitel'stve gorodov." *Pravda*, November 4, 1929.

Sabsovich, L. *Goroda budushchego i organizatsiia sotsialisticheskogo byta*. Moscow: Gosudarstvennoe tekhnicheskoe izdatel'stvo, 1929.

——. "Problema goroda." *Planovoe khoziaistvo*, no. 7 (1929): 37–58.

——. *Sotsialisticheskie goroda*. Moscow: Gosizdat RSFSR "Moskovskii rabochii," 1930.

——. *SSSR cherez 15 let: Gipoteza generalnogo plana, kak plana postroeniia sotsializma v SSSR*. 2. izd. ed. Moscow: "Planovoe khoziastvo," 1929.

——. "'Vzbesivshiisia melkii burzhua' ili kommivoiazher avtomobil'noi firmy." *Ekonomicheskaia zhizn'*, December 20, 1929, 3.

Scott, John, and Stephen Kotkin. *Behind the Urals: An American Worker in Russia's City of Steel*. Bloomington: Indiana University Press, 1989.

Serebrovskii, A. P. *Neftianaia i gazovaia promyshlennost' v Amerike. Chast' pervaia*. Moscow: Tsentral'noe upravlenie pechati VSNKh, 1925.

Shibaev, D. E. "Za sotsialisticheskii gorod Magnitorgosk." *Sovetskaia arkhitektura*, May–June (1933): 25–30.

Shtange, A. "Planirovka Magnitogorska i ego raiona." *Planirovka i stroitel'stvo gorodov*, no. 10 (1934): 13–22.

Shub, I. V. "Stroitel'stva v gody vosstanovitel'nogo protsessa (1923/24–1926/27)." *Planovoe khoziaistvo*, no. 10 (1926): 43–56.

——. "Problemy stroitel'stva v kontrol'nykh tsifrakh na 1927/28 god." *Planovoe khoziaistvo*, no. 8 (1927): 135–56.

Shub, I. V., and Ia. I. Rabonovich. "Zhilishchnoe stroitel'stvo v pitatiletnem perspektivnom plane." *Planovoe khoziaistvo*, no. 1 (1928): 123–36.

Sitte, Camillo. *The Birth of Modern City Planning*. Edited by George R. Collins and Christiane Crasemann. New York: Rizzoli, 1986.

Smurgis, Iu. "Voprosy stroitel'nogo dela." *Planovoe khoziaistvo*, no. 11 (1928): 102–14.

Sosfenov, I. "Novyi Baku: Putevye zametki." *Arkhitektura SSSR*, no. 6 (1934): 36–45.

Strong, Anna Louise. *From Stalingrad to Kuzbas*. New York: International Pamphlets, 1932.

Strumilin, S. G. *Ocherki sovetskoi ekonomiki: Resursy i perspektivi*. Moscow: Gosudarstvennoe izdatel'stvo, 1928.

Swajian, Leon A. "Building the Kharkov Tractor Plant." *Economic Review of the Soviet Union* 6 (1931): 413–15.

Trotskii, L. "Ot staroi sem'i—K novoi." *Pravda*, July 13, 1923.

——. "Chtoby perestroit byt', nado poznat' ego." *Pravda*, July 11, 1923.

Tsentral'nyi bank kommunal'nogo khozaistva i zhilishchnogo. *Proekty rabochikh zhilishch*. Moscow: Izdanie Tsekombanka, 1929.

Tsvetaev, V. D. *Sovremennaia fabrichno-zavodskaia arkhitektura*. 2nd ed. Moscow: Gosstroiizdat, 1933.

Unwin, Raymond Sir. *Town Planning in Practice: An Introduction to the Art of Designing Cities and Suburbs*. London: T. F. Unwin, 1909.

Vegman, G. "Ukrupnennoe zhil'e." *Sovremennaia arkhitektura*, no. 1 (1927): 12–20.

Vesnin, V. A., and A. A. Vesnin. "Predposylki stroitel'stva novykh gorodov." *Ekonomicheskaia zhizn'*, December 6, 1929, 2.

Vlasenko, S. "Bol'shoi Baku: Rekonstruktsiia Baku—Vazhneishaia zadacha obshchesoiuznogo znacheniia." *SoReGor*, no. 3–4 (1932): 64–67.

Witkin, Zara, and Michael Gelb. *An American Engineer in Stalin's Russia: The Memoirs of Zara Witkin, 1932–1934*. Berkeley: University of California Press, 1991.

Yanovits'kiy, G., and A. Sanovich. "Pro Kharkiv stariy i noviy." *Arkhitektura radians'koi Ukrainy*, no. 10–11 (1938): 18–21.

Zaporozhets, I. K. "Kommunal'noe stroitel'stvo v piatiletnem perspektivnom plane." *Planovoe khoziaistvo*, no. 1 (1928): 112–22.

Zelenko, A. "Problema stroitel'stva sotsialisticheskikh gorodov." *Planovoe khoziaistvo*, no. 12 (1929): 16–31.

Zuev, P. M. *Poselki sady: Planirovka*. Kiev, 1918.

Secondary Sources

Alekperov, Vagit. *Oil of Russia: Past, Present and Future*. Translated by Paul B. Gallager and Thomas D. Hedden. Minneapolis: EastView Press, 2011.

Altstadt, Audrey L. *The Azerbaijani Turks: Power and Identity under Russian Rule*. Stanford: Hoover Institution Press, 1992.

Altstadt-Mirhadi, Audrey "Baku: Transformation of a Muslim Town." In *City in Late Imperial Russia*, edited by Michael F. Hamm, 282–318. Bloomington: Indiana University Press, 1983.

Anderson, Richard. "The Future of History: The Cultural Politics of Soviet Architecture, 1928–41." PhD diss., Columbia University, 2010.

Applebaum, Anne. *Red Famine: Stalin's War on Ukraine*. New York: Doubleday, 2017.

Aslanov, S. *Aleksandr Serebrovskii: Biograficheskii ocherk*. Baku: Azerbaidzhanskoe gos. izd-vo, 1974.

Astafieva-Dlugach, M. "Proekt raionnoi planirovki apsheronskogo poluostrova." *Arkhitektura SSSR*, no. 10 (1971): 42–43.

Austin, Richard Cartwright. *Building Utopia: Erecting Russia's First Modern City, 1930*. Kent: Kent State University Press, 2004.

Bailes, Kendall E. "The American Connection: Ideology and the Transfer of American Technology to the Soviet Union, 1917–1941." *Comparative Studies in Society and History* 23, no. 3 (1981): 421–48.

Barkhina, A. G. *G. B. Barkhin*. Moscow: Stroizdat, 1981.

Bater, James H. *The Soviet City: Ideal and Reality*. Explorations in Urban Analysis, vol. 2. Beverly Hills: Sage, 1980.

Blau, Eve, Ivan Rupnik, and Iwan Baan. *Baku: Oil and Urbanism*. Zurich: Park Books, 2018.

Bliznakov, Milka. "The Realization of Utopia: Western Technology and Soviet Avant-Garde Architecture." In *Reshaping Russian Architecture: Western Technology, Utopian Dreams*, edited by William C. Brumfield, 145–75. Washington, DC: Woodrow Wilson Center Press, 1990.

——. "Urban Planning in the USSR: Integrative Theories." In *The City in Russian History*, edited by Michael F. Hamm, 243–56. Lexington: University Press of Kentucky, 1976.

Bocharnikova, Daria. "Inventing Socialist Modern: A History of the Architectural Profession in the USSR, 1932–1971." PhD diss., European University Institute, 2014.

Bosma, Koos, and Helma Hellinga, eds. *Mastering the City: North European City Planning, 1900–2000*. 2 vols. Rotterdam: NAI Publishers, 1998.

Boym, Svetlana. *Common Places: Mythologies of Everyday Life in Russia*. Cambridge: Harvard University Press, 1994.

Brinegar, Sara G. "Baku at All Costs: The Politics of Oil in the New Soviet State." PhD diss., University of Wisconsin, 2014.

Brown, Bay. "Albert Kahn: The Russian Legacy." *Proekt Rossiia = Project Russia* 7b (1997): 92–96.

Brumfield, William Craft. *Reshaping Russian Architecture: Western Technology, Utopian Dreams*. Washington, DC: Woodrow Wilson Center Press, 1990.

——. *The Origins of Modernism in Russian Architecture*. Berkeley: University of California Press, 1991.

Brumfield, William Craft, and Blair A. Ruble. *Russian Housing in the Modern Age: Design and Social History*. Washington, DC: Woodrow Wilson Center Press, 1993.

Buber, Martin. *Paths in Utopia*. New York: Macmillan, 1950.

Buchli, Victor. *An Archaeology of Socialism*. Oxford: Berg, 1999.

——. "Moisei Ginzburg's Narkomfin Communal House in Moscow: Contesting the Social and Material World." *Journal of the Society of Architectural Historians* 57, no. 2 (1998): 160–81.

Bur'ianova, Iuliia. *Velyki ochikuvannia, nezdiisneni mrii: Znikaiuchi bagatstva arkhitektury konstruktivizmu v Ukraini ta Azherbaidzhani*. Kyiv: Tirazh, 2003.

Carr, Edward Hallett. *Foundations of a Planned Economy, 1926–1929*. Edited by R. W. Davies. London: Macmillan, 1969.

Castillo, Greg. "Stalinist Modern: Constructivism and the Soviet Company Town." In *Architectures of Russian Identity: 1500 to the Present*, edited by James Cracraft and Daniel Rowland, 135–49. Ithaca: Cornell University Press, 2003.

Chase, William. "Voluntarism, Mobilisation and Coercion: Subbotniki 1919–1921." *Soviet Studies* 41, no. 1 (1989): 111–28.

Chepelik, Viktor. *Ukrains'kiy arkhitekturniy modern.* Kyiv: Kyivs'kiy national'niy universitet budivinstva i arkhitekturi, 2000.

Cheredina, Irina. "Stroitel'stvo goroda Magnitogorska 1930-e gody. K istorii voprosa." *Budownictwo* no. 17 (2011): 30–35.

Cherkasova, E. T. "Idei i realiztsiia plana sotsialisticheskoi rekonstruktsii Khar'kova." In *Sovetskoe grad-stroitel'stvo 1920–1930kh godov: Novye issledovaniia i materialy*, edited by Yu. L. Kosenkova. Moscow: Librokom, 2010.

Choay, Françoise. *The Rule and the Model: On the Theory of Architecture and Urbanism.* Edited by Denise Bratton. Cambridge: MIT Press, 1997.

Clark, Katerina. *Moscow, the Fourth Rome: Stalinism, Cosmopolitanism, and the Evolution of Soviet Culture, 1931–1941.* Cambridge: Harvard University Press, 2011.

——. *Petersburg, Crucible of Cultural Revolution.* Cambridge: Harvard University Press, 1995.

Cohen, Jean-Louis. *Building a new World: Amerikanizm in Russian Architecture.* New Haven: Yale University Press, 2020.

——. *Le Corbusier and the Mystique of the USSR: Theories and Projects for Moscow, 1928–1936.* Princeton: Princeton University Press, 1992.

Cohen, Yves. "Circulatory Localities: The Example of Stalinism in the 1930s." *Kritika: Explorations in Russian and Eurasian History* 11, no. 1 (2010): 11–45.

——. "The Soviet Fordson. Between the Politics of Stalin and the Philosophy of Ford, 1924–1932." In *Ford, 1903–2003, the European History*, edited by Hubert et al Bonin, 531–58. Paris: Plage, 2003.

Collier, Stephen J. *Post-Soviet Social: Neoliberalism, Social Modernity, Biopolitics.* Princeton: Princeton University Press, 2011.

Colton, Timothy J. *Moscow: Governing the Socialist Metropolis.* Cambridge: Belknap Press of Harvard University Press, 1995.

Companjen, Françoise, László Marácz, and Lia Versteegh. *Exploring the Caucasus in the 21st Century: Essays on Culture, History and Politics in a Dynamic Context.* Amsterdam: Amsterdam University Press, 2012.

Cooke, Catherine. *Russian Avant-Garde Theories of Art, Architecture and the City.* London: Academy Editions, 1995.

——. "The Town of Socialism." PhD diss., University of Cambridge, 1974.

Corner, James. "The Agency of Mapping: Speculation, Critique and Invention." In *Mappings*, edited by Denis Cosgrove, 213–52. London: Reaktion Books, 1999.

Crawford, Christina E. "From the Old Family—to the New." *Harvard Design Magazine* 41: Family Planning (2015): 38–45.

——. "From Tractors to Territory: Socialist Urbanization through Standardization." *Journal of Urban History* 44, no. 1 (2017): 54–77.

——. "The Innovative Potential of Scarcity in SA's Comradely Competition for Communal Housing, 1927." *ArchiDOCT* 1, no. 2 (2014): 32–65.

Croissant, Michael P., and Bülent Aras. *Oil and Geopolitics in the Caspian Sea Region.* Westport: Praeger, 2000.

Crowley, David, and Susan Emily Reid. *Socialist Spaces: Sites of Everyday Life in the Eastern Bloc.* Oxford: Berg, 2002.

Dalrymple, Dana G. "The American Tractor Comes to Soviet Agriculture: The Transfer of a Technology." *Technology and Culture* 5, no. 2 (1964): 191–214.

Davidovich, V. G., and Tatiana Aleksandrovna Chizhikova. *Aleksandr Ivanitskii.* Mastera arkhitektury. Moscow: Stroiizdat, 1973.

DeHaan, Heather D. *Stalinist City Planning: Professionals, Performance, and Power.* Toronto: University of Toronto Press, 2013.

Dobrenko, E. A. *Political Economy of Socialist Realism.* New Haven: Yale University Press, 2007.

Dobrenko, E. A., and Eric Naiman. *The Landscape of Stalinism: The Art and Ideology of Soviet Space.* Seattle: University of Washington Press, 2003.

Efendizade, R. M. *Planirovka i zastroika zhilykh raionov Baku (1920–1967 gg.).* Baku: Elm, 1971.

Fainstein, Norman, and Susan Fainstein. "New Debates in Urban Planning: The Impact of Marxist Theory in the United States." *International Journal of Urban and Regional Research* 3, no. 3 (1979): 381–403.

Fatullaev-Figarov, Sh. S. *Arkhitekturnaia entsiklopediia Baku.* Baku: Mezhdunrodnaia akademiia arkhitektury stran vostoka, 1998.

——. *Gradostroitel'stvo Baku XIX–nachala XX vekov.* Leningrad: Stroiizdat, 1978.

Fedosikhin, V. S., and V. V. Khoroshanskii. *Magnitogorsk—Klassika sovetskoi sotsialisticheskoi arkhitektury 1918–1991.* Magnitogorsk: Magnitogorskii gosudarstvennyi tekhnicheskii universitet, 1999.

Flierl, Thomas. "'Possibly the Greatest Task an Architect Ever Faced': Ernst May in the Soviet Union (1930–1933)." In *Ernst May, 1886–1970*, edited by Claudia Quiring, Helen Barr, Eckhard Herrel, Peter Cachola Schmal, and Wolfgang Voigt, 157–95. Munich: Prestel, 2011.

Frolov, D. Ia. *Inzhener O.I. Nerovets'kii.* Kyiv: Budivel'nik, 1967.

Gerschenkron, Alexander. "Economic Backwardness in Economic Perspective." In *Economic Backwardness in Economic Perspective: A Book of Essays*, 5–30. New York: Praeger, 1962.

Ginzburg, Alexey. *Dom narkomfina restavratsiia, 2016–2020.* Moscow: Departament kul'turnogo naslediia goroda Moskvy, 2020. https://www.mos.ru/upload/documents/files/3458/Narkomphin.pdf?fbclid=IwAR2VKSV1wjZ4U6a9CAYlc6vzjc6q-gDuW8eyFbCnHBDmsxoQZgpgj40e3M8.

Golovko, G. V., ed. *Narysy istorii arkhitektury Ukrainskoi RSR (radianskyi period)*, vol. 2. Kyiv: Derzh. vyd. lit. z bud. i arkh., 1962.

Gorvitz, G. "Stanovlenie arkhitektury sovetskogo Kharkova." *Arkhitektura SSSR*, no. 5 (1974): 42–48.

Gough, Maria. "John Heartfield's Biography of Soviet Petroleum." In *Magazines, Modernity and War*, edited by Jordana Mendelson, 75–97. Madrid: Ministerio de Cultura, Museo Nacional Centro de Arte Reina Sofia, 2008.

——. *The Artist as Producer: Russian Constructivism in Revolution.* Berkeley: University of California Press, 2005.

Gozak, A. *Ivan Leonidov: The Complete Works.* Edited by Andrei Leonidov, Catherine Cooke, and Igor Palmin. New York: Rizzoli, 1988.

Grace, John D. *Russian Oil Supply: Performance and Prospects.* Oxford: Oxford University Press, 2005.

Greenstein, David E. "Assembling Fordizm: The Production of Automobiles, Americans, and Bolsheviks in Detroit and Early Soviet Russia." *Comparative Studies in Society and History* 56, no. 2 (2014): 259–89.

Groys, Boris. *The Total Art of Stalinism: Avant-Garde, Aesthetic Dictatorship, and Beyond*. Princeton: Princeton University Press, 1992.

Hall, Peter. *Cities of Tomorrow: An Intellectual History of Urban Planning and Design in the Twentieth Century*. 3rd ed. Oxford: Blackwell, 2002.

Harries, Karsten. *The Ethical Function of Architecture*. Cambridge: MIT Press, 1998.

Harris, Chauncy D. "Urbanization and Population Growth in the Soviet Union, 1959–1970." *Geographical Review* 61, no. 1 (1971): 102–24.

Harris, Steven E. *Communism on Tomorrow Street: Mass Housing and Everyday Life after Stalin*. Washington, DC: Woodrow Wilson Center Press, 2013.

Henderson, Susan R. *Building Culture: Ernst May and the Frankfurt Initiative, 1926–1931*. Bern: Peter Lang, 2013.

Hewryk, Titus. "Planning of the Capital in Kharkiv." *Harvard Ukrainian Studies* 16, no. 3/4 December (1992): 325–60.

Hoffmann, David L. *Peasant Metropolis: Social Identities in Moscow, 1929–1941*. Ithaca: Cornell University Press, 1994.

Holliday, George D. *Technology Transfer to the USSR, 1928–1937 and 1966–1975: The Role of Western Technology in Soviet Economic Development*. Boulder: Westview Press, 1979.

Hudson, Hugh D. *Blueprints and Blood: The Stalinization of Soviet Architecture, 1917–1937*. Princeton: Princeton University Press, 1994.

———. "Terror in Soviet Architecture: The Murder of Mikhail Okhitovich." *Slavic Review* 51, no. 3 (1992): 448–67.

Igolkin, A. A. *Russkaia neft' o kotoroi my tak malo znaem*. Moscow: Olimp-Biznes, 2003.

Igurskaia, N. "Progressivnye cherty v zastroike poselka KhTZ (k 30-letiiu Khar'kovskogo traktornogo zavoda)." *Stroitel'stvo i arkhitektura*, no. 10 (1961): 10–13.

Kasim-Zade, Envar. *Problemy razvitiia Azerbaidzhanskoi sovetskoi arkhitektury na sovremennom etape*. Baku: Azerbaidzhanskoe gos. izd-vo, 1967.

Kazarinova, V. I., and Vaslii Ivanovich Pavlichenkov. *Magnitogorsk: Opyt sovetskoi arkhitektury*. Moscow: Gos. izd. lit. po stroitel'stvu, arkhitekture i stroit. materialam, 1961.

Kazus', I. A. *Sovetskaia arkhitektura 1920-kh godov: Organizatsiia proektirovaniia*. Moscow: Progress-Traditsiia, 2009.

Khan-Magomedov, S. O. *Arkhitektura sovetskogo avangarda*. Moscow: Stroiizdat, 1996.

———. *Mikhail Okhitovich. Tvortsy avangarda*. Moscow: Russkii avangard, 2009.

Khan-Magomedov, S. O., and Aleksandr Aleksandrovich Vesnin. *Alexander Vesnin and Russian Constructivism*. London: Lund Humphries, 1986.

Khan-Magomedov, S., and Catherine Cooke. *Pioneers of Soviet Architecture: The Search for New Solutions in the 1920s and 1930s*. New York: Rizzoli, 1987.

Khazanova, V. E. *Sovetskaia arkhitektura pervoi piatiletki: Problemy goroda budushchego*. Moscow: Izdatel'stvo nauka, 1980.

Khmel'nitskii, D. M. "Leonid Sabsovich ili kto pridumal obobshchestvlenie byta?" In *Sem'ia v traditsionnoi kul'ture i sovremennom mire*, edited by Iu. M. Smirnov Vladimir: Transit IKS, 2011. http://archi.ru/lib/publication.html?id=1850569891&fl=5&sl=1.

Khmel'nitskii, Dmitrii, and Ekaterina Miliutina. *Arkhitektor Nikolai Miliutin*. Moscow: Novoe literaturnoe obozrenie, 2013.

Khrushchev, Nikita. "On the Extensive Introduction of Industrial Methods, Improving the Quality and Reducing the Cost of Construction (December 7, 1954)." *Volume* 21, no. 3 (2009): 26–34.

Kiaer, Christina. *Imagine No Possessions: The Socialist Objects of Russian Constructivism*. Cambridge: MIT Press, 2005.

Kolli, N. "Pamiati Anatoliia Vasil'evicha Samoilova." *Arkhitektura SSSR*, no. 12 (1954): 37.

Konysheva, Evgeniia, and Mark Meerovich. "Bereg levyi, bereg pravyi: Ernst Mai i otkrytye voprosy istorii sovetskoi arkhitektury." *Arkhitekton: Izvestiia vuzov*, no. 30 (June 2010). http://archvuz.ru/2010_2/13/.

Konysheva, Evgeniia Vladimirovna, and M. G. Meerovich. *Ernst Mai: Proektirovanie sotsgorodov v gody pervykh piatiletok (na primere Magnitogorska)*. Moscow: URSS, 2012.

Konysheva, Evgeniia, Mark Meerovich, and Thomas Flierl. "Ernst May v istorii sovetskoi industrializatsii." *Proekt Baikal* 8, no. 27 (2011): 137–41.

Konyseva, Evgenija, Thomas Flierl, and Mark G. Meerovic. *Linkes Ufer, rechtes Ufer: Ernst May und die Planungsgeschichte von Magnitogorsk (1930–1933)*. Berlin: Theater Der Zeit, 2014.

Kopelev, Lev. *The Education of a True Believer*. New York: Harper & Row, 1980.

——. *To Be Preserved Forever*. Translated and edited by Anthony Austin. Philadelphia: Lippincott, 1977.

Kopp, Anatole. *Constructivist Architecture in the USSR*. London: Academy Editions, 1985.

——. *Town and Revolution: Soviet Architecture and City Planning, 1917–1935*. New York: G. Braziller, 1970.

Kotkin, Stephen. *Magnetic Mountain: Stalinism as a Civilization*. Berkeley: University of California Press, 1995.

——. "The Search for the Socialist City." *Russian History / Histoire Russe* 23, no. 1–4 (1996): 231–63.

Kravchenko, Volodymyr. "Kharkiv: A Borderland City." In *Cities after the Fall of Communism: Reshaping Cultural Landscapes and European Identity*, edited by John Czaplicka, Nida M. Gelazis, and Blair A. Ruble, 219–54. Washington, DC: Woodrow Wilson Center Press, 2009.

——. *Khar'kov—Kharkiv: Stolitsa pogranich'ia*. Vilnius: Evropeiskii gumanitarnyi universitet, 2010.

Lane, Barbara Miller. *Architecture and Politics in Germany, 1918–1945*. Cambridge: Harvard University Press, 1985.

Lefebvre, Henri. *The Production of Space*. Oxford: Blackwell, 1991.

——. *The Urban Revolution*. Minneapolis: University of Minnesota Press, 2003.

Lewin, Moshe. *The Making of the Soviet System: Essays in the Social History of Interwar Russia*. London: Methuen, 1985.

Liber, George. *Soviet Nationality Policy, Urban Growth, and Identity Change in the Ukrainian SSR, 1923–1934*. Cambridge: Cambridge University Press, 1992.

Link, Stefan. "Transnational Fordism. Ford Motor Company, Nazi Germany and the Soviet Union in the Interwar Years." PhD diss., Harvard University, 2012.

Lubetkin, Berthold. "Soviet Architecture: Notes on Development from 1917–1932." *Architectural Association Journal*, May (1956): 260–64.

Meerovich, Mark. "Al'bert Kan v istorii sovetskoi industrializatsii." *Proekt Baikal*, no. 20 (2009). https://archi.ru/lib/publication.html?id=1850569787.

——. "Giprogor: Organizatsiia i Liudi." *Archi.Ru*, May 20, 2014, https://archi.ru/russia/54884/istoriya-otechestvennogo-gradostroitelstva-giprogor-1929-1932-gg.

——. *Gradostroitel'naia politika v SSSR (1917–1929): Ot goroda-sada k vedomstvennomu rabochemu poselku*. Moscow: Novoe literaturnoe obozrenie, 2017.

——. *Nakazanie zhilishchem: Zhilishchnaia politika v SSSR kak sredstvo upravleniia liudiami, 1917–1937.* Moscow: ROSSPEN, 2008.

——. "Neoffitsial'noe gradostroitel'stvo: Tainyi aspekt sovetskoi industrializatsii (1928–1932)." In *Problemy otchestvennoi istorii: Istochniki, istoriografiia, issledovaniia,* edited by M. V. Drusin, 395–414. St. Petersburg: Sankt Peterburgskii institut istorii RAN, 2008.

——. "Razdroblennoe proektirovanie (pismo Ernsta Maia Iosifu Stalinu)." *Arkhitekton: Izvestiia vuzov,* no. 38 (2012): 112–29. http://old.archvuz.ru/PDF/%23%2038%20PDF/ArchPHE%2338(Art11) pp112-129Meerovich.pdf.

Meerovich, M. G., Evgeniia Vladimirovna Konysheva, and Dmitrii Khmelnitskii. *Kladbishche sotsgorodov: Gradostroitel'naia politika v SSSR 1928–1932.* Moscow: ROSSPEN, 2011.

Melnikova-Raich, Sonia. "The Soviet Problem with Two 'Unknowns': How an American Architect and a Soviet Negotiator Jump-Started the Industrialization of Russia, Part I: Albert Kahn." *IA: The Journal of the Society for Industrial Archeology* 36, no. 2 (2010): 57–80.

——. "The Soviet Problem with Two 'Unknowns': How an American Architect and a Soviet Negotiator Jump-Started the Industrialization of Russia, Part II: Saul Bron." *IA: The Journal of the Society for Industrial Archeology* 37, no. 1–2 (2011): 5–28.

Meuser, Philipp, and Dmiitrij Zadorin. *Towards a Typology of Soviet Mass Housing: Prefabrication in the USSR 1955–1991.* Berlin: DOM Publishers, 2015.

Miller, Mervyn. *Raymond Unwin: Garden Cities and Town Planning.* Leicester: Leicester University Press, 1992.

Miller, Robert F. "Soviet Agricultural Policy in the Twenties: The Failure of Cooperation." *Soviet Studies* 27, no. 2 (1975): 220–44.

Mullin, John Robert. "City Planning in Frankfurt, Germany, 1925–1932. A Study in Practical Utopianism." *Journal of Urban History* 4, no. 1 (November) (1977): 3–28.

Mokrousova, Alena. "Biblioteka Pavla Aleshina." *Antikvar* 101, no. March–April (2017). https://antikvar.ua/biblioteka-pavla-alyoshina/.

Mumford, Eric Paul. *The CIAM Discourse on Urbanism, 1928–1960.* Cambridge: MIT Press, 2000.

Murawski, Michal. "Actually-Existing Success: Economics, Aesthetics, and the Specificity of (Still-) Socialist Urbanism." *Comparative Studies in Society and History* 60, no. 4 (2018): 907–37.

Mykhailenko, Halyna. "Diial'nist' O. I. Nerovets'koho v haluzi promyslovnoho ta tsivil'noho budivnitstva v Ukraini v 1922–1936 rokakh." *Doslidzheniia z istorii tekhniki* 22 (2016): 4–8.

Nassibli, Nasib. "Azerbaijan: Oil and Politics in the Country's Future." In *Oil and Geopolitics in the Caspian Sea Region,* edited by Michael P. Croissant and Bülent Aras, 101–30. Westport: Praeger, 2000.

Oblastnoi ispolnitel'nyi komitet. Arkhivnyi otdel Cheliabinsk. *Iz istorii Magnitogorskogo metallurgicheskogo kombinata i goroda Magnitogorska, 1929–1941 gg.; Sbornik dokumentov i materialov.* Cheliabinskaia oblast': Iuzhno-Ural'skoe knizhnoe izd-vo, 1965.

Paden, Roger. "Marxism, Utopianism, and Modern Urban Planning." *Utopian Studies* 14, no. 1 (2003): 82–111.

Paperny, Vladimir. *Architecture in the Age of Stalin: Culture Two.* Cambridge: Cambridge University Press, 2002.

Parkins, Maurice Frank. *City Planning in Soviet Russia: With an Interpretative Bibliography.* Chicago: University of Chicago Press, 1953.

Porotto, Alessandro. *L'intelligence Des Formes: Le Projet de Logements Collectifs à Vienne et Francfort.* Geneva: Mētispresses, 2019.

Quiring, Claudia, Helen Barr, Eckhard Herrel, Peter Cachola Schmal, and Wolfgang Voigt, eds. *Ernst May, 1886–1970*. Architekturmuseum Deutsches and Gesellschaft Ernst May. Munich: Prestel, 2011.

Rogger, Hans. "Amerikanizm and the Economic Development of Russia." *Comparative Studies in Society and History* 23, no. 3 (1981): 382–420.

Ruble, Blair A. "From Khruchsheby to Korobki." In *Russian Housing in the Modern Age*, edited by William Craft Brumfield, 232–70. Washington, DC: Woodrow Wilson Center Press, 1993.

Schlögel, Karl. *Moscow, 1937*. Edited by Rodney Livingstone. Cambridge: Polity, 2012.

Schultz, Kurt Stephen. "The American Factor in Soviet Industrialization: Fordism and the First Five-Year Plan, 1928–1932." PhD diss., Ohio State University, 1992.

Schwarzenbach, Sibyl A. *The Marxian Concept of Praxis. Constructivism and Practice: Toward a Historical Epistemology*. Edited by Carol C. Gould. Lanham: Rowman & Littlefield, 2003.

Scott, James C. *Seeing Like a State: How Certain Schemes to Improve the Human Condition Have Failed*. New Haven: Yale University Press, 1998.

Sedak, I. N. *Arkhitektura Sovetskoi Ukrainy = Architecture of the Soviet Ukraine*. Moscow: Stroizdat, 1987.

Senkevich, Anatole Jr. "Albert Kahn's Great Soviet Adventure." *Dimensions* 10 (1996): 35–49.

Shpara, P. E. *Zapiski arkhitektora*. Kyiv: Budivel'nyk, 1988.

Shpotov, B. M. *Amerikanskii biznes i sovetskii soiuz v 1920–1930-e gody: Labirinty ekonomicheskogo sotrudnichestva*. Moscow: URSS, 2013.

Shpotov, Boris M. "The Case of Us Companies in Russia-USSR: Ford in 1920s–1930s." In *American Firms in Europe: Strategy, Identity, Perception and Performance (1880–1980)*, edited by Hubert Bonin and Ferry de Goey, 435–55. Geneva: Librairie Droz, 2009.

Siegelbaum, Lewis H. *Cars for Comrades: The Life of the Soviet Automobile*. Ithaca: Cornell University Press, 2008.

Smith, Mark B. *Property of Communists: The Urban Housing Program from Stalin to Khrushchev*. DeKalb: Northern Illinois University Press, 2010.

Sorensen, Charles E. *My Forty Years with Ford*. Detroit: Wayne State University Press, 2006.

Sosnovy, Timothy. "The Soviet Housing Situation Today." *Soviet Studies* 11, no. 1 (1959): 1–21.

Stanek, Lukasz. *Architecture in Global Socialism: Eastern Europe, West Africa, and the Middle East in the Cold War*. Princeton: Princeton University Press, 2020.

Starr, S. Frederick. "The Revival and Schism of Urban Planning in Twentieth-Century Russia." In *The City in Russian History*, edited by Michael F. Hamm, 222–42. Lexington: University Press of Kentucky, 1976.

——. "Visionary Town Planning During the Cultural Revolution." In *Cultural Revolution in Russia, 1928–1931*, edited by Sheila Fitzpatrick, 207–40. Bloomington: Indiana University Press, 1978.

Stites, Richard. *Revolutionary Dreams: Utopian Vision and Experimental Life in the Russian Revolution*. New York: Oxford University Press, 1989.

Suny, Ronald Grigor. "A Journeyman for the Revolution: Stalin and the Labour Movement in Baku, June 1907–May 1908." *Soviet Studies* 23, no. 3 (1972): 373–94.

——. *The Baku Commune, 1917–1918: Class and Nationality in the Russian Revolution*. Princeton: Princeton University Press, 1972.

Sutton, Antony C. *Western Technology and Soviet Economic Development 1917 to 1930*. Hoover Institution Publications, vol. 1. Stanford: Hoover Institution on War, Revolution and Peace, 1968.

——. *Western Technology and Soviet Economic Development 1930 to 1945*. Hoover Institution Publications, vol. 2. Stanford: Hoover Institution on War, Revolution and Peace, 1971.

Swenarton, Mark. "Rationality and Rationalism: The Theory and Practice of Site Planning in Modern Architecture 1905–1930." *AA Files*, no. 4 (July 1983): 49–59.

Swietochowski, Tadeusz. *Russian Azerbaijan, 1905–1920. The Shaping of National Identity in a Muslim Community.* Cambridge: Cambridge University Press, 1985.

Tafuri, Manfredo. *Architecture and Utopia: Design and Capitalist Development.* Cambridge: MIT Press, 1976.

——. *The Sphere and the Labyrinth: Avant-Gardes and Architecture from Piranesi to the 1970s.* Cambridge: MIT Press, 1987.

Takao, Chizuko. "The Origin of the Machine Tractor Station in the USSR: A New Perspective." *Acta Slavica Iaponica* 19 (2002): 117–36.

Udovicki-Selb, Danilo. "Between Modernism and Socialist Realism: Soviet Architectural Culture under Stalin's Revolution from above, 1928–1938." *Journal of the Society of Architectural Historians* 68, no. 4 (2009): 467–95.

——. *Soviet Architectural Avant-Gardes: Architecture and Stalin's Revolution from Above, 1928–1938.* London: Bloomsbury, 2020.

Utkin, I. V., and I. V. Chepkunova. *Arkhitektor Vegman.* Ekaterinburg: Tatlin Publishers, 2008.

Viola, Lynne. *Peasant Rebels under Stalin: Collectivization and the Culture of Peasant Resistance.* Oxford: Oxford University Press, 1996.

Vujosevic, Tijana. *Modernism and the Making of the Soviet New Man.* Manchester: Manchester University Press, 2017.

Wagner, Phillip. "Facilitating Planning Communication across Borders: The International Federation for Housing and Town Planning in the Interwar Period." *Planning Perspectives* 31, no. 2 (2016): 299–311.

Widdis, Emma. *Visions of a New Land: Soviet Film from the Revolution to the Second World War.* New Haven: Yale University Press, 2003.

Zarecor, Kimberly Elman. "What Was so Socialist about the Socialist City? Second World Urbanity in Europe." *Journal of Urban History* 44, no. 1 (2018): 95–117.

Zubovich, Katherine. *Moscow Monumental: Soviet Skyscrapers and Urban Life under High Stalinism.* Princeton: Princeton University Press, 2020.

INDEX

Page numbers followed by *f*, n, or nn indicate illustrations or notes.